TO

NEW★YORK

2007

KAREN MARCHBANK
with AMANDA STATHAM

foulsham
LONDON • NEW YORK • TORONTO • SYDNEY

foulsham

The Publishing House, Bennetts Close, Cippenham,
Slough, Berkshire, SL1 5AP, England

Foulsham books can be found in all good bookshops or direct from
www.foulsham.com

Dedication

To Nicki Grihault for helping out with all of the research.

ISBN-13: 978-0-572-03277-7
ISBN-10: 0-572-03277-3

Series title, format, logo, artwork and layout design
© 2006 W. Foulsham & Co. Ltd

Text copyright © 2006 W. Foulsham & Co. Ltd

The moral right of the authors has been asserted

Maps by PC Graphics (UK) Limited

A CIP record for this book is available from the British Library

While every effort has been made to ensure the accuracy of all the information
contained within this book, neither the author nor the publisher can be liable for
any errors. In particular, since prices, times and any holiday or hotel details change
on a regular basis, it is vital that individuals check relevant information for
themselves.

Look out for the latest editions in this series:
A Brit's Guide to Las Vegas and the West, Karen Marchbank
A Brit's Guide to Orlando and Walt Disney World, Simon and Susan Veness
A Brit's Guide to Disneyland Resort Paris, Simon and Susan Veness
A Brit's Guide to Choosing a Cruise, Simon Veness

Printed in Dubai

Contents

Acknowledgements

With grateful thanks for all their help to Jonathan Sloan, Suzanne Seyghal and Vicky Aykroyd at Hillsbalfour PR, which represents NYC & Co in the UK. All at NYC Visit.com, Niagara Falls Convention and Visitors Bureau and the New York State Department of Economic Development.

My thanks also to the Lower East Side Tenement Museum, the Metropolitan Museum of Art, Ellis Island Immigration Museum, the Museum of Modern Art, the Museum of Jewish Heritage, the Whitney Museum of American Art, Intrepid Sea-Air-Space Museum, the Frick Collection, the Skyscraper Museum, the National Museum of the American Indian, the Children's Museum of Manhattan, the Empire State Building, the American Museum of Natural History, the New York Stock Exchange, the Brooklyn Museum of Art, NY Waterways, the Sex And The City Tour, Harlem Spirituals, the Big Apple Greeters, David Watkins and Ponycabs, the Queens Jazz Trail, Gangland Tours, Big Onion Walking Tours, Rabbi Beryl Epstein and the Hassidic Discovery Center, former NYPD cop Gary Gorman, Gray Line, Food Tours of Greenwich, Ryan Hawkins (known as jazz aficionado Ed Lockjaw), The Ritz-Carlton at Battery Park, The Warwick, The Mark, Waldorf Astoria, Le Parker Meridien, The Marriott Marquis, The Wellington, The Doral, Le Cirque, The Bull & Bear, The View at the Marriot Marquis, American Park at the Battery, Serafina Fabulous Grill, The Boathouse, Picholine, Sylvia's Restaurant, The River Café, The Water Club, World Yacht Dining Cruise, Europa Grill, The 21 Club, Tavern on the Green, Zoe's Restaurant and ONE c.p.s.

Thanks also to the following individuals who were a fount of great knowledge: Loraine Heller, Neal Smith, Russell Brightwell, Maria Pieri, the divine Kirsty Hislop, Annie Davies, Colin Macrae, Dale Burg and Neil Wadey.

New York public library

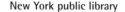

Introduction

Welcome to the 2007 edition of the *Brit's Guide to New York*, the guide that is like your very own personal tour guide to this amazing city.

We hope the guide will inspire you to want to visit the Big Apple again and again. For this is a city that really does capture the heart. Very few people visit once and don't return, simply because they're always left with the feeling that there's so much more to see and do. Once you've ticked off your list the major sights – such as the Empire State Building, Statue of Liberty and Central Park – you can start investigating the cosmopolitan neighbourhoods of the likes of SoHo, Greenwich Village and Chelsea and, in each new place you venture into, you'll discover a veritable treasure of shops, cafés, hotels and bars and witness the 'zoo' of residents going about their daily business.

A record 41 million visitors flocked to the city last year, demonstrating that the dark day of 11 September 2001, when terrorists

7th Avenue Garment District

INTRODUCTION

THE NEW YORK STATE OF MIND

While New York is undoubtedly a melting pot of cultures and religions (Italians, Chinese, Jews, Africans, Irish and French to name but a few) there is one thing that unites everyone living in this cosmopolitan city – attitude. Resident New Yorkers are a breed unto themselves, unlike other American states where you're constantly instructed to 'have a nice day', they're not prone to saccharine sweetness. Here's how to spot a genuine New Yorker: on face value, they tend to have a sort of totally cheesed-off-with-the-world, don't-mess-with-me look. They also speak incredibly quickly as if they were eating their own words, so it can be hard to understand them.

Scratch the surface, though, and you just have your ordinary, everyday kind of person with the same kind of worries, fears and doubts as the rest of us. We've discovered two things that work a treat: firstly, smiling like mad and being genuinely polite; secondly, the British accent. You can see them looking at you askance when you smile (smile? Who on earth does that in New York?), but then deciding that you must be one of those British eccentrics they've heard about. It does the trick, though, because more often than not they'll respond in a helpful way.

And don't go thinking that all New Yorkers will tell you to f*** off if you ask for directions. Many are happy to help and we've even had people stop to help us work out where we're going when they've spotted us studying a map. This heady mix of rudeness and helpfulness is no better demonstrated than in the following anecdote from New York author Douglas Kennedy:

'On a crosstown bus I noticed two visitors from Japan having difficulty with the exact change for the fare,' he recounts. 'The driver, an overweight guy with a scowl, started giving them a hard time. "Like can't you read English or what?" he said loudly. "It says a buck-fifty. Surely they teach you how to count in Japan."

'The Japanese looked as if they wanted to commit hara-kiri on the spot until an elegantly dressed woman in her late sixties seated opposite the door came to their defence. Out of nowhere she turned to the driver and said: "Hey asshole, be polite".'

destroyed the twin towers of the World Trade Center and killed nearly 3,000 people, has done nothing to deter people's appetite for the Big Apple. The physical destruction it caused the city has long since been cleared to make way for some fabulous new buildings that are now emerging from the dust and ash. It's typical of the spirit of this vibrant, beautiful city that it has come back stronger than ever before; foreign visitors from all over the world continue to pour into the Big Apple, trade is booming and it's brimming with life and excitement in whichever neighbourhood you venture into.

★ ★ ★ ★ **BRIT TIP** ★ ★ ★ ★
★ ★
★ **If you do want to pay your respects** ★
★ **at Ground Zero, remember that this** ★
★ **is also an ideal place from which to** ★
★ **visit Wall Street and the Statue of** ★
★ **Liberty, so give yourself time to** ★
★ **explore Lower Manhattan.** ★
★ ★

The city has always been about regeneration, about removal of the old to make way for the new and, hopefully, the bigger and the better. In fact, in the 1960s, that is exactly what the Twin Towers themselves were all about.

There has been much discussion over the last five years as to what would fill the space that has been left by the fall of the Twin Towers, but it seems that agreement has finally been reached and redevelopment is under way at last. A 52-storey 7 World Trade Center is set for completion at the end of 2006 and construction of a new state-of-the-art transit centre beneath the area has started. Still in the planning stages is the three-level memorial, Reflecting Absence, designed by architects Michael Arad and Peter Walker in conjunction with associate architect Max Bond. The 541m (1,776ft) Freedom Tower is expected to finally open in 2010 and feature 242,000 sq m (2.6m sq ft) of office space, a rooftop restaurant and observation deck.

In the meantime, the city has continued its constant process of renewal, regeneration and regrowth. The Big Apple really cranked up the pace in 2006 with a dizzying array of new hotel rooms, global cuisine, blockbuster Broadway shows, exceptional exhibitions and incomparable shopping. The record number of visitors flocking to the city proves that it really is back on its feet and that the insatiable demand for New York continues to climb. With more than 5,000 new and renovated hotel rooms on track for 2007, the world's most exhilarating city is set to welcome the world. Enjoy!

PLANNING YOUR HOLIDAY

One of New York's greatest charms is its cosmopolitan nature, its hugely diverse ethnic mix. In this city you will find any type of cuisine, often available at any time of the day or night. Where music is concerned, everything from jazz and R&B to techno and rap is out there on any night of the week and the many nightclubs are among the hottest and most stylish of any in the world.

The drawback is that it may seem a bit overwhelming and it doesn't help that everyone gives the impression of being in the biggest hurry ever and far too busy to help. But beneath the ice-cool veneer of most New Yorkers you'll find people who will be willing to answer any question or plea for help.

BRIT TIP

If you really want to get an insight into how a New Yorker thinks, read the Metropolitan Diary in Monday's edition of the *New York Times*. It's full of stories of New York life supplied by the locals.

In this book, we hope not only to provide all the information you need about the sights, sounds and attractions, but also to give an insight into what makes the city tick and how to get the most out of it. The book is filled with tips and insider information,

HOW TO USE YOUR GUIDEBOOK

We've tried to help you with your choices in as many ways as possible. For instance, the top sights and museums have been put in order of importance so you can go straight to the ones you will most likely want to see, and in each case the area they are in has been specified – again to help you plan your day. Be sure to look out for our 'Top Fives', which are scattered throughout the chapters. They are designed to give you instant snippets of information – for example the best restaurants with an outside garden area, or the five best shops for accessories – and provide a certain degree of insider knowledge. The same is true for our Brit Tips, which give you extra titbits of facts and advice that you probably won't find elsewhere.

Most of the main Broadway shows are easy enough to plan for because they tend to be in the Theater District, and the restaurant chapter gives an alphabetical area-by-area guide that makes light work of planning lunch and dinner. We've also provided a complete outline of all the different transport systems in New York and how to use them, plus a description of the different neighbourhoods so that you will be able to get the most out of what each one offers.

The accommodation chapter has been placed towards the back of the book because choosing a hotel should be one of your final decisions. If the sights, sounds, shops and museums you want to see are all in a particular area, then you should try to find a hotel or accommodation as close to it as possible. That way you can reduce the time and money you spend on getting around. Unless, of course, the hotel is the reason you're travelling to the city; for some people the experience of staying in exclusive accommodation such as The Waldorf is worth a visit to NYC before they've even thought about sightseeing.

We've tried to include everything we believe the average Brit will be interested in visiting in New York, but if you come across a sight, museum, shop, gallery, coffee shop, club, hotel or restaurant not in this book, which you think is worth including, email us at **amanda@mrhoppy.freeserve.co.uk**.

Finally, we'd just like to wish you a wonderful trip to what is still one of the greatest cities in the world.

but we are always open to hearing other people's views and are happy to receive suggestions by email at amanda@ mrhoppy.freeserve.co.uk.

Once you have decided to go to New York, the next step is to work out what you want to do there, otherwise you could end up wasting a lot of valuable time. The city is so big and diverse and everyone's tastes are so different that each visit to New York is a unique experience. Are you a museum buff? Do you like to get off the beaten track? Want to see a great Broadway show and some of the outstanding sights of the city? Your priorities will reflect not only your tastes but also whether it is your first or second visit to the Big Apple, or whether you are becoming an old friend, as well as the time you have available. Whatever the case, the key to making the most of your time is in the planning.

★ ★ ★ ★ **BRIT TIP** ★ ★ ★ ★
★   ★
★   Make the most of your time by   ★
★   planning each day carefully – but ★
★   don't try to do too much, and give ★
★   yourself enough breaks each day to ★
★   recharge your batteries.   ★
★   ★
★ ★

The thing we emphasise most is the importance of location. When you fly into New York, seeing all the skyscrapers from your lofty perch makes Manhattan look pretty small, but do not be fooled by this. It

Met Life Tower and the Flatiron Building

is a narrow island, but it's longer than it looks from high in the sky – 21km (13 miles) in fact – so don't be duped into believing it is easy to walk from Downtown to the Upper East Side. Nothing could be further from the truth.

It's also the case that the city's subway is nowhere near as fast as our much-maligned tube system in London, nor is it that good for getting from east to west or vice versa. That means using buses is often the better option and they, like taxis, can get stuck in heavy traffic. So, when planning your activities for the day, it is a good idea to stick to one particular area so that walking everywhere – the best way to see the city – won't be so tiring.

Most New York trips are for between two and seven days. For the former, it's like dipping your toes in the water; for the latter it's a big commitment to getting to know the city. Regardless of how many days you have, though, you won't be able to see everything, so you'll need to be selective.

View of Manhattan from the Mandarin Oriental

CHAPTER 1

Knowing New York

So what is New York all about? Due to the vast number of movies set in different periods of the city, many of the key people in its history, sights and areas are familiar to us Brits, though you may be a little hazy as to their whereabouts or true influence.

A BRIEF HISTORY OF NEW YORK

Understanding a little of the city's history is a good way of understanding its modern-day psyche, and to familiarise yourself with the different areas of New York and the buildings named after its great movers and shakers. Many of them were men and women of great vision and courage and their contributions to New York's rich and diverse culture, business and entertainment are all part of what makes the city so remarkable today.

The great story of New York started in 1524 when Florentine Giovanni da Verrazano arrived on the island now known as Manhattan. It was a mixture of marshes, woodland, rivers and meadows and was home to the Algonquin and Iroquois tribes of Native Americans.

No one settled on the island, though, until British explorer Henry Hudson arrived in 1609. Working for the Dutch West India Company, he discovered Indians who were happy to trade in furs, skins, birds and fruit. In 1613, a trading post was set up at Fort Nassau and by 1624 the Dutch West India Company was given the right to govern the area by the Dutch government.

Dutch settlers soon began to arrive; Manhattan was named New Amsterdam and governor Peter Minuit bought the island for $24-worth of trinkets and blankets. The Dutch, of course, thought they had a bargain. The irony is that they were trading with a tribe of Indians who were simply passing through the area! Peaceful relations between the Europeans and Native Americans were disturbed, however, by the settlers' insistence on taking over the land,

and a costly and bloody war ensued, lasting two and a half years. Finally Peter Stuyvesant was hired by the Dutch West India Company to restore peace.

Stuyvesant was an experienced colonialist and went about establishing a strong community with a proper infrastructure. One of the first things he did was to order the building of a defensive wall and ditch along what we know today as Wall Street. The new settlement prospered and even doubled in size, but Governor Stuyvesant was not well liked. He introduced new taxes, persecuted Jews and Quakers, and even limited the amount of alcohol people could drink. Trouble followed, and the locals became less and less inclined to obey him. By the time four British warships sailed into the harbour in late 1664, he had no alternative but to surrender to Colonel Richard Nichols without a shot being fired. The colony was immediately renamed New York in honour of the Duke of York, brother to the English king, and thereafter remained mostly in the hands of the British until the end of the American Revolution.

The Chrysler Building

WHAT'S IN A NAME?

The Big Apple has become synonymous with New York City, but came into being during the 1920s when horse-racing writer John Fitzgerald popularised the term. On assignment in New Orleans for *The Morning Telegraph*, he overheard stablehands refer to New York City racing tracks as The Big Apple and decided to call his column on New York's racing scene 'Around the Big Apple'.

A decade later, jazz musicians adopted the term to refer to New York City. The favourite story of Big Onion tour guides is related to Small's Big Apple jazz club in Harlem. The story goes that when the musicians from the club went on tour around America they'd say to each other: 'I'll see you in the Big Apple'. But the term was still relatively unknown until it was adopted by the New York Convention and Visitors' Bureau in 1971, when they launched The Big Apple campaign.

So there you have it – the name Big Apple is a marketing device invented by the city to lure in visitors and it certainly seems to work as more than 34 million business people and tourists arrive each year.

Many New Yorkers also like to call the city Gotham – taken from the Batman stories that are based in Gotham City and believed by many to be a thinly veiled reference to New York. The name Manhattan is derived from Mannahatta, the name given to the island by its first inhabitants, the Algonquin Indians.

A NEW VOICE

By 1700, the population had reached 20,000, made up of immigrants from England, Holland, Germany, Ireland and Sweden. It was already the rich melting-pot of cultures and religions that it remains today. Over the next 74 years, the colony gradually began to establish itself and there was a growing belief among well-educated and powerful Americans – including Thomas Jefferson and Benjamin Franklin – that the government should be fair and democratic.

In 1764, following the Seven Years War between the British and French, the Brits passed a number of laws, including the Stamp Act, allowing them to raise taxes in the colony. In response, Americans from all over the country banded together and rescinded Britain's right to collect taxes from them. The Stamp Act was repealed but it seemed that the Brits hadn't learned their lesson. They introduced the Townshend Act, which imposed taxes on various imports and led to a bloody confrontation in 1770. In 1774, the Americans set up the Continental Congress, made up of representatives from each of the colonies. Later that year, those representatives urged all Americans to stop paying their taxes and just two years later the Declaration of Independence was drawn up, largely by Jefferson.

During the War of Independence that inevitably followed, New York was considered strategically vital as it stood between the New England colonies and those in the south. In 1776, British commander Lord Howe sailed 500 ships into the harbour and occupied the city. George Washington's army was defeated and forced to leave. The peace process began in 1779 and led to a treaty in 1783. The Brits, who had remained in New York since the end of the war, left just before George Washington returned to claim victory.

New York then became the country's first capital and George Washington its first president, taking his oath of office in 1789. The city was capital for just one year, but business boomed. The New York Stock

TOP FIVE BOOKS ON NEW YORK HISTORY

Herbert Asbury: *The Gangs of New York; An Informal History of the Underworld*, Arrow Books (2003)

Sanna Feirstein: *Naming New York*, New York University Press (2000)

Kenneth T Jackson: *The Encyclopedia of New York City*, Yale University Press (1995)

Mike Wallace and Edwin G Burrows: *Gotham: A History of New York City to 1898*, Oxford University Press Inc. USA (1999)

Shaun O'Connell: *Remarkable, Unspeakable New York*, Beacon Press (1997)

Exchange, established under a tree on Wall Street by Alexander Hamilton in 1792, positively buzzed with activity as new companies were set up, bought and sold.

As the city grew, it became clear that a proper infrastructure and sanitation system was needed, so the governors introduced a grid system throughout the entire island. North of 14th Street, it abandoned all the existing roads except for Broadway, which followed an old Indian trail, and set up wide avenues that ran south to north and streets that ran between the rivers. Everything, it seemed, was pushing the city north, from illness to prosperity: while the grid system was being put on paper, a series of epidemics drove residents from the old Downtown into what is now known as Greenwich Village.

THE RICH GET RICHER...

By 1818, reliable shipping services between New York and other American cities and Europe were well established and trade was booming. It was boosted further by the opening of the Erie Canal in 1825, which, together with the new railroads, opened trade routes to the Midwest. With so much spare cash to play with, businessmen started to build large summer estates and mansions along 5th Avenue up to Madison Square. At the same time, many charities and philanthropic institutions were set up and great libraries were built, as education was seen as being very important.

But the divide between rich and poor was getting wider. While water supplies, indoor plumbing and central heating were being installed in the 5th Avenue mansions, thousands of immigrant families – particularly from Ireland – had no choice but to live in the appalling tenement buildings that were being erected on the Lower East Side of Manhattan.

These people were forced to eke out a wretched existence in the old sweatshops by day and contend with the punitive living conditions of the tenements by night. Entire families were crammed into one or two rooms that had no windows, no hot water, no heat and, of course, no bathroom. Toilet facilities had to be shared with neighbours.

The impending Civil War over the question of slavery became a major issue for the poor of New York, who couldn't afford to buy their way out of conscription. Uppermost in their minds was the concern

that freed slaves would be going after their jobs. The fear reached fever pitch and led to America's worst-ever riot, a four-day-long affair in which over 100 people died and thousands, mostly blacks, were injured. By 1865, however, the abolitionists won the war, finally freeing four million black people from the plight of slavery.

BOOM TIME FOR IMMIGRATION

At the same time, New York and Boston were being hit by great tidal waves of immigrants. In the 1840s and 1850s it was the Irish fleeing famine; in the 1860s it was the Germans fleeing persecution; and in the 1870s it was the Chinese, brought into America specifically to build the railroads. In the 1880s it was the turn of the Russians, along with 1.5 million Eastern European Jews. Over 8 million immigrants went through Castle Clinton in Battery Park between 1855 and 1890. Then the Ellis Island centre was built in 1892 and handled double that number. Between 1880 and 1910, 17 million immigrants passed through the city and, by 1900, the population had reached 3.4 million.

Most of the new arrivals who chose to stay in New York ended up in the crowded tenements of the Lower East Side. Finally in 1879, after the terrible conditions were brought to light, the city passed new housing laws requiring landlords to increase water supplies and toilets, install fire escapes and build air shafts between buildings to let in air and light. The introduction of streetcars and elevated railways also helped to alleviate the transport problem.

THE GILDED AGE

Meanwhile, the wealthy were enjoying the Gilded Age, as Mark Twain dubbed it. Central Park opened in 1858 and more and more mansions were built on 5th Avenue for the likes of the Whitneys, Vanderbilts and Astors. Row houses were also being built on the Upper West Side for wealthy European immigrants. Henry Frick, who made his fortune in steel and the railroads, built a mansion (now a museum) on the east side of the park at 70th Street, just 10 blocks from the new Metropolitan Museum of Art. Luxury hotels such as the original Waldorf Astoria and the Plaza opened, as did the original Metropolitan Opera House. The Statue of Liberty, St Patrick's Cathedral, the Brooklyn Bridge and Carnegie Hall were all built at this time.

Those were the days of the people whose names we associate with New York but don't necessarily know why – like Cornelius Vanderbilt, a shipping and railroad magnate; Andrew Carnegie, a steel and railroad baron; and John D Rockefeller, who made his millions in oil. The names of many of these millionaires live on in the gifts they gave back to the city: they provided concert halls, libraries and art museums, and donated entire collections to put in them. Carnegie built and donated Carnegie Hall to the city, Rockefeller was one of three major backers behind the opening of the Museum of Modern Art, and the Whitneys created a museum containing their own collection of modern American works of art.

At the same time, the structure of the city itself was undergoing a transformation. In 1904, the IRT subway opened 135km (84 miles) of track, which meant that people could move away from the polluted downtown areas, and by 1918 the New York City Transit System was complete.

The turn of the century also saw the birth of another phenomenon – the skyscraper. First to be built, in 1902, was the Flatiron Building, which was constructed using the new technology for the mass production of cast iron. Frank Woolworth's Gothic structure followed in 1913. The beautiful Chrysler Building went up in 1929 and the Empire State Building was completed in 1931.

Ritz Carlton Hotel

PROHIBITION ARRIVES

In the meantime, the Volstead Act of 1919 banned the sale of alcohol at the start of the Roaring Twenties. Fuelled by lively speakeasies, illegal booze, gangsters, the Charleston and jazz, this was the real heyday of famous venues like Harlem's Cotton Club and the Apollo Theater. After several glittering years, the fun and frolics came to an abrupt end with the collapse of the Wall Street stock market on 29 October 1929. It destroyed most small investors and led to huge unemployment and poverty across the whole of America. Things started to turn for the better only after President Franklin D Roosevelt introduced the New Deal, employing people to build new roads, houses and parks.

In New York, Fiorello LaGuardia was elected mayor and set up his austerity

USEFUL WEBSITES

www.cityguideny.com The online site of the weekly *City Guide* that is provided to hotels.

www.citysearchnyc.com Packed with information on New York, events and what's happening.

www.clubnyc.com Complete list of what's cool, where and why.

www.downtownny.com Directory of places to visit in Downtown.

www.halloween-nyc.com The official Halloween Parade site with history.

www.nyctourist.com An official tourism site for the city.

www.nycvisit.com The New York Convention and Visitors' Bureau's comprehensive listing includes suggested itineraries for where to stay and shop and what to do.

www.nytab.com The New York Travel Advisory Bureau's site is helpful for trip planning and gives information on major savings.

www.nytimes.com The online site for the *New York Times*.

www.villagevoice.com The online site of *The Village Voice*.

BEAT IT

The 1950s' Beat Movement was a partly social, partly literary phenomenon with three centres – Greenwich Village in New York, the North Beach district of San Francisco and Venice West in Los Angeles. Socially, the movement was all about rejecting middle-class values and commercialism and embracing poverty, individualism and release through jazz, sexual experience and drugs. The term 'beat' conveys both the American connotations of being worn-out and exhausted, but also suggests 'beatitude' or 'blessedness'. The chief spokesmen were Allen Ginsberg, Jack Kerouac, whose most famous novel is *On The Road*, Gregory Corso, William S Burroughs, Lawrence Ferlinghetti and Gary Snyder.

programme to enable the city to claw its way back to financial security. During his 12 years in office, LaGuardia worked hard at fighting corruption and organised crime in the city, and introduced a massive public housing project.

★ ★ ★ ★ **BRIT TIP** ★ ★ ★ ★

★ One of the most famous speakeasies
   during Prohibition was Jack &
   Charlies 21. You can visit it today as
   the rather more respectable 21 Club
   at 21 West 52nd Street.

These were also the days of a great literary and artistic scene in the city. Giants of the spoken and written word, including Dorothy Parker and George Kaufman, would meet at the famous Round Table of the Algonquin Hotel, where they were joined by stage and screen legends Tallulah Bankhead, Douglas Fairbanks and the Marx Brothers.

The Second World War was another watershed for New York, as people fled war-ravaged Europe and headed for the metropolis. Both during and after the war, huge new waves of immigrants arrived, fleeing first the Nazis and then the Communists. New York was as affected by McCarthy's hunt for 'reds' among the cultural and intellectual elite as the rest of the country, but it bounced back when a

new building boom followed the election of President Harry S Truman, whose policies were aimed specifically at helping the poor.

The Port Authority Bus Terminal was finished in 1950, the mammoth United Nations Building was completed in 1953, and in 1959 work started on the huge Lincoln Center complex – built on the slums of the San Juan district that were the setting for *West Side Story*.

FROM BOOM TO BUST

By the 1950s, a new period of affluence had started for the middle classes of New York. The descendants of the earlier Irish, Italian and Jewish immigrants moved out to the new towns that were springing up outside Manhattan, leaving space for a whole new wave of immigrants from Puerto Rico and the southern states of America. It was also the decade of the Beat generation, epitomised by Jack Kerouac and Allen Ginsberg, which evolved into the hippy culture of the 1960s. This was when Greenwich Village became the centre of a new wave of artists extolling the virtues of equality for all.

By the 1970s, however, this laissez-faire attitude, coupled with New York's position as a major gateway for illegal drug importation and the general demoralisation of the working classes and ethnic groups, led to an escalation in crime. Muggings and murder were rampant, and the city was brought to the brink of bankruptcy.

Chaos was averted only by the introduction of austerity measures, which unfortunately primarily affected the poor. But good news was just around the corner, as new mayor Ed Koch implemented major tax incentives to rejuvenate New York's business community. A boom followed, reflected in the erection of a series of

The Waldorf Astoria

mammoth new skyscrapers, including the World Trade Center and Trump Tower.

The transformation was completed in the 1990s with Mayor Giuliani's clean-up operation. This was unpopular with the more liberal New Yorkers but many believe it was his policies that turned New York into a city fit for the new millennium.

From the time of the earliest immigrants, New York has represented a gateway to a new life, a place of hope: the American dream offered a future filled with happiness and success. And nowadays New York still draws in people in their thousands. After all, as the song goes, 'If you can make it there, you'll make it anywhere.'

THE BEST TIMES TO GO

January to March and July and August are best for accommodation and good for flights. Just bear in mind that July and August are the hottest months, though it is not as bad as you might expect because all the shops and cabs have air-conditioning and you get blasts of lovely cool air from the shops as you pass.

In the run-up to Christmas it is very difficult to find accommodation in Manhattan, as it is in September and October when there are a lot of conventions. Surprisingly, the times around Thanksgiving and between Christmas and New Year are good times to go because people tend to be already at home with their families. April to June should be pleasantly cool (though it can also be surprisingly warm) and is a popular time to go.

Check Chapter 13, Festivals and Parades (page 254) to find out when the major events are happening in the city, as it tends to be more crowded at these times.

WHAT TO WEAR

Layers are the key to comfortable clothes in New York, no matter what time of year you go.

In summer the air-con in buildings can get pretty cold, while outside it is stiflingly hot. If you take a lightweight, rainproof jacket, you'll be covered for all eventualities, including the odd shower.

In winter it is the other way round –

AT-A-GLANCE HISTORY

1524 Giovanni da Verrazano arrives on Manhattan
1613 Trading post is set up at Fort Nassau
1624 Dutch West India Company establishes rule and settlers name Manhattan New Amsterdam
1626 Peter Minuit buys Manhattan for trinkets worth $24
1664 Dutch surrender to the British and New Amsterdam is renamed New York after the Duke of York
1776 War of Independence and battle for New York begins
1785 New York becomes the nation's capital
1792 New York Stock Exchange is founded
1811 Grid plan for Manhattan is introduced
1827 Slavery is officially abolished in New York
1858 Work on Central Park begins
1883 Brooklyn Bridge opens
1886 Statue of Liberty is built
1892 Ellis Island opens
1902 The Fuller (Flatiron) Building becomes the world's first skyscraper
1904 New York's first subway line opens
1919 Prohibition Act sees alcohol sales banned in New York
1923 Yankee Stadium opens
1929 New York stock market crashes
1931 Empire State Building opens
1950 United Nations building completed
1970 First New York City Marathon
1993 A terrorist bomb in the World Trade Center kills six and injures 1,000
1994 Rudy Giuliani appointed mayor and brings crime to an all-time low
2001 World Trade Centre Twin Towers hit by terrorists, killing 3,000

SEASONAL WEATHER

Month	Temp	Rainfall
Jan	-3-3°C (27-38°F)	8cm (3in)
Feb	-3-5°C (27-40°F)	8cm (3in)
Mar	1-9°C (34-49°F)	11cm (4¹/₄in)
Apr	7-16°C (44-61°F)	10cm (4in)
May	12-22°C (53-72°F)	10cm (4in)
June	17-27°C (63-80°F)	8cm (3in)
July	20-29°C (68-85°F)	10cm (4in)
Aug	19-29°C (67-85°F)	10cm (4in)
Sep	16-25°C (60-77°F)	9cm (3¹/₂in)
Oct	10-19°C (50-66°F)	9cm (3¹/₂in)
Nov	5-12°C (41-54°F)	11cm (4¹/₄in)
Dec	-1-6°C (31-42°F)	10cm (4in)

warm buildings and cold streets – so it's best to have an overcoat of some sort, but nothing too heavy unless you're planning to be out of doors a lot. Also make sure you have a hat, scarf and gloves in your bag for times of emergency. At any time of the year, the skyscrapers of the city act as a kind of wind tunnel and unless you're in the sun it can get nippy pretty quickly – another reason to make sure you have a cardigan or lightweight jacket in the summer.

★ ★ ★ ★ **BRIT TIP** ★ ★ ★ ★
★ Don't worry if you spill wine all over ★
★ your favourite outfit – most hotels ★
★ have a valet service that can clean it ★
★ for you overnight or there are plenty ★
★ of dry cleaners throughout the city. ★
★ Ask at the hotel reception desk. ★
★ ★

DISABLED TRAVELLERS

According to the disabled people we've spoken to, New York is one of the easier destinations to tackle – and certainly puts Britain to shame. Most of the road corners, for instance, have kerbs that dip to the ground, making it a lot easier to wheel yourself about the city. Again, for the wheelchair-bound, bus platforms can be lowered to the same level as the pavement to allow easy access and, where possible, some of the subway stations have had

elevators installed. To find out which 59 stations are accessible to wheelchair passengers, check the MTA site www.mta.nyc.ny.us. For up-to-date information on the accessibility status of lifts and escalators, call 800 734-6772 or 718-596 8273 around the clock.

If you'd like to travel in style, Vega Transportation (tel 718-507 0500, www.vegatransportation.com) offers the luxury of a chauffeur-driven car for those in a wheelchair. And you can rent a wheelchair on arrival (7 day, 24-hour service) from ScootAround (tel 888-441 7575, www.scootaround.com).

One of our favourite New York tales comes from Colin Macrae, a disabled person who regularly travels all over the world with his wife Joan. They were in New York one cold Christmas and Colin was sitting in his wheelchair all by himself, huddled up against the biting wind, while his wife went off to sort out tickets for the Circle Line cruise. As he waited, Colin was approached by a tramp, who pressed a quarter into his hand saying: 'I don't have much, but you can have what I've got.' Then he rushed off before Colin could reply or give him his money back. Just goes to show, the most unexpected and heart-warming things can happen in this amazing city.

Anyway, to make your life as easy as possible, here are the main organisations that deal with different aspects of travel for the disabled.

RESOURCES FOR THE DISABLED

Note: TDD or TTY = Telecommunications devices for the deaf.

Hospital Audiences Inc (HAI): 3rd Floor, 548 Broadway. Tel 212-575 7676 or 888-424 4685, www.hospaud.org. Publishes a book, *Access for All* ($5), which gives comprehensive information on venue access, toilet facilities and water fountains at a whole range of cultural centres from theatres to museums and major sights.

In addition, it has audio description services for people who are blind or visually impaired. Called Describe, this contains Program Notes, which describe all aspects of a show and staging in an audio cassette you can listen to before the performance. It also transmits a live Audio Description, during a pause in the dialogue, to audience members who have a small receiver. Reservations for both the tickets, which have to be bought either through HAI or the theatre, and receivers, which are provided free of charge, must be made through HAI. For more information call Describe on 212-575 7663.

New York Society for the Deaf: 817 Broadway at 12th Street. Tel 212-777 3900. Provides advice and information on facilities for the deaf.

Big Apple Greeter Access Coordinator: 1 Center Street, Room 2035, New York, NY 10007. Tel 212-669 2896 (voice) or 212-669 8273 (TDD), www.bigapplegreeter.org. Will provide a free tour guide for anyone with a disability. Reserve though, three to four weeks ahead.

SIGN LANGUAGE INTERPRETED PERFORMANCES

The Theater Access Program: TAP is specifically for Broadway shows and is run by the Theater Development Fund. Tel 212-669 8159 (voice) or 212-719 4537 (TDD), www.tdf.org. Reservations for infrared headsets or neckloops for Broadway shows can be made by calling Sound Associates. Tel 212-582 7678, www.soundassociates.com.

Lighthouse Incorporated: 111 East 59th Street. Tel 212-821 9200 (voice) or 212-821 9713 (TTY), www.lighthouse.org. Provides help and advice for blind people living in or visiting the city.

COMMUNICATIONS

The American ringing tone is long and the engaged tone is very short and high-pitched, almost like a beep.

PHONES

To call New York from abroad: Dial 001 and the prefix – for instance, the main prefix for Manhattan is 212 and the new one is 646 – then dial the 7-digit number.

West Village

To call abroad from New York: Dial 011 + country code + area code (dropping the first 0) + local number. The code for Britain is 44.

To call any number in New York from New York: Always dial 1 + the area code + the number.

Useful numbers:

Operator: 0

Directory enquiries: 411 (free from payphones)

Long distance directory enquiries: 1 + area code + 555 1212

Free numbers directory: 1 + 800 + 555 1212 (no charge)

MOBILE PHONES

It is now possible to get a mobile phone for use in New York. Cellhire USA supplies competitively priced mobiles (or cell phones in American-speak) to international business travellers to the city. Tel 212-376 7373, www.cellhire.com.

★ ★ ★ ★ BRIT TIP ★ ★ ★ ★
★   ★
★   If you make any calls at all from   ★
★   your hotel you will pay a   ★
★ tremendous premium. To avoid this, ★
★   you can either get a whole bucket   ★
★   of quarters to use in a public   ★
★   payphone or buy an international   ★
★ phone card before you leave home. ★
★   Local call costs a minimum of 25c.   ★
★ ★

POST

To send a postcard costs 70c, to send a letter costs 80c for the first 25g (1oz). You can buy stamps in shops – the Duane Reade chain of chemists has machines – but there is a mark-up. If you don't want to pay over the odds for the convenience of these stamps, then go to one of the many post offices dotted around the city (call 800-275 877 or visit www.usps.com).

The main post office on 34th Street at 8th Avenue is a beautiful Beaux Arts building and incredibly large. If the queues are long, you can buy stamps from the vending machines.

Post boxes are square, dark blue metal boxes about 1.2m (4ft) tall with a rounded top that has a pull-down handle. They have a sign saying *US Mail* and a striking big American eagle logo on the side and can be found on street corners.

THE INTERNET

easyEverything: 234 West 42nd Street between 7th and 8th Avenues. Tel 212-398 0724, www.easyinternetcafe.com. Subway A, C, E, 1, 2, 3, 7, 9, S, B, D, F, Q to 42nd Street/Times Square. Area: Theater District. Open 24 hours, the world's largest internet cafe has 648 computers, plus scanners. Prices start at just $1 and it is open 7 days a week, 7am–1am.

Cybercafé: 273 Lafayette Street at Prince Street. Tel 212-334 5140, www.cyber-cafe.com. Subway 6 to Bleecker Street, 4, 5, 6 to Spring Street and N, R to Prince Street. Area: NoLiTa/SoHo. It's open 8.30am–10pm and costs $6.40 for half an hour on the internet. One of many dotted around the city.

AMERICAN–SPEAK

It has often been said that the Brits and Americans are two races divided by a common language and when you make an unexpected faux pas you'll certainly learn how true this is. For instance, never ask for a packet of fags as this is the American slang word for gays! There are plenty of other differences, too, which may not necessarily cause offence but which will cause confusion, so to help you on your way, here is a guide to American-speak.

General:

English	American
Air hostess	Flight attendant
Anti-clockwise	Counterclockwise
At weekends	On weekends
Autumn	Fall
Behind	In back of
Camp bed	Cot
Cinema	Movie theater
City/town centre	Downtown (not Lower Manhattan)
Coach	Bus
Cot	Crib
Diary (appointments)	Calendar
Diary (records)	Journal
Football	Soccer
From... to...	Through
Lift	Elevator
Long-distance call	Trunk call
Nappy	Diaper
Ordinary	Regular, normal
Paddling pool	Wading pool
Plaster	Band Aid
Post, postbox	Mail, mailbox
Pram, pushchair	Stroller
Receptionist	Desk clerk

Tap	Faucet
Toilet	Restroom (public) or bathroom (private)

Money:

English	American
Banknote	Bill
Bill	Check or tab
Cashpoint/cash machine	ATM
Cheque	Check
1 dollar	Single
25 cents	Quarter
10 cents	Dime
5 cents	Nickel
1 cent	Penny

★ ★ ★ ★ **BRIT TIP** ★ ★ ★ ★

There are no ground floors in America; what we call the ground floor, they call the first floor. It may seem a silly point, but it can cause confusion!

Food and drink:

One of the biggest disappointments we had on our first trip to America was to order our breakfast eggs 'sunny-side up', only to end up with what seemed like a half-cooked egg! The Americans don't flick fat over the top of the egg when frying it, but turn it over to cook on both sides. So for eggs cooked on both sides but soft, order eggs 'over easy' and if you like yours well done, then ask for eggs 'over hard'.

There are plenty of other anomalies. Many standard American dishes come with a biscuit – which is a corn scone to us. Breakfast may also include grits, a porridge-like dish of ground, boiled corn, and hash browns – grated, fried potatoes. You'll find foods and food terms that are specific to New York on page 176.

Canal Street, Chinatown

KNOWING NEW YORK

English	American
Aubergine	Eggplant
Biscuit (savoury)	Cracker
Biscuit (sweet)	Cookie
Chick pea	Garbanzo bean
Chips	(French) fries
Choux bun	Cream puff
Clingfilm	Plastic wrap
Cornflour	Cornstarch
Courgette	Zucchini
Crayfish	Crawfish
Crisps	Chips
Crystallised	Candied
Cutlery	Silverware or place-setting
Demerara sugar	Light-brown sugar
Desiccated coconut	Shredded coconut
Digestive biscuit	Graham cracker
Double cream	Heavy cream
Essence (eg vanilla)	Extract or flavouring
Filled baguette	Sub or hero
Fillet (of meat/fish)	Filet
Fizzy drink	Soda
Golden syrup	Corn syrup
Grated, fried potatoes	Hash browns
Grilled	Broiled
Icing sugar	Powdered/ confectioners' sugar
Jam	Jelly/conserve
Jelly	Jello
Ketchup	Catsup
King prawn	Shrimp
Main course	Entrée
Measure	Shot
Mince	Ground meat
Off-licence	Liquor store
Pastry case	Pie shell
Pips	Seeds (in fruit)
Plain/dark chocolate	Semi-sweet or unsweetened chocolate
Pumpkin	Squash
Scone	Biscuit
Shortcrust pastry	Pie dough
Single cream	Light cream
Soda water	Seltzer
Sorbet	Sherbet
Soya	Soy
Spirits	Liquor
Sponge finger biscuits	Lady fingers
Spring onion	Scallion
Starter	Appetiser
Stoned (cherries etc)	Pitted
Sultanas	Golden raisins
Sweet shop	Candy store
Takeaway	To go
Tomato purée	Tomato paste
Water biscuit	Cracker

★ ★ ★ ★ **BRIT TIP** ★ ★ ★ ★

New Yorkers may consider themselves broad-minded but, like any American, will be genuinely shocked if you ask where the toilet is. Ask for the restroom in a public place and the bathroom if you're in someone's house.

Shopping:

English	American
Braces	Suspenders
Bumbag	Fanny pack
Chemist	Drug store
Flip-flops	Thongs
Ground floor	First floor
Handbag	Purse
High street	Main street
Jumper	Sweater
Knickers	Panties
Muslin	Cheesecloth
Queue	Line, line up
Suspenders	Garters
Tights	Pantyhose
Till	Check-out
Trainers	Sneakers
Trousers	Pants
Underpants	Shorts, underwear
Vest	Undershirt
Waistcoat	Vest
Zip	Zipper

Travelling around:

English	American
Aerial	Antenna
Articulated truck	Semi
Bonnet	Hood
Boot	Trunk
Caravan	House trailer
Car park	Parking lot
Carriage (on a train)	Car
Car silencer	Muffler
Crossroads/junction	Intersection
Demister	Defogger
Dipswitch	Dimmer
Dual carriageway	Four-lane (or divided) highway
Flyover	Overpass
Give way	Yield
Jump lead	Jumper cables
Layby	Pull-off
Lorry	Truck
Manual transmission	Stickshift
Motorway	Highway, freeway, expressway

Pavement	Sidewalk
Petrol	Gas
Request stop	Flag stop
Ring road	Beltway
Roundabout	Traffic circle
Slip road	Ramp
Subway	Pedestrian underpass
Turning	Turnoff
Underground	Subway
Walk	Hike
Wheel clamp	Denver boot
Windscreen	Windshield
Wing	Fender
Zebra crossing	Cross walk

★ ★ ★ ★ **BRIT TIP** ★ ★ ★ ★

While you're at the NYC visitor centre in New York, pick up a copy of the *City Guide* magazine. It has up-to-date listings on Broadway shows plus various money-off coupons.

TOURIST INFORMATION

NYC & COMPANY CONVENTION & VISITORS BUREAU

www.nycvisit.com
London: Tel 020 7202 6368 (line open Mon–Fri 9.30am–5.30pm).
New York City's official tourism agency – call to discuss any queries you have with the information officers or ask them to send you a Visitors' Guide.

New York: 810 Seventh Avenue at 53rd Street. Tel 212-484 1222. Mon–Fri 8.30am–6pm; Sat and Sun 8.30am–5pm. Subway N, R, S, Q to 57th Street, B, D, E to 7th Avenue/53rd Street or 1, 9 to 50th Street/Rockefeller Center.
Area: Midtown. There are also visitors' centres in Downtown, Chinatown and Harlem.
A state-of-the-art visitors' information centre with touch-screen kiosks that provide up-to-date information on the city's attractions and events accompanied by a detailed map. There is also a cashpoint and a souvenir shop, plus an incredible range of brochures covering hotels, shops, museums, sights, tours and Broadway shows.

NEW YORK TALK

Of course, in addition to the differences between American and Brit-speak, the locals have a dialect and phraseology all their own, influenced mainly by the Brooklyn accent, Mafia-speak and the fact that people often talk so quickly that words run into each other. Here are just a few examples that you may well come across:

All right already: Stop it, that's enough!
Big one: A $1,000 bill
Bloomies: Bloomingdale's
Capeesh: Pronunciation of capisce, Italian for 'understand'
Cattle call: A casting call at a Broadway theatre
Dead soldier: Empty beer can or bottle
Do me a solid: Do me a favour
Don't jerk my chain: Don't fool with me
DPh: Damned fool, based on transposing PhD
Eighth Wonder of the World: Brooklyn Bridge
Finger: Pickpocket (also mechanic, dip, cannon, goniff or moll buzzer)
Fuggedaboduid: No way
Guppies: Gay yuppies
JAPs: Jewish American princesses
Jocks: Sporty types, after their straps
Mazuma: Slang for money
Meet me between the lions: A favourite meeting place: the lion statues at the New York Public Library
Met: The Metropolitan Opera House or the Metropolitan Museum
No problem: You're welcome
Nudnik or nudge: A persistently dull and boring person
On account: Because
On line: Stand in a queue
Out in left field: Weird, unorthodox
Ozone: Very fresh, pure air
Shoot the works: Gamble or risk everything
Straphanger: Subway commuter
Suit: Businessman
Yard: Back garden

NEW YORK TRAVEL ADVISORY BUREAU

www.nytab.com
An independently run tourism agency, which is most famous for its own pocket guide to New York, the NYPages, and the NYCard, which gives discounts to hotels,

museums and attractions – check the website for the latest update on all their available discounts. It also has downloadable walking maps.

LOST YOUR PASSPORT?

If you lose your passport or have any big problems, call the emergency number at the New York British Consulate on 212-745 0202 option 2, www.britainusa.com.

CURRENCY

Exchange rate for the US dollar at the time of writing is around $1.80/£1. UK banks' and travel agencies' rates vary, so shop around to find the best. Also check the commission – some will charge for both selling and buying back, but many will only charge once so you can return unused dollars you bought from them free of charge. Travel agencies tend to compete with each other on rates and don't charge commission. The Post Office and Marks & Spencer do not charge commission.

★ ★ ★ ★ **BRIT TIP** ★ ★ ★ ★
★ For a quick currency converter go to ★
★ www.xe.com/ucc/ which also offers ★
★ free currency exchange rates. ★

A lot of people use travellers' cheques, but it is often a real palaver to cash them, especially at banks in New York. Many banks simply won't take them, and if they do they'll need photo ID so you'll have to carry your passport around with you. Chase Bank, Manhattan has more than 400 branches and doesn't charge a fee for exchanging currencies. Phone 212-935 9935 or visit www.chase.com to find a branch.

★ ★ ★ ★ **BRIT TIP** ★ ★ ★ ★
★ You must have plenty of change and ★
★ singles ($1 notes) as you'll be tipping ★
★ everyone for everything, and you'll ★
★ also need change for the buses. ★

The alternative is to exchange a reasonable amount of cash in one hit to use for tips, buses and in cafés, then use your credit card as much as possible (the exchange rate is generally reasonable). If

you need extra cash, make sure you know your PIN number for your credit card and you'll be able to use any of the many cashpoints (ATMs) around the city, for which there is usually a fee.

DISCOUNT DIVAS

NYC & Co (www.nycvisit.com) (see page 21) runs various money-off campaigns in association with the American Express Card that cover restaurants, hotels, theatres and sightseeing tours. The main one is Paint the Town Red, which runs from early January until the end of March.

Each year the popular Summer Restaurant Week takes place for two weeks from mid-July when you can get three-course meals at more than 150 of the city's top restaurants for around $25 (excluding tip, tax and drinks). Many restaurants also continue serving their prix-fixe lunches to the end of August. Establishments include Nobu, Gramercy Tavern, Union Square Café, La Caravelle and Montrachet. For further information visit www.nycvisit.com/restaurantweek or phone either 1-800 NYC VISIT (toll-free within America) or 212-484 1222.

TIPS ON TIPPING

You won't get a lunch, drink, ride or even a taxi door being opened for you without a tip being involved in America and it can add quite a lot to your overall expenses when you're on holiday. It's something that doesn't come naturally to us Brits, but you need to get used to it quickly.

Bartender: $1 a round.

Hotel doormen: $1 for hailing a cab.

Maid service: $2 per day when you leave your accommodation.

Porters: $1 per bag.

Taxi drivers: 15 per cent, and if you travel by private car or limousine they'll automatically add 20 per cent to the bill.

Waiters: General rule of thumb is 15–20 per cent. The best way to work it out is to double the sales tax, which will come to 17 per cent, and add a little more if you are very impressed. Just remember, at a posh restaurant the tip alone can come to more than the price of a decent meal!

CHAPTER 2

On the Move

When most people talk about New York, they actually mean Manhattan, which is the long, thin sliver of an island in the middle of the four outer boroughs of Staten Island, Queens, the Bronx and Brooklyn.

You'll find diagrammatic maps, such as the one below, dotted throughout the book to help you focus on the basic geography of the area. Once you get the hang of roughly where everything is, you'll find it easier to use the subway and bus maps on the inside front and back covers, and the street maps in the centre pages.

ORIENTATION

Manhattan is 21km (13 miles) long and 3.2km (2 miles) wide for the most part and almost all of it above 14th Street is on the grid system that was introduced quite early on in New York's history. The main exceptions are Chinatown and Greenwich Village, which, like Downtown, had already established its eccentric random arrangement of streets (like ours in the UK) before urban planning and refused to get on the grid system. The other exception is Broadway, which follows an old Indian trail that runs largely north to south on the west side of the island, then cuts across to the east side as it runs down towards Downtown.

Here are a few basic rules about the geography of Manhattan; it is useful to acquaint yourself with them as soon as possible, then you'll be able to walk around with confidence.

➡ Manhattan is divided into three main areas: Downtown, which includes neighbourhoods south of 14th Street; Midtown, the area between 14th and 59th Streets; and Uptown, areas north of 59th Street.

➡ All the roads going across Manhattan east to west are streets and all the roads going north to south are avenues.

➡ The city is divided between east and west by 5th Avenue and all the street numbers begin there. This means that 2 West 57th Street is just a few steps to the west of 5th Avenue while 2 East 57th Street is just a few steps to the east of 5th Avenue.

★ ★ ★ ★ **BRIT TIP** ★ ★ ★ ★

To New Yorkers, 'downtown' does not mean the city centre, but means south, while 'uptown' means north. You will need to get used to these terms if you are planning to use the subway – which is simpler to use than it looks at first!

➡ Most streets in Manhattan are one-way. With a few exceptions, traffic on even-numbered streets travels east and traffic on odd-numbered streets travels west. Traffic on major 'cross-town' streets – so-called because they are horizontal on the street maps of Manhattan – travels in both directions. From south to north, these include Canal, Houston (pronounced Howston), 14th, 23rd, 34th, 42nd, 57th, 72nd, 79th, 86th and 96th Streets.

Areas of New York

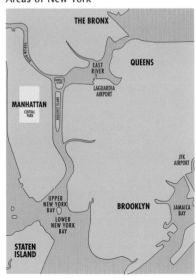

➡ When travelling north to south or vice versa, remember that traffic on York Avenue goes both ways, 1st Avenue goes from south to north, 2nd Avenue goes south and 3rd goes north mostly, though there is a small two-way section. Lexington goes south, Park goes in both directions, Madison goes north and 5th Avenue goes south. Central Park West goes both ways, Columbus Avenue goes south, Amsterdam Avenue north, Broadway goes in both directions until Columbus Circle, after which it continues southbound only to the tip of Manhattan. West End Avenue and Riverside Drive go in both directions.

➡ Numbered avenue addresses increase from south to north.

★ To calculate the distance from one ★ place to another, 20 north-south ★ blocks or 10 east-west blocks equal ★ about 1.6km (1 mile). This rule does ★ not apply to the Financial District or ★ Greenwich Village.

ARRIVING BY AIR

JOHN F KENNEDY INTERNATIONAL AIRPORT
Tel 718-244 4444
www.panynj.gov

JFK is in the borough of Queens and is the best place to enter or leave New York by air. It is 24km (15 miles) from Midtown Manhattan, a journey that will take you 50–60 minutes.

Taxi
The cost of a yellow medallion taxi into town is a fixed rate of $45 (per taxi) as set by the New York Taxi and Limousine Commission (www.nyc.gov/taxi). Bridge and tunnel tolls are extra (around $4 and you can pay at the end of the journey) as is the 15 per cent tip. So think around $50.

Train
The AirTrain JFK (212-435 7000, www.airtrainjfk.com) is a flat $5 enter/exit fare. They run every 4–8 minutes from 6am to 11pm and will take you to the Howard Beach Station from where you connect to the A subway to head into town.

Bus
New York Airport Service Express Bus (Westside & Eastside): Tel 718-875 8200, www.nyairportservice.com. Catch one from the Airport Bus Center. They run from 6.15am to 10.10pm daily every 15–30 minutes, cost $15 (or $27 round trip) and will drop you off Midtown west or east.

Trans-Bridge Lines: Tel 1-800 962 9135 or 610-868 6001. $12 (one way) which leaves at 3.30, 5.30 and 7pm daily.

Private hire car
Classic Limousine: Tel 1-800-666-4949 or 631-567 5100, www.classictrans.com.

Supersaver by Carmel: Tel 1-800-924-9954 or 212-666 6666, www.carmellimo.com.

SuperShuttle: Tel 212-209 7000, www.supershuttle.com. A door-to-door minibus service from the airport to your hotel operating 24 hours a day year round. Look for the blue van! Costs $13–22.

NEWARK LIBERTY INTERNATIONAL AIRPORT
Tel 973-961 6000
www.newarkairport.com

Taxi
The journey from Newark to central Manhattan takes around 40 minutes, but add at least 30 minutes in the rush hour. Set taxi fares range from $45 to the Battery Park area to $60 and above to 185th Street. There's a $5 extra charge for all destinations to the east side of Manhattan. For more information contact the Newark Taxi Commission. Tel 973-733 8912, www.nyc.gov/taxi.

Train
AirTrain: Tel 1-888-397 4636, www.airtrainnewark.com. This $415-million link connecting the airport terminals with Newark Liberty International Airport Train Station opened in 2003. You can get to Manhattan from the station by taking an NJ Transit or Amtrak train to New York Penn Station, from where you can connect to the city's subways and buses with ease.

Bus
PATH: Tel 800-234 PATH. Rapid transit from Newark to Penn Station (but you must take a taxi to the bus station from the airport – $13) to stops in Downtown and Midtown Manhattan. Operates 24 hours, fare $1.50.

AIRPORT SECURITY

Since September 11, the relaxed security systems that operated in most American airports have been seriously tightened up. Expect longer queues and subsequent waiting times getting through immigration and baggage checks. Remember that it is prohibited to carry any sharp items in your hand luggage, so make sure you put scissors, tweezers and nail files in your main check-in luggage. You should also be prepared to be asked to open your bags for inspection and to be frisked by a security guard with a hand-held scanner.

Olympia Trails Airport Express Bus:
Tel 212-964 6233, www.olympiabus.com. Operates between Newark and three Manhattan locations – Penn Station (34th Street/8th Avenue), Port Authority Bus Terminal (42nd Street/8th Avenue) and Grand Central (41st Street between Lexington and Park Avenues). Also operates a hotel shuttle to all Midtown points between 30th and 65th Streets. Departs every 15 minutes, fare $13. Kids under 12 ride free or only pay $4 for hotel shuttle. 4am–11.45pm.

Private hire car and SuperShuttle services: As from John F Kennedy International Airport (see page 24).

★ If you're worried about getting lost in New York, click on to www.hopstop.com for online subway and walking directions around the city.

LAGUARDIA AIRPORT (LGA)
Tel: 718-533 3400
www.panynj.gov
This is the airport you'll probably arrive at if you've taken an internal domestic flight from another state. TWIA, United Airlines and Continental Airlines all operate here. It's situated about 13km (8 miles) from the centre of Manhattan, between Queens and the Bronx.

Taxi
You'll find a clearly marked taxi rank outside the main terminals. Unlike JFK you pay by the meter rather than a flat rate, and you will also be charged tolls. A basic guide is $25–30 plus tolls ($4-6) and tip, and the journey should take about 20–25 minutes.

Bus
New York Airport Express Bus: Tel 718-875 8200, www.nyairportservice.com. A far cheaper option into town than taxi, taking around 40–50 minutes. The fare costs only $12 (or $21 round trip) and buses run daily (7.20am–11pm), leaving every 30 minutes. To catch your ride into town, follow the Ground Transportation signs out of the terminal and wait at the M60 or Q33 bus stop sign by the curb.

GETTING AROUND

There are lots of options for getting around Manhattan and the outer boroughs. The yellow cabs that you'll see in abundance are the fastest and most efficient way of getting to a destination, but they're not the cheapest. The subway in New York is easy to use and perfect for people with a limited budget, as well as being under cover when it's raining. If you'd rather see the sights,

METROCARD
The flat fare to travel on the subway is $2. However, you can no longer buy single fares; the cheapest ticket you can now get is the $10 MetroCard. This magnetically encoded card debits the fare when you swipe it through the turnstile in the subway or the farebox on a bus. You can purchase the cards from subway ticket offices (cash only), vending machines in most subways, from drugstores such as Rite Aid and Hudson News or from the Times Square Visitors Center at 1560 Broadway between 46th and 47th Streets. Some hotels also sell them at the reception desk.

A $10 card gives you six rides for the price of five. The $20 MetroCard gives you 12 rides for the price of 10. Both of these tickets can be used by up to four people though, so if there are two of you, you only need buy one MetroCard.

Unlimited Ride MetroCards include the 1-Day Fun Pass for $7 (which lasts until 3am the following day), the 7-Day card for $24, the 30-Day card for $76 and the 7-Day Express Bus Plus for $33. For more details, phone 1-800-638 7622 or visit www.mta.info.

then jump on a bus, though progress can be slow in rush hour. And then there's the oldest mode of transport, your feet. Walking around Manhattan is a joyful experience and thoroughly recommended; just don't forget to pack some comfy shoes.

TAXI

No trip to Manhattan would be complete without a ride in a yellow cab. It's the preferred means of transport for many visitors largely because there are so many about and the fares are reasonable. However, be warned. Even though the fares are much cheaper than in London, the cost still mounts up pretty quickly. Fares start at $2.50 and increase 40c every 0.32km ($^1/_5$ mile), or 20c per minute in stopped or slow traffic, with a 50c surcharge at night (8pm–6am) and $1 in peak hour (Mon–Fri 4-8pm). It's not just the cost of the ride that you have to take into consideration, but the $1 tip to the hotel doorman and the 15 per cent tip to the driver. It can work out to be an expensive option if used too often.

In any case, you will need to have a good idea of where you are going and how to get there, as most of the cab drivers in New York are the latest immigrants to have arrived and have very little clue about how to get around the city. The best way to ensure you don't get into any difficulties is to always carry the full address of where you're going, preferably with a map reference too. Fortunately, thanks to the grid system, it is relatively easy to educate yourself about where you are going and so you can give them directions!

➡ First off, never expect the driver to be the kind of chirpy, chatty Cockney character that you're used to in London. Most speak very little English and are not interested in making polite conversation, and many can be downright rude.

➡ Secondly, make sure you get into a taxi heading in the direction that you want to be going. If you are travelling uptown but you're on a road heading downtown, walk a block east or west so you'll be pointing in the right direction. It saves time and money, and if you don't, the taxi driver will know immediately that you're a tourist.

➡ Hailing a taxi is not necessarily as easy as it looks – you have to be aware of the lighting system on the top of the yellow medallion taxis. If the central light is on, it means the taxi driver is working and available. If all the lights are out, it means the driver is working but already has a fare. If the outer two lights or all three lights are on, it means that the taxi driver is off-duty – look carefully and you'll see the words. The best method for actually hailing a cab is to hold out your arm while standing at the curb.

➡ When you get to a toll, expect the taxi driver to turn around and demand the cash to pay for it, but you are quite within your rights to ask him to add it to your final fare.

➡ Beware of trying to get a cab at around 4pm. Not only is it the approach of rush hour, it's also when most drivers change shifts so getting a taxi is well nigh impossible as they don't want to go anywhere but home! If you really need a taxi at this time, be sure to call a car service company.

➡ Do not expect a taxi driver to change any bill larger than $20.

➡ In addition to the medallion on the roof, a legitimate taxi will have an automatic receipt machine mounted on the dashboard so that you can be given an immediate record of your trip.

➡ If you find yourself below Canal Street after business hours or at the weekend, you may have difficulty finding a yellow cab. Your best bet is to phone one of the many companies listed under Taxicab Service in

Areas of Manhattan

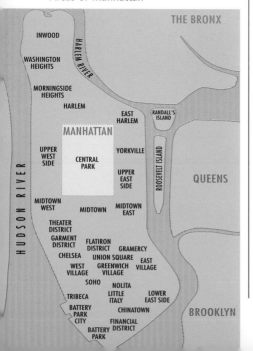

the Yellow Pages. Fares are slightly higher than for the metered cabs, but they are a safer option.

➡ There is no extra charge per person or for luggage, but a licensed taxi won't be able to take more than four people.

➡ Fasten your seatbelt once in the cab. All taxis are now required by law to provide them and passengers in the front seat have to wear them.

CAR SERVICE COMPANIES

When you need to be certain you have a taxi ride to the airport or some other destination, here are the companies you can phone, all of which provide a 24-hour service:

Carmel: Tel 212-666-6666, www.carmellimo.com.

Dial 7: Tel 212/1-800-777 7777, www.dial7.com.

Tel-Aviv: Tel 212-777 7777/1-800-222 9888.

Tri-State Limousine: Tel 212-777 7171.

ON THE SUBWAY

The first time you take a look at a subway map of New York, you can be forgiven for thinking you need a degree in the whole system to get anywhere. Plus the signposts – both outside and inside the stations – can easily be missed.

★ Generally, if you're going downtown, use subway entrances on the west side of the road and if you're going uptown, use subway entrances on the east side. This way you should be heading in the right direction, but do always check before entering.

In addition, the Metropolitan Transportation Authority (MTA) is undergoing a billion-dollar rejuvenation programme of many subway stops and has introduced new, clean trains on to the network, though New Yorkers aren't convinced that will last! On the old subway trains, the conductor would always announce stops and interchanges. These, for the large part, were unintelligible, but the new trains have pre-recorded announcements in a non-New York accent that can be understood.

THE SUBWAY MAP

There are subway maps on the inside front cover of this book. You can also get hold of free MTA maps in most subways stations, hotel lobbies and information centres.

➡ The subway lines are all indicated on the map by a colour but, unlike the London Underground, the colours are not used in the stations and on the trains. The important bit is the number or letter. Below the name of every stop you will find the letters and numbers of lines that stop there, such as 7, S Grand Central/42nd Street.

➡ When examining a subway map, a number or letter in a diamond means rush-hour service, in a circle it denotes normal service and a square indicates the end of a line. Black and white lines connecting white and black circles indicate a free subway transfer. White circles on coloured lines indicate express stops (express trains skip about three stops for every one that they make).

➡ If the numbers against your destination on the subway map are printed in a lighter tone, they are peak-time only.

RIDING THE SUBWAY

The good news is that New York's subway system is one of the cheapest to ride in the world. Before you can start getting around on the subway you'll need to buy a MetroCard (which also works on buses). You can buy these from a booth inside the entrance to the station or from a MetroCard vending machine, which you'll easily spot as they're brightly coloured. The machines accept cash, debit and credit cards. There are two types of ticket, pay-per-use and unlimited-ride 9 (see page 25).

➡ Don't look for obvious signs indicating a subway; instead look for either the very discreet 'M' signs in blue or the signature red and green glass globes – red means the entrance is not always open and green means it's staffed 24 hours a day.

➡ Before going down a subway entrance, check it is going in the right direction for

59th Street subway

you – many entrances take you to either 'downtown' or 'uptown' destinations, not both. It means that if you make the mistake of going in and swiping your ticket before you realise you're going in the wrong direction, you will have to swipe your card again to get in on the right side – so you'll end up paying double. The alternative is to travel in the wrong direction until you get to one of the larger subway stations (such as 42nd Street) and then change.

➡ If you're in one of the outer boroughs the same rules apply, but instead of looking for a Downtown or Uptown sign, look for one that says Manhattan.

➡ Some trains are express – they stop only at selected stations. At some stations you have to go down two flights to get to the platforms for express trains, while at others you don't, and it is easy to get on an express train by mistake.

★ ★ ★ ★ **BRIT TIP** ★ ★ ★ ★

Changes to subway schedules often occur at the last minute, so pay attention to posters on subway station walls and any announcements you hear on the platforms.

➡ There are conflicting opinions (hotly debated by the locals) as to whether it is worth waiting for an express. On the plus side, they move quickly, but on the down side you could end up waiting 10 minutes for one, so you won't have saved any time in the end.

➡ There are many different lines going to the same destinations, but they don't all exit at the same place. For example, if you arrive at Fulton Street on the New York subway and head for the exit you can come out at four completely different locations. The Red Line exits at Fulton and William Streets, the Brown Line exits at John and Nassau Streets, the Blue Line exits at Fulton and Nassau Streets, and the Green Line exits at Broadway and John Street – all of which are quite a long way from each other.

➡ The locals consider that the subway is safe to travel on until around 11pm. After that opinions vary, but when making up your mind to travel do be aware that the subway service after 11pm is generally incredibly slow.

➡ The subway does have one very good point: because the island of Manhattan is largely made up of granite, they did not have to dig as deep as we have to in London to find the really strong foundation level. This means you generally only have to go down one flight of steps to find the line.

➡ If you've been to New York before but not for a few years, bear in mind there have been a few changes to the subway network – and all for the better – thanks to a $17-billion expansion and renovation programme. These are the new lines:

➡ The L line runs almost the full width of Manhattan along 14th Street from 8th Avenue in the west to 1st Avenue in the east on its way to Queens. Other stops in Manhattan include 6th Avenue, Union Square and 3rd Avenue.

➡ The S line should not be confused with the shuttle between Times Square and Grand Central Station. It is another good east–west train linking West and East Villages in Greenwich and runs from West 4th Street to Grand Street.

➡ In Manhattan, the new peak-time V line largely runs in conjunction with the F line and includes new stops at 5th Avenue and 53rd Street as well as Lexington Avenue and 53rd Street.

ON THE BUSES

Travelling by bus is always a little more nerve-wracking because you can never be sure whether you've arrived at your destination, but most people are pretty helpful if asked a direct question. We thought that taking to the buses would be more difficult than travelling by subway, but two of our friends put paid to that notion by going everywhere by bus on their first visit.

FINDING A BUS

Our Manhattan bus map inside the front cover will come in handy as often there are no route maps at the bus stops. However, as a general rule buses run north to south, south to north, east to west or west to east.

➡ You can recognise bus stops by a yellow-painted curb next to a blue and white sign. Look at the Guide-a-Ride information at the stop, which should show the route and service schedule.

ON THE MOVE

RIDING THE BUSES

➡ Get on the bus at the front and click in your MetroCard or feed in $2. Exact change is essential – and it must be all in coins as no dollar bills are accepted.

➡ Although there are bus exits at the back, you can also get off at the front.

➡ Requesting a stop may be a little confusing – there are no clearly marked red buttons to press; instead there are black strips that run the full length of the bus between the windows or at the back along the tops of the handles. Simply press one of these to request the next stop.

➡ If the bus says 'Limited Stopping' it means it stops only at major stops, such as the cross-town streets of 14, 23, 34, 42, 50, 57, 68, 72, 79 and 86.

➡ The main bus routes used by tourists are: M1, which travels from 5th Avenue and Central Park to Madison Avenue; M7, which runs from Union Square to Broadway through the Theater District; and M6, which takes in Carnegie Hall to SoHo.

BRIT TIP

★ Our favourite MetroCard is the $20
★ pass. It offers 12 trips for the price
★ of 10, up to four people can use it
★ at one time and if you transfer to a
★ bus you only have to swipe the
★ ticket once and it will register for
★ everyone. You can also top it up in
★ amounts as small as $5 (page 25).

TOURIST ROUTES

Certain bus routes link key attractions, so if your feet are killing you, jump on one of the following buses to continue your trawl of Manhattan sights shown here in brackets:

M1: 5th Avenue (Central Park), 5th Avenue/84th Street (Metropolitan Museum of Art) 5th Avenue/49th–50th Streets (Rockefeller Centre) Madison Avenue/East 43rd Street (Grand Central Terminal/Chrysler Building).

M6: 7th Avenue/West 57th Street (Carnegie Hall), 7th Avenue/West 42nd Street (Times Square), Herald Square/Broadway (Empire State Building), Broadway/East 8th–9th Streets (Greenwich Village), South Street/Whitehall Street (Battery Park, ferry to Ellis Island & Statue of Liberty).

BY WATER TAXI

For a completely different way of getting around, you can go by water taxi. A commuter service runs around the lower part of Manhattan but the most useful is a hop on-hop off service designed for sightseeing from 1 May to 15 October. The three bright yellow catamarans with black and white check are easy to spot and there are six stops from DUMBO to West 44th Street, all easily accessible from the subway and bus stops. The service runs 11am–3pm on weekdays, stopping en route at South Street Seaport, Battery Park, World Financial Center, West Village and Chelsea Piers. At weekends, it runs each hour 11.22am–6.22pm from Hunters Point, stopping at East 34th Street, Schaeffer Landing, Fulton Ferry Landing, South Street Seaport, Red Hook, Battery Park, World Financial Center, Pier 45, West 23rd Street and West 44th Street. The other direction, from West 44th Street, it runs each hour 10.52am–6.52pm. Tickets cost $25 adults, $15 children and seniors.

A Gateway to America Harbor Tour runs every weekend, on the hour 11am–4pm taking in the Statue of Liberty, the Brooklyn Bridge and Manhattan Skyline. This costs $20 for adults, $18 for seniors and $12 for children 12 and under. For more information, phone 212-742 1969 or visit www.nywatertaxi.com. If you're on a budget or here in winter, check out the commuter route and times.

DRIVING IN NEW YORK

A word of advice: don't even think about it. Most of the streets will be jam-packed, while parking is extremely scarce and astronomically expensive at $8–10 an hour. You can park on the street, but watch out for what is known as alternate-side-of-the-street parking. This means you have to know which day of the week the cleaning truck comes past so you move the car over at the right time. Double parking is common, so it is easy to get boxed in, and frustrated drivers simply get in their cars and honk the horn until the guilty owner moves their car. As one New Yorker told us: 'People do not know how to park here. New Yorkers are not good drivers and are the wildest parkers.'

If you plan to take a trip upstate and wish to do so by car, then there are some dos and don'ts about car hire. Firstly, never

DRIVING TIPS

➡ Most streets in New York are one-way, so be sure to look out for signs before you head down a street.
➡ Drivers have to wear seatbelts by law, as do front-seat passengers and children aged 4–10 in the back.
➡ Speed limits are 30mph around town, 55mph on highways and freeways.
➡ Private parking facilities are available in the city but they cost $25–40 per day.
➡ Illegally parked cars will be towed away and there's a $150 fine plus $15 per day to be paid. Collect your car from Pier 76, West 38th Street at 12th Avenue (Midtown West). Tel 212-971 0772. It's open 24 hours a day Mon–Sat.

hire a car in Manhattan unless you want to pay around $160 a day. Take a ferry to the state of New Jersey and hire a car from there for around $85 for a medium-sized car with unlimited mileage. Secondly, don't consider hiring a car in the summer or at weekends because that's what most New Yorkers will be doing and they'll be difficult to come by. Cars are also snapped up in the autumn when New Yorkers like to go to see the autumn foliage.

★ ★ ★ ★ ★ BRIT TIP ★ ★ ★ ★ ★
★ Overtaking is permitted on the ★
★ inside and outside lanes of ★
★ interstate highways, so if you're ★
★ driving to Manhattan from one of ★
★ the airports, be sure to use both of ★
★ your wing mirrors to look for ★
★ passing cars. ★

CAR HIRE

If you do decide to take the plunge and drive around the city, there are a number of car hire companies to choose from. Most are based at the major airports, so you can simply pick them up when you arrive. Prices vary enormously, from a one-day rental costing from $90 to a week rate of $225–300. Remember that to rent a car you'll need to be over 25, have a valid driver's licence, have your own insurance and some photo ID. You'll also need to have a credit card (or very large cash deposit) to be able to rent a car and most rental companics add sales tax of around 8.6 per cent.

Car hire companies

Alamo: Tel 1-800-462 5266, www.alamo.com.

Argus Rentals: Tel 353-1-490 6173, www.argusrentals.com.

Avis: Tel 1-800-331 1212, www.avis.com.

Dollar: 1-800-800 3665, www.dollar.com.

Hertz: Tel 800-654 3131, www.hertz.com.

Independent (and often cheaper) car rental companies: www.cartental express.com.

FINDING A WC

It's worth raising this subject early as you'll probably be spending quite a lot of time walking around and you could easily get caught out. It is wise to know that public lavatories are thin on the ground in New York. In addition, subway loos – if they are actually open – are dangerous and unhygienic. It is considered impolite to use the word 'toilet'; in America a public toilet is always the 'restroom'.

So you're in the middle of Greenwich Village, you're desperate, and you don't want to pay through the nose for a beer so you can use the bar's facilities. What do you do? We have it on good authority from those New Yorkers in the know that you can go to the following places:

Barnes & Noble: This is a chain of bookstores that offers restrooms because the company wants people to treat the stores as public meeting places.

Department stores: The restrooms are hidden away, however, and you have to ask where they are (this is to deter street people from using them).

Government buildings: Try places like the United Nations, though you'll have to go through a security check.

Hotels: The restrooms are usually on the ground floor or you can ask.

Lincoln Center: There are ten 'stalls' open to the public, close to the entrance.

McDonald's and Burger King: Unisex toilets that are usually clean and modern because they are built to the company's spec rather than the typical New York building spec.

Public libraries: They all have public loos.

Restaurants: Some have signs saying 'For customers only', but if you ask authoritatively enough and look okay, they'll probably let you use them.

Statue of Liberty: In the gift shop.

CHAPTER 3

The New York Neighbourhoods

It's worth getting to know the neighbourhoods of Manhattan as each one has a distinct flavour and is filled with its own unique sights and sounds. From the historic Downtown area of the Financial District to the charming cobbled streets of Greenwich Village and the vibrancy of Times Square, every one is well worth visiting in its own right.

Here's an outline of what you'll find in each neighbourhood, what makes them so special and how to make the most of your time there. They are placed in alphabetical order for ease of reference.

34TH STREET

You'll have two major reasons for coming to this part of New York (Map 3) – the divine **Empire State Building** (page 61) and the shopping. **Macy's** is here (page 89), as well as a range of chains and most importantly a lot of retail outlets for the nearby Garment District. This was once a pretty seedy area but, thanks to the efforts of the 34th Street Business Improvement District Partnership (BID), it has been transformed.

Now the streets are constantly maintained, clean and lined with pretty flower tubs and green benches. The BID has even installed some smart green telephones with a semi enclosure to block out some of the street noise. The kiosk at Herald Square is in matching green, as is the city's one and only automatic pay toilet next door. It's pretty swanky and, most importantly, it's clean! The size of the average New York bedroom, you've enough room to swing a cat if you feel like it and 25c gives you 20 minutes inside.

If you plan to do the Empire State Building, make it your first port of call before the crowds and queues build up. Take the B, D, F, N, Q, R, V, W to 34th Street and walk one block east to 5th Avenue where you'll find the beautiful Art Deco entrance.

Once you've come back down to earth, take a cheap coffee break at the little-known **Graduate Center** (www.gc.cuny.edu/)

at 365 5th Avenue on the corner of 34th Street, diagonally opposite the Empire State Building. Here you can buy filtered coffee or a luscious latte with a croissant and sit in relative piece at any time of the day before 4pm, which is when the graduates start pouring in. The building used to be a department store, which is why there are ribbons and ties sculpted into the exterior columns. Now it is used as a research centre for students and holds free concerts. Anyone can sign up to use a computer here for up to two hours for free.

Empire State Building

HERALD SQUARE

Herald Square, which is named after the now defunct newspaper, is home to the famous **Macy's** (www.macys.com), the world's largest retail outlet (the best subways for East 34th Street are the B, D, F, N, Q, R, V, W to 34th Street/Herald Square). Prior to Macy's opening in 1901, the area was down-at-heel, with lots of bordellos and seedy clubs. The opening of the department store was a fashion moment and improved the entire district.

The store's top-sellers among the Brits are the extremely well-priced Levi's and beauty products, while the seventh floor is dedicated to children's goods and it even has a McDonald's – the only department store in town to make such a proud boast.

For the grown-ups there is the wonderful **Cucina & Co.** (page 114) in the basement. A combination of buffet foods to eat in and take away, a grill restaurant and a coffee shop, it also has a sandwich station, pasta station and take-aways at incredible prices. Bearing in mind the average New Yorker spends $10 for a sandwich-style lunch and drink, Cucina's lunches are amazing value, as are their meal specials.

But don't expect it to look cheap; this is a wonderful space filled with fabulously fresh food in an indoor-market setting. Adjacent to it is **Macy's Cellar**, where a complete dinner for two costs $24.95.

SHOPPERS' PARADISE

Between 5th and 8th Avenues on 34th Street is a shopper's paradise and one of the highlights is the **Sephora** beauty emporium, which has branches all over the city (page 103). With its sparkling floor-to-ceiling windows and stylish displays, this is a pristine shrine to beauty products and fragrances.

Other great shops in the area include **Old Navy**, the high-value end of the **Banana Republic** chain, **Kids R Us**, **Daffy's** and its amazingly cheap designer selection, plus **HMV**, **H&M** and **Kmart**.

PENN STATION

One block south on 33rd Street and 7th Avenue is the entrance to **Penn Station**, short for Pennsylvania Station (subways 1, 2, 3, 9 to 34th Street–Penn Station). Before you enter you'll see a **Lindy's** pastry shop. The original Lindy's in the theatre area was famous for its cheesecake, and this and the other branch (in Times Square), trade off the name but they're pricey and not unique.

★ ★ ★ ★   **BRIT TIP**   ★ ★ ★ ★
★   ★
★ If you're on the west side of Penn ★
★ Station, you're just a stone's throw ★
★ from the block-long B&H Photo &   ★
★ Video store (www.bhphotovideo.   ★
★ com) on 9th Avenue from 33rd to   ★
★ 34th Street (page 112). It has 625 ★
★ staff over its four floors selling   ★
★ thousands of items to both   ★
★ amateurs and professionals.   ★
★ ★

As you enter Penn Station, you'll see a handy Duane Reade (think Boots the Chemist) on the left. Walk down to the round area that sits under the **Madison Square Garden** building and on your left you'll see the information booth for the **34th Street BID Partnership**. All around are coffee shops, bakeries and a sit-down restaurant called **Kabooz**. None of them is a patch on Cucina & Co. or the Graduate Center, though. The restrooms are terrible; they have running water, but it just happens to be all over the floor! A good alternative is to head for the **Hotel Pennsylvania** on 7th Avenue opposite Penn Station, where you'll find clean WCs situated on the ground floor.

★ ★ ★ ★   **BRIT TIP**   ★ ★ ★ ★
★   ★
★ There's a free tour of Penn Station ★
★ on the fourth Monday of each   ★
★ month starting from the 34th Street ★
★ Partnership Information Kiosk at   ★
★ 12.30pm. Tel 212-484 1222.   ★
★ ★

The main taxi ranks for Penn Station are on 7th Avenue opposite the Pennsylvania Hotel and on 8th Avenue opposite the majestic Beaux Arts General Post Office building. If you want a taxi from here, it's best to walk a block north as the queues can get quite long, or use the A, C, E, 1, 2, 3, 9 subways at 34th Street–Penn Station.

CHELSEA

This neighbourhood is only likely to be on your list of places to see if you like art galleries, want to go clubbing or you're gay. However, it's actually worth a visit if you want to see an up-and-coming area in the process of 'gentrification'. Once the enclave of slaughterhouses and the working classes, it has a mixture of sought-after brownstone townhouses and warehouses that have made it a perfect target for artists priced out of SoHo, and although it's still rough around the edges, many of the quaint streets and buildings have been restored.

It is bounded by 6th Avenue (Avenue of the Americas) in the east, the Hudson River in the west, 16th Street in the south and 29th Street in the north. If you get off the A, C, E line at 14th Street and walk north on **8th Avenue**, you'll see the main drag of restaurants, shops, bars and gyms. Along the way you'll notice an abundance of Chippendale-type male bodies – the neighbourhood's gay boys, who love to flaunt their pecs in the local nightclubs.

At the corner of 19th stands the **Joyce Theater** (www.joyce.org), famous for dance and its fancy Art Deco building. Just a little further north and you're not only in the **Chelsea Historic District** – the blocks around 9th and 10th Avenues at 20th, 21st and 22nd Streets – but at the heart of the new gallery community that lies between 10th and 12th Avenues.

First port of call should be the **Dia Center for the Arts** (www.diacenter.org), a four-storey, 3,700 sq m (40,000 sq ft) warehouse, which opened in 1987 and still plays a pivotal role in the art world. Other great galleries nearby include **LFL, Leslie Tonkonow, Max Protetch Gallery, 303 Gallery** and the **D'Amelio Terras Gallery**. Two blocks north on 24th Street is the 1,950 sq m (21,000 sq ft) **Gagosian Gallery, Barbara Gladstone Gallery** and the **Andrea Rosen Gallery**. Photographer Annie Leibovitz's studio is on 26th. Appropriately enough, given the area's new-found propensity for art, it now has its first art museum – the Chelsea Art Museum (page 121), which can be found on West 22nd Street at 11th Avenue.

CHELSEA HOTEL

One of the most infamous of all of New York's hotels, the red-brick **Chelsea Hotel** (or Hotel Chelsea as it's officially known, www.hotelchelsea.com, page 244) is not only still going strong but is also in the midst of a great revival. Before Sex Pistols frontman Sid Vicious moved in with his girlfriend Nancy Spungen and allegedly killed her back in the 1970s, famous inhabitants included Mark Twain, Dylan Thomas, William S Burroughs, Arthur Miller

and Arthur C Clarke.

Built in 1883 and named an historic landmark in 1966, its lobby walls are covered with plaques commemorating venerated guests and their artworks, while the Spanish **El Quijote** restaurant is famous for its lobster specials.

CHINATOWN AND FIVE POINTS

The sprawling mass that is Chinatown (Map 1) has spread its wings north into the remnants of Little Italy, east into the Lower East Side and south in the Civic Center area. It is also home to the infamous Five Points area, once the most dangerous part of New York city.

Until recently only history books and tour guides referred to Five Points. The name is derived from the five streets that intersect next to Colombus Park. Originally called Orange, Mulberry, Anthony, Little Water and Cross Streets, they are now known as Bayard, Park, Worth, Mulberry and Baxter.

In the 1820s, a pond graced a lovely area where the rich had their country homes, but they started sub-letting to tanners, who polluted the lake. Attempts to get rid of the dreadful smells from the lake by building a canal down Canal Street failed, and in the end only the poorest came to live in the area, which included freed slaves and immigrant blacks.

★★★★ **BRIT TIP** ★★★★
★ ★
★ Have a game plan when visiting ★
★ Chinatown – it's so crowded that it's ★
★ easy to feel daunted by all the ★
★ hustle and bustle. ★
★★★★★★★★★★★★★★★★★★★★★★★★★

Irish immigrants arrived in the 1850s, then Italians and Eastern Europeans in the 1880s. Poverty was rife, and gangs flourished to such an extent that the streets were too unsafe for the police to patrol, and at least one person was killed each night. For almost a hundred years, Five Points was considered the worst slum in the world and even shocked Charles Dickens. During that time the gangs were schools for criminals and politicians such as Johnny Torrio, Charles 'Lucky' Luciano, Al Capone and Frankie Yale. Paul Kelly set up boxing gyms to teach them how to be gangsters, use guns and extort money. Amazingly, the

Restaurant Row, 46th Street and 9th

gangs even produced flyers with their 'services': $100 for the big job (murder), $50 for a slash on the face or $15 for an ear chewed off.

★ ★ ★ ★   **BRIT TIP**   ★ ★ ★ ★

Take advantage of Big Onion's Gangs of New York walking tour (page 84).

The appalling violence, corruption and history of this era has been brought to life by Martin Scorsese's movie *Gangs of New York*, which starred Leonardo DiCaprio and Daniel Day-Lewis. It genuinely gives a true insight into the psyche of the early American immigrants.

Fortunately, now it's a very different place. Many of the overcrowded tenements were pulled down at the turn of the 20th century to build a park. Since then, they've also built the Criminal Court Building nearby, retaining a contact with the area's violent past!

The original Chinese immigrants to New York in the 1850s huddled around Pell Street. Sadly, it was not long before the Tongs, with their extortion rackets, illegal gambling and opium dens, gave the area a new reputation for violence.

As a result, the US Government passed the Exclusion Act in 1882, which banned Chinese from entering America. That all changed in 1965 with the new Immigration Act and a new wave of Chinese immigrants arrived. Very quickly the women, in particular, were snapped up for poorly paid work in the garment industry, which gradually moved from its old Garment District above 34th Street into Chinatown. In more recent years, there have been more changes as a new wave of immigrants from the Fujian province of China has once again changed the face of the area. Now many of the well-off Cantonese have moved to Queens and the Mandarin-speaking Fujinese have the upper hand.

The best way to get to Chinatown by subway is to take the A, C, E, J, M, N, Q, R, W, Z, 6 to Canal Street.

At 277 Canal Street at Broadway and up some rickety old stairs you will find Pearl River Mart, Chinatown's idea of a department store, stocking everything from crockery to Buddhas, pretty lacquered paper umbrellas, clothes, shoes and slippers.

Back on the street again, you could be forgiven for feeling a little overwhelmed by the licensed and unlicensed street traders of Chinatown, who sell anything from fake watches to jewellery and handbags. It's often impossible to walk on the pavements, but also dangerous to step too far into the. incredibly busy Canal Street!

★ ★ ★ ★   **BRIT TIP**   ★ ★ ★ ★

You'll have a hard time getting a taxi on Canal Street – they just don't make it into Chinatown that often. Head toward The Bowery and try to hail a taxi as it comes off the Manhattan Bridge, or use the subway stations at Canal and Broadway.

Further down the road, you can get another real insight into the local lifestyle by visiting the **Kam Man** grocery store at 200 Canal Street. It offers a wide range from plucked ducks to squid. Try a bag of Konja, which is filled with deliciously refreshing bite-sized pots of lychee jelly.

Mott Street is the main thoroughfare of Chinatown. Here, along with Canal, Pell, Bayard, Doyers and The Bowery, is a host of restaurants plus tea and rice shops.

South towards Doyers Street you'll find the **Church of the Transfiguration** – one of two so named in New York – which perfectly portrays the changing nature of the immigrant population here. The oldest Catholic church building in New York, it was built in the early 19th century and Padre Felix Varela Morales, a Cuban priest who helped form the Ancient Hibernian Order, preached here. But between 1881 and 1943, no Chinese were allowed into it, apart from some wealthy merchants. It was first used by the Irish immigrants, then the Italians, but is now, finally, used by the Chinese and has services in Chinese.

★ It's pointless arriving at Chinatown ★
★ before 10am as only the local ★
★ McDonald's will be open. ★

May May restaurant at 35 Pell Street serves up fabulous dim sum. The chicken and shrimp combo is delicious. Dim sum, incidentally, means the 'little delicacy that will lighten up your heart' – and it certainly does when it's good! Next door is the **Chinese Gourmet Bakery and Vegetarian Food Center**, from where you can buy enough ingredients to make your own picnic to eat sitting in the nearby **Confucious Plaza**.

You should try to visit the beautiful **Bowery Savings Bank** on Bowery Street at Grand. When it was built in the 1890s, people liked to save locally and so the bankers tried to create the feeling that their building was a safe place for people to leave their money by making their banks stunningly beautiful inside. The neo-classical exterior is an incongruous sight here in Chinatown but it's worth having a peek at it.

DOWNTOWN

This is where the history of New York started and where some of the most important financial sites in the world were founded. The Downtown area covers the whole of the Financial District and the Civic Center, stretching from river to river and reaching as far north as the Brooklyn Bridge/Chambers Street (Map 1).

Today, the winding, narrow streets of the true Downtown – a square mile area south of Chambers Street that stretches from City Hall to the Battery – are a dizzying juxtaposition of colonial-era buildings and towering temples of capitalism. In the beginning, they were the location of some of the most important events in American history. This is where the Bill of Rights was signed, where George Washington was inaugurated as the first president and where

★ ★ ★ ★ Look out for people wearing red ★ ★ ★ ★
★ jackets with red, white and black ★
★ carts. Employed by the Downtown ★
★ Alliance, they clean the streets and ★
★ public areas, are an added level ★
★ of security and will answer queries ★
★ on the area. ★

UN and Chrysler Buildings

millions arrived to begin their search for the American Dream.

Visit www.downtownny.com for more information on free events and services.

THE WALL STREET SHUFFLE

The Dutch were the first to arrive and it was Peter Stuyvesant, New York's first governor, who ordered the building of a wooden wall at the northern edge of what was then New Amsterdam to protect the colonialists from possible attacks from Indians and the British. The name stuck and today it is known as **Wall Street**. This aspect of New York's history is presented in an exhibition in the Ionic-looking **Federal Hall National Memorial** (26 Wall Street, tel 212-825 6888), built on the site of New York's original City Hall. Cross the road into Broad Street and you're at the neo-classical entrance to the **New York Stock Exchange** (page 69).

Other fascinating landmarks include the **Federal Reserve Bank** in Liberty Street at Maiden Lane, which stores one-quarter of the world's gold bullion, and the neo-Gothic **Trinity Church**, where Alexander Hamilton, the country's first secretary of the treasury, was buried after losing a duel. There has been a church on this site since the end of the 17th century and, for the first 50 years after it was built, Trinity was actually the tallest structure in New York.

★ ★ ★ ★ **BRIT TIP** ★ ★ ★ ★
★ The Bowling Green end of Broadway ★
★ is lined with coffee shops, cafés and ★
★ pizza parlours. A freshly cooked slice ★
★ eaten in or taken to go makes a ★
★ perfect pit stop. ★

Just off Wall Street at 25 Broadway is probably one of the poshest post office buildings in the world. Known as the old **Cunard Building**, it was once home to the booking offices of the steamship company in the days before aeroplanes took over the transportation needs of the masses from large liners, and the interior walls of the building are still lined with marble. There are other signs of its former use, too, with murals of ships and nautical mythology around the ceiling.

And it seems only fitting that the former headquarters of John D Rockefeller's Standard Oil Company at 28 Broadway

should now be the home of one of New York's newest museums, the **Museum of American Finance** (page 128).

The best subway lines are the 2, 3, 4, 5 to Wall Street.

BOWLING GREEN

Blink and you'll miss this oval of greenery at the end of Broadway. You know you're there by the presence of the Greek revival-style US Customs House, which is now the **National Museum of the American Indian** (page 130) and has the world's largest collection devoted to North, Central and South American Indian cultures. Bowling Green was the site of the infamous business deal between the Dutch colony of New Amsterdam and the Indians, who were conned into selling Manhattan for a bucket of trinkets.

In the 18th century, the tiny turfed area was used for the game of bowls by colonial Brits on a lease of 'one peppercorn per year'. The iron fence that encloses it now is the original and was built in 1771, though, ironically, the once-proud statue of King George III was melted into musket balls for use in the American Revolution.

Here you'll also find the 3,175kg (7,000lb) life-sized **bronze bull**. A symbol of the Financial District's stock market, it appeared overnight outside the New York Stock Exchange in 1989. Now it is a tradition to rub him!

The nearest subways to take you to Bowling Green are the 4, 5 line to Bowling Green or R, W to Whitehall.

BATTERY PARK AND CASTLE CLINTON

Thanks to hundreds of years of landfill, the whole Downtown area is quite different to how it once was. Years ago, State Street houses looked over Upper New York Bay, and Water and Pearl Streets were named because they were at or near the water's edge. The excavation works required to build the deep foundations for the World Trade Center in the 1960s, destroyed by terrorists on 11 September 2001, created enough granite blocks of earth to form 9 hectares (23 acres) of new land, which then became home to Battery Park City and the World Financial Center.

In the Battery Park area, **Castle Clinton** originally stood on an island. Built in 1811 as one of several forts that defended New York harbour, it is now part of Manhattan. It has been an opera house, an aquarium and the original immigration sorting office, dealing with 8 million immigrants before the opening of Ellis Island. It is now used as the ferry ticket office.

The opening of a plethora of new shops and cafés and the remodelling of the Battery Park public spaces has given the area a whole new lease of life.

The best subways to take here are the 1, 9 to South Ferry or 4, 5 to Bowling Green.

★ ★ ★ ★   ★ ★ ★ ★
★   ★
★   **Battery Park is a beautiful spot**   ★
★   **for a picnic.**   ★
★ ★ ★ ★ ★ ★ ★ ★ ★ ★ ★ ★ ★ ★ ★ ★ ★ ★ ★ ★

BATTERY PARK CITY

North-west of Battery Park, you'll find a relatively new area of land known as **Battery Park City**, which is actually the area created by landfill. It's still pretty much a quiet district, though there has been plenty of development. This is home to two of New York's newer museums. The **Museum of Jewish Heritage** (page 129) has been so successful, it already has plans for an extension.

★ ★ ★ ★   ★ ★ ★ ★
★   ★
★   **For more fantastic views of Dame**   ★
★   **Liberty and the harbour, treat**   ★
★   **yourself to a drink in the chic bar,**   ★
★   **Rise, on the 14th floor of the**   ★
★   **Ritz-Carlton Hotel in West Street**   ★
★   **(page 200).**   ★
★ ★ ★ ★ ★ ★ ★ ★ ★ ★ ★ ★ ★ ★ ★ ★ ★ ★ ★ ★

At 39 Battery Place is the **Skyscraper Museum** (page 133), which tells the fascinating story of the creation of all those famous buildings. On the southern tip of the 'City' is the recently landscaped **Robert Wagner Junior Park** with a café, some WCs and street vendors selling food and drink – it is a wonderful place to sit and gaze out at the harbour.

To the north is the **World Financial Center**, which has four tower blocks and a full calendar of fairs and festivals. It's worth coming here for the Winter Garden (page 69), a huge, glass-ceilinged public plaza decorated by massive palm trees. From here you can see the fancy private boats docked in **North Cove**.

The nearest subways are the A, C, 1, 2, 3, 9 to Chambers Street (for the World Financial Center) or the 1, 9 to South Ferry (for the museums and park).

EAST OF BATTERY PARK

To see what life was like in 18th-century Manhattan, head for the **Fraunces Tavern Block Historic District**, which has 11 early 19th-century buildings that escaped the fire of 1835. The three-storey Georgian brick house that is home to the **Fraunces Tavern Museum** (page 124) on the corner of Pearl and Broad Streets was built in 1904 and houses an exhibition on the site's history.

A little further north-east along Water Street to the Old Slip, you'll see the tiny **First Precinct Police Station**, which was modelled on an Italian mansion and which has been used for exterior shots for both *Kojak* and *The French Connection*. Fittingly, this is now the permanent home of the **New York City Police Museum** (page132). Down on the water's edge of South Street is to be the new home of the **Guggenheim's Downtown Museum** project, a Frank Gehry design that will include a water garden, an ice rink and a public plaza. It is expected that the new museum will attract more than three million visitors a year.

★ ★ ★ ★   ★ ★ ★ ★
★   ★
★ **Don't miss the free outdoor concerts** ★
★ **at the South Street Seaport Museum** ★
★   **(page 133), held almost nightly**   ★
★   **throughout the summer.**   ★
★ ★ ★ ★ ★ ★ ★ ★ ★ ★ ★ ★ ★ ★ ★ ★ ★ ★ ★ ★

Just off Water Street at 70 Pine Street is the incredibly beautiful Art Deco wedding-cake-shaped **American International Building**. It has one of the most beautiful Art Deco-designed lobbies in New York and visitors are welcome to come inside to have a look.

A little further north at piers 16, 17 and 18, you find yourself in the heart of the **South Street Seaport** (page 65), which has a museum, a shopping and restaurant complex and the 150-year-old **Fulton Fish Market**, open midnight–8am daily.

Best subways to the area are the R, W to Whitehall Street, J, M, Z to Broad Street or the 2, 3 to Wall Street.

CITY HALL PARK AND THE CIVIC CENTER

City Hall Park is right opposite the entrance to Brooklyn Bridge and is also the dividing point between the Financial District and Chinatown. From here you can stroll across the **Brooklyn Bridge** or visit the neo-Gothic **Woolworth Building** (page 70) on Broadway at Barclay Street, which

BRIT TIP

★ ★ ★ ★ ★ ★
There is a farmers' market each
Tuesday and Friday (April to
December, 8am–6pm) in the City
Hall Park where you can buy fresh
fruits, vegetables and bread – a
great way to create a picnic.
★ ★ ★ ★ ★ ★

is likely to be your main reason for swinging by. Check out the lobby's vaulted ceilings and its magnificent mosaics and mail boxes. When it was first built it was the tallest structure in New York and Mr Woolworth paid cash for it!

Back in the 1930s, when Prosecutor Dewey decided to target organised crime, he made the Woolworth Building his base and during that time he locked up 15 prostitutes in the building for four months. In the end, he worked out that the prostitutes were controlled by Lucky Luciano and successfully prosecuted him for white slavery. 'Lucky' got 32 years in prison, but lived up to his name by serving just ten before he was pardoned for his efforts on behalf of the American government during the Second World War. Just north of City Hall Park are the **Police Plaza, US Courthouse, New York County Courthouse** and **Criminal Court Building**.

It's useful to note that there is a Lower Manhattan information kiosk in City Hall Park where you can find information on

City Hall

Brooklyn Bridge

attractions and upcoming events plus maps and directions.

The best subways to take are the R, W to City Hall or the 4, 5, 6 to Brooklyn Bridge/ City Hall.

EAST VILLAGE

Forget the picturesque cobbled streets of Greenwich and the West Villages. Once you cross The Bowery (otherwise known as Skid Row) and head up to St Mark's Place you are in the heart of the **East Village** (Map 2) and an area more reminiscent of the Lower East Side than a village. No matter where you are in New York, it's easy to spot an East Villager – they have long hair and more metal in their face than a jewellery shop window display. You also know when you've entered the neighbourhood by the many tattoo studios, along with boutiques selling punk and leather outfits.

Where Greenwich Village has become upper middle class, the East Village retains its roots as a Bohemian enclave of free-thinkers and non-conformists, though the tramps are gradually being replaced by a more genteel set attracted by newly built apartment blocks and the comparatively reasonable, though not low, rents.

This was once the home of Beat Generation writer Allen Ginsberg (on East 7th Street) and was frequented by Jack Kerouac and other radical thinkers of the 1950s. Amazingly, one of the area's oldest clubs, **CBGB** on The Bowery, is still going strong. The punk-rock club is famous for hosting Blondie, the Ramones, Talking Heads and the Police.

Now the area is most well known for its

Battery Park promenade

THE NEW YORK NEIGHBOURHOODS

★ ★ ★ ★ **BRIT TIP** ★ ★ ★ ★
★   ★
★ Check out the sales section of New ★
★ York's *Time Out* magazine for up-to- ★
★   date information on designer   ★
★ sample sales in the Garment District. ★
★ ★

second-hand shops, which can be found all along 7th Street and 2nd and 3rd Avenues. There's a tiny Little India on 6th Street, where you'll find a row of curry houses, but the most famous eating outlets is the **Yaffa Café** (page 161) on St Mark's Place heading towards Tompkins Square Park.

The formerly dangerous area of Alphabet City (Avenues A, B, C and D) has been much cleaned up, but the muggers and drug pushers still frequent the area beyond B later in the evening.

The best subways are the I, N, Q, R, W, 4, 5, 6 to 14th Street/Union Square and the L to 3rd Avenue and 1st Avenue.

GARMENT DISTRICT

From 34th Street to 42nd Street between 6th and 8th Avenues, you'll find the **Garment District** of New York (Map 3). Having shrunk a little in the past – a lot of work disappeared overseas or moved to the cheap labour available in Chinatown – the area is once again up-and-coming, as

designers are now choosing to have their clothes manufactured in New York. If you wander around this area – and you may well if you're in search of sample sales – you'll see racks of clothes being pushed around the streets. Some are going to showrooms and warehouses, but as no one manufacturer makes an entire piece of clothing, many of the garments are being shunted from company to company to have different bits sewn on at each place!

GRAMERCY PARK

Two blocks south and two blocks east of the Flatiron Building on East 20th and 21st at **Irving Place** (Map 3) is one of the prettiest squares in New York City (the nearest subway is the 6 to 23rd Street). The park itself was once a swamp but has now been beautifully laid out, though you won't be able to go in unless you are staying with a resident of the surrounding square or at the **Gramercy Park Hotel**.

The most famous building in the neighbourhood is **The Players** at 16 Gramercy Park, a private club created for actors and theatrical types by actor Edwin Booth when Gramercy Park was the centre of the theatre scene. Booth was the greatest actor in America in the 1870s and 1880s and opened the Gothic revival-style house

St Mark's Place, East Village

as a club in 1888 so that actors and literary types could meet in private to interact. One tragic event overshadowed the end of Booth's life – his brother John Wilkes Booth assassinated Abraham Lincoln.

GREENWICH VILLAGE

This is one of the prettiest areas of New York and, although the radical free-thinkers have gone, its quaint cobbled and tree-lined streets, shops and Federal and Greek-style buildings are well worth a visit.

Greenwich Village proper (Map 2) is bounded in the north by 14th Street, in the south by Houston, in the east by Broadway and in the west by 7th, where it becomes the West Village, which stretches west to the Hudson River.

When the Dutch first arrived in Manhattan, 'the Village' as it is known in New York, was mostly woodland, but was turned into a tobacco plantation by the Dutch West India Company. Then in the early 1800s people started fleeing from a series of cholera and yellow fever epidemics in the unhygienic Downtown.

When the wealthy moved into their 5th Avenue mansions at the end of the 19th century, though, rents came down and a whole new breed of artists, radicals and intellectual rebels moved in, creating a kind of Parisian Left Bank feel to the neighbourhood. Over the years it has been home to such literary lions as Mark Twain, Edgar Allen Poe, Dylan Thomas, Eugene O'Neill and Jack Kerouac.

Now the writers and artists have largely been forced out by the soaring rents – a tiny two-bed apartment costs at least $2,500 a month and to buy a shoebox of a studio is at least $275,000 – and in their place have come upper middle-class Americans for whom making money is the abiding principle. Yet there is still the sense of a community spirit, many restaurants cater mostly to locals rather than tourists (in New York, only Village restaurants seem filled with people who are in no particular rush) and a great variety of off-Broadway shows and other cultural events can be seen in this neighbourhood.

WASHINGTON SQUARE PARK

If you take the A, B, C, E, F or V subway to West 4th Street and Washington Square, you'll find yourself in what many people

---

GREAT TOURS OF THE VILLAGE

If eating's your thing, then you'll love the **Foods of New York** tour (page 80) of Greenwich Village and West Village, which not only shows you the sights, food shops, restaurants and architectural secrets of the area, but will also give you a chance to taste the foods that are unique to this corner of New York. Other great tours are the **Literary Pub Crawl** (page 84), which takes you to the watering holes once frequented by the literary giants who lived here, and **Haunted Greenwich Village** (page 81) shows you places with a legendary past.

---

consider to be the heart of the Village – and in one of the very few genuine squares in Manhattan. The first thing you'll notice is the Stanford White-designed marble square **Triumphal Arch** at the bottom of 5th Avenue, built in 1892 to commemorate George Washington's inauguration as the first US president.

You may also become aware of how dingy it all looks and you may be even a little concerned about the 'grungy' nature of many of the people there, but this area is considered 'alternative' rather than dodgy. It's full of locals skating, playing chess and just hanging out, plus students from the nearby **New York University**. It used to be a place where a lot of people took drugs, but that problem is largely in the past.

★ ★ ★ ★ BRIT TIP ★ ★ ★ ★

Tomoe Sushi, on Thompson Street (page 163), looks pretty unappealing from the outside but has incredible queues – and not without reason. You can get the best sushi in New York here for about a tenth of what it would cost you at Nobu.

A little-known fact is that the park was once used by City officials to conduct public hangings until they were moved to Sing Sing penitentiary. Apart from the arch and the people, the other main point of interest in the park is the **Dog Run**. A uniquely New York phenomenon, the idea is that instead of taking your dog for a walk along the roads, you bring them to dog runs where they can literally run around off the lead. It's rather like a parent taking their child to the swings – hilarious and has to be seen to be believed!

North from the park on 6th Avenue between Waverly Place and 9th Street is **Bigelow's Pharmacy**, the oldest traditional chemist in America. Across the street is the beautiful **Jefferson Market Courthouse**, which is now used as a library, and just off 10th Street is one of the most famous rows of mews houses in the Village – **Patchin Place**, which has been home not only to many a writer, including e e cummings and John Reed, but also to Marlon Brando.

BLEECKER STREET

Effectively the main drag of the Village, this is one of the best places to be in New York, filled as it is with sidewalk cafés, shops, restaurants and clubs. The corner of Cornelia and Bleecker Streets gives you access to some of the finest food shops and restaurants in Manhattan. To get here, take the 6 to Bleecker Street or B, D, F, V to Broadway/Lafayette Street.

At 259 Bleecker is **Zito's** old-fashioned Italian bread shop, which still uses the ovens that were built here in the 1860s and were once used by the whole community. They are particularly famous for focaccia with different toppings, such as onions and olive oil and rosemary, and their prosciutto bread is unique to them.

Next door is **Murray's Cheese Shop** (page 113) with more than 350 cheeses from around the world. Nothing is pre-cut and they have great names such as Wabash Cannonball, Crocodile Tears, Mutton Buttons and Cardinal Sin, a British cows'-milk cheese. They also have 15 different types of olives and sell chorizos, pâtés and breads. Opposite at 260 Bleecker is **Faicco's** (page 113), a landmark shop that has been here since 1900. Its famous range of sausages is made every morning and sold not only to local residents but to many of the local restaurants. It also sells home-cooked ready-made meals and offers a huge deli selection.

Around the corner is Cornelia Street, home to four of the best restaurants in the Village. The **Cornelia Street Café** (pages 162 and 193) hosts jazz, readings and other events (from $6 to $11), while **Home Restaurant** specialises in American comfort food with a gourmet twist, **le Gigot** is a traditional country French restaurant and **Little Havana** offers great Cuban food.

Bleecker Street has two more incredible bakeries with their own seating areas. **Pasticceria Bruno** is run by popular chef Biagio. He produces an amazing range of tarts and mousses for $2 to $3 with names like Kiss Cream, Wildberries, Green Apple and Apricot. The café itself has a lot of atmosphere and old world charm. Next door is **Rocco's**, run by Rocco, who used to be a head pastry chef at Bruno's until 1972 when he opened his own place here. An entire Italian cheesecake made of ricotta cheese costs just $12.50. The interior is much more modern, with steel-framed chairs, mirrors and more seats than Bruno's (page 114).

HAMILTON HEIGHTS

The Hamilton Heights neighbourhood (Map 6) is up on the high ground north of Morningside Heights and is effectively the middle-class enclave of Harlem. It takes its name from **Alexander Hamilton**, the first secretary of the treasury to the newly formed United States of America. He lived here from 1802 until he was killed in a duel in 1804.

The area is now the home of **City College**, one of the senior colleges in the New York university system. It was founded in the 19th century to educate the children of the working classes and immigrants and used to be known as the poor man's Columbia. It used to be free, but now it charges $3,200 per year, though that is still a lot cheaper than private universities in America, which charge an average of $27,400 per year.

Further north on West 145th Street off Amsterdam is the area known as **Sugar Hill**, which was made famous in the Duke Ellington song 'Take the A Train [to Sugar Hill]'. Now a conservation area, it is filled with beautiful brownstone townhouses, and was dubbed Sugar Hill because life here was considered to be so sweet.

HARLEM

Harlem is a huge area that covers a substantial part of the northern reaches of Manhattan above Central Park, though it has various subsections. What we refer to when we use the name Harlem is actually the African-American area, which stretches from 8th Avenue in the west to 5th Avenue in the east and goes north to the East River (Map 6). The area from East 96th Street east of 5th Avenue going up to the East River is **Spanish Harlem**, known as El Barrio and populated largely by Puerto Ricans.

Named after the Dutch town of Haarlem, the area received its first Dutch settlers in the mid-19th century when it was used as farmland and as an escape from the dust and traffic of Midtown. Better-off immigrant families started moving here following the arrival of the railroad link and the building of attractive brownstone townhouses. Then property speculators, eager to take advantage of the new subway heading for Harlem, started building good-quality homes for the upper middle classes in the early 1900s. But they'd got a little ahead of themselves. A couple of mini depressions and Harlem's distance from Midtown Manhattan put the dampers on hopes of a major middle-class movement into the area.

★★★★ **BRIT TIP** ★★★★
★ **Many avenues and streets in Harlem** ★
★ **have two names that reflect both** ★
★ **historical and more modern** ★
★ **influences. For instance, Lenox** ★
★ **Avenue is known as Malcolm X** ★
★ **Boulevard and 7th Avenue is known** ★
★ **as Adam Clayton Powell Junior** ★
★ **Boulevard – both named after major** ★
★ **African-American activists.** ★
★★★★★★★★★★★★★★★★★★★★★★★★★

The African-American estate agents spotted a golden opportunity, bought up a whole batch of empty homes cheaply and started renting them out to blacks eager to escape the gang warfare of the West 40s and 50s in Hell's Kitchen and Clinton. This was the beginning of Harlem as the capital of the black world and when African-Americans started migrating from America's southern states, they headed straight here.

★★★★ **BRIT TIP** ★★★★
★ **Instead of going to the somewhat** ★
★ **touristy Sylvia's Restaurant on 125th,** ★
★ **try the M&G Soul Food Diner on** ★
★ **West 125th at Morningside Avenue** ★
★ **for a truly traditional southern meal** ★
★ **to the background sounds of great** ★
★ **soul singers (page 183).** ★
★★★★★★★★★★★★★★★★★★★★★★★★★★★

And it's no wonder really. Brits are frequently shocked to discover that the blacks may have been freed from slavery by the end of the 19th century, but there was still segregation until the 1960s. Black people were not allowed to sit on the same benches as whites, they had to drink at different water fountains and in church they were forced to wait until after the whites for Communion. When great black musicians such as **Duke Ellington** and **Louis Armstrong** went on tour, they had to stay at black-only hotels and eat at black-only restaurants.

Back in Harlem, at least, there was some

SoHo café

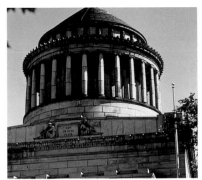

Grant's Tomb in Harlem

★ ★ ★ ★ ★ ★ ★ ★
★ **To experience the life and times of** ★
★ **Harlem, pick up a copy of** *Harlem's* ★
★ *Culture: Guide to Great Events*, ★
★ **available at cultural institutions** ★
★ **such as the Schomburg Center.** ★
★ ★ ★ ★ ★ ★ ★ ★ ★ ★ ★ ★ ★ ★ ★ ★ ★

semblance of belonging and thanks to the influx of political activists, professionals and artists to the area following the opening of the subway lines between 1904 and 1906, many African-American organisations had sprung up by the early 1920s. They included the **National Urban League**, which helped people who were moving into the area to get training for jobs, and the **White Rose Mission**, which helped African-American female migrants coming to New York from the South. They were followed by the political **Universal Negro Improvement Association** and the **Union Brotherhood of Sleeping Porters**, whose leader Phillip Randolph was at one time considered by the government to be the most dangerous black in America.

THE GLORY DAYS OF HARLEM

The 1920s and 1930s were a great time for the neighbourhood, filled as it was with poets, writers, artists, actors and political activists. The combination of prohibition and great jazz musicians such as **Count Basie, Duke Ellington** and **Cab Calloway** made famous nightspots like the **Cotton Club** attractive to the upper middle classes who came in their droves to enjoy Harlem's speakeasies.

But all this was hardly doing anything for the lot of the average African-American who lived in the area. The speakeasies were strictly for whites only and even **WC Handy**, who co-wrote a song with Duke Ellington, was not allowed into the Cotton Club to hear it being played for the first time. Then there was the matter of the racism on **125th Street** – Harlem's very centre – which runs from Frederick Douglas Boulevard to Malcolm X Boulevard. The white-owned shops and hotels here,

which were used by the African-Americans, were staffed by whites and it was impossible for blacks to get anything but the most menial jobs.

In 1934 Adam Clayton Powell Junior, preacher at the Abyssinian Baptist Church, organised a boycott of these businesses, entitled Don't Buy Where You Can't Work. The campaign was successful and the shops started hiring blacks. You can still see the remnants of those businesses along 125th.

You can start your experience of Harlem with a tour round the **Apollo Theater** on 125th (page 191), which was the focal point for African-American entertainment between the 1930s and 1970s. Known for its legendary **Amateur Night**, which is now broadcast on TV, it has launched the careers of Ella Fitzgerald, Marvin Gaye, James Brown and even The Jackson Five.

At the corner of 7th Avenue stands the former **Theresa Hotel**, now an office block, but which was once considered to be the Waldorf of Harlem. Back in the days of segregation **Josephine Baker** stayed in the penthouse with its vaulted ceiling and views of both rivers. Malcolm X's Unity organisation was based here in the 1950s and 1960s and, in a show of support for African-Americans, Fidel Castro moved his entire entourage to the Theresa when he

NYC & Co. Visitor Information Kiosk

came to New York In 1960 for a United Nations conference.

★ ★ ★ ★ **BRIT TIP** ★ ★ ★ ★

For soul food, try Miss Maude's Spoonbread, Malcom X Boulevard (Lenox Avenue) at 137th Street or visit Manna's Too at 134th Street (or Manna's at 8th Avenue and West 125th Street) for a great selection of well-priced fresh food and drinks.

A little further down the street is **Blumsteins**, once the largest department store in Harlem. With its dilapidated frontage and peeling paintwork, it's now hard to imagine this as once being the Macy's of the area.

Another major location in Harlem is up on 135th to 137th Streets between Powell Boulevard and Malcolm X Boulevard. You can either walk from 125th Street or take the 2, 3 subway to 135th Street station. Once there you'll find yourself right outside the **Schomburg Center**, which chronicles the history of black people in North America, South America and the Caribbean. Opposite is the **Harlem Hospital Center** where Martin Luther King was operated on after being shot. It was the first hospital in New York to be integrated.

A couple of blocks north and you'll find the famous **Abyssinian Baptist Church** at 132 West 138th Street. It was originally founded in 1808, and as the blacks moved from the Lower East Side to Greenwich

★ ★ ★ ★ **BRIT TIP** ★ ★ ★ ★

To experience a gospel choir in action, *the* place to go is the Abyssinian Church on 138th Street, but you'll need to arrive early because it gets packed. Another great place is the Second Canaan Baptist Church on 110th Street and Lenox Avenue.

Village, then up to the West 50s and 60s before finally finding a home in Harlem, the church moved with them. This church was built in 1923 and, with Adam Clayton Powell Junior as its preacher for many years

before he became a senator, it was a centre of political activity, particularly in the 1920s.

One block west on 138th and 139th Streets between Powell and Frederick Douglas Boulevards are the four rows of Stanford White houses built in 1891 and known as **Striver's Row** because this is where the middle and upper classes strove to live. The houses were filled by doctors, lawyers, nurses from Harlem Hospital, jazz musicians and politicians such as Malcolm X. Boxer Harry Wills, known as the Brown Panther, lived here. He was paid $50,000 not to fight Jack Dempsey when the mayor banned the fight because he thought a black boxer fighting a white man would lead to riots.

★ ★ ★ ★ **BRIT TIP** ★ ★ ★ ★

A terrific variety of tours of Harlem are available from Harlem Heritage Tours (tel 212-280 7888, www.harlemheritagetours.com).

The alleys at the back of these buildings were originally created for parking horses and carriages. Houses were usually built back to back so the alleys are a rarity, but a boon for the current occupants to park their BMWs. You can still see the old signs that say 'Walk your horses' or 'Park your carriages'.

DECLINE AND FALL
Sadly, the good times didn't last long and, from the 1940s to the 1960s, Harlem declined into an urban no-man's land as a result of a lack of government support and racial conflict. The once-fine apartment blocks grew shabbier as landlords were either too unscrupulous or unable to afford to maintain them on the cheap rental income.

★ ★ ★ ★ **BRIT TIP** ★ ★ ★ ★

If you're concerned about wandering the streets of Harlem by yourself, try either a Big Onion walking tour (page 82) or a Harlem Spirituals bus tour (page 76).

Eventually City Hall and certain businesses started investing in the area. In

1976 the city began reclaiming properties abandoned by landlords who couldn't afford to pay their taxes. You can still buy one of these blocks for $1 if you have the $2 million needed to renovate it. Fortunately, many have already been refurbished and, with the influx of banks and even Starbucks, a small but important step towards 'gentrification' is taking place.

For some time the brownstones of **Hamilton Heights** and other local neighbourhoods have been targeted by those trying to escape the substantial rents elsewhere in Manhattan. There have been other developments, too. Former president Bill Clinton has his offices on 125th Street between Lenox and 5th (the one with the huge Gap advert down the side). He's always been a favourite with African-Americans because he did a lot for racial equality and was invited to move his offices to Harlem from Carnegie Hall. Former baseball star **Magic Johnson** has also been doing much to encourage a sense of pride in the community.

RENAISSANCE

Now many people are predicting a renaissance for Harlem and suggest house prices could sky-rocket within the next few years, though it's unlikely that would help the really poor people. Old nightspots once frequented exclusively by the African-Americans have also been bought up and are being earmarked for renovation, including the **Renaissance Ballroom**, once a neighbourhood institution. Everyone would watch the Harlem Rennies basketball team early in the evening, then clean up to hit the nightclub. It was shut in the 1940s, but is now owned by the Abyssinian Church, which is hoping to renovate it.

Another major venue was **Small's Big Apple** jazz club. Its sister establishment, **Small's Paradise**, was a restaurant in the 1930s and 1940s. It was so popular and the dance floor so small that it was said people had to dance on a dime here. It enjoyed a revival from the 1960s and was where Professor du Bois, who once ran the National Association for Advancement of Coloured People, held a birthday party in the 1980s. It closed in the same decade, but is now owned by the Abyssinian Church and there's a chance it may re-open as a tourist centre.

LITTLE ITALY

The best subway to Little Italy (Map 1) is the N, R, Q, W, 6 to Canal and then walk east to Mulberry, or take the 6 to Spring and walk south. Head along Grand Street towards Mott and Mulberry Streets to **Di Palo's** (page 114), which marks the beginnings of what is left of Little Italy. Di Palo's shop at 210 Grand Street was founded 80 years ago and is still famous for its Mozzarella, Italian sausages and salamis. It has its own cheese-ageing room and gets very crowded. A little further on is **Ferrara's** (page 164), the oldest and most popular pastry café in Little Italy.

★ ★ ★ ★   **BRIT TIP**   ★ ★ ★ ★

Ferrara's in Grand Street, near Mulberry, is a perfect spot for a coffee and pastry break, and you'll find the restrooms on the first floor. You'll also get a real slice of the Italian lifestyle.

It has to be said that Little Italy is now little more than a tourist attraction, with the Italians having done a deal with the Chinese community to retain **Mulberry Street** between Hester and Kenmare Streets. It's actually an area that was formerly home to Italians from the Naples area of Italy and, as such, it has taken St Gennaro, the patron saint of Naples, as its own saint. Every year in the third week of September, Italians flock from far and wide to celebrate the **Feast of St Gennaro**. Food carts line each side of Mulberry Street and there is much laughing, dancing and drinking until the early hours of the morning.

★ ★ ★ ★   **BRIT TIP**   ★ ★ ★ ★

Little Italy is at its finest at the weekend in warm weather when the restaurants put their tables outdoors. Arrive early – around noon – to get a seat outside, or late in the afternoon.

Little Italy's best feature is its wonderful restaurants with outdoor seating where you can watch the world go by while tucking into some great dishes. The restaurants have a reputation for being on the pricey side, but plenty have pasta and pizza specials for

Dining al fresco in Little Italy

a more economical $8.95.

Just a little bit of gruesome history for you: Da Gennaro on the corner of Mulberry and Hester Streets was the original home of **Umberto's Clam House** (which is now further south on Mulberry). This was a favoured haunt of gangster Crazy Joey Gallo and where he was murdered in 1972 while celebrating his birthday.

Further north at 247 Mulberry between Spring and Kenmare Streets is the former home of the **Ravenlight Club** and Mafia headquarters for John Gotti. He was once known as the Teflon Don because no charges could be made to stick and this was where he made the policemen and judges on his payroll come to pay their respects.

The FBI were so determined to put him away they not only bugged the Ravenlight but also all the parking meters around the streets – but still they got nowhere. Then Gotti's underboss, Sammy Gravano, became a supergrass. He had killed 19 people but got away with all those murders because he did a deal with the FBI that helped them put Gotti away.

Shops at Columbus Circle

LOWER EAST SIDE

One of the seedier parts of town, the **Lower East Side** has a fascinating history but is now known for its trendy nightclubs and bargain shopping. The Lower East Side stretches from the East River ostensibly to Chrystie Street (though Chinatown is encroaching) and south from Canal Street to East Houston in the north, while Delancey is its main thoroughfare (Map 2).

The best way to get there by subway is by taking the J, M, Z, F trains to Delancey or Essex Streets.

In many respects the history of the Lower East Side is the history of America's immigration which, in turn, has played a pivotal role in the country's development.

★ ★ ★ ★ **BRIT TIP** ★ ★ ★ ★
★   ★
★   The Lower East Side Business   ★
★   Improvement District runs FREE   ★
★   two-hour walking tours of the   ★
★   historic Orchard Street Shopping   ★
★   District at 11am on Sundays from   ★
★   April to December. Call 866-224   ★
★   0406 for details.   ★
★ ★

At one time this was the most densely populated area in the world with 1,000 inhabitants crammed into a square mile, but more of that later. Almost from the word go, the Lower East Side was a settlement for new arrivals to New York because of its cheap housing and its proximity to where people disembarked. Once these immigrants had established themselves they moved on, leaving space for a new wave of arrivals. Street names such as Essex, Suffolk and Norfolk point to the origins of their first tenants. Since then streets have been named anything from a Kleine Deutschland to a Little Italy or Ireland.

★ While you're in the neighbourhood, don't miss Katz's Deli (page 165) on East Houston Street at Ludlow Street. It's a real institution.

With each new wave of immigrants came friction between new and old arrivals, which often led to violence. The Protestant English were angry, for instance, when the Roman Catholic Irish built St Mary's on Grand Street in 1828 and burned it down. That led to the formation of the **Ancient Order of Hibernians** in 1830 – the organisation that started the St Patrick's Day parade. The Hibernians rebuilt the church and put walls around the outside. It is still in existence, but now runs a kosher soup service for local Jewish people.

Check out www.lowereastsideny.com for information on events and discounts.

SWEATSHOPS AND TENEMENTS

Other tenants of the early 1800s were relatively well-off Jews from Germany, who eventually moved further north. This was a pattern that was to be repeated again and again with each new wave of immigrants. But perhaps the saddest were the incredibly poor Jewish immigrants who started arriving from Eastern Europe in the 1860s and 70s. They were forced to eke out a miserly existence in sweatshops and live in tenement buildings. Whole families were crowded into 1.8m (6ft) square rooms with no heating or running water and often little light. Visit the **Lower East Side Tenement Museum** (page 126) in Orchard Street for their full story.

During this period **Hester Street** was the main thoroughfare and it was filled with shops and pedlars selling their wares – meat, fruit and vegetables. The pedlars did very well, though, as they paid no tax and had no overheads such as rent. Often they made more than three times as much as teachers did. But the shopkeepers were unhappy with the unfair competition and by the 1930s the city had banned pedlars and created the Essex Market. Famous for its fresh meats, produce and other products, the market has recently been renovated at a cost of $1.5 million. It is open Monday to Friday 8am–6pm.

★ The Lower East Side was once known as a mugger's paradise. It's no longer so bad but, as in any city, you still need to be careful.

A NEW DAWN

The main language in Hester Street between the 1880s and 1920s was Yiddish – a mixture of Hebrew, German and Slavic. The local newspaper, called *Forward*, was published in Yiddish and each edition sold 200,000 copies. Now the area is very quiet. There are still many Jews left, but the new waves of immigrants include Puerto Ricans and Latinos from the Dominican Republic.

Staten Island ferry

If you want to see some real action you need to go to **Delancey** and the big shopping area around Orchard and Ludlow Streets. Here you'll find bargain basement products and cutting-edge designer fashions – many young designers have started in the Lower East Side before moving uptown. **Orchard and Ludlow** between Delancey and East Houston Streets are also the main drags for the new bars and clubs that have been opening in the area. The best day to experience the Lower East Side is Sunday, when the market is open and the whole area is buzzing with people. A large chunk of it is still closed on Saturday to mark the Jewish Sabbath, but that is gradually changing due to the arrival of the Latinos.

★ ★ ★ ★ **BRIT TIP** ★ ★ ★ ★
★   ★
★   ★
★ **For excellently priced and clean** ★
★ **accommodation in Lower East Side,** ★
★ **stay at the Howard Johnson Express** ★
★ **Inn (page 248) on East Houston.** ★
★ ★

An outstanding sight on Delancey is **Ratner's Dairy Restaurant** at 138 Delancey near Essex Street. Although it's still a dairy restaurant, it's now also home to **Lansky Lounge** (page 000), the chic nightspot that celebrates the place where mob boss Meyer Lansky used to hold court. The entrance is at 104 Norfolk Street.

MADISON SQUARE

It's a weird but true fact that the ugly Madison Square Garden building, constructed above Penn Station on 33rd Street (pages 67, 192 and 252), is the latest (and probably least attractive) of the four Madison Square Gardens that have been built in New York. But only the first two were, in fact, located at Madison Square (Map 3), which is where Madison Avenue begins and is the site of the recently renovated **Madison Square Park**. Facing the square is Cass Gilbert's **New York Life Building**, which was erected in 1928. In its shadow is The **Little Church Around the Corner** just off 5th Avenue at 29th Street. Its real name is the **Episcopal Church of the Transfiguration** and its stained glass windows commemorate famous actors such as Edwin Booth, who frequented the church

at a time when being an actor was not considered to be a very honourable profession. The nearest subways are the N, R, W, 6 to 28th Street.

MEATPACKING DISTRICT

The Meatpacking District is to be found in the north-western corner of the West Village, south of West 14th Street to West 12th Street and from West Street to Hudson Street on the east side (Map 2). The nearest subway is the A, C, E to 14th Street. Cattle are not actually slaughtered in this area, but large carcasses of beef are cut up in wholesale markets and distributed throughout the city from here.

However, many of the old warehouses are no longer in use and the lofts are being used as nightclubs. One of the trendiest is **Hogs & Heifers** (page 198), which is frequented by a mix of motorcycle groups and celebrities. Many women leave their bras on the ceiling as a memento.

Another great hang-out is **Tortilla Flats** in Washington Street on the corner of West 12th Street. It's a cool, grungy café famous for its hula-hooping-for-tequila-shots on a Wednesday night. Also home to the wonderful **Florent** restaurant (page 166) is Gansevoort Street. The area was until lately very edgy and still a hang-out for transvestite prostitutes – as depicted in *Sex And The City* when the man-eating Samantha moved here from the Upper East Side. This also where Carrie's boyfriend Aiden worked at the Furniture Company. But it's rapidly gentrifying, with expensive stores like **Jeffrey's** and **Stella McCartney's** highly fashionable shop.

MIDTOWN

Technically Midtown starts at 34th Street, but for the purposes of this area guide, we're starting at the more realistic 42nd Street (Map 3). From this point up to about 59th Street are some of the most beautiful and famous shops, hotels and buildings in the world, both to the east and west and on 5th Avenue itself (page 88). At the northern end of the Midtown area, 5th Avenue is lined with marvellous institutions such as **Saks**, **Bergdorf Goodman**, **Tiffany's** (our favourite jeweller) and **Trump Tower** (page 69).

Fabulous hotels in Midtown include the media den of the **Royalton** (page 221) and the famous **Algonquin** (page 245). Opposite **St Patrick's Cathedral** (page 71) on 5th Avenue is the main entrance into the **Rockefeller Center** complex of 19 statuesque buildings with the famous ice-skating rink in the middle of its central plaza (page 64). There's so much to do here, from browsing in the shops to checking out the architecture or visiting the beautifully restored Art Deco **Radio City Music Hall** (page 64). Further north on 57th Street is **Carnegie Hall** (pages 121 and 191).

MIDTOWN EAST

The area between 5th Avenue and East River, **Midtown East** (Map 3) has its fair share of New York landmarks. No visit to the city would be complete without seeing the magnificent, marble **Grand Central Station** (page 67) at 42nd Street, which has been restored to its former glory. It may be overshadowed by the **MetLife Building** from the outside, but nothing can detract from its gorgeous interior. The ceiling has been painted to show the sky as seen by God from above.

To the east is the stunning **Chrysler Building** (page 66) and down by the river is the monolithic **United Nations Building** (page 69). And no visit to Park Avenue would be complete without a drink at the **Waldorf Astoria** (page 229). Out of its many cocktail bars, the lobby bar is best for people-watching with a drink.

MIDTOWN WEST

TIMES SQUARE AND THE THEATER DISTRICT

If you arrive at **Times Square** (Map 3) by day when all the lights and motion are less distracting, you may actually notice the lack of a square. Like Greeley and Herald Squares, Times Square is no more than a junction where Broadway crosses 7th Avenue. The **Theater District** starts on the boundary with the Garment District at 41st Street, goes north to 53rd Street and is bounded by 6th and 8th Avenues. The best way to get there is to take the 1, 2, 3, 7, 9 N, Q, R, S, W to Times Square/42nd Street.

The Theater District came into being at the end of the 19th century – previously the theatres could all be found in the Union Square area and then Chelsea – when Oscar Hammerstein I (father of the great lyricist) built his opulent but long-gone Olympia Theater on Broadway between 44th and 45th Streets. Until then, it had been an unfashionable area known as Long Acre Square, housing the city's stables and blacksmiths.

In 1904, when the *New York Times* set up shop in what is now 1 Times Square, the area was renamed in its honour (it's since moved offices to around the corner). That same year a massive fireworks display on New Year's Eve became the precursor to the now famous annual countdown watched by millions of people. The surrounding Theater District, home to the Ziegfeld Follies at the **New Amsterdam Theater**, **Minsky's** and **Gypsy Rose Lee**, blossomed in the 1920s. In fact, so many theatres burst on to the scene that even though many were converted into cinemas in the 1940s, during a clean-up of the burlesque shows by Mayor LaGuardia, 30 theatres still remain.

BAD TIMES COME

Sadly, by the 1960s, Times Square had lost its shine and the economic problems of the 1970s and 1980s compounded the situation. If you've seen Martin Scorsese's film *Taxi Driver*, you'll have some idea of the level of drugs, prostitution and seedy strip joints that crowded the area. Crime rose dramatically and until fairly recently it was not a safe place to be.

Things started to change in the early 1990s, helped by the establishment of the **Times Square Business Improvement District**, which worked hard to clean things up and pay for security guards, and the discovery of an age-old law that prevents sex shops from operating within a certain distance of schools or churches. Since then crime in the area has dropped by 60 per cent and many New Yorkers have even complained of its relative cleanliness. The arrival of the Disney company, which spent millions renovating the New Amsterdam Theater to put on *The Lion King* (page 188), was the last nail in the coffin.

In all honesty, these dirt purists shouldn't fret too much – there is still definitely an edgy vibe to the neighbourhood, while the contant stream of traffic and the gruginess of many visitors stops Times Square from being what some people think of as a squeaky-clean environment.

44th Street and 9th

The Rockefeller Center

All the same, it's safe enough for the most part, attracts tenants who pay the same rents as on more elegant 5th and Madison Avenues, and has plenty to offer everyone. New hotels have sprung up and corporate companies have moved into the neighbourhood including media giants Viacom, MTV, VH-1 studios, ABC TV's *Good Morning America*, Condé Nast Publications and Reuters news service.

★ ★ ★ ★ **BRIT TIP** ★ ★ ★ ★
★ ★
★ For dining after the show with a ★
★ good chance to spot celebrities, ★
★ book into Angus McIndoe, 258 West ★
★ 44th Street. Tel: 212-221 9222. ★
★ ★
★★★★★★★★★★★★★★★★★★★★★★★★★★

There's the huge new **ESPN Zone**, a 3,900 sq m (42,000 sq ft) sports, dining and entertainment complex, **Nasdaq MarketSite** with its massive sign – the largest video screen in the world – and **Madame Tussaud's** (page 63). In between are the **Virgin Megastore** (page 112), the Coco Chanel-style beauty emporium of **Sephora** (page 103) and the **World Wrestling Federation** entertainment and dining complex, which includes a restaurant and hot new nightclub. Oh, and, of course, there are the 30 theatres and nearly 50 cinema screens...

HELL'S KITCHEN/CLINTON

Running up the west side of Midtown from 34th Street to 57th from around 8th Avenue to the river is an area known as **Hell's Kitchen**. In the latter part of the 19th century, many poor Irish immigrants settled here, creating a ghetto. They were later joined by blacks, Italians and Latinos and inevitably gangs formed. The big employers were the docks (see *On the Waterfront*, starring Marlon Brando, for an insight into the lifestyle; although set in Brooklyn, it is equally true of all the dock areas), but when container ships came into play many lost their jobs. Other local industries included slaughterhouses and glue and soap factories.

★ ★ ★ ★ **BRIT TIP** ★ ★ ★ ★
★   ★
★ If you have an evening out on the   ★
★ World Yacht (pages 76 and 139),   ★
★ you'll find yourself walking through ★
★ Hell's Kitchen/Clinton in search of a ★
★ taxi. Adopt 'the New York walk'   ★
★ (walk quickly and confidently) and   ★
★ head east to 7th or 6th Avenues   ★
★ where it's easiest to pick up a cab. ★
★ ★

A lot of the gangs were put out of business by the police in 1910, but it remained a scary area until fairly recently. It was renamed Clinton in 1959 to hide its violent past – which is long before Bill came on the scene, so there's no link to the former president. Now a lot of people living there work in the Theater District and it's moving up in the world. 9th and 10th Avenues are full of restaurants, the **Intrepid Sea-Air-Space Museum** (page 118) is on the river and, on the whole, the area is pretty safe until around 11pm.

MORNINGSIDE HEIGHTS

Further north the terrain gets hilly as you reach **Morningside Heights** (Map 6) home to the **Cathedral of St John the Divine** (page 70) and **Columbia University**, one of the most exclusive universities in America where a year's tuition fees, room and board will set you back around $38,000. Even so, it has 20,000 students, of whom 4,000 are undergraduates. This is a beautiful area, which is bounded by 8th Avenue to the east and West 125th Street to the north.

Street food vendor

★ ★ ★ ★ **BRIT TIP** ★ ★ ★ ★
★   ★
★ A great pit-stop in the Columbia   ★
★ University area is Tom's Restaurant ★
★ on Broadway at 112th Street (page   ★
★ 184). If you recognise the diner's   ★
★ exterior, that's because it was used ★
★ in *Seinfeld*.   ★
★ ★

MURRAY HILL

It's a testimony to man's desire to tame his environment that the majority of Manhattan is flat. This is a result of the zoning plans created in the early 19th century, when the streets and avenues were laid out north of Downtown, except for the Village. At the same time, the City flattened the majority of Manhattan except for what is now Morningside Heights and Harlem, as nobody believed anyone would live up there! The only other area that has kept its contours is **Murray Hill** (Map 3), a largely residential neighbourhood for New York's gentry, which lies between 5th and 3rd Avenues and 32nd and 40th Streets.

Columbia University

The most famous resident of the area was the multi-millionaire JP Morgan. His son lived in a brownstone on the corner of 37th Street and Madison Avenue, which is now the headquarters of the **Lutheran Church**. JP Morgan lived in a house next door until he had it knocked down to make way for an expansion of his library. Now known as the **Morgan Library** (page 128), it has a unique collection of manuscripts, paintings, prints and furniture, which the financier collected on his trips to Europe. The nearest subways are the 6 to 33rd Street or the 4, 5, 6, 7, S to Grand Central/42nd Street.

NOHO

Wedged between Greenwich Village and the East Village is a small section of streets now known as **NoHo** – North of Houston Street (Map 2). Bounded by Broadway to the west, Bowery to the east, Astor Place to the north and East Houston Street to the south, it's a tiny triangular-shaped area cut off from both of the villages, yet teeming with bars, cafés and shops. The boutiques here are a match for nearby SoHo and some are just as pricey, but for innovative and unique designs, they're streets ahead of many areas, with the exception of NoLiTa.

Get here via the 6 subway to Astor Place or Bleecker Street or the F, V, S to Broadway/Lafayette Street.

NOLITA

NoLiTa stands for North of Little Italy and stretches from Kenmare Street in the south, to Houston in the north and from Crosby Street in the west to Elizabeth Street in the east (Map 2). The best subways to take are the 6 to Spring Street, the F, V, S to Broadway/Lafayette Street and the F, V to 2nd Avenue.

A fairly new part of town, it's filled with funky coffee shops, bars and restaurants. In a very short space of time Elizabeth, Mott and Mulberry Streets have seen a rapid growth in up-and-coming designers. Ultra cool and cutting edge, some are pricey, but most still charge moderate prices. It's difficult to know how long that will last, though, as many of the boutiques are now frequented by celebrities in search of chic, one-off designs.

SOHO

SoHo means south of Houston, pronounced 'Howston'. It is bounded by Lafayette Street at its eastern border, 6th Avenue to the west and Canal Street to the south (Map 2). The best subways are 6, C, E to Spring Street and N, R to Prince Street.

The main drag is on **West Broadway**, though Spring and Prince Streets are major shopping havens too, and the whole area is reminiscent of Hampstead Village in London. Okay, so there are no hills and the roads are wider, but it has the same boutiquey, picturesque, funky design-conscious element.

★ ★ ★ ★   **BRIT TIP**   ★ ★ ★ ★

★ **If you're looking for a delicious latte** ★
★ **and snack in SoHo, try the aptly** ★
★ **named Space Untitled in Green** ★
★ **Street between Houston and** ★
★ **Prince Streets.** ★

It's hard to imagine the totally trendy and oh-so-expensive SoHo as a slum, yet just over 30 years ago this was the case. Despite the arrival of cutting-edge artists in the 1940s, who'd spotted the great potential of the massive loft spaces once used by manufacturers and wholesalers, the whole area was run-down and shabby.

Then, in the 1960s, those same artists

TASTES GOOD TO ME

SoHo is home to a complete first in New York City – a shop that can sell both wine and food. **Vintage New York** at 482 Broome Street at Wooster Street (212-226 9463) is owned by a vineyard from New York State, which means it can open on Sundays and sell proper alcoholic wine and food together – both of which are otherwise illegal in New York. The true secret to this little gem is that you can get five 1oz tastes of different wines for just $5, which actually works out to be one of the cheapest glasses of wine going in Manhattan! All the wines, incidentally, are from vineyards in the state of New York. Best time to visit Vintage is during the week when there are stools to sit on at the tasting bar.

were forced to fight for their very homes when the city decided to pull down all the buildings because they were only supposed to be used for light industry and definitely NOT for living in. The artists successfully argued that the architecture of the cast-iron buildings was too valuable to be destroyed and the whole of SoHo was declared a historic district.

★ There is a cracking restaurant just
★ off the beaten track in MacDougal –
★ Provence (page 173) – where you'll
★ get a delicious meal in a romantic
★ setting. For good fare at reasonable
★ prices, locals frequent Jerry's on
★ Prince Street.

In the 1970s, art galleries first started moving into the area and the art boom of the 1980s truly transformed it. In 1992 the Guggenheim opened a downtown site on Broadway at Prince Street. These events coincided with a kind of bubble-bursting feeling for the more cutting-edge artists, especially those who could no longer afford SoHo's sky-rocketing rents. Many have now moved on to Chelsea and TriBeCa, and SoHo has become a wealthy residential neighbourhood occupied by anyone rich enough to afford the large loft spaces that are prevalent.

However, there are still plenty of art galleries – certainly a higher density than most areas of Manhattan – but the nature of the area has changed quite substantially (and we think for the better). Designers, clothes boutiques and dedicated beauty shops have arrived en masse, though the emphasis still lies heavily on style and art in terms of presentation and decor. The Guggenheim has shut up shop to be replaced by Prada's stunning flagship store (page 97). Coffee shops, bars and restaurants that normal mortals can afford are now in better supply and the beauty boutiques with their wooden flooring, high ceilings and gleaming, glistening displays are wonderful places to get expert beauty advice on the cheap.

While MoMA's **New Museum of Contemporary Art** (page 131) is the only remaining art museum in the area, a formidable sense of style remains and can

be seen daily at the fashionistas' **SoHo Grand Hotel** haunt (page 232).

★ For a well-priced, delicious lunch al
★ fresco, head to the Gourmet Garage
★ on the corner of Broome and Mercer
★ Streets. It has a wonderful deli with
★ ready-made salads to take away.

TRIBECA

TriBeCa (Map 1) like other acronyms such as SoHo, is a shortening of the area's location. In this case it means the triangle below Canal Street. It is bounded by Canal to the north, Murray to the south, West Broadway to the east and the Hudson River. To get here on the subway, use the 1, 9 to Canal or Franklin Streets or the 1, 2, 3, 9 to Chambers Street.

TriBeCa provides a good idea of what SoHo looked like 20 years ago. With the increasing pressure to find affordable housing, the empty warehouses of TriBeCa were ripe for the 'gentrification' process that has been happening all over New York, including SoHo, the East Village and even the Lower East Side to a certain extent. And the area certainly has its fair share of pretty cast-iron buildings and quaint cobbled streets. Along **Harrison Street** is a row of well-preserved Federal-style townhouses and the area around White Street is particularly picturesque.

In the late 1970s, the former industrial buildings were targeted by estate agents for residential dwellings, but it was not really until the late 1980s that the area became a favourite with artists priced out of SoHo. Now TriBeCa is home to a variety of media and artistic businesses such as galleries, recording studios and graphic companies.

Its most famous film company, the **TriBeCa Film Center** at 375 Greenwich Street, which is part-owned by Robert De Niro, has production offices and screening rooms and is used by visiting film-makers. They, of course, frequent De Niro's extremely expensive **TriBeCa Grill** on the ground floor of the building. Visiting film-makers have also been given a boost by the opening of the triangular-shaped **TriBeCa Grand Hotel**, which has its own private screening room.

THE NEW YORK NEIGHBOURHOODS

Now the area is deemed quite hip – being home to Harvey Keitel and Naomi Campbell among others – it has attracted a lot of upper middle-class families, while restaurants and nightclubs are frequented by residents from the nearby Battery Park City. It is also home to the **TriBeCa Film Festival**, which showcases independent movies during the second week of May.

UNION SQUARE

Take the L, N, Q, R, W, 4, 5, 6 to Union Square at 14th Street (Map 2). This area was once pretty run down and overrun with drug pushers and muggers, but now it's one of the trendiest neighbourhoods in New York. The stretch of Park Avenue South between 14th and 23rd Streets is filled with some truly hip eateries and is known as **Restaurant Row**.

★ ★ ★ ★ BRIT TIP ★ ★ ★ ★
★ The West Hotel Union Square on ★
★ Park Avenue South at 17th Street is ★
★ home to Underbar, one of the most ★
★ stylish nightclubs in New York ★
★ (page 206). ★

Along here you'll find **Tammany Hall**, the most corrupt City Hall in New York's history. It was home to Jimmy Walker, ostensibly a popular mayor, but a man who had been elected by the gangsters in the 1920s, which is effectively how organised crime was born in America. The gangsters were impossible to prosecute because they knew all the judges, cops and politicians in New York and virtually lived at Tammany Hall. Walker even had showers installed for them. Eventually, in the face of mounting

Park Avenue apartments

SoHo

financial problems in the city, Walker was forced to resign and his successor, Fiorello LaGuardia (pronounced La-gwar-dia), decided to go after the gangs.

★ ★ ★ ★ BRIT TIP ★ ★ ★ ★
★ Create an instant picnic by buying ★
★ farm-fresh produce, home-made ★
★ breads, cheeses and drinks from the ★
★ Union Square Farmers' Market every ★
★ Monday, Wednesday, Friday and ★
★ Saturday. ★

In the middle of Union Square is **Luna Park**, a great casual place for a bite to eat in the summer, with outdoor seating (page 251). Further north on Broadway to Madison Square Park, you'll find **Theodore Roosevelt's birthplace** at 28 East 20th Street. It's not the original building, but it does house some great memorabilia from the former president's life (open Wed–Sun 9am–5pm; $3). Just around the corner is the wonderful, triangular **Flatiron Building** (page 66), at the end of what was once known as **Ladies Mile**, the city's most fashionable shopping district along Broadway and 6th Avenue from 14th Street.

UPPER EAST SIDE

One of the most conservative areas of New York, the **Upper East Side** (Map 4) stretches from Central Park South to 98th Street and is centred on 5th, Madison, Park and Lexington Avenues. It came into being after Central Park was finally completed in 1876 and the rich and famous of the Gilded Era – the Whitneys, Carnegies, Fricks, Vanderbilts and Astors – decided to build their mansions alongside. It was a time when neo-classicism was the favourite architectural design, but many of the houses left standing are not the originals as the grandiose properties were built and rebuilt in an ever-more opulent style or replaced with apartment blocks.

★ ★ ★ ★   **BRIT TIP**   ★ ★ ★ ★
★   ★
★   ★
★ Jim's Shoeshine on East 59th Street ★
★ between Madison and Park Avenues ★
★ is a real institution that has existed ★
★   since the 1930s.   ★
★ ★

Two things have always remained the same, though. The neighbourhood is known as the Silk Stocking District because of the vast family fortunes represented in the area, and the grand old apartment houses are known as 'white glove' buildings because of the uniforms of the doormen. People still pay a fortune to live there. For instance, Jackie Onassis's former 14-room apartment at 1040 5th Avenue near East 86th Street sold some years ago for a whopping $9 million. The mansion on the corner of East 86th is one of nine once owned by the Vanderbilts. Nearby residents include Michael J Fox and Bette Midler.

If you're serious about designer clothes, then you'll be visiting the designer stores that line **Madison Avenue**. If you're clever you won't buy, just gather information on what's new for when you go rummaging through the designer selections at **Daffy's** or the sample sales (pages 39, 92 and 93).

This area is also full of museums, with a staggering array to choose from. They range from the world's largest and, arguably, most magnificent – the **Metropolitan Museum of Art** (page 119) – to the jewel of the **Frick Collection** (page 124), housed in the magnate's former mansion. Near to the Frick is the joyous **Whitney Museum of American Art** (page 134), with its emphasis on contemporary art.

Further north is the beautiful-looking **Guggenheim** (page 120), as well as the **Cooper-Hewitt** (page 122), the **Jewish Museum** (page 126) and the **International Center of Photography** (page 124). Finally, up on the borders of East Harlem, populated by Latin Americans, are the **Museum of the City of New York** (page 129) and **El Museo del Barrio** (page 123).

UPPER WEST SIDE

Central Park divides the Upper East and West Sides not only geographically but in terms of attitude, too. If the East Side is upper crust, conservative old money, then the West Side (Map 5) is more artistic. It's a vibrant neighbourhood filled with bars, restaurants, shops, museums and, of course, the culture of the Lincoln Center.

The area is now anchored by the amazing new **AOL Time Warner Center**'s twin towers at Columbus Circle, which house a mixture of offices, hotel, shopping and cultural centres. The $1.7-billion complex includes the **Mandarin Oriental Hotel and Spa**, the new home of jazz at the **Lincoln Center** (pages 192 and 193), broadcast facilities for live transmission of CNN, apartments and **The Palladium**, a massive space for shops, restaurants and entertainment venues (nearest subway is the A, B, C, D, 1, 9 to 59th Street/Columbus

Bleeker Street and 7th, West Village

BAG YOURSELF A BAGEL

Among the best places for bagels:

Bagelry: 1324 Lexington Avenue between East 88th and 89th Streets on the Upper East Side and many other locations around the city.

Ess-A-Bagel: 359 1st Avenue at 21st Street.

H&H: 80th Street and Broadway and other locations. Ships bagels worldwide.

Murray's Bagels: 500 7th Avenue at West 12th Street.

Pick-A-Bagel: 200 West 57th Street at 7th Avenue and other locations.

Yonah Schimmel's: 137 East Houston Street between Forsyth and Eldridge Streets in the Lower East Side, near to Katz's Deli. Knishes – pastries stuffed with savoury fillings – are the major speciality here.

Circle). As you navigate the traffic lights to cross the roads at Columbus Circle, you can ponder on the fact that this is where Joe Colombo, the boss of one of the five Mafia families of New York, was shot.

★ ★ ★ ★ **BRIT TIP** ★ ★ ★ ★
★   ★
★   A new place to take a break is ★
★ Whole Foods, a huge market selling ★
★ a dazzling array of prepared foods, ★
★ on the basement level of AOL Time ★
★ Warner Center. Either dine at one of ★
★ the tables there or eat in Central ★
★   Park across the street.   ★
★ ★

Up Broadway and left down West 63rd Street you'll find the **Lincoln Center**. This was once filled with the slums that housed poor Puerto Ricans (the setting for the 1961

WHICH MET'S THE MET?

Traditionally, the Metropolitan Opera House, with its crystal chandeliers and red-carpeted staircases, has been known as the Met. Increasingly, though, the Metropolitan Museum of Art is being referred to by the same moniker, which is causing a certain amount of confusion. It probably depends which establishment you stumble across first. For us the museum will always be the Met!

movie *West Side Story*) until Robert Moses proposed the building of various cultural centres that include the **Metropolitan Opera House**, the **New York State Theater** and **Avery Fisher Hall**. To see more, join one of the popular backstage tours or enjoy the free lunchtime music supplied by visiting jazz and folk bands during the summer months.

BUILT TO LAST

The Upper West Side is well known for its beautiful buildings including the Beaux Arts **Ansonia Hotel** on Broadway between 73rd and 74th Streets, which has been called home by both Babe Ruth and Igor Stravinsky in its time. Starting on the southern tip of Central Park West, which runs all the way up Central Park, is the Art Deco stunner at No 55, which was used as the setting for the film *Ghostbusters*.

On 67th Street near Central Park West is the **Hotel des Artistes** which, as the name suggests, was built for the artistic types who used its studios. Over the years it has been home to such celebrities as Noel Coward and Isadora Duncan. Today you can dine at the elegant **Café des Artistes** there (page 182). Back on Central Park West between 71st and 72nd Streets is the yellow façade of the Art Deco **Majestik** apartment house, which was built in 1930.

★ ★ ★ ★ **BRIT TIP** ★ ★ ★ ★
★   ★
★ Once you cross West 59th Street ★
★ going north, 8th, 9th, 10th and 11th ★
★ Avenues become Central Park West, ★
★ Columbus, Amsterdam and West End ★
★   Avenues respectively.   ★
★ ★

Across the way is the famous **Dakota Building**, which was the first apartment block ever to be built on the Upper West Side in 1884, and was named after the distant territory to indicate its remoteness from anything else on the West Side. Of course, since then it has had a long line of famous inhabitants including Leonard Bernstein, Judy Garland and Boris Karloff. Its most famous resident of all, **John Lennon**, was gunned down outside the building by a crazed fan in 1980. His widow Yoko Ono still lives here – she owns several apartments – and she donated money to build the Strawberry Fields memorial to the star in

Central Park, just across the road.

A couple of blocks north between 73rd and 74th is the neo-Renaissance style **Langham**, which was built in 1905, and between 74th and 75th is the **San Remo**, built in 1930, where Rita Hayworth died of Alzheimer's in 1987. Several blocks north, on the corner of 81st Street and Central Park West, stands the elegant **Beresford**. Between them, these grand apartment blocks have housed a huge number of celebrities, including such names as Lauren Bacall, Dustin Hoffman, Steve Martin and Jerry Seinfeld, who bought Isaac Stern's sprawling apartment home.

★ ★ ★ ★ **BRIT TIP** ★ ★ ★ ★
★   ★
★   ★
★ Just a few blocks from the museums ★
★   is Zabar's (page 114) on Broadway ★
★   at West 80th Street, the famous ★
★ food emporium seen in Friends, and ★
★   Fairway, on West 75th Street. Both ★
★   are jam-packed with all the   ★
★   ingredients needed for a picnic in ★
★   nearby Riverside or Central Parks. ★
★ ★

MUSEUM HALF MILE

On Central Park West at 77th Street is the **New York Historical Society** (page 132), which was formed in 1804 and was the only art museum in the city until the opening of the Metropolitan Museum of Art in 1872. It was founded to chronicle New York's history but still houses the world's largest collection of Tiffany stained-glass shades and lamps and two million manuscripts, including letters sent by George Washington during the War of Independence.

Next door is the real big boy of museums, the **American Museum of Natural History** (page 117), which was the brainchild of scientist Albert Smith Bickmore. It first opened at the New York Arsenal in Central Park in 1869, but by 1874 had moved to these bigger premises. Architect Calvert Vaux, who was also responsible for the Met Museum and largely responsible for Central Park, created the bulk of the building, which has since had a Romanesque-style façade added to its 77th Street side and a Beaux Arts-style frontage on the Central Park West side.

This is a favourite museum of ours. It's crammed with well laid-out exhibitions that really bring the world of science, scientific discovery and expeditions to life, while the **Rose Center** and **Big Bang Theater** attract major crowds to see the 13-billion-year history of the universe.

The Upper West Side's Museum Half Mile also includes the **Children's Museum of Manhattan** (page 122) on 83rd Street between Broadway and Amsterdam Avenue, where interactive exhibits keep the wee ones happy.

West 106th Street, at the top end of the neighbourhood, is now known as **Duke Ellington Broadway**. This is where the great musician lived, premiered many of his songs and was buried in 1974. Over 10,000 people came to his funeral and there is a memorial to him on 5th Avenue at West 110th by Central Park's Harlem Meer.

WEST VILLAGE

The West Village, on the other side of 7th Avenue, has an amazingly pretty collection of cobbled streets lined with picturesque homes and trees. These are among some of the oldest remaining houses in New York, many being built in the 1820s and 1850s, and quite a few have the one thing that is so rare in Manhattan – a back garden, albeit tiny. To get here take the 1, 9 to Christopher Street or the A, C, E to 14th Street or the L subway to 8th Avenue.

FAMOUS SPEAKEASY

On the corner of Bedford Street, number 86 is one of the most famous former speakeasies in New York. Known as **Chumley's** (page 199), it doesn't have its name advertised anywhere outside, but there is a back entrance on Barrow Street that will take you directly into the bar. The front entrance merely has the old grille, used for checking over potential customers during Prohibition, and the number 86.

In the old days a dumb waiter took two people at a time to the gambling den upstairs, and the best table in the house was right by the entrance to the cellar, where people could hide if there was a raid. Now Chumley's does fish and chips and shepherd's pie-type food and usually has a roaring fire in the winter, while the walls are still lined with all the book jackets donated by many of the writers who once frequented it.

★ ★ ★ ★ **BRIT TIP** ★ ★ ★ ★
★　　　　　　　　　　　　　★
★　　　　　　　　　　　　　★
★ **Crossing Bedford is Barrow Street,** ★
★ **where you'll find One If By Land,** ★
★ **Two If By Sea. It's in the oldest** ★
★ **building housing a restaurant in** ★
★ **Manhattan, a former carriage house** ★
★ **built in 1726. Great food, service** ★
★ **and decor. If you're in the mood for** ★
★ **a romantic splurge, this is the place.** ★
★ **Tel 212-228 0822.** ★
★ ★ ★ ★ ★ ★ ★ ★ ★ ★ ★ ★ ★ ★ ★ ★ ★ ★ ★ ★

At the corner of **Grove Street** is the oldest wooden house in the West Village. Built in 1822, it's the most exclusive cottage in the area and costs $6,000 a month to rent, but it does have its own little garden – what a bargain! All around Grove Street the houses are covered in a network of vines, which blossom in May and have grown in the area for 150 years.

A MATTER OF RIGHTS

Christopher Street, the main drag of the West Village, is the heart of the gay community and a shopping paradise for antique lovers. **Sheridan Square**, one of the Village's busiest junctions, has been the scene of two major riots. First were the New York Draft Riots of 1863, sparked off by the requirement to join the army for the Civil War. The rich could buy their way out, but the poor had no choice and were fearful they would lose their jobs to the newly freed black slaves.

The second riot is the more famous and is known as the Stonewall Riot. This was sparked in 1969 by the police raiding the Stonewall gay bar and arresting its occupants – an event that frequently occurred at the many gay watering holes in the area. This time the community decided to fight back and, over a period of three nights, the gay community held its ground

Christopher Park

in the Stonewall as it was surrounded by police. It was the crucial first step made by gay people in standing up for their rights.

Christopher Street is still filled with bars, restaurants and bookstores that are used by gays – though not exclusively – but many members of the gay community have moved on to Chelsea.

YORKVILLE

Between Lexington Avenue and the East River from East 77th to 96th Streets is the working- to middle-class enclave of **Yorkville** (Map 5) (subway 4, 5, 6 to 86th Street), which has an interesting mix of cultures, singles and families.

★ ★ ★ ★ **BRIT TIP** ★ ★ ★ ★
★　　　　　　　　　　　　　★
★ **Fancy the idea of a picnic by the** ★
★ **river? Then stop off at The Vinegar** ★
★ **Factory in 91st Street (page 114),** ★
★ **where you'll find an extensive** ★
★ **selection of cheeses, meats, breads** ★
★ **and salads, and head for the nearby** ★
★ **Carl Schurz Park.** ★
★ ★ ★ ★ ★ ★ ★ ★ ★ ★ ★ ★ ★ ★ ★ ★ ★ ★ ★ ★

It was originally populated by German–Hungarians, who moved northwards from their first stopping point in the East Village's Thompkins Square with the arrival of Italian and Slavic immigrants. Now, though, you'd be hard-pressed to find the few remnants of German culture, as most left the neighbourhood during the Second World War to avoid anti-German feelings.

★ ★ ★ ★ **BRIT TIP** ★ ★ ★ ★
★　　　　　　　　　　　　　★
★ **Do like the locals and head to the** ★
★ **cosy DT UT coffee bar on 2nd** ★
★ **Avenue between 84th and 85th** ★
★ **Streets. For a real American Girl** ★
★ **Scouts' adventure, try some 's'mores'** ★
★ **(short for 'I want some more') –** ★
★ **toasted marshmallows with Hershey** ★
★ **chocolate and a biscuit on top.** ★
★ ★ ★ ★ ★ ★ ★ ★ ★ ★ ★ ★ ★ ★ ★ ★ ★ ★ ★ ★

The most famous resident in the area is the mayor, who lives in the official residence at Gracie Mansion (page 66) overlooking the East River and the lovely Carl Schurz Park at East 89th Street.

CHAPTER 4

What to See and Do

There is so much to see and do in the city that never sleeps that it can all feel a bit daunting when you first step out of your hotel, guide book in hand. Therefore it's a good idea to make a plan of what you'd really like to see before you're back on the plane and heading home. The major sights are often the number one priority – especially for the first-time visitor – so, to try to make your life a little easier, we have indicated the location of each of the following sights. It would be advisable to read Chapter 3 first so you get a good feel for each of the neighbourhoods and that way you can make the most of your time by planning your days in specific areas of the city. For instance, if you plan to see the Empire State Building, bear in mind it is deep in the heart of the 34th Street shopping district. The section entitled Orientation (page 23) will also help you make sense of the streets of New York and get to know the intricacies of the grid system and the distances involved. Having said all of that, do make sure you leave a little time in your schedule for simply wandering. Even if it's only for a couple of hours, the feeling of walking along the streets of New York like a local and discovering a charming café or cool local shop as yet unearthed by a guidebook is marvellous.

PART ONE – THE SIGHTS

This section gives you our Top Five must-see sights, plus all the major sights in New York. You can either visit them under your own steam or take advantage of the many and varied tours that are listed in the second part of this chapter.

★ ★ ★ ★ BRIT TIP ★ ★ ★ ★

Security at many sights and buildings has been tightened following the tragic events of September 11, so allow extra time for this when planning your schedules.
★ ★

A-Z OF SIGHTS

CENTRAL PARK

Think of New York and Central Park is likely to spring to mind. It's the New Yorkers' playground and a wonderful place to spend time during your stay. For a complete description of the park and all its facilities, see pages 249–250. For family fun and activities, see pages 212–215.

Ellis Island Immigration Museum

TOP FIVE SIGHTS

There are plenty of exciting things to see and do in New York, but some are simply unmissable, particularly if you're visiting for the first time. Below is our definitive guide to the top sights, and whatever else you do when you are in the city, these are the ones you mustn't miss:

Central Park: pages 212 and 249

Ellis Island Immigration Museum: with Statue of Liberty (below)

Empire State Building: 34th Street (page 61)

Statue of Liberty: ferry from Battery Park (below)

Times Square: Midtown West (Chapter 8, page 185)

ELLIS ISLAND IMMIGRATION MUSEUM AND THE STATUE OF LIBERTY

Battery Park

☎ 212-269 5755
Fax 212-363 9810

🖱 www.circlelinedowntown.com

🚗 Statue of Liberty and Ellis Island Ferry, which leaves every 20-30 minutes from Gangway 5 in Battery Park. Subway 1, 9, 4, 5 to Bowling Green

🕐 9am–3.30pm

$ $11.50 adults, $9.50 seniors, $4.50 children (4–12), under 3s free. Credit cards accepted.

⋆ Don't spoil your day of sightseeing
⋆ by missing the boat. The last boat
⋆ leaves from Liberty Island at 5pm
⋆ and Ellis Island at 5.15pm and the
⋆ museum closes at 5.30pm.

The Statue of Liberty (www.nps.gov/stli), one of the biggest attractions in New York is reached by a ferry, which also takes you to the Ellis Island Museum where you learn the immigration story of America. Ferry tickets are sold at Castle Clinton, the low circular brownstone building in Battery Park (open 8.30am–4.30pm). Luggage, including backpacks, is not permitted and the security checks can take up to an hour.

The Statute of Liberty originally came to New York in 1886, as a gift from France. You can enjoy the panoramic views from the observation deck, about 16 storeys above ground, and tour the museum in the pedestal. A limited number of time passes are now available for an 'insider's view' into this work of art (www.statue reservations.com). The rest of the statue will continue to be off-limits, however, including the statue's interior spiral staircases, but you can stroll along the promenade above the star-shaped former fort on which the statue and its pedestal rise some 30 storeys above the harbour.

The Statue of Liberty café is extremely small and there are simply not enough loos. There is space to eat outside, but not very much. At Ellis Island, however, you'll find plenty of WCs on all the different levels, a large café and a huge amount of outdoor seating that looks right out over to the Statue of Liberty and the skyscrapers of Lower Manhattan.

⋆ When leaving the Statue of Liberty
⋆ to go on to Ellis Island DO NOT get
⋆ on the ferry that takes you to New
⋆ Jersey. That is on the left. It IS
⋆ clearly signposted, but it is very easy
⋆ to get disorientated!

The Ellis Island Immigration Museum (www.ellisisland.com) is the most visited museum in New York, particularly beloved by crowds of Americans who want to see where their immigrant ancestors arrived. In

TICKET TO RIDE

The CityPass is an excellent way to avoid long queues and save money if you visit at least three of the participating attractions. These are the American Museum of Natural History, the Empire State Building and New York Skyride, the Intrepid Sea-Air-Space Museum, the Guggenheim Museum, the Museum of Modern Art and a harbour tour with the Circle Line. You can buy a CityPass from any of the attractions, which will save you queuing again. Prices are $63 (a $59.50 saving on normal admission prices) for adults and $46 for 6–17s. Call 208-787 4300 or you can buy online at www.citypass.com.

use from 1892 to 1954, it 'processed' up to 10,000 immigrants a day. Each person was examined and then interviewed to find out if they could speak English. An unfortunate 2 per cent were turned away.

Visitors follow the immigrants' route as they entered the main baggage room and went up to the Registry and then the Staircase of Separation. Poignant exhibits include photos, video clips, jewellery, clothing, baggage and the stark dormitories. The Immigrant Wall of Fame lists half a million names, including those of the grandfathers of Presidents Washington and Kennedy.

This is a great museum and well worth allocating a good portion of your day to. All the films and the guided tour are free. The Ranger Tours last 45 minutes and leave at regular times throughout the day (times posted in the information booth). At 2pm there is a re-enactment of a board of inquiry, which decides an immigrant's fate. Immigrants tell their stories in the movie *Island of Hope, Island of Tears*, which runs frequently in two theatres. Free tickets are available at the desk. Audio tours are available for $6. A play, *Ellis Island Stories*, is also presented regularly. Tickets are $2 and $3.

★★★★ **BRIT TIP** ★★★★
The tour, film and play on Ellis Island are free but you need to get tickets for each of them from the information desk (just to the left on your way in). Busiest times are obviously just after a boat has arrived, so try to be the first off the ferry and head straight for the desk.
★★★★★★★★★★★★★★★★★★★★★★★★

The museum is very well laid out, has lots of benches everywhere and is so big it never feels too crowded. There is a cashpoint (ATM) in the corridor on the way to the café, which is on your right as you enter the building. The café is a little pricey but you could bring your own picnic and sit outside and enjoy the fabulous views.

FREE SIGHTS AND ATTRACTIONS

Cathedral of St John the Divine. Upper West Side/Morningside Heights (page 70)

Central Park: (pages 212 and 249)

Federal Reserve Bank: Financial District (page 66)

Gracie Mansion: Upper East Side (page 66)

Grand Central Station: Midtown East (page 67)

New York Public Library: Midtown (page 68)

Rockefeller Center: Midtown (page 64)

South Street Seaport: Financial District (page 65)

Staten Island Ferry: Battery Park (page 65)

Times Square: Midtown West (Chapter 8, page 185)

The Winter Garden: Battery Park City (page 69)

Woolworth Building: Civic Center/Financial District (page 70)

EMPIRE STATE BUILDING
34th Street

✉ 350 5th Avenue at 34th Street
☎ 212-736 3100
🖰 www.esbnyc.com
🚇 Subway B, D, F, Q, N, R, V, W to 34th Street
🕐 8am–midnight, last lifts go up at 11.15pm
$ $18 adults, $16 seniors and youth (12–17), $12 children (6–11), under 5s free. Tickets can be bought online.

It is hard to believe that the Empire State, which was for almost 40 years the world's tallest building, was nearly not built at all. Just weeks after its building contract was signed in 1929, the Wall Street Crash brought the financial world to its knees. Fortunately, the project went ahead and was even completed 45 days ahead of schedule, rising to 443m (1,454ft) in 1931. The lobby interior features Art Deco design incorporating rare marble imported from Italy, France, Belgium and Germany.

★ ★ ★ ★ **BRIT TIP** ★ ★ ★ ★

Fancy a coffee when you're in the Empire State Building? To avoid the pricey snack bars, get back down to ground level and visit Starbucks next door.

There are two observation decks, one on the 86th floor and another on the 102nd floor. Sadly, the higher deck is now closed. Your best bet is to arrive as early in the morning as possible to avoid long waits for tickets. Weekends, of course, get really crowded. Once you reach the 86th floor you can enjoy some fabulous views of Manhattan and the outer boroughs and really get your bearings. If you like you can hire the ESB Audio Tour for $6. You buy your tickets on the concourse level below the main lobby, but don't have to use them on the same day.

★ ★ ★ ★ **BRIT TIP** ★ ★ ★ ★

If you've a CityPass booklet (page 60), you can avoid the ticket queues at the Empire State Building. Walk straight past the crowds on the ground floor and turn right to go up one flight.

Empire State Building

Ellis Island ferry

The **New York SkyRide** is on the second floor and is open seven days a week 10am–10pm. It simulates a thrilling flight around the skyscrapers and bridges of New York. Entrance $18 adults, $14 youth (12–17) and $13 seniors and children (5–11). For a combined New York Skyride and Empire State Building ticket, the prices are $28 adults, $18 seniors and youth and $20 for children. Tel 212-279 9777 or buy online www.skyride.com.

GROUND ZERO – MEMORIAL FOUNDATIONS AT WORLD TRADE CENTER
Financial District
- ✉ West Street between Liberty and Vesey Streets
- 🖰 www.groundzero.nyc.ny.us
- 🚇 Subway N, R, W to Cortlandt Street; 1, 9 to Rector Street

After a lengthy public consultation, in 2002 the Lower Manhattan Development Corporation (LMDC) began a worldwide search for a suitable design concept for the 6.5 hectare (16 acre) former World Trade Center site. There were 400 submissions from around the globe, which were whittled down to seven and exhibited at the Winter

---

NEW YORK PASS
As well as the CityPass, the New York Pass offers discounted entry to over 40 sights and also gives discounts and extras at a range of shops and restaurants and for some tours, plus free access to the subway and buses. One day costs $54, phone 877-714 1999 or visit www.newyorkpass.com.

The Woolworth Building

Garden. More than 100,000 visitors saw the exhibition– generating 8,000 comments– and another eight million looked at the plans on the internet. Finally, after three public meetings, Studio Daniel Libeskind's Memory Foundations design was chosen in early 2003.

Originally, Libeskind planned to divide the 'superblock' formed by the World Trade Center into four parts. His plan included a sunken memorial site on the spot where the Twin Towers had stood, and around the memorial he envisioned five irregularly shaped towers of which the tallest would be a 541m (1,776ft) towering spire of glass called the Freedom Tower.

Eventually, Libeskind redesigned the towers to be slimmer, taller and squarer, in order to provide more office space. Then, the site developer brought in architect David Childs, who changed Libeskind's glass Freedom Tower into a larger, heavier building but retained the spire. Wind turbines will harness the wind and generate the building's energy. The occupied portion will be 60 storeys high. The 1,776ft Freedom Tower is expected to open in 2010.

In January 2004, a jury chose Michel Arad's memorial design, Reflecting Absence, which differed from Libeskind's. It includes a forest of trees planted throughout a plaza around the footprints of the Twin Towers; reflecting pools deep within the footprints, with constantly falling water to mark the voids; exposure of the bedrock-and-slurry wall to reveal the scale of the site and the disaster; and chambers for unidentified remains of the dead, as well as relics of the disaster. Peter Walker, a Californian landscape architect, is designing a park on the broad, open street-level plaza.

Santiago Calatrava, designer of the transportation hub, has incorporated Libeskind's Wedge of Light feature. His steel-and-glass train station will allow a shaft of light to fall between its wings without a shadow each year on September 11 between the hours of 8.46am, when the first plane hit, and 10.28am, when the second tower collapsed, in perpetual tribute to altruism and courage.

★ ★ ★ ★ ★ BRIT TIP ★ ★ ★ ★
★ Always carry water around with you ★
★ whether you are sightseeing or ★
★ shopping. No matter what the ★
★ weather, it is incredibly easy to get ★
★ dehydrated. Take a small bottle and ★
★ refill along the way. ★

The design concept is being built in several phases, and includes better street and pedestrian layouts, better connections between subway and PATH train systems, easily accessible shops and restaurants at street level, particularly along Fulton and Church Streets, plus better bus and car parking. There will be a mix of office space, shops and other amenities. The new transit centre is currently under construction but there is as yet no completion date for the memorial plan.

MADAME TUSSAUD'S
Times Square
- ✉ 234 West 42nd Street between 7th and 8th Avenues
- ☎ 800-246 8872
- 🖰 www.madame-tussauds.com
- 🚌 Subway A, C, E, 1, 2, 3, 7, 9, N, Q, R, S, W to Times Square/42nd Street
- 🕐 Daily 10am–8pm. Last tickets 6pm. Holiday hours until 10pm – check website for dates.
- $ $29 adults, $26 senior, $23 children, under 4s free

Madame Tussaud's has been spreading its wings around the globe and has recently opened attractions in Las Vegas, Hong Kong, Amsterdam and this one in New York. If wax

Radio City Music Hall

models (extremely well done) are your thing, it is worth visiting this sight in the heart of New York's Times Square as the celebs portrayed reflect personalities associated with the city, such as Woody Allen, Leonard Bernstein, Jacqueline Kennedy Onassis, John D Rockefeller, Yoko Ono, Donald Trump, Andy Warhol and former mayor Rudolph Giuliani among others.

NBC TOURS
Rockefeller Center/Midtown

✉ Lobby level of 30 Rockefeller Plaza at 49th Street between 5th and 6th Avenues

☎ 212-664 7174 tickets, 212-664 3700 information

🖰 www.nbcuniversalstore.com

🚋 Subway B, D, F, V to 47th–50th Streets/ Rockefeller Center

🕐 Mon–Thurs 8.30am–5.30pm every 30 minutes, Fri and Sat 8.30am–5.30pm every 15 mins, Sun 9.30am–4.30pm every 15 mins.

$ $18.50 adults, $15.50 seniors and children (6–12), no children under 6. For a small extra fee, combine with Rockefeller Center Tour (below).

You get a 30-minute look behind the scenes at NBC, the major television network headquartered in New York.

RADIO CITY MUSIC HALL
Midtown at 6th Avenue

✉ 1260 6th Avenue at 50th Street

☎ 212-247 4777

🖰 www.radiocity.com

🚋 Subway B, D, F, V to 47th–50th Streets/ Rockefeller Center

🕐 Tours daily 11am–3pm

$ $17 adults, $14 seniors, $10 under 12s.

While you're at the Rockefeller Center you won't want to miss out on this fabulous building, which has been fully restored to its original Art Deco movie palace glory and is

★★★★ **BRIT TIP** ★★★★

★ You can no longer get tickets for TV ★
★ shows by sending away for them, ★
★ but you can join the crowd outside ★
★ the *Today Show*'s walled studio ★
★ Mon–Fri 7am–10am at 49th Street ★
★ and Rockefeller Plaza. For other TV ★
★ shows you can attend, visit ★
★ www.nycvisit.com. Click on 'Visitors' ★
★ and 'Things to Do'. ★

utterly beautiful. This is where great films such as *Gone With The Wind* were given their premieres and it has the largest screen in America. Make a point of visiting the loos – they have a different theme on each floor, from palm trees to Chinese and floral. There are even cigar-theme loos for the boys. The tour takes you around the whole building and you get to meet a Rockette.

★★★★ **BRIT TIP** ★★★★

★ Buy your ticket for the Radio City ★
★ Music Hall in the morning to find ★
★ out what time your tour is. It is well ★
★ worth planning your day around. Or ★
★ you can now see it as part of the ★
★ Rockefeller Center Tour. ★

ROCKEFELLER CENTER
Midtown

✉ Midtown at 5th Avenue – West 48th to West 50th Streets between 5th and 6th Avenues

☎ 212-664 3700

🖰 www.RockefellerCenter.com

🚋 Subway B, D, F, V to 47th–50th Streets/ Rockefeller Center

🕐 Tours Mon–Sat 10am–5pm, Sun 10pm–4pm every hour, departing from the NBC experience store (see above).

$ $12 adults, $10 seniors and children (6–16), no children under 6. Reservations are necessary on 212-664 7174.

Built in Art Deco style in the 1930s, this was named after the New York benefactor whose fortune paid for its construction. As well as Radio City Music Hall, it houses opulent office space, restaurants, bars, shopping on several levels and even gardens. In November 2005 the Top of the Rock observation deck at 30 Rockefeller Plaza was re-opened offering visitors spectacular 360-degree views of the city. The observation deck, first opened in 1933, has been redeveloped into a 55,000 sq ft, multi-level complex with state-of-the-art features such as new transparent safety glass panels that allow completely unobstructed views of the city's landmarks. To help you find your way round the 19 buildings, collect a map at the lobby of the main building (30 Rockefeller Center). The central plaza, a restaurant in summer, is turned into an ice rink in winter, and a

★ ★ ★ ★ ★ ★ ★ ★
Lovers of the Metropolitan Museum
shops can get their fix at one of its
branches in the heart of the
Rockefeller Center. It's just off the
main plaza by the ice rink.
★ ★ ★ ★ ★ ★ ★ ★

massive Christmas tree with 8km (5 miles) of fairy lights draws huge crowds.

You can either wander around the plaza or take the 75-minute Rockefeller Center Tour. This takes in The Channel Gardens, Radio City, the ice rink, NBC and more, while giving an insight into the Center's history, architecture and more than 100 pieces of artwork that create the world's most amazing public collection of Art Deco.

SOUTH STREET SEAPORT
Financial District
✉ Water Street to the East River between John Street and Peck Slip
☎ 212-732 7678
🖰 www.southstreetseaport.com
🚇 Subway A, C, J, M, Z, 2, 3, 4, 5 to Fulton Street/Broadway Nassau

You don't have to go into the South Street Seaport Museum (page 133) to get a feeling of the maritime history of the city– the ships are all around you. So are the shops. The Seaport is a rare New York approximation of a typical American shopping mall. Most shops are open Mon– Sat 10am–9pm, Sun 11am–8pm, and there are dining options at all prices, indoors and out, some with a view of the Brooklyn Bridge. The port was previously home to the 150-year-old Fulton Fish Market, but this has now been moved to the Bronx.

STATEN ISLAND FERRY
Battery Park
✉ Ferry Terminal, 1 Whitehall Street at South Street
☎ 718-815 2628
🖰 www.siferry.com
🚇 Subway 4, 5 to Bowling Green; R, W to Whitehall Street
$ Free

Probably the best sightseeing bargain in the world, it passes close to the Statue of Liberty and gives dramatic views of Downtown. Runs regularly 24 hours a day.

TIMES SQUARE AND THE THEATER DISTRICT
Another iconic area of New York and a must-see place. Full details of what to see and do here are given in Chapter 8, Shows, Bars and Clubs.

THE OUTER BOROUGHS

BRONX ZOO
A wonderful zoo, which combines conservation and ecological awareness with Disney-style rides and a children's zoo. Further details are given on page 265.

HISTORIC RICHMOND TOWN AND ST MARK'S PLACE, STATEN ISLAND
The two top historical sites on Staten Island, both give a unique insight into the New York of yesteryear. Further details are given on pages 271 and 272.

NEW YORK BOTANICAL GARDEN
Home to the Bronx River Gorge, it not only gives a fascinating insight into the geological history of New York, but also has acres and acres of beautiful gardens. Further details are given on page 215.

AMAZING ARCHITECTURE

Whether you have an interest in architecture or not, you won't fail to appreciate just how beautiful many of the buildings of New York are. The fact that Manhattan is an island has been key to so many of the designs over the last 200 years: when space is a premium the only way to go is up. New York gave the world skyscrapers and it's these soaring buildings that have given the city its sensational skyline that is recognised the world over.

BROOKLYN BRIDGE
This Gothic creation was considered one of the modern engineering feats of the world

★ ★ ★ ★ ★ ★ ★ ★
For a completely different 'insider' view of the modern-day history of Brooklyn Bridge, try Gary Gorman's Big Onion Brooklyn Bridge Jumper Tour (page 82). A former member of the NYPD, he relates fascinating stories of talking down would-be suicide victims.
★ ★ ★ ★ ★ ★ ★ ★

when it was completed in 1883 after 16 long years of construction, and at the time was both the world's largest suspension bridge and the first to be built of steel.

The original engineer, John A Roebling, died even before the project began and his son, who took over, had to oversee the building from his Brooklyn apartment after being struck down by the bends. In all, 20 people died during the construction of the bridge. Take the A or C train to High Street station and stroll back along the walkway – a great way to see some incredible views of the Downtown skyscrapers.

CHRYSLER BUILDING
Midtown East
- ✉ 405 Lexington Avenue at 42nd Street
- 🚇 Subway S, 4, 5, 6, 7 to Grand Central/ 42nd Street

Opened in 1930, this was William van Alen's homage to the motor car. At the foot of the Art Deco skyscraper are brickwork cars with enlarged chrome hubcaps and radiator caps. Inside, see its marble and chrome lobby and inlaid-wood elevators. Its needle-like spire is illuminated at night and the building vies with the Empire State for the most stunning.

★ ★ ★ ★ **BRIT TIP** ★ ★ ★ ★
★ Just across the way from the Federal ★
★ Reserve Bank is probably the ★
★ poshest McDonald's in the world at ★
★ 160 Broadway. It has doormen, a ★
★ chandelier and a grand piano ★
★ upstairs. ★

FEDERAL RESERVE BANK
Financial District
- ✉ 33 Liberty Street between William and Nassau Streets
- ☎ 212-720 6130
- 🖥 www.ny.frb.org
- 🚇 Subway 2, 3, 5 to Wall Street

Yes, this really is the place where billions of dollars' worth of gold bars are stashed (as stolen by Jeremy Irons in *Die Hard 3*) on

The Flatiron Building

behalf of half the countries of the world, and where money is printed. Security, as you can imagine, is tight, but you can still do a free one-hour tour which runs Mon–Fri at 9.30am, 10.30am, 11.30am 1.30pm and 2.30pm that takes you deep into the underground vaults, providing you reserve at least five days in advance. Your name will be placed on a computer list, but the minimum age is 16. Passport or picture identification is essential.

FLATIRON BUILDING
Flatiron District
- ✉ 175 5th Avenue between 22nd and 23rd Streets
- ☎ 212-477 0947
- 🚇 Subway F, V, N, R, 6 to 23rd Street

The Renaissance palazzo building was the first-ever skyscraper when it was completed in 1902 and is held up by a steel skeleton.

GRACIE MANSION
Yorkville
- ✉ Carl Schurz Park, 88th Street at East End Avenue
- ☎ 212-570 4751
- 🖥 www.historichousetrust.org
- 🚇 Subway 4, 5, 6 to 86th Street
- ⊘ Tours Tues, Wed, Thurs pm: phone ahead to reserve
- $ $7 adults, $4 seniors, under 12s free

Now the official residence of the mayor, the tour takes you through the mayor's living room, a guest suite and smaller bedrooms. The best part, though, is the view down the river.

UN Building and city skyscrapers

Grand Central Station

GRAND CENTRAL STATION
Midtown East

✉ East 42nd Street between Lexington and Vanderbilt Avenues
🔗 www.grandcentralterminal.com
🚇 Subway S, 1, 2, 3, 4, 5, 6, 7, 9, N, Q, R, to Grand Central/42nd Street

Even if you're not going anywhere by train, this huge, vaulted station, which was opened in 1913, is well worth a visit. A $196-million, two-year renovation programme was recently completed and the ceiling once again twinkles with the stars and astrological symbols of the night skies,

★★★★ **BRIT TIP** ★★★★

★ If you go to Grand Central Station
★ on a Friday at 12.30pm, you can go
★ on a free tour sponsored by the
★ Grand Central Partnership (tel 212-
★ 883 2420, www.grandcentral
★ partnership.org) – meet in the
★ sculpture court of the Whitney
★ Museum. Wednesdays at 12.30pm,
★ the tour is given by The Municipal
★ Arts Society (tel 212-935 3960) –
★ meet at the Center info booth on
★ the main concourse.
★★★★★★★★★★★★★★★★★★★★★★★★

and the chandeliers, while the marble balusters and clerestory windows gleam in the main concourse. Inside you will find a Mediterranean restaurant, Michael Jordan's Steakhouse and a cocktail lounge modelled on a Florentine palazzo. The lower level dining concourse offers inexpensive meals and takeaways, while main floor shopping outlets include Banana Republic, Godiva chocolates and Kenneth Cole. Complete your trip to this elegant edifice by tucking in at the Oyster Bar & Restaurant.

MADISON SQUARE GARDEN'S ALL ACCESS TOUR
34th Street

✉ 4 Pennsylvania Plaza at 33rd Street and 7th Avenue
☎ 212-465 MSG1 (information); 212-307 7171 (ticketmaster)
🔗 www.thegarden.com
🚇 Subway A, C, E, 1, 2, 3, 9, D, F, B, V, N, Q, R, W to 34th Street/Penn Station
$ $17 adults, $12 children (12 and under), 1-hour tours operate every day every 30 minutes from 11am to 3pm.

This is the round building that sits right on top of Penn Station and the entrance is on 7th Avenue at 33rd Street. It occupies the site of the original Pennsylvania Station, an architectural masterpiece that was even more beautiful than Grand Central Station, but which was razed in the 1960s. (One good thing came out of its destruction, though, the creation of the Landmarks Preservation Commission, which has helped to protect many buildings and areas in New York from developers.)

Madison Square Garden's arena is 10 storeys tall, covers 3.24 hectares (8 acres) and is famous for its circular ceiling, which is suspended by 48 bridge-like cables. Every year it hosts 600 events from concerts to boxing, wrestling, basketball and hockey,

Madison Square Garden

FILM LOCATIONS

New York is one of the most filmed and photographed cities in the world – that's one of the reasons why we feel we know it so well. Many of the most popular films and TV series around the globe have been set in the city, so here's a taster of locations to visit, ranging from the famous to the plain weird. For an organised tour of Manhattan's locations, turn to page 79. For TV locations see boxes on pages 71 and 74.

Annie Hall: The roller coaster next to where Alvy Singer (Woody Allen) grows up is the one on Coney Island. Lots of other scenes from this classic 1977 movie starring Allen and Diane Keating are shot all over the city.

Breakfast at Tiffany's: Audrey Hepburn immortalised 5th Avenue's most famous jewellery store in this 1961 film (727 5th Avenue at 57th Street. Tel 212-755 8000, www.tiffany.com).

Home Alone 2: Lost in New York: The hotel where Macaulay Culkin fights off the baddies is The Plaza, but sadly it has been made into condos.

Love Story: Ali MacGraw and Ryan O'Neal's ice-skating scenes were filmed in Central Park.

Maid in Manhattan: Jennifer Lopez and Ralph Fiennes filmed scenes in the Roosevelt Hotel (East 45th Street at Madison Avenue. Tel 212-661 9600, www.theroosevelthotel.com).

Men in Black 2: A scene from the Will Smith blockbuster was filmed in the Art-Deco eatery Empire Diner (210 10th Avenue at 22nd Street. Tel 212-924 0011).

Serendipity: You can reconstruct Kate Beckinsale and John Cusack's elevaor race at the Waldorf-Astoria Hotel (301 Park Avenue at 50th Street. Tel 212-355 3000, www.waldorfastoria.com) where the film's couple meet, split and reunite.

Sleepless in Seattle: Meg Ryan and Tom Hanks fall for each other at the top of the Empire State Building (350 5th Avenue at 34th Street. Tel 212-736 3100, www.esbnyc.com).

When Harry Met Sally: The canteen scene where Meg Ryan fakes an orgasm in front of Billy Crystal was filmed at Katz's Delicatessen (205 East Houston Street at Ludlow Street. Tel 212-254 2246, www.katzdeli.com).

---

bringing in five million people. Its most famous residents are the New York Knickerbockers basketball team (known as the Knicks), the New York Rangers ice hockey team and the New York Liberty women's pro basketball team.

Below the arena are the theatre, exhibition centre, box office and two club restaurants. Incidentally, this is actually the fourth Madison Square Garden building. The first two were built at Madison Square on the site of the current New York Life Building; the third was built on 8th Avenue between 49th and 50th Streets, where the Worldwide Plaza stands. This building opened in 1968 with a gala featuring Bob Hope and Bing Crosby.

During the course of the one-hour tour, you will hear about its history, see the inner workings and the Walk of Fame, and gain access to the locker rooms of both the Knicks and the Rangers.

MORRIS–JUMEL MANSION
Harlem

✉ Roger Morris Park, 65 Jumel Terrace at 160th Street
☎ 212-923 8008
🖰 www.morrisjumel.org
🚇 Subway A, C to 163rd Street
🕐 Wed–Sun 10am–4pm
$ $5 adults, $3.50 seniors and children; various tours offered (over 12)

Built by British colonel Roger Morris in 1765, this is the oldest house in Manhattan. It was confiscated by George Washington in 1776 and briefly used as his war headquarters until the Brits kicked him out of New York. Charles Dickens visited it, too.

NEW YORK PUBLIC LIBRARY
Midtown

✉ 5th Avenue at 42nd Street
☎ 212-869 8089
🖰 www.nypl.org/research

★ ★ ★ ★ **BRIT TIP** ★ ★ ★ ★

Visit the library on a Monday afternoon from June to August (Tuesdays if it rains) and you can enjoy free outdoor movies and other events at Bryant Park (page 250).

🚇 Subway B, D, F, V, 7 to 42nd Street
Opened in 1911, this is one of the best examples of the city's Beaux Arts architecture. Inside you'll find more than 8.5 million volumes guarded by the twin marble lions of Patience and Fortitude. The steps up to the library are a sun trap during the day and serve as a meeting place. Alternatively, they make a great place for a sandwich or drink stop.

NEW YORK STOCK EXCHANGE
Financial District
✉ 20 Broad Street at Wall Street
☎ 212-656 3000
🖥 www.nyse.com
🚇 Subway 6, 4, 5 to Wall Street; J, M, Z to Broad Street
Amazing fact: the stock exchange was founded by 24 brokers meeting beneath a tree; now more than 1,300 members crowd on to the building's trading floor. It's still an interesting place to visit. At the time of going to press, the Stock Exchange was closed to the public, though this may yet change, so call to check.

SEAGRAM BUILDING
Midtown
✉ 375 Park Avenue at 53rd Street
☎ 212-572 7000
🚇 Subway 6 to 51st Street
The New York City mile's only Mies Van Der Rohe building, and widely recognised as one of the finest architectural skyscrapers in the world. It ignited a passion for plazas that you can still see in NY today. Tours are offered on Tuesdays at 3pm.

TRUMP TOWER
Midtown
✉ 725 5th Avenue between 56th and 57th Streets
🚇 Subway F, N, R, Q, W to 57th Street
Donald Trump's monument to opulence includes an extravagant pink marbled atrium with waterfalls and plenty of upmarket shops. This is not to be confused with Trump International Hotel and Tower at Columbus Circle.

UNITED NATIONS BUILDING
Midtown East
✉ 1st Avenue at 46th Street
☎ 212-963 8687 for tour reservations
🖥 www.un.org/tours
🚇 Subway 4, 5, 6, S, 7 to Grand Central/42nd Street
🕐 Mon–Fri 9am–4.45pm, Sat and Sun 10am–4.30pm (not at weekends Jan and Feb)
$ $12 adults, $8.50 seniors, $8 students, $6.50 children (5–14)
Tours of the General Assembly, the Economic and Social Council and other areas every half hour. Tours last around 45 minutes. Despite its fame, this is not the most exciting tour in the world! No children under 5.

WINTER GARDEN AT THE WORLD FINANCIAL CENTER
Battery Park City
✉ 250 Vesey Street at West Street
☎ 212-945 0505
🖥 www.worldfinancialcenter.com
🚇 Subway 1, 2, 3, 9, A, C to Chambers Street; N, R to Cortlandt Street
The World Financial Center is actually the main focal point for the northern end of Battery Park City, a strip of land running down the west side of Lower Manhattan from Chambers Street to South Park. It was created by landfill from the digging work required to build the foundations for the

★ ★ ★ ★ **BRIT TIP** ★ ★ ★ ★

The Winter Garden is not just a pretty place to enjoy a drink or two – it also holds a series of free concerts and fairs.

World Trade Center. The World Financial Center has a complex of four office towers, but is most famous for the beautiful glass-roofed Winter Garden that looks over the boats moored in North Cove. Filled with palm trees, it houses upscale shops including Ann Taylor, Urban Athletics and Gap. Or enjoy the free summer events held outdoors. Check the website for schedules.

WOOLWORTH BUILDING
Civic Center/Financial District
- ✉ 233 Broadway at Park Place
- 🚇 Subway 2, 3 4 to Park Place; N, R to City Hall

There is no official tour of the city's second skyscraper, which was built in 1913 at a cost of $13.5 million, but it's worth sneaking a look inside the lobby. Incidentally, one-time shop assistant FW Woolworth's building was derided as a 'cathedral of commerce' when it opened, but the millionaire took this as a compliment. Just to prove a point, he can be spotted counting out his money in the carved ceilings.

Ground Zero

RELIGIOUS BUILDINGS

CATHEDRAL OF ST JOHN THE DIVINE
Upper West Side/Morningside Heights
- ✉ 1047 Amsterdam Avenue at 112th Street
- ☎ 212-316 7540 (info); tours 212-932 7347
- 🖳 www.stjohndivine.org
- 🚇 Subway 1 to 110th Street
- ⌚ Mon–Sat 7am–6pm, Sun 7am–7pm. Public tours Tues–Sat 11am, Sun 1pm.
- $ Free but tours cost $5 adults, $4 seniors and students

The world's largest Gothic cathedral has one of the world's biggest rose windows with 10,000 pieces of glass. Even more amazing are the main bronze doors, which weigh 3,000 tonnes each and are opened only for an official visit by the bishop. An Episcopal church built in 1892, its grounds cover 4.9 hectares (12 acres) of land and include a school and accommodation for the clergy. A lot of people will tell you that the church, according to its original plans, is still not complete. The reality is the building never will be 'finished' because the church funds are channelled into helping the poor and needy. Still, it's not as if they are ever going to run out of space. It has a capacity to seat 3,000 people but, because it holds so many art and performing art events, they have chairs rather than pews.

One of the highlights of the cathedral's calendar is the Feast of Assisi when real animals, including an elephant and a llama, are ceremonially taken up to the altar to be blessed by the cathedral clergy. Inspired by St Francis of Assisi, whose life exemplified living in harmony with the natural world, the feast usually takes place on the first Sunday in October.

At the back of the cathedral, behind the main altar are seven different chapels, which represent different countries in Europe. These are used for weddings, christenings and the services (at least two a day). The shop is also at the back on the left-hand side and money raised from it is put towards the church's housing and other ministries. There are plenty of WCs at the back of the shop along with drinks machines for general use.

The Cathedral of St John the Divine

Trinity Church and Wall Street

GRACE CHURCH
Union Square
✉ 800 Broadway
🖰 www.gracechurchnyc.org
🚇 Subway N, R, L, 4, 5, 6 to Union Square
A beautiful example of the Gothic Revival period that was occurring in the city when this was built by James Renwick in 1846. The church's original wood steeple was replace by marble in 1888, and it is a landmark on the skyline if you gaze along Broadway from Downtown. Tours take place on the first Sunday of the month after the 11am service.

★★★★ BRIT TIP ★★★★
It is appropriate to tip your guide around 15 per cent of the cost of the ticket, if you are happy with the service you received.
★★★★★★★★★★★★★★★★★★★★★★★★

RIVERSIDE CHURCH
Morningside Heights
✉ 490 Riverside Drive at 120th Street
☎ 212-870 6700
🖰 www.riversidechurchny.org
🚇 Subway 1, 9, B, C to 116th Street
Famous for having the world's largest tuned bell and its Carillon Concerts on Sundays at 10.30am, 12.30pm and 3pm. You can also go for the great views of Upper Manhattan and the Hudson River. Nearby is the Union Theological Seminary at West 120th and Broadway. Woody Allen uses this façade in many of his movies.

FRIENDS
Although most of the filming was actually done in California, the many *Friends* series, starring Jennifer Aniston and co, were set in New York. There are some locations you may recognise:

The place where Ross and Rachel consummated their relationship was filmed in one of the old-school dioramas in The American Museum of Natural History (page 117).

The Central Park Café where the six friends meet every day was based on Manhattan Café, now Grille, in West Village. Tel 212-888 6556, www.themanhattangrille.com.

ST PATRICK'S CATHEDRAL
Midtown
✉ 14 East 51st Street between 50th and 51st Street (entrance 5th Avenue)
☎ 212-753 2261
🚇 Subway 6 to 51st Street; E, V to 5th Avenue/53rd Street
The seat of New York's Roman Catholic Archdiocese, the cathedral was begun in 1857 and the stained-glass windows weren't completed until l930. However, the magnificent results have definitely been worth the wait.

★★★★ BRIT TIP ★★★★
The steps leading up to St Patrick's create a perfect picnic spot for a lunch or snack stop.
★★★★★★★★★★★★★★★★★★★★★★★★

St Patrick's Cathedral

PART 2 –
TOUR NEW YORK

Time is a precious commodity when visiting New York, so you need to make sure that any tour you take pays for itself both financially and in terms of time. Your choice of tours will depend on whether it is your first or second visit or you are a regular. Newcomers need to get their bearings and two ways of doing this are to take a boat tour and a bus tour. The boat trip goes in a semi-circle around Manhattan from Midtown on one side to Midtown on the other; the bus tour, such as Gray Line's Manhattan Essential New York tour, is known as New York 101 (101 being slang for a first-year university course) because it covers so much of the city in one day. An alternative is the New York Visions tour, which takes a lot less time, is cheaper and is generally more fact-filled.

Bus tours are useful when you want to visit an area such as Harlem or the Bronx, but are unsure of your personal safety, in which case the Harlem Spirituals/New York Visions tours are your best bet. Then there are helicopter tours, which will certainly give you breathtaking views, but won't show you the full ins and outs of each area.

★ ★ ★ ★ BRIT TIP ★ ★ ★ ★

★ If you take a tour of New York, you ★
★ are likely to hear the word 'stoop'. ★
★ This is taken from a Dutch word by ★
★ original settlers and refers to the ★
★ steps up to a townhouse, such as a ★
★ brownstone – another New York ★
★ term, this time for much sought- ★
★ after townhouses, though they are ★
★ as likely to be made out of grey ★
★ stone as brown stone. ★

★ ★

The reality is that the best way to see New York, get to know the city and find those interesting nooks and crannies is on foot, which possibly explains why the Big Onion Walking Tours are so popular – or it could be that they are just so darned good– and why so many people take advantage of the Big Apple Greeters, who can show you any area or sight you wish to visit. There is also a wide choice from bike tours to gangland tours and a reasonable selection of food tours.

The following categories of tour have been put in alphabetical order for ease of use. Within each category, what we consider are the most important or useful tours have been put first.

AIR TOURS

LIBERTY HELICOPTER TOURS
Chelsea
✉ VIP Heliport, West 30th Street and Hudson River
☎ 212-967 6464
⌐ www.libertyhelicopters.com
🚇 Subway A, C, E to 34th Street/Penn Station

This is a fantastic, if pricey, way to see New York, and perfect if you're looking for a once-in-a-lifetime experience. There are lots of tours to choose from, such as the Taste of New York, $69 per person for 5–7 minutes, Lady Liberty, $69 for 5–7 minutes and, if you really want to push the boat out, there's the Romance Over Manhattan tour which is 15 minutes and costs $849 for private hire of the whole helicopter, maximum four people.

BIKE TOURS

BIKE THE BIG APPLE
☎ 212-201 837 1133
⌐ www.bikethebigapple.com
$ $49-60 includes bike rental for tours and helmet rental.

Licensed guides take you through a variety of neighbourhoods, to see both historic and hip sides of the city. Tours can be customised to your interests and are taken at a gentle pace.

CENTRAL PARK BICYCLE TOURS AND RENTALS
Colombus Circle
✉ 59th Street and Broadway
☎ 212-541 8759
⌐ www.centralparkbiketour.com
🚇 Subway A, B, C, D, 1, 2 to Columbus Circle/59th Street
$ $40 adults, $20 children (15 and under) includes bike rental for tours; bike rental only is $20 for two hours, $25 for 3 hours and $35 all day.

A two-hour bike tour of Central Park from April to November starting at 10am, 1pm and 4pm daily and 9am and 11am on summer weekends, which includes stops at the Shakespeare Garden, Strawberry Fields,

SEX AND THE CITY

Okay, so the series has sadly finished, but we know there are legions of fans out there with box sets of DVDs who still emulate the fabulous lifestyles of the *Sex And The City* girls Carrie Bradshaw, Samantha Jones, Charlotte York and Miranda Hobbs. If you still yearn to learn more about where they were filmed, we can give you an insight. For organised tours around the girls' haunts, see page 78.

Shopping

Patricia Field (page 93): Patricia Field is the designer who created all the fabulous fashion for the TV series, so anyone who emulates Carrie's style has to pay a visit. You can stock up on the cool bags and jewellery that the cast has carried and worn, in particular the Mia and Lizzie diamond horseshoe necklaces that Carrie has been seen in. In the basement you'll find a bijou beauty counter with a complete guide to the make-up used by the girls. Choose your favourite!

Tracey Feith (page 96): When Sarah Jessica Parker wore one of Feith's red and blue silk creations in the series, the shop sold out of the style in days.

Manolo Blahnik (page 95): No true *Sex And The City* experience would be complete without wearing a pair of towering Manolo heels. Check out the SJP ankle-strap stiletto named after the show's star. SATC trivia: SJP is petite as petite can be, yet her shoe size is $7\frac{1}{2}$ ($6\frac{1}{2}$ in UK size)!

Jimmy Choo (page 95): Another of Carrie's favourites, Jimmy's shoes are so exclusive they are sold in only four Jimmy Choo shoe shops around the globe, plus a few Saks and Bergdorf Goodman stores.

Bars

Monkey Bar: 60 East 54th Street between Madison and Park Avenues. Tel 212-838 2600. Subway E, V to 5th Avenue. Area: Midtown. The venue Mr Big and Carrie chose to discuss how to stay 'just friends' after their affair. It's very upmarket – think dark wood and a resident pianist – plus it has some extraordinary original murals of frolicking monkeys dating back to the 1930s.

Tortilla Flats: 767 Washington Street at West 12th Street. Tel 212 243 1053. Subway 1, 9 to Christopher Street. Area: West Village. The ice-breaking date between Carrie and Aidan, accompanied by Miranda and Steve, was filmed at this Mexican party spot. Margaritas are the fashionable tipple here.

Restaurants

Park View at the Boathouse (page 140): The episode where Mr Big and Carrie fell into the boating lake was shot in Manhattan's oasis of calm, Central Park. The Boathouse is often cited as one of the most romantic places in town by those in the know. You can have dinner, rent a boat or act like the locals and sip a drink while the sun goes down over the skyscrapers.

Eleven Madison Park (page 161): One of New York's hottest eateries, this is where Mr Big chose to tell Carrie he was getting married to Natasha (the stick with no soul) over dinner. Carrie had one too many Cosmopolitans, the girl's favourite cocktail, and fell down the stairs as she walked out.

Other locations

The Church of the Transfiguration (page 35): Also known as The Little Church Around The Corner, this was the location for shooting the 'Friar F**k' episode, though on the show it was called the All Souls Center. The Episcopal church – famous for being a haven for actors – got a nice donation towards a wall renovation for its trouble.

Meisel Gallery: In Prince Street just off West Broadway, this is where Charlotte worked. The show paid $18,000 for the first shoot in the gallery, $28,000 for the second and $37,000 for the third. In the end, the producers decided to find Charlotte a new job!

Also ... the **Blue Water Grill** on Union Square and 16th Street (page 177) where Miranda said she was an 'everything but girl'; **Luna Park Café** in the middle of Union Square (page 54) is where Carrie met up with Stamford, and **Faicco's Sausage Store** in Cornelia Street (page 113) is where Samantha wanted to spank her boyfriend before going up to his apartment.

SATC **trivia:** nearly all the show's scenes are filmed on location in New York except for when they are in their apartments or eating. The only two places that refused to be used for filming are the Hudson Hotel and the Intrepid Sea-Air-Space Museum!

Belvedere Castle and other sights, plus bike rentals for your own use. Other tours on offer include Central Park Movie Scenes Tour, Central Park Picnic Tour and the 3½-hour Manhattan Island Bike Tour.

★★★★ BRIT TIP ★★★★

★ Once you have your bike, don't feel
★ you have to cycle everywhere as you
★ can take bikes on the subway. A
★ long list of bike rental shops and
★ cycle events around the city can be
★ found on www.bikenewyork.org.

CANAL STREET BICYCLE SHOP
Chinatown
- ✉ 417 Canal Street between 6th Avenue and Grand Street
- ☎ 212-334 8000
- 🚇 Subway A, C, E to Canal Street

Rent your bike and head off to the Financial District, where the streets are usually almost deserted on a Sunday.

THE HUB
SoHo
- ✉ 517 Broome Street at Thompson Street
- ☎ 212-965 9334
- 🚇 Subway A to Canal

Tandems, recumbents and electric bikes along with standard types.

METRO BICYCLES
Upper West Side and Upper East Side
- ✉ 96th Street at Broadway and 87th Street at Lexington
- ☎ 212-766 9222
- 🖰 www.metrobicycles.com
- 🚇 Subway 1, 2, 3, A, C, B, D to West 96th Street; 4, 5, 6 to East 87th Street

If you want to check out the Upper West Side along the river or the Upper East side, rent from here. (They have other locations such as 1311 Lexington Avenue at 88th Street (212-427 4450) too.) Open daily 9.30am–6.30pm.

Gray Line double-decker bus

Pedicab in Times Square

HUB STATION/PONY PEDICAB
SoHo
- ✉ 517 Broome Street at Thompson Street
- ☎ 212-254 8844
- 🚇 Subway C, E to Spring Street; N, R to Prince Street
- ⏰ Open Tues–Sun 11am–7pm
- $ $15 for 30 minutes, $30 for 1 hour

Technically not bicycles, but three-man tricycles or 'pedicabs' (one 'driver' to pedal and two passengers!). So amazing looking that even seen-it-all-before New Yorkers stop to stare. That may be a little off-putting for some, but I found them an excellent way to see SoHo without breaking into a sweat or breaking the bank! You may even be able to hail one of these after the theatre in the Times Square area. Don't forget to tip – 'drivers' earn their money! In good weather only. You can either reserve in advance and arrange a meeting point or turn up at the hub. You get $5 off with NYTAB's NYCard (page 21).

THE SOPRANOS
Most of the locations for this ultra-popular series are shot in New Jersey, a short bus ride from main Manhattan. For a more comprehensive tour, see page 79.

Pizzaland: 260 Belleville Turnpike, North Arlington, NJ, can be seen in the opening sequence of every episode as Tony Soprano drives past it on his way home.

Satin Dolls: 230 State Route 17 South, Lodi, NJ. (tel 201-845 6494) is a real-life dancing club where scenes for the Bada Bing Club are filmed.

Circle Line cruise on East River

BOAT TOURS

ADIRONDACK
Chelsea Pier
- ✉ Pier 62, 22nd Street at Hudson River
- ☎ 212-209 3370 to book
- 🖰 www.sail-nyc.com
- 🚌 Subway C, E to 23rd Street
- $ Tickets $35 for day sails; $45 for evening and Sunday brunch sails.

A sail on this three-masted replica of a 19th-century schooner is unforgettable. It sails from Chelsea Pier to Battery Park, allowing you the chance to catch a glimpse of Ellis Island and the Statue of Liberty, Governor's Island and Brooklyn Bridge, while sipping your complimentary glass of wine.

CIRCLE LINE
West Midtown
- ✉ Pier 83, West 42nd Street
- ☎ 212-563 3200
- 🖰 www.circleline42.com
- 🚌 Any subway to 42nd Street, then transfer to an M42 bus heading west
- $ From $19 adults, $11 children; combo packages available

Choose from a 3-hour full island cruise, $29 adults and $16 children, or a 2-hour semi-circle or sunset/harbour lights cruise, $24 adults and $13 children. Or you can take a 3-hour Latin DJ dance cruise, a full-day cruise to Bear Mountain ($45 adults, $40 seniors and $30 for children 12 and under) or a 1½-hour Liberty Island cruise ($19 adults, $16 seniors and $11 children) from May to October.

Alternatively, you can go for a spin on *The Beast*, a speedboat that takes you on a quick and memorable 30-minute tour. Sights fly by as you reach a speed of 64kph (45mph) and stop at the Statue of Liberty for photos. May to Oct daily on the hour noon–dusk ($17 adults, $11 children).

NY WATERWAY
Financial District
- ✉ Pier 78 at West 38 Street and 12th Avenue
- ☎ 800-533 3779
- 🖰 www.nywaterway.com
- 🚌 Any subway to 42nd Street, transfer to M42 bus heading west
- $ Harbour cruise prices from $22 adults, $19 seniors and $12 children, without service charge, and baseball cruises from $18 adults and $11 children, no service charge; children under 3 free on both.

Offers a wide variety of sightseeing options all year round, including New York harbour cruises and evening cruises with on-board entertainment. Also available in the summer are day trips to Sandy Hook Beach and, for baseball fans, cruise packages that include a round-trip sail on the *Yankee Clipper*, tickets, souvenirs and the ubiquitous hot dog.

★ ★ ★ ★ **BRIT TIP** ★ ★ ★ ★

The harbour cruises are very informative and give a great insight into Manhattan and beyond, but it can sometimes be hard to hear the commentary from the upper deck. If you want to hear everything, it's probably best to stay inside.

Manhattan Bridge from Washington Street

WHAT TO SEE AND DO

BATEAUX NEW YORK
Chelsea

✉ Pier 62 at Chelsea Piers

☎ 212-727 2789 or 866-211 3806 (toll-free)

🖱 www.spiritcitycruises.com

🚗 Subway C, E, 1, 9, 4, 5, 6 to 23rd Street, transfer to cross-town bus heading west

$ Brunch ticket around $50, dinner from $110-125, $5 tax excluded

Indulge in a dinner (7.30-10.30pm daily) or brunch (noon-2pm) while cruising around Lower Manhattan (note – boarding an hour earlier).

WORLD YACHT DINNER CRUISES
Midtown West

✉ Pier 81 at West 41st Street and Hudson River

☎ 212-630 8100

🖱 www.worldyacht.com

🚗 Any subway to 42nd Street, then transfer to M42 bus heading west

🕐 Daily Apr–Dec; Feb Sat, Sun; Mar Fri–Sun only; board at 6pm, sail 7–10pm

$ From $106 in the high season, including a 3-hour cruise with dancing to live music Sun-Thur, $96.50 in low season

With four-course menus created by a selection of New York's best chefs, linen tablecloths, live music, a dance floor and world-class videos, this is an upmarket experience you are sure to enjoy. The cruise lasts 3 hours and also provides spectacular views of the harbour. Note that the dress code is smart and that jackets are required, so make sure you allow yourself plenty of time to put on your glad rags.

BUS TOURS

HARLEM SPIRITUALS/ NEW YORK VISIONS
Midtown

✉ 690 8th Avenue between West 43rd and West 44th Streets

☎ 212-391 0900

🖱 www.harlemspirituals.com or www.harlemheritagetours.com

🚗 Subway A, C, E, 1, 2, 3, 7, 9, S, N, Q, R, S, W, B, F, D, V to 42nd Street/Times Square

$ Varies, see below.

One of the most reputable tour companies in New York, the guides are highly qualified, great founts of knowledge and very friendly,

while the buses are modern and comfortable with the all-important air-conditioning. Tours by the Harlem Spirituals include:

Harlem Gospel Tour: A combined walking (though not too far!) and riding tour of Harlem on Sundays and Wednesdays, during which you attend a church service, hear a gospel choir and have the option of having lunch or brunch at a soul food restaurant. Prices are $45-49 adults/$85-89 with meal, $29-35 children (5–11)/$65-69 with meal. Tours 9.30am–1.30pm Sundays, 9am–1pm Wednesdays.

Soul Food and Jazz: A chance to relive the heyday of Harlem, thanks to the return of jazz to the area. This combines a walking and riding tour through Harlem's historical sites with a soul food meal and the chance to see a jam session at a local jazz club. Tours are available on Monday, Thursday and Saturday 7pm–midnight and cost $115-119 for adults and children.

The New York Visions Manhattan Sightseeing Tour New York New York: An excellent four-hour introduction to all the major sights including Times Square, Central Park, Rockefeller Center, Greenwich Village, SoHo, Little Italy, Chinatown and the Wall Street area. Tours leave on Mondays, Thursdays and Saturdays at 9.30am. Prices are $45 adults, $29 children. Pay an extra $11 (adults and children) and you also get tickets for the ferry to the Statue of Liberty and Ellis Island Immigration Museum (you'll be dropped off at Battery Park) plus an MTA Fun Pass for 24-hour use on the subways and buses (page 25).

GRAY LINE NEW YORK SIGHTSEEING
West Midtown

✉ 777 8th Avenue between 47th and 48th Streets

☎ 212-445 0848/800-669 0051

🖱 www.graylinenewyork.com

🚗 Subway C, E to 50th Street

🕐 Daily 8.30am–5pm

$ Varies, see below; prices are with $5 online booking discount

The oldest sightseeing bus company in New York, it has much to offer, although the average tour guide gives very little information in comparison with the New York Visions tours. Still, if you don't want to be overwhelmed by information on your first visit to New York, then try the

Major sights in Manhattan

The Statue of Liberty

Essential New York Tour ($89 adults, $61 children). A double-decker bus tour with 40 hop-on, hop-off stops, it comes with a choice of 1-hour harbour cruises or ferry with close-up views of the Statue of Liberty and Ellis Island, a ticket to the Empire State Building and a Fun Pass to New York's subway and bus systems (page 25).

Gray Line also offers 'Loops', which run around Downtown, Midtown, uptown and Brooklyn. You can do as few or as many as you like, so you can spend as long as you want in each area, giving you plenty of flexibility. The Downtown loop is $34; best value is a 48-hour pass for $44 or a 3-day pass for $104.

The **Showbiz Insiders Tour** ($74) is a 6-hour daily extravaganza giving a behind-the-scenes look at New York's TV and Broadway shows. You'll visit the New Amsterdam Theatre, home of *The Lion King*, before taking the Stage Door Tour at Radio City Music Hall and lunch at Planet Hollywood. The tour ends with a private performance given by a current Broadway actor and the opportunity for some photos and autographs.

The Time Warner Center

LOCATION TOURS

Upper East Side
☎ 212-209 3370
🖰 www.sceneontv.com
The best company in New York for fun and informative bus tours around the sights and attractions seen in two of the city's most famous shows, *Sex And The City* and *The Sopranos*, plus a general TV and movie tour and one of Central Park movie sites. Details are as follows:

SEX AND THE CITY
✉ Meet by the Pulitzer Fountain on 5th Avenue at 58th Street
🚇 Subway 4, 5, 6, to 59th Street/ Lexington Avenue; N, R, W to 5th Avenue
🕐 Daily 11am and 3pm, Sat–Sun 10am, 11am and 3pm
$ $36 (plus $2 ticket fee)
Here's a chance to check out the stomping grounds of the girls from *Sex And The City* even now the show has ended. During the 3-hour bus tour, you'll visit D&G in SoHo, where Carrie shopped for shoes, and the New York Sports Club where Miranda worked out, plus bars such as O'Neil's and Tao where Carrie, Samantha, Charlotte and Miranda did their flirting. Most important of all, you'll get some behind-the-scenes scoops on the show and the actors. This is a really fun experience, which gets into the spirit of the show and gives everyone plenty of browsing and chatting opportunities. You'll also get to eat a cupcake from the famous Magnolia Bakery, though be warned, they are incredibly sweet! By the end, you should be fluent in *Sex And The*

Bagel vendor

out quickly, so reserve your place as far in advance as possible.

MANHATTAN TV AND MOVIE TOUR

✉ Bus departs from Ellen's Stardust Diner, 1650 Broadway at 51st Street

🚇 Subway 1, 9 to 50th Street; N, W, R to 49th Street

🕐 Daily in summer or Thurs–Sun 11am

$ $32 (plus $2 ticket fee)

Takes you to over 40 different locations seen in TV shows and movies such as *Friends, You've Got Mail, Ghostbusters, The Bill Cosby Show* and Woody Allen's *Manhattan* in around 3 hours.

CENTRAL PARK MOVIE TOUR

✉ Meet at the entrance to Central Park, 59th Street between 5th and 6th Avenues

🚇 Subway N, R to 5th Avenue

🕐 Fri 3pm, Sat noon

$ $15 (plus $2 ticket fee)

Take some snaps of the Boathouse Café seen in *When Harry Met Sally* and *Sex And The City*, check out Tavern in the Green that featured in *Ghostbusters* and feed pigeons in the park à la Macaulay Culkin in *Home Alone 2*, plus many more choice spots in the park. Tour takes 2 hours and, for the novelty, you could do it by bike (see page 74).

City-speak and know your Manhattan Guy (a genetically mutant strain of single man that feeds on Zabar's and midnight shows at Angelika) from your Trysexual (someone who will try everything once) or a 'We' Guy (a man who refers to your potential future relationship by using 'we' statements such as 'we' can cook etc, thus faking a future with you to get what he wants in the present). This tour is busy, so book at least a week in advance.

THE SOPRANOS

✉ Bus departs from the 'Button' statue on 7th Avenue at 39th Street

🚇 B, D, F, V to 42nd Street; N, Q, R, S, W, 1, 2, 3, 7, 9, S to Times Square

🕐 Sat and Sun 2pm

$ $40 (plus $2 ticket fee)

Get the 'shakedown' on a tour of 15 sites used in *The Sopranos* including Satriale's Pork Store, the cemetery where Livia Soprano is buried, the Bada Bing nightclub and the diner where Chris was shot. The 4-hour tour also includes a guide to New Jersey Mafia-speak, a stop for cannolis – traditional Italian pastries – and six other stops along the way. The tours tend to sell

★ ★ ★ ★ **BRIT TIP** ★ ★ ★ ★

★
★
★ **Pace yourself. There's no point in** ★
★ **trying to pack so much into your** ★
★ **day that you arrive back at your** ★
★ **hotel exhausted with your head** ★
★ **spinning. Less can often be more!** ★
★ ★

Autumn in Central Park

FOOD TOURS

ENTHUSIASTIC GOURMET
Chinatown
- ✉ 245 East 63rd Street
- ☎ 646-209 4724
- ⌗ www.enthusiasticgourmet.com
- ⏰ 10am and 2pm. Different days for different tours; check website for times and availability
- $ $45 per person

The Chinatown Discovered Tour explores the neighbourhood's grocery stores, meat and fish markets and produce stands for 2-3 hours. If you're still hungry, head for Jing Fong Restaurant (20 Elizabeth Street, 212-964 5256) for more pan-Asian cuisine. There are lots of other gourmet tours to be enjoyed, such as the kosher NY Nosh, and a taste of Hispanic, Jewish, Chinese and Italian on the Melting Pot.

FOODS OF NEW YORK
Greenwich Village
- ✉ 4th Floor, 9 Barrow Street, meet near 6th and Bleecker Street
- ☎ 212-209 3370/917-408 9539
- ⌗ www.foodsofny.com
- ⏰ Daily, year round 11am–2pm (but varies so check website)
- $ $38 per person

A great-value 3-hour tour, considering the amount of food you eat along the way, and with a friendly atmosphere as they take a maximum of 16.

★ ★ ★ ★ **BRIT TIP** ★ ★ ★ ★
★   ★
★ **In the unlikely event you still** ★
★ **feel peckish after the Foods of New** ★
★ **York tour, head back to Fish at** ★
★ **280 Bleecker Street where you can** ★
★ **have six oysters and a glass of wine** ★
★ **or beer at the bar for an** ★
★ **unbelievable $8.** ★
★ ★

In Greenwich Village you'll stop to sample the wares of Zito's old-fashioned bread shop, Murray's famous cheese shop and Faicco's world-famous pork shop, and you'll end up at Vintage New York on Broome Street, where you get the chance to taste five wines from New York State. And, as well as all you'll learn about the food of New York, especially of the Italian community, you'll gain hints about architecture and properties in the Village and visit a real speakeasy. Alternatively, you can choose to go on a tour of the Chelsea Gourmet Market and the West Village Meatpacking area (Fri–Sun).

SAVORY SOJOURNS
Chelsea
- ✉ 144 West 13th Street
- ☎ 212-691 7314
- ⌗ www.savorysojourns.com
- $ $95–165

For a unique insight into the fine foods and culinary skills of some of New York's finest restaurants, Savory Sojourns promises to give you an insider's guide to New York's best culinary and cultural destinations followed by a great slap-up meal. Some even include a cookery lesson and can last around 4 hours. Areas covered include Upper East Side, Chinatown, Little Italy, Greenwich Village, Flatiron and Chelsea Market. New last year (2006) was Harlem.

INSIDER TOURS

Some of the most interesting New York tours are led by residents who have unique inside perspectives that they are willing to share on everything from shopping to a haircut. Here is a fascinating selection:

KRAMER'S REALITY TOUR
West Midtown
- ✉ The Producer's Club, 358 West 44th Street between 8th and 9th Avenues
- ☎ 212-268 5525
- ⌗ www.kennykramer.com
- 🚇 Subway A, C, E to 42nd Street/Penn Station
- ⏰ Sat at noon, Sun (on holiday weekends) at noon (check site for winter availability)
- $ $37.50 (plus $2 service charge)

The real Kramer behind the *Seinfeld* character has come out of the woodwork and invented his own 3-hour tour based on all the *Seinfeld* spots in the city. Kenny Kramer will answer questions, share backstage gossip and the real-life incidents behind the show. Book early as this tour sells out weeks in advance.

MYSTICAL WORLD OF HASSIDIC JEWS
Brooklyn
- ✉ Chassidic Discovery Welcome Center, 305 Kingston Avenue
- ☎ 718-953 5244
- ⌗ www.jewishtours.com

🚇 Subway 3 to Kingston Avenue
🕐 Sun 10am–1pm for individuals or
Sun–Fri for groups
$ $36 adults, $18 children (12 and
under); includes a Kosher deli lunch

★★★★ **BRIT TIP** ★★★★

It's easy to get to the Hassidic
Discovery Welcome Center by the
3 train (the red line). Allow an hour
from Midtown. The subway exit is
right by the synagogue and you
simply walk a few yards up Kingston
Avenue to two brown doors just
by a bookshop. There is no dress
code, but it would be inappropriate
for a woman to turn up in a
sleeveless top.

The Lubavitcher Jews in Crown Heights,
Brooklyn, are focused on sharing what they
have with the outside world, providing a
unique opportunity to get an insight into a
Hassidic community. Guided by Rabbi Beryl
Epstein – a person with a charming manner
and great sense of humour – you'll hear
about the history of the Hassidic Jews; visit
the synagogue to learn about some of the
Jewish customs and traditions; watch a
scribe working on a Torah scroll; and see the
Rebbe's library, a Matzoh bakery and a
Hassidic art gallery. A real insight into a
fascinating culture.

★★★★ **BRIT TIP** ★★★★

The Kingston Avenue subway stop
for the Hassidic tour is just one
away from Eastern Parkway, the stop
for the Brooklyn Museum of Art
(page 262) and the Botanic Garden
(page 250) – both great places to
visit on a Sunday afternoon.

ROCK N ROLL WALKING TOUR
East Village
☎ 212-696 6578
🖱 www.rockjunket.com
🕐 Mon–Fri by appointment; Sat 1pm.
$ Tickets $20
Die-hard rockers and liggers Bobby Pinn and
Ginger Ali lead these fun tours around East
Village's legendary punk, rock and glam
nigtspots.

SAVOR THE APPLE
Village and Harlem
✉ PO Box 914, Ansonia Station, New York,
NY 10023
☎ 212-877 2903
$ Prices vary
Marlayna gives her personal tours of
different parts of the city, but is particularly
knowledgeable about Greenwich Village, the
East Village and Harlem, where she has
many contacts.

WALKING TOURS

ADVENTURE ON A SHOESTRING
✉ 300 West 53rd Street
☎ 212-265 2663
🕐 Every day, rain or shine
$ $5
The 'granddaddy' of walking tours,
Adventure has been going strong for nearly
45 years, offering 90-minute tours of many
Manhattan neighbourhoods as well as
outlying areas that are less familiar to
tourists, such as Astoria, the Greek section
of the borough of Queens, and Hoboken, a
new artists' centre in New Jersey. Two of the
most popular tours are Haunted Greenwich
Village and Hell's Kitchen. Theme tours, such
as those based on Marilyn Monroe's New
York and Jacqueline Kennedy Onassis's New
York are also favourites.

ALLIANCE FOR DOWNTOWN
NEW YORK
Financial District
✉ Tours start at the steps of the National
Museum of the American Indian,
1 Bowling Green
☎ 212-606 4064
🖱 www.downtownny.com
🚇 Subway 4, 5 to Bowling Green
🕐 Thurs and Sat at noon
Free 90-minute walking tour for individuals
and groups exploring the 'birthplace' of
New York, including the Customs House,
Trinity Church, Wall Street and the Stock
Exchange, among others. The Alliance has
been doing much work on sprucing up the
entire district and employs red-hatted
security staff/cleaners who are there to help
you find your way around.

BIG ONION WALKING TOURS
Brooklyn

✉ 476 13th Street, Brooklyn, NY 11215
☎ 212-439 1090
🖰 www.bigonion.com
◷ Wed–Sun (Jun–Aug), Thurs–Sun (Sept–May) 1pm. Always call after 9.30am on the morning of your tour to verify schedule as it will change if the weather is bad
$ $15 adults, $12 seniors, $10 students

Amazingly informative ethnic, architectural and historic walking tours, which you can just turn up to (apart from the multi-ethnic eating tour, which needs to be reserved). Led by American history graduates, they're not for the faint-hearted – you'll be on your feet for a full two hours – but they are informative and gem packed. Tours are offered on a rotating basis and begin in different spots. Call the main number or check the website to see what's on the schedule. Options include the East Village, Central Park, Gay New York, Financial District, Gramercy Park and Union Square, Greenwich Village, Historic Lower Manhattan, Historic TriBeCa, the Jewish Lower East Side, Presidential New York, Revolutionary New York, Roosevelt Island, SoHo and NoLiTa and the Upper East Side. 'Big Onion' was the nickname given to New York in the 19th century by non-New Yorkers who believed it smelled of the immigrants' heavily spiced cooking!

Big Onion's Multi-ethnic Eating Tour:
Meet on the corner of Essex and Delancey Streets in front of Olympic Diner. Subway J, M, Z to Essex Street; F to Delancey Street.

Wall Street news stand

★ ★ ★ ★ **BRIT TIP** ★ ★ ★ ★
Some Big Onion tours can get a little crowded. If so, make sure you stand as close to the guide as possible to hear their pearls of wisdom and you'll still get good value for money.

This is one of the more popular tours, which covers the Lower East Side, Chinatown and Little Italy, and it is offered frequently. You pay a $4 supplement for nosh, which includes delicious spicy tofu,

South Street Seaport

Brooklyn Bridge

Mozzarella and Italian sausage, chicken and shrimp and vegetarian dim sum, plus other food favourites of the locals, all eaten outdoors in the streets. The tour also provides a good way to get an insight into areas you may find confusing to wander around on your own.

★★★★ **BRIT TIP** ★★★★
★ ★
★ If you need to visit the loo before ★
★ you start this tour, head for the ★
★ McDonald's diagonally opposite the ★
★ meeting point. ★
★ ★
★★★★★★★★★★★★★★★★★★★★★★★

It gives a fascinating insight into the history of the area and what modern-day life is like – for instance what was once a very high-density Jewish area is now populated by Puerto Rican immigrants. And before the Jews and Chinese, there were the English, Irish and Italians.

You'll end the tour deep in the heart of Chinatown outside a vegetarian food centre and the Chinese Gourmet Bakery. It may be good to stop for a drink before you head off to the nearest subway stations at Canal Street, where you have the choice of the A, C, E, J, M, N, Q, R, W, 6 lines to take you just about anywhere in Manhattan.

Big Onion's Historic Harlem Tour: Meet at the Schomburg Center at 135th Street and Lenox Avenue. Subway 2, 3 to 135th Street. A brilliant way to get to know a major chunk of Harlem, its history, politics and modern-day life through the eyes of a history graduate.

★★★★ **BRIT TIP** ★★★★
★ ★
★ For a cheap and delicious meal ★
★ before the Harlem tour, head for ★
★ Mannas at 486 Lenox Avenue at ★
★ 134th Street. After the tour you'll ★
★ find yourself outside the Apollo ★
★ Theater. Just a few metres east ★
★ is a clean McDonald's with TVs on ★
★ one wall (and a loo on the ★
★ opposite side). ★
★★★★★★★★★★★★★★★★★★★★★★★

Ponycab

GREETINGS FROM THE BIG APPLE

It's certainly a novel idea and it's also a winner – the Big Apple Greeters are ready to take you on a personalised and entirely customised tour of any part of New York any day of the week and it costs absolutely nothing. The idea is simple: New Yorkers who are proud of their neighbourhoods and have some spare time will spend between two and four hours with you. They will take you round any area you like and help you do just what you want to do, be it shopping, sightseeing or eating and drinking, rain or shine. Just make your request at least ten working days (preferably 3-4 weeks) in advance and confirmation will be awaiting you upon your arrival at your hotel. The service is entirely free and no Big Apple Greeters worth their salt will take a tip, but I found that it was no problem to get them to agree to letting me pay for a spot of brunch or lunch. And they're well worth it. Tel 212-669 8159, fax 212-669 3685, email visitrequest@bigapple greeter.org, www.bigapplegreeter.org.

You'll hear about Martin Luther King and other African-American activists, local literary salons and gospel churches. You'll learn about the old neighbourhood joints of the Renny and Savoy, how the Apollo Theater and Cotton Clubs were only open to rich white folk looking for an 'authentic black' experience, the campaign to allow black people to work in the shops they bought their food and clothes from, Striver's Row, the architecture and the old black pressure groups, two of whose buildings now house beauty parlours.

Gangs of New York Tour: Meet on the south-east corner of Broadway and Chambers Street at City Hall Park, Sundays at 1pm. Subway 1, 2, 3, 9, A, C to Chambers Street.

This very popular tour is (like the movie of the same name) inspired by Herbert Asbury's 1927 classic book *The Gangs of New York*, which explores every aspect of the city's dark and brutal gang culture that had its centre at Five Points.

★★★★ **BRIT TIP** ★★★★
★ ★
★ A 21st-century version of the audio ★
★ walking tour is available any time ★
★ you want by mobile phone from ★
★ Talking Street (212-505 8687, ★
★ www.talking street.com). The sultry ★
★ tones of Sigourney Weaver will ★
★ show you around Lower Manhattan ★
★ and the World Trade Center. ★
★★★★★★★★★★★★★★★★★★★★★★★★★

Led in conjunction with Miramax Films, the tour paints a vivid and detailed picture of life for the immigrants in the 1800s and includes stops at Paradise Square,

Murderer's Alley and other sites associated with Bill 'The Butcher' Poole, William Tweed and the police and draft riots. Before you get too carried away with any notions of glamour, just bear in mind that the area then was so unsafe the police refused to go anywhere near it. There was at least one murder a night and ordinary people were so scared of leaving their tenements they even buried their dead in their buildings.

JOYCE GOLD HISTORY TOURS OF NEW YORK
Chelsea
✉ 141 West 17th Street
☎ 212-242 5762
🖰 www.nyctours.com
⏱ Various starting times for 2–3 hours, no reservations needed
$ $12

Specialists in unusual, in-depth weekend forays into many of the city's distinctive neighbourhoods. Fascinating tours include the East Village, culture and counter-culture, Downtown graveyards and Greenwich Village highlights.

LITERARY PUB CRAWL
West Village
✉ Meet at the White Horse Tavern, 567 Hudson Street at 11th Street
☎ 212-613 5796
🖰 www.bakerloo.org/pubcrawl
🚇 Subway A, C, E, L to 14th Street
⏱ Sat 2 pm
$ $15 adults; $12 students/seniors

Tour four pubs in the Village area that attracted writers, poets and artists, among them Dylan Thomas, Ernest Hemingway, John Steinbeck, e e cummings, Jack Kerouac, Jackson Pollock and Frank McCourt.

MUNICIPAL ART SOCIETY
Midtown

📫 457 Madison Avenue between East 50th and East 51st Streets
☎ 212-439 1049/212-935 3960
🖰 www.mas.org
🚇 Subway 6 to 51st Street
$ $12 weekdays, $15 weekends

Walking tours taking in both historic and architectural sites. Well-run, informative and very enjoyable. Telephone or visit their website for more information.

TALK-A-WALK

📫 30 Waterside Plaza, NY 10010
☎ 212-686 0356
   Fax 212-689 3538
$ $9.95

Walking tour guides on cassettes – they're an excellent way to learn about the city. It's best to order them before you leave home and they will be posted to you. There is a

---

BRIT'S GUIDE AWARDS FOR SIGHTSEEING TOURS
Best overview of city:

By bus: New York Visions (page 76)
By boat: Circle Line (page 75)

Best walking tours:
The Big Onion (page 82)

Best for thrills:
The Beast speedboat (page 75)
Liberty Helicopter Tours (page 72)

Most eye-opening experiences:
The Mystical World of Hassidic Jews (page 80)

Best for foodies:
Foods of New York around Greenwich Village and Chelsea Gourmet Market (page 80)

Best for free:
Big Apple Greeters (see opposite)

Best for romance:
Bateaux New York dinner cruises around Manhattan (page 76)

Best TV show tours:
Sex and the City (page 78)
Kramer's Reality Tour (page 80)

Most offbeat:
Hub Station/Pony Pedicabs (page 74)

Best musical tour:
Harlem Gospel Tour (page 76)
Soul Food And Jazz (page 76)

---

choice of four, each looking at the history and the architecture of historic Downtown.

TYING THE KNOT IN NEW YORK

If you're thinking about getting married in the city, then you've picked a top spot, because the Big Apple is one of the most popular places for Brits to marry abroad thanks to an abundance of romantic venues.

WHERE TO WED
There's no shortage of exceptional places to marry in New York, but it's best to get it all booked before you go. Most upmarket hotels will accommodate weddings, so be sure to contact the ones we've listed in our accommodation section (Chapter 11) for some of the best in town.

★ To get a better grasp of all the great NYC wedding venues check out the Great Places Directory at www.greatplacesdirectory.com, which features lots of ceremony and reception locations.

As well as hotels, other places you may want to investigate include Gotham Hall (1356 Broadway, 212-244 4300, www.gothamhallevents.com), a historic landmark in Midtown Manhattan that is a great venue for occasions such as weddings, holding from 25 to more than 1,000 guests. There's also **The Lighthouse** and **Pier Sixty** at Chelsea Piers (23rd Street at 12th Avenue, 212-336 6144, www.piersixty.com) for an intimate affair to remember. Or how about **New York Aquarium** (West 8th Street at Surf Avenue, Brooklyn, 718-265 3474, www.nyaquarium.com) for a more unusual location?

For an outdoor ceremony, the obvious place is Central Park, and it's not as tricky to organise as you may imagine. The Central Park Conservancy (212-310 6600, www.centralparknyc.org) grants the permits for wedding ceremonies and photography in venues throughout the park including the lovely Conservatory Garden and Shakespeare Garden.

THE KNOW-HOW
For all of the legal aspects of a wedding in New York, such as the minimum age, documentation and costs, contact the NYC

WHAT TO SEE AND DO

Marriage Bureau (City Clerk of New York in Manhattan, Municipal Building, 1 Center Street, 2nd Floor South, NY 10007. Tel 212-669 2400, www.nycmarriagebureau.com.

View from the Four Seasons

TOP FIVE PLACES TO PROPOSE

Just in case you haven't got down on one knee yet, here are some of the most idyllic spots to ask for her (or his) hand:

Top of the Empire State Building before sunset (page 61)

By the boating lake in Central Park (page 249)

In a helicopter flying over the city (page 72)

The penthouse suite of the Four Seasons (page 231)

A $10,000 Martini at the Algonquin Hotel (page 245) – it's a mix of vodka, vermouth, olive and ice, except that the ice is a sparkling diamond from the hotel's jeweller!

Manhattan at sunset

CHAPTER 5

Shopping and Beauty

For many people New York equals shopping. Yes, there are jaw-dropping buildings, amazing museums and exciting nightlife, but when it comes down to it New York City is one of the best places in the world to indulge in a spot of retail therapy. You can get a taste of fantastic American service at the fabulous and famous department stores, and shop until you drop for cheaper CDs, clothes, shoes and cameras. Although the city does have some real American malls like the one at the South Street Seaport, it is better known for its many boutiques.

The distinct atmosphere of each New York neighbourhood is reflected in the type of shopping available there. The upper section of 5th Avenue in the Midtown area is where you will find all the best department stores and other posh shops. Even posher – exclusive, actually – is Madison Avenue, which is where the top American and European designers such as Prada, Valentino and Versace are based.

★ ★ ★ ★ **BRIT TIP** ★ ★ ★ ★

New Yorkers in the know head to Aaron's in Brooklyn at 627 5th Avenue (tel 718-768 5400, www.aarons.com) where you can buy in-season women's designer fashions with up to 33 per cent discount.
★ ★

The Villages are excellent for boutique shops that tend to open late but stay open late, too. In **Greenwich Village** you'll find jazz records, rare books and vintage clothing and the **West Village's** tree-lined streets are full of fine and funky boutiques and popular restaurants that cater to a young, trendy crowd. On the major shopping streets of Bleecker, Broadway and 8th, you'll find everything from antiques to fashion and T-shirt emporiums. There are plenty of up-and-coming designers and second-hand shops in the **East Village**. Try 9th Street for clothes and 7th for young designers.

The **Flatiron District** around 5th Avenue from 14th to 23rd Streets is full of wonderful old buildings that are brimming with one-of-a-kind shops and designer boutiques. **SoHo** has lots of boutiques selling avant-garde fashion and art, plus restaurants and art galleries, all housed in handsome cast-iron 1850s buildings. West Broadway is the main drag, but other important shop-lined streets include Spring, Prince, Green, Mercer and Wooster. High-profile recent openings include Prada and Earl Jeans.

In **TriBeCa** you will find trendsetting boutiques such as the fantastic Issey Miyake flagship store, art galleries and restaurants in an area that combines loft living with commercial activity.

Last but not least is the **Lower East Side**, which is to bargains what Madison Avenue is to high-class acts. Many of the boutiques offer fashion by young designers – some of whom go on to open outlets in the posher areas – and famous-name gear at huge discounts. This whole area reflects the immigrant roots of New York and stands out as a bargain hunter's paradise particularly when the market is open on Sundays. Orchard Street from Houston to Delancey Streets is well known for leather goods, luggage, designer clothes, belts, shoes and fabrics. Ludlow Street is famous for trendy bars, and boutiques filled with clothes by flourishing new designers.

Macy's

TOP FIVE SHOPPING TIPS

If you're on a really tight schedule, call ahead and book appointments with the **personal shoppers** at major stores. They're very helpful and their service is absolutely free. Bargain! Call Macy's on 212-560 3618, Bloomingdale's on 212-705 2000 and Saks on 212-940 4650.

You have a right to a **full refund** on goods you return within 20 days with a valid receipt unless the shop has signs saying otherwise. Always check, though, especially if the item is in a sale.

Call in advance for **opening hours**. Smaller shops downtown – in SoHo, the Villages, Financial District and Lower East Side – tend not to open until noon or 1pm, but are often open as late as 8pm. Many are also closed on Mondays.

You can **avoid sales tax** if you arrange to have your purchases shipped outside of New York State – a facility that is available at larger stores and those that are more tourist orientated.

Watch out for 'Sale' signs on the Midtown section of 5th Avenue in the streets 30s and 40s. Here most of the shop windows are filled with signs that say 'Great Sales!', 'Going Out Of Business!' – yet they have been around for years and are still going strong. In fact, most of what is on sale there can be bought cheaper elsewhere and with a guarantee.

DEPARTMENT STORES

The big department stores in New York City are reliable places to buy good quality, brand-named merchandise at fair prices. These stores usually sell a variety of men's, women's and children's clothing, including designer label items. You can also expect to find cosmetics, small appliances, electronics and household goods. Department stores usually hold end-of-season clearance sales with significant price reductions. Most of the following are in the Midtown area either in or near 5th Avenue. Standard opening times are Monday to Friday 10am–8pm, Saturday 10am–7pm and Sunday noon–6pm.

★ The voltage system is different in
★ America so any plug-in electrical
★ goods will not work properly in the
★ UK without an adaptor.

5TH AVENUE

Bergdorf Goodman: 754 5th Avenue at 57th Street. Tel 212-753 7300, www.bergdorfgoodman.com. Subway N, R, W to 5th Avenue/59th Street; F to 57th Street.
An air of understated elegance pervades every department – not surprising, given

that it has been around for generations. This department store is not only still going strong, but it is positively booming and has even opened a Bergdorf Goodman Men on the opposite side of the street.

★ The only major department store
★ NOT open on a Sunday is Bergdorf
★ Goodman, but it's still well worth a
★ visit on any other day.

Lord and Taylor: 424 5th Avenue at 39th Street. Tel 212-391 3344, www.maycompany.com. Subway B, D, F, V to 42nd Street; 7 to 5th Avenue.
Good service at cheap prices. The store is famous for its animated window displays at Christmas time.

Saks 5th Avenue: 611 5th Avenue at 50th Street. Tel 212-753 4000, www.saksfifthavenue.com. Subway E, V to 5th Avenue/53rd Street.
Not only is this one of the finest shopping institutions in New York, it also has fabulous views of the Rockefeller Centre and is right next door to the beautiful St Patrick's Cathedral. Saks is a classic and has all the big names. There is a fabulous beauty area on the ground floor where you can get a personal consultation and a makeover.

Takashimaya: 693 5th Avenue between 54th and 55th Streets. Tel 212-350 0100. Subway N, R to 5th Avenue; 4, 5, 6 to 59th Street.

An elegant spot for tea is to be found in The Tea Box, a café in the basement of Takashimaya. It has a superb range of teas and a great selection of teapots to buy.

Hugely expensive, but filled with truly gorgeous things laid out in a six-storey townhouse building.

MEATPACKING DISTRICT
Jeffrey: 449 West 14th Street between 9th and 10th Avenues. Tel 212-206 1272. Subway N, R to 5th Avenue/59th Street.
A boutique department store sounds like an oxymoron, but this little gem, on the edge of the gritty up-and-coming Meatpacking District is packed full of tremendously hip clothes and accessories. It attracts A-list celebrities – note the limousines waiting at the front – and great labels like Dries Van Noten and Balenciaga. The women's shoe department is one of the best in New York.

MIDTOWN–34TH STREET
Macy's: Herald Square at 151 West 34th Street, 6th Avenue and Broadway. Tel 212-695 4400, www.macys.com. Subway B, D, F, N, Q, R, V, W to 34th Street.

Macy's is the venue for the Thanksgiving Day Parade, Fourth of July Fireworks and a Spring Flower Week in April.

This is a beast of a gigantic store, filling as it does an entire city block, so you can be forgiven for getting yourself lost. If you enter from the Herald Square side, you'll find the Visitors' Center on the mezzanine level up to your left. Here you can pick up your free Macy's tote bag or rucksack with any purchase over $35, on production of a special voucher – try the leaflet rack at your hotel. Along the way you'll pass the delightful Metropolitan Museum Shop. A favourite area with Brits is the jeans

department and, of course, the beauty counters that throng the ground floor. If you're with children, head for the seventh floor where all their needs are catered for, along with the only McDonald's inside a department store in New York. Don't miss the coffee shops, restaurant and food store run by Cucina & Co (page 114).

UPPER EAST SIDE
Barneys: 660 Madison Avenue at 61st Street. Tel 212-826 8900, www.barneys.com. Subway N, R, W to 5th Avenue; 4, 5, 6 to Lexington. Open until 8pm every weekday night.
A truly up-to-the-minute fashion outlet, this store is filled with all the top designers and a good selection of newer ones. There isn't really a Brit equivalent; the nearest would be Harvey Nichols, but it doesn't come close. It has eight floors of fashion where there's everything from big-name designers to more obscure, but very hip, small labels. There is a branch called Coop on 18th Street in Chelsea, and another one at the World Financial Center in Downtown, but this is the $100-million megastore. Don't miss it!

If you plan to be in New York in August or March, get on down to the Barneys Warehouse Sale – call ahead for locations or check the website (above).

Bloomingdale's: 1000 3rd Avenue between 59th and 60th Streets. Tel 212-705 2000, www.bloomingdales.com. Subway 4, 5, 6 to 59th Street; N, R to Lexington Avenue.
This is probably the most famous of all 5th Avenue's department stores. You can't go wrong with anything you buy from here, and if you spend over $50, claim your free gift from the brand new state-of-the-art visitors' centre. A truly glitzy shop filled with all the right designers, you can now also sample its delights at the new SoHo branch (page 96).

DISCOUNT STORES
Century 21: 22 Cortlandt Street between Church Street and Broadway. Tel 212-227 9092, www.c21stores.com. Subway 1, 2, 4, 5, A, C to Fulton Street/Broadway Nassau. Area: Financial District.

TAXES AND ALLOWANCES

US taxes: Be aware that local taxes will be added to the cost of your purchases when you pay at the till, so don't get too carried away by the often seemingly very low price tags. New York sales tax is 8.625 per cent, though it has now been dropped on clothes and shoes costing under $110, while New York state tax is 5 per cent.

UK allowances: Your UK duty-free allowance is just £145 and, given the wealth of shopping opportunities, you're likely to exceed this, but don't be tempted to change receipts to show a lesser value as, if you are rumbled, the goods will be confiscated and you'll face a massive fine. In any case, the prices for some goods in America are so cheap that, even once you've paid the duty and VAT on top, they will still work out cheaper than buying the same item in Britain.

Duty can range from 3.5 to 19 per cent depending on the item: for example, computers are charged at 3.5 per cent, golf clubs at 4 per cent, cameras at 5.4 per cent and mountain bikes at a massive 15.8 per cent. You pay this on goods above £145 and then VAT of 17.5 per cent on top of that. Keep your eye on the newspapers though, as chancellor Gordon Brown is considering raising the figure to a more reasonable £1,000 – enough for a couple of iPods!

Duty free: Buy your booze from US liquor stores – they're better value than the airports – but remember your allowance is only 1 litre of spirits and two bottles of wine.

Excellent discounts on everything from adult's and children's clothing to goods for the home. Arrive early to avoid the lunchtime rush or mid-afternoon.

Daffy's: 462 Broadway (corner Grand). Tel 212-334 7444, www.daffys.com. Subway J, M, Q, W, 2, 6 to Canal Street. Area: Soho. 335 Madison Avenue at 44th Street. Tel 212-557 4422. Subway S, 4, 5, 6, 7 to 42nd Street/Grand Central. Area: Midtown East. 1311 Broadway at West 34th Street. Tel 212-736 4477. Subway B, D, F, N, Q, R to 34th Street. Area: 34th Street. 125 East 57th Street between Lexington and Park Avenues. Tel 212-376 4477. Subway 4, 5, 6 to 59th Street; N, R, W to Lexington Avenue. Area: Midtown East.

You'll find an amazing range of designer stock from all over the world at all four outlets of this famous discount store, and a hunt could result in a real bargain.

Filene's Basement: 620 6th Avenue between 18th and 19th Streets. Tel 212-620 3100, www.filenesbasement.com. Subway F, V, L to 6th Avenue/14th Street. Area: Union Square.

Bloomingdales

Part of the Boston-based bargain-basement company which is one of the country's oldest off-price chains. There's also an outlet on Broadway at West 79th Street in the Upper West Side.

Gabay's Outlet: 225 1st Avenue between 13th and 14th Streets. Tel 212-254 3180, www.gabaysoutlet.com. Subway F, V, L to Ave 1.

An East Village gem offering high-end designer fashion at seriously discounted prices. Its shoes and bags are coveted by the fashion pack and often include Manolo, Christian Louboutin and Tod's.

INA: 21 Prince Street between Thompson and Spring Streets. Tel 212-334 9048. Subway C, E to Spring Street; N, R, W to Prince Street. Area: NoLiTa.

A designer resale stock that changes daily and offers discounts of 30–50 per cent per item. You'll be able to get your hands on plenty of model cast-offs, from Manolo shoes to Prada.

Loehmann's: 101 7th Avenue between 16th and 17th Streets. Tel 212-352 0856, www.loehmanns.com. Subway 1, 9 to 18th Street. Area: Chelsea.

A five-storey building filled with bargains – typically 30–65 per cent off – for men and women. Head straight to the top floor for designer labels such as Donna Karan, Calvin Klein and Versace. The other floors feature accessories, bags, clothing and shoes all at great prices.

★★★★ **BRIT TIP** ★★★★
★ To find out about more bargain
★ outlets before you go log on to to
★ http://gonyc.about.com/od/shopping
★ /tp/discount_shop.htm
★★★★★★★★★★★★★★★★★★★★★★★★★

SHOPPING TOURS

Arrange a shopping tour of everything from Saks 5th Avenue to little boutiques in SoHo. They're lots of fun, really good value and a must-do for any shopaholic. **Pamela Parisi's Tightwad Treks** aim to have you dressing like a diva on a tight budget. Call her on 631-841 2111, www.theelegant tightwad.com. Rebecca Merritt of **Shop Gotham** will help you get under the city's skin with shopping trips around areas like SoHo and NoLiTa, speed shop the big department stores and get huge discounts in the Garment Center. Call 212-209 3370, www.shopgotham.com. Tours cost from $30.

★★★★ **BRIT TIP** ★★★★
★ If you don't want to go on an
★ organised shopping tour, create your
★ own using the Shopping Walking
★ Tour Map at http://gonyc.about.com.
★ Expect to walk two miles in about
★ an hour-and-a-half.
★★★★★★★★★★★★★★★★★★★★★★★★★

FASHION

You can find everything in New York from top designers to up-and-coming newcomers. The main shopping areas for fashion are the Upper East Side (for posh), SoHo (for designer), the East Village and Lower East Side (for cheap designer). Call ahead for opening times as many shops do not open until late – but they stay open later in the evening.

CHELSEA

Balenciaga: 542 West 22nd Street at 11th Avenue. Tel 212-206 0872, www.balenciaga.com. Subway C, E to 23rd Street.
The New York flagship store of this popular womenswear label often spotted on the backs of supermodels such as Kate Moss.

Camouflage: 139–141 8th Avenue at 17th

BEST FOR BRIDES

If you're a bride-to-be on the look out for your dream dress during your trip to the Big Apple, make a beeline for **Kleinfeld** (110 West 20th Street. Tel 212-352 2180, www.kleinfeldbridal.com). This venerable institution has just moved to a new location in the Chelsea neighbourhood and features the world's largest selection of wedding dresses from American and European designers. There's also **Kleinfeld Bridesmaids**, Loft (270 West 38th street, 212-398 5255) to check out if you're travelling with friends. You'll find almost 400 samples in every style, size and fabric imaginable. If you've got money to burn then you'll also want to make a trip to the Upper East side to visit the **Vera Wang Bridal Salon** (991 Madison Avenue, 212-628 3400, www.verawang.com). The queen of wedding gowns is renowned the world over for her amazing creations and boasts customers such as Sharon Stone. There's also **Vera Wang Maids** on Madison at 980 Madison Avenue, 212-628 9898.

Street. Tel 212-691 1750. Subway A, C, E to 14th Street.
Designer men's wear store that offers the highlights of the season from labels like Michael Kors, Etro and Marc Jacobs.

Comme des Garcons: 540 West 22nd Street between 10th and 11th Avenues. Tel 212-604 0013. Subway C, E to 23rd Street. Japanese designer Rei Kawakubo's stark designs are worn by fashion's elite, and the high prices reflect that.

Co-op Store: 236 West 18th Street between 7th and 8th Avenues. Tel 212-716 8816. Subway 1, 2 to 18th Street. One of the best stores in New York.

agnès b

EAST VILLAGE

A Cheng: 443 East 9th Street at 1st Avenue. Tel 212-979 7324, www.achengshop.com. Subway L to 1st Avenue.
A mix of smart and street styles from this trendy designer.

Enelra Lingerie: 48 East 7th Street. Tel 212-473 2454. Subway F, V to 2nd Avenue. Madonna's haunt 20 years ago. Now worth checking out at Halloween when the window displays feature items like full-length latex devil outfits!

Himalayan Vision: 127 2nd Avenue at 7th Street. Tel 212-254 1952. Subway 6 to Astor Place.
Tibetan-style dresses, silk skirts, trousers, tops and hand-knit hats from around $40 can be found in this serene shop.

Jill Anderson: 331 East 9th Street at 1st Avenue. Tel 212-253 1747. Subway 6 to Astor Place.
The sweeping coat-dresses and girly slips are in keeping with the bohemian vibe of the artsy East Village.

Religious Sex: 7 St Mark's Place between 2nd and 3rd Avenues. Tel 212-477 9037, www.religioussex.com. Subway 6 to Astor Place.
If you're feeling outrageous (sequinned thong, anybody?), you'll find the clothes that you're after here.

Suzette Sundae: 182 Avenue near 11th Street. Tel 212-777 7870, www.suzettesundae.com. Subway L to 1st Avenue.
Lady-like dresses crossed with punk rock is the name of the game at this wonderfully named store. There's a private-label collection hanging alongside pieces from hot designers of the moment.

Trash and Vaudeville: 4 St Mark's Place between 2nd and 3rd Avenues. Tel 212-982 3590. Subway 6 to Astor Place.
You'll get the East Village look in no time if you step into this punk/grunge paradise. Here you'll find outrageous rubber dresses and shirts, black leather outfits and plenty of studded gear and footwear to match.

GREENWICH VILLAGE

American Apparel: 712 Broadway at Washington Place (and 12 other outlets in New York). Tel 212-383 2257, www.americanapparel.net. Subway N, R to 8th Street.
Stocks a huge selection of slogan T-shirts.

Bang Bang Boutique: 53 8th Street near Broadway. Tel 212-475 8220, www.bangbang.com. Subway 6 to Astor Place.

HOW TO FIND A REAL BARGAIN

Goods at normal prices in New York are cheaper than in the UK, but it is possible to find whatever you are looking for at an even better price.

➡ If **shopping bargains** are your main reason for visiting New York, then bear in mind that the major sales are held in March and August. The winter sales seem to start earlier and earlier and may even begin before Christmas.

➡ Visit **www.NYSale.com** for all the vital information on when the latest designer and sample sales are about to take place. Hot sale action is also listed on www.daily candy.com, www.citylaunch.com and www.thebudgetfashionista.com.

➡ Check out the **Sales and Bargains** section of *New York Magazine*, the ads in the *New York Times* and the Check Out section of *Time Out*.

➡ Get the **S&B Report** on www.lazarshopping.com.

➡ Bear in mind that many of the **vintage clothing outlets** are excellent for barely worn designer clothes and some even specialise in never-worn-before sample sales.

➡ Head for the premium shopping bargain outlet of **Woodbury Common**, just an hour out of New York in the Central Valley, tel 845-928 4000, www.premiumoutlets.com. It has discounts of between 25 and 65 per cent at a huge number of factory outlets for designers and department stores such as Ann Taylor, Banana Republic, Barneys, Betsey Johnson, Burberry, Calvin Klein, Christian Dior, Donna Karan, Gap, Giorgio Armani, Gucci, Nike, Saks and Versace. Do you want me to go on? For more information on Woodbury Common, see pages 278–279.

Fun, way-out clubbing and party gear for men and women.

Patricia Field: 10 East 8th Street between 5th Avenue and University Place. Tel 212-254 1699. Subway A, C, E, F, V, S to West 4th Street.
Once only famous for her outrageous club clobber, Patricia is the designer who creates all the fashion for the *Sex And The City* girls. So if you want to emulate Carrie, Mia or Lizzie, then come here to stock up on cool bags and jewellery worn by the cast.

Untitled: 26 West 8th Street between 5th and 6th Avenues. Tel 212-505 9725. Subway A, C, E, F, V, S to West 4th Street.
Contemporary clothing and accessories from exclusive New York designers as well as the likes of Vivienne Westwood.

LOWER EAST SIDE
Edith and Daha: 104 Rivington Street at Ludlow Street. Tel: 212-979 9992. Subway F to Delancey Street.

★ ★ ★ ★ **BRIT TIP** ★ ★ ★ ★
For info on sample sales in the Lower East Side area, go to www.lowereastsideny.com.

This pair of women's wear designers make a maximum of only 12 copies of each item, so you're pretty much guaranteed not to meet anyone else wearing your cool dress or skirt. A nice touch is that you can watch the clothes being created at the back of the shop.

Nova USA: 100 Stanton Street at Ludlow Street. Tel 212-228 6844. Subway J, M, Z, F to Delancey Street.
Great for basic but brilliant sportswear, Cameron Diaz and Helena Christensen are just two of the many women who stock up on these casually cool bits of kit when they're in Manhattan.

MEATPACKING DISTRICT
Alexander McQueen: 417 West 14th Street between 9th Avenue and Washington Street. Tel: 212-645 1797, www.alexandermcqueen.com. Subway A, C, E to 14th Street, L to 8th Avenue.
British fashion guru who made his name at Givenchy before designing for Gucci. The clothes are way out and very expensive.

An Earnest Cut & Sew: 821 Washington Street at Gansevoort Street. Tel: 212-242 3414, www.earnestsewn.com. Subway A, C, E to 8th Avenue.
High-end denim label Earnest Sewn's opened its first stand-alone store in 2005 and it has been a major hit with trendy young New Yorkers. The major hook here is

---

TOP FIVE MOST-WANTED AMERICAN LABELS
East Village
Mark Montano: 434 East 9th Street between 1st Avenue and Avenue A. Tel 212-505 0325. Subway 6 to Astor Place.
Drew Barrymore, Johnny Depp and Kate Moss are all fans of the funky designer who uses bright, often vintage, fabrics to create designs with style.

SoHo
Earl Jeans: 160 Mercer Street between Houston and Prince Streets. Tel 212-226 8709, www.earljean.com. Subway N, R to Prince Street; 6 to Spring Street.
Self-taught California designer Suzanne Costas has not only created jeans that actually fit women, but made them sexy too. Her ultra-low-slung jeans have been the definitive favourites of stars like Cameron Diaz and Kate Moss for some time and now visitors to New York can get their hands on them too.

Marc Jacobs: 163 Mercer Street between Houston and Prince Streets. Tel 212-343 1490, www.marcjacobs.com. Subway N, R to Prince Street.
The darling of supermodels and superwomen, such as movie director Sophia Coppella, Jacobs' style is minimalist and luxurious.

Upper East Side
Calvin Klein: 654 Madison Avenue at 60th Street. Tel 212-292 9000, www.calvinklein.com. Subway N, R to Lexington Avenue; 4, 5, 6 to 59th Street.
CK's leading outlet seems to have enjoyed as much attention from the designers as the clothes themselves!

Donna Karan: 819 Madison Avenue between East 68th and 69th Streets. Tel 212-861 1001, www.donnakaran.com. Subway 6 to 68th Street.
A leading American designer who is best known for her elegant, simple outfits for women. The floating staircase is worth popping in for.

its customising– you can have pockets, buttons or zips tweaked and fabric added to ensure you get a genuine one-off garment. The service takes 2 hours and costs $300–350.

Diane von Furstenberg: 385 West 12th Street between Washington Street and West Side Highway. Tel 646-486 4800, www.dvf.com. Subway A, C, E to 8th Avenue.
Flagship store of the queen of the classically sexy silk jersey wrap dress. The dramatic shop, with its draped changing rooms, is worth a visit in its own right.

Stella McCartney: 429 West 14th Street. Tel 212-255 1556, www.stellamccartney.com. Subway A, C, E to West 14th Street.
The famous daughter of a Beatle moved on from shaking up fashion at Chloe to designing under her own label to great acclaim. Her first store in this cool district sees the likes of Liv Tyler and Gwyneth Paltrow when they are shopping in town.

★ ★ ★ ★ **BRIT TIP** ★ ★ ★ ★
★ ★
★ **If you long to wear Armani but** ★
★ **don't have the bank balance to** ★
★ **match, then hunt out one of five** ★
★ **AIX Armani Exchange stores in** ★
★ **Manhattan, which offer the label's** ★
★ **chic, well-made clothes at a fraction** ★
★ **of the cost of Armani – www.armani** ★
★ **exchange.com. Stores are at 645** ★
★ **and 656 5th Avenue, Time Warner** ★
★ **Center (10 Columbus Circle), 129** ★
★ **5th Avenue and 568 Broadway.** ★
★ ★

MIDTOWN
BOSS Hugo Boss: 717 5th Avenue at 56th Street. Tel 212-485 1800, www.hugoboss.com. Subway N, R to 5th Avenue.

Earl Jeans

Flagship floor of this fashionable menswear label. It has a wide range of the brand's goodies, from sharp suits to coveted watches.

Burberry: 9 East 57th Street between 6th and Madison Avenues. Tel 212-407 7100, www.burberry.com. Subway 4, 5, 6 to 59th Street.
The opening of this fabulous flagship store reflects the resurgence of the great British classic as a trendsetting force in recent years. There's something for everyone here – men, women, teenagers and even children since the introduction of the new tots' clothing line.

Chanel: 15 East 57th Street between 5th and Madison Avenues. Tel 212-385 5050, www.chanel.com. Subway E, V to 5th Avenue.
The enduring French label offers you the chance to buy all the classics from thousand dollar suits to quilted handbags and, of course, No 5 perfume.

Gianni Versace: 647 5th Avenue between 51st and 52nd Streets. Tel 212-317 0224, www.versace.com. Subway E, V to 5th Avenue/53rd Street.
A beautiful shop, housed in the former Vanderbilt mansion, selling beautiful clothes for the rich and famous.

Gucci: 685 5th Avenue at 54th Street. Tel 212-826 2600, www.gucci.com. Subway E, V to 5th Avenue/53rd Street.
So you may not be able to afford anything on display, but it's essential to know what 'look' you are trying to achieve when you browse through the copy-cat shops downtown.

Lacoste: 575 Madison Avenue near 56th Street. Tel 212-750 8115, www.lacoste.com. Subway 6 to 51st Street. Also at 608 5th Avenue and 134 Prince Street.
The alligator-logoed polo shirts are a classic item to snap up while you're in the Big Apple.

Levi's: 536 Broadway, between Prince and Spring Streets. Area: SoHo. Tel 646-613 1847, www.levi.com. Also at 750 Lexington Avenue. Area: Upper East Side.
If you've ever had trouble finding a pair of jeans that fit you perfectly, come here to be measured and have your jeans custom-made and sent to you.

Liz Claiborne: 650 5th Avenue at East 52nd Street. Tel 212-956 6505,

TOP FIVE MIDTOWN SHOPS FOR ACCESSORIES

Bottega Veneta: 699 5th Avenue between 54th and 55th Streets. Tel 212-371 5511, www.bottegaveneta.com. Subway E, V to 5th Avenue/53rd Street.
Who wouldn't covet the gorgeous soft leather, logo-free handbags offered at this Italian designer store.

Ferragamo on Madison: 655 Madison Avenue at 52nd Street. Tel 212-759 3822. Subway V to 5th Avenue.
The largest Ferragamo store in the world has an amazing 23,000-plus shoes as well as handbags, scarves and ties.

Jimmy Choo: 645 5th Avenue at 51st Street. Tel 212-593 0800, www.jimmychoo.com. Subway E, V to 5th Avenue/53rd Street.
Originally part of Jimmy's upscale ready-to-wear 'chain' of stores – think London, Paris, Los Angeles and New York – the designer has sold up most of his shares and gone back to his couture clients. Now the thongs (flip-flops), slingbacks and skinny high-heeled shoes are designed by his daughter Sanda, but still remain the favourites of celebs like Madonna and Sarah Jessica Parker. A pair of women's shoes are upwards of $450. Men's loafers, sneakers and thongs start at around $300.

Lingerie & Company: 1217 3rd Avenue at 70th Street. Tel 212-737 7700. Subway 6 to 68th Street.
A user-friendly shop for a wide choice of gorgeous undies.

Manolo Blahnik: 31 West 54th Street between 5th and 6th Avenues. Tel 212-582 3007. Subway E, V to 5th Avenue/53rd Street.
Anyone serious about their shoe collection wouldn't miss this mecca for celebs. In fact, Manolo has even designed the SJP – an ankle-strapped stiletto named after Sarah Jessica Parker.

www.lizclaiborne.com. Subway 6 to 51st Street; E, F to Lexington Avenue.
Career and sportswear with plenty of style for women.

NOHO

Avirex Cockpit Store: 652 Broadway between Bleecker and Bond Streets. Tel 212-925 5456, www.avirex.com.
Great for flight and varsity jackets.

Urban Outfitters: 628 Broadway between Houston and Bleecker Streets. Tel 212-475 0009, www.urbanoutfitters.com. Subway F, V, S to Broadway/Lafayette Street; 6 to Bleecker Street.
The last word in trendy, inexpensive clothes. Also has vintage urban wear. There's one in London now so it's not as special as it used to be, but still worth a visit for its mix of hip clothes, accessories, toys and other whatnots.

NOLITA

Calypso Christiane Celle: 280 Mott Street between East Houston and Prince Street. Tel 212-965 0990, www.calypso-celle.com. Subway 6 to Spring Street.
A French boutique with a Caribbean influence, this shop is filled with designs from Christiane Celle. There's a riot of sexy silk slip dresses, tie-dye tops and cute beaded cardigans. Her newest store is at 654 Hudson Street in the trendy Meatpacking District.

Maverick: 262 Mott Street near Prince Street. Tel 212-965 1150. Subway 6 to Spring Street.
Rebecca Romero's store is full of feminine pieces perfect for an uptown look. Think floral-print pencil skirts and pinstripe shirt dresses.

Selvedge: 250 Mulberry Street near Prince Street. Tel 212-219 0994. Subway 6 to Spring Street.
Known as a laboratory for denim, it sells everything from funky reproductions of cult

Manolo Blahnik

CLOTHES SIZES

Clothes sizes for men and women are one size smaller in America, so a dress size 10 in the US is a size 12 in the UK, a jacket size 42 is a UK 44. But it's the opposite with shoes – an American size 10 is our size 9.

classics like 501s through to the Levi's Red collection.

Tracey Feith: 209 Mulberry Street between Spring and Kenmare Streets. Tel 212-334 3097. Subway 6 to Spring Street.
Tucked away in the hip NoLiTa, here you can get a dress made to order if you've $550 to burn. Just remember, Sarah Jessica Parker wore one of Feith's red and blue silk creations in *Sex And The City*.

SOHO

Adidas Originals Store: 136 Wooster Street near Prince Street. Tel 212-673 0398, www.adidas.com. Subway C, E to Prince Street.
If you have a penchant for old-school trainers and sportswear then this is the place to head for.

agnès b: 103 Greene Street between Spring and Prince Streets. Tel 212-925 4649, www.agnesb.com. Subway N, R to Prince Street.
Superb designs for women and children here – simple but stunning and beautifully cut.

Anna Sui: 113 Greene Street between Prince and Spring Streets. Tel 212-941 8406, www.annasui.com. Subway N, R to Prince Street.
Get the glamour-with-a-hint-of-grunge look with Anna's dresses, skirts, blouses, boots and scarves. The small collection for men includes trousers, shirts and jackets from the outrageously loud to the quite positively restrained.

A.P.C.: 131 Mercer Street near Prince Street. Tel 212-966 9685, www.apc.fr. Subway N, R to Prince Street.
Men's and women's Euro-hip functional city clothes, such as shirt dresses, crisp shirts and jackets and trench coats, sold in a trendy loft space.

A Uno: 198 Spring Street near Thompson Street. Tel 212-343 2040. Subway C, E to Spring Street.
Edgy sportswear and versatile women's clothing.

Banana Republic: 552 Broadway between Spring and Prince Streets. Tel 212-925 0308, www.bananarepublic.com. Subway N, R to Prince Street.
A classy and reputable chain, famous for classic clothing in feel-good fabrics such as cashmere, suede, velvet and soft cotton at affordable prices. Nevertheless, the best buys are in the frequent sales.

Betsey Johnson: 138 Wooster Street between Houston and Prince Streets. Tel 212-995 5048, www.betseyjohnson.com. Subway C, E to Spring Street; N, R to Prince Street.
A wonderful presentation of a combination of party and working clothes that are thrilling to wear.

★ ★ ★ ★ **BRIT TIP** ★ ★ ★ ★

★ SoHo is the place to take a trip to if
★ you're looking for quirky, one-off
★ clothing that you can be sure no
★ one back home will have. Its streets
★ are lined with boutique designer
★ shops and has stores from some of
★ the world's leading designers.

Bio: 29 Prince Street near Elizabeth Street. Tel 212-343 3006, www.bio-nyc.com. Subway B, D, F, V to Broadway and Lafayette Street.
Owner Au Vu stocks fabulous suits and matching coordinates for well-heeled city women who want to look professional but fashionable.

Bloomingdale's: 504 Broadway between Spring and Broome Streets. Tel 212-729 5900, www.bloomingdales.com. Subway N, R to Prince Street.
Aimed at Lower Manhattan's trendy set, this brand-new, six-level SoHo branch of the world-famous store offers something for everyone, with plenty of different designer lines.

Burberry: 131 Spring Street between Greene and Wooster Streets. Tel 212-925 9300, www.burberry.com. Subway C, E to Spring Street.
Don't miss this younger, hipper outlet of the super trendy British company for rainwear, leather, trench dresses, bags, shoes and casual wear.

Catherine Malandrino's: 468 Broome Street at Greene Street. Tel 212-925 6765, www.catherinemalandrino.com. Subway 6 to Spring Street.

The designer's own sexy French knitwear in block colours stands alongside more tailored knitted skirts and jackets.

Club Monaco: 520 Broadway at Spring Street. Tel 212-941 1511, www.clubmonaco.com. Subway 6 to Spring Street.

Once a Canadian company offering high fashion at high street prices, Ralph Lauren loved it so much he bought it.

D&G: 434 West Broadway between Prince and Spring Streets. Tel 212-965 8000, www.dolcegabbana.it. Subway N, R to Prince Street.

Shop for jeans, suits, bags and dresses to a background of (loud) pop music. *Sex And The City*'s Carrie's favourite shop!

Earl Jeans: See page 93.

Helmut Lang: 80 Greene Street near Prince Street. Tel 212-925 4519, www.helmutlang.com. Subway C, E to Spring Street; N, R to Prince Street.

A stark, white gallery-like space that contrasts well with the designer's dark creations for men and women. It's pricey, think $500 upwards, but items like tuxedo jackets and shoes are exquisite.

Hotel Venus: 302 Bowery. Tel 212-966 4066, www.patriciafield.com.

One of Patricia Field's outlets. Her trendsetting club and streetwear are so outrageous they attract a large following among the drag queen and stripper crowd. But don't let that put you off if you fancy a corset, fake fur coat, bodysuit or bikini that's completely OTT. Patricia, by the way, is now known for dressing Sarah Jessica Parker of *Sex And The City*.

J Crew: 99 Prince Street between Mercer and Greene Streets. Tel 212-966 2739, www.jcrew.com. Subway N, R to Prince Street.

American-style men's and women's clothes plus shoes and accessories.

Keiko: 62 Greene Street between Spring and Broome Streets. Tel 212-226 6051, www.keikonewyork.com. Subway N, R to Prince Street.

Designer swimwear for all tastes – and you may recognise the odd supermodel shopping here.

Le Sportsac: 176 Spring Street between West Broadway and Thompson Streets. Tel 212-625 2626, www.lesportsac.com. Subway C, E to Spring Street.

Beloved of Japanese trendoids and US out-of-towners, not to mention Brit hipsters, Le Sportsac offers great nylon bags in every style, size, colour and pattern and they're reasonably priced, too. Worth a visit as the range isn't available in the UK.

Marc Jacobs: See page 93.

Operations: 60 Mercer Street at Broome Street. Tel: 212-334 4950. Subway N, R to Prince Street.

The quirky work-style clothing, like red trucker jackets with black elbow patches, hang off meat hooks, while the changing rooms are industrial-sized freezers.

Phat Farm: 129 Prince Street between West Broadway and Wooster Street. Tel 212-533 7428, www.phatfarmstore.com. Subway C, E to Spring Street.

If you're into hip-hop baggies, you'll find everything you need here.

Philosophy di Alberta Ferretti: 452 West Broadway near Prince Street. Tel: 212-460 5500, www.philosophy.it. Subway C, E to Spring Street.

The younger, more affordable line from top designer Alberta Ferretti.

Pleats Please: 128 Wooster Street at Prince Street. Tel: 212-226 3600, www.pleatsplease.com. Subway N, R to Prince Street.

Issey Miyake's tightly pleated skirts, tops, scarves and trousers can be found here.

Prada New York Epicenter: 575 Broadway at Prince Street. Tel 212-334 8888, www.prada.com. Subway N, R, W to Prince Street.

Art is the byword of this incredible $40 million flagship store for Prada. Once the Guggenheim's SoHo museum, the two-level space has been designed by architect Rem Koolhaas and includes a zebrawood 'wave' in the entry hall and shoe display steps that can be converted into auditorium seating. Other neat design elements include dressing rooms behind a wall that switches from translucent to transparent (be warned!) and clothes suspended from the ceiling in metal cages. And therein lies one of the main drawbacks of the store from a punter's point of view. Prada's entire collection is to be found here, yet all the empty areas make people feel as if there isn't that much to buy. On top of that, the store has taken being 'cool' so seriously that the staff are positively frosty. Deal with them by either telling yourself that you earn a lot more than they do, or as one woman put it: 'You can have fun by asking the sales people for things from the storage rooms and keep them running!'

★★★★ **BRIT TIP** ★★★★
★ ★
★ **A great place for a pit stop is the** ★
★ **Universal News and Café Corp (tel** ★
★ **212-965 9042, www.universal** ★
★ **newsusa.com) at 484 Broadway** ★
★ **between Broome and Grand Streets,** ★
★ **where you'll not only be able to find** ★
★ **a snack, but also check out their** ★
★ **range of 7,000 magazine titles!** ★
★★★★★★★★★★★★★★★★★★★★★★★★★★

Sean: 132 Thompson Street near Prince Street. Tel 212-598 5980, www.seanstore.com. Subway 1, 9 to Houston.
A superb range of menswear for work and play at low prices, from colourful shirts to wool sports jackets.

Stüssy Store: 140 Wooster Street between West Houston and Prince Streets. Tel 212-274 8855, www.stussy.com. Subway N, R to Prince Street.
Everything you could want if you're after a West Coast look.

TRIBECA

Buffalo Chips Boot Company: 426 Washington Street near Vestry Street. Tel 212-965 0300. Subway 1, 9 to Franklin Street.
Pop star Sheryl Crow is just one of the celebrities who have got in touch with their inner cowgirl and gone on a spending spree at this cowgirl-kitsch store. Cowboy boots, handmade leather pants and Western shirts are just some of the fun items on offer.

Rival: 225 Hudson Street near Canal Street. Tel 212-929 7222, www.225hudson.com (still under construction). Subway 1, 9 to Canal Street.
Skatewear for grown-ups best describes this store, which is packed full of great labels such as Burton and Oliver Spence. Best of all, you don't have to be under 18 to get the attention of staff; customer service here is excellent, even if your days of whizzing along on a snow or skateboard are well behind you.

Steven Alan: 103 Franklin Street between Church Street and West Broadway. Tel 212-343 0692, www.stevenalan.com. Subway 1 to Franklin Street.
A small but perfectly formed boutique filled to the rafters with up-and-coming designers such as Kayatone Adeli's cute disco top and Daryl K's hipster trousers.

Tribeca Issey Miyake: 119 Hudson Street at North Moore Street. Tel 212-226 0100, www.isseymiyake.com. Subway 1, 2 to Franklin Street.
The new Prada store got the old Guggenheim Museum space in SoHo: Issey Miyake got Frank Gehry, the architect of the amazing Guggenheim Museum in Bilbao. Now serious shoppers mingle with art buffs who come to see the titanium tornado that swirls through this two-storey, 279 sq m (3,000 sq ft) boutique, plus art by Gehry's son Alejandro. Fortunately, the purpose of the shop (sorry, but that's what it is) has not been forgotten and the entire Issey collection is here including the Pleats Please, Haat, A/POC and fragrance lines. What's more, the staff are actually helpful. A truly wonderful experience – especially if you can afford $1,600 for a shirt. Otherwise wait for the sales!

UPPER EAST SIDE

Anne Fontaine: 687 Madison Avenue near 62nd Street. Tel 212-688 4362, www.annefontaine.com. Subway 4, 5, 6 to 59th Street.
The place in New York to snap up the perfect white shirt.

Betsey Johnson: 1060 Madison Avenue. Tel 212-734 1257, www.betseyjohnson.com. Subway 6 to 77th Street.
Eclectic mix of rock chick chic and artsy boudoir designs.

Billy Martin's Western Wear: 220 East 60th Street. Tel 212-861 3100, www.billymartin.com. Subway 6 to 68th Street.
Everything for the posh cowboy.

Calvin Klein: See page 93.

Cantaloup: 1036 Lexington Avenue at 74th Street. Tel 212-249 3566. Subway 6 to 77th Street.
This candy-coloured boutique is a magnet for trendspotters thanks to its display rails filled with edgy designers like True Religion.

D&G: 825 Madison Avenue between 68th and 69th Streets. Tel 212-249 4100,

TOP FIVE STORES FOR MENSWEAR

Ascot Chang: 7 West 57th Street between 5th and 6th Avenues. Tel 212-759 3333, www.ascotchang.com. Subway F to 57th Street.
Known as New York's finest shirtmaker, the store also makes suits and overcoats too. It's a real investment buy as Ascot Chang items don't date, last for ever – but they are pricey. If you're not feeling flush, there are off-the-rack pieces too, from shirts to pyjamas.

Brooks Brothers: 346 Madison Avenue between 44th and 45th Streets. Tel 212-682 8800, www.brooksbrothers.com. Subway S, 4, 5, 6, 7 to 42nd Street/Grand Central.
A very famous American label known for its preppy and Ivy League type customers. It offers a great range of luxurious suits, shirts and jackets along with cashmere sweaters, polo shirts and blazers. This is the place to come if you're looking for sophisticated menswear with a unique American style.

Duncan Quinn: 8 Spring Street between Bowery and Elizabeth Streets. Tel 212-226 7030, www.duncanquinn.com. Subway C, E to Spring Street.
For those that believe exciting clothes shopping isn't just for women. This menswear treasure is packed full of brightly patterned suits, ties and shirts all expertly crafted. There are also some excellent shoes on offer.

Sean: 224 Columbus Avenue between 70 and 71st Streets. Tel 212-769 1489, www.seanstore.com. Subway 1, 2, 3, 9 to 72nd Street.
Posh menswear that's just the right side of cool. Think well-made wool suits, brightly coloured shirts and silk ties. There's some younger, funkier bits too such as parkas and corduroy trousers.

Sean John: 475 5th Avenue at East 41st Street. Tel: 212-220 2633, www.seanjohn.com. Subway B, D, F, V to 42nd Street.
Lots of sportswear for the hip-hop look, but plenty of other bits to ensure you look cool even at special occasions, such as white linen suits and pink polo shirts. There's also toiletries, ties, watches and belts for a complete bling style.

www.dolcegabbana.it. Subway 6 to 68th Street.
Shop for jeans, suits, bags and dresses to a background of (loud) pop music.

Diesel: 770 Lexington Avenue at 60th Street. Tel 212-308 0055, www.diesel.com. Subway N, R to Lexington Avenue 4, 5, 6 to 59th Street.
A massive store in which you'll find everything from denim to vinyl clothing, shoes and accessories.

Donna Karan: See page 93.

Emporio Armani: 601 Madison Avenue between 57th and 58th Streets. Tel 212-317 0800. Subway N, R to 59th Street.
Armani's line for younger people.

Giorgio Armani: 760 Madison Avenue at 65th Street. Tel 212-988 9191, www.giorgioarmani.com. Subway 6 to 68th Street.
A huge boutique, which sells all three of Armani's lines. Come here to find well-tailored classics.

Nicole Farhi: 10 East 60th Street near Madison Avenue. Tel 212-223 8811, www.nicolefarhi.com. Subway 4, 5, 6 to 59th Street.
Elegant, simple designs for men and women. It also sells homeware.

Prada: 841 Madison Avenue at 70th Street. Tel 212-327 4200, www.prada.com. Subway 6 to 68th Street.
Check out the season's look before you head for the bargain basement stores.

Ralph Lauren: 867 Madison Avenue at East 72nd Street. Tel 212-606 2100, www.polo.com. Subway 6 to 68th Street.
Worth a visit just to see the store – it's in an old Rhinelander mansion and is decorated with everything from Oriental rugs to riding whips, leather chairs and English paintings. The clothes are of excellent quality too.

D&G

TOP FIVE PLACES TO GET YOUR CLOTHES MADE-TO-MEASURE

Frida's Closet: Carroll Gardens, 296 Smith Street, Brooklyn. Subway F, G, 2, 3, 4, 5 to Preisdent Street. Tel 718-855 0311, www.fridascloset.com.
An amazing store run by Sandra Paez who has based her shop on the style of inspirational Mexican artist Frida Kahlo; think long peasant skirts, soft blouses and gorgeous leather bags. Dresses, skirts and blouses are custom made for you in the shop.

Lee Anderson: 23 East 67th Street between 5th and Madison Avenues. Tel 212-772 2563. Subway 4, 5, 6 to 68th Street.
This is where the businesswomen of New York go to get their classic suits, separates and eveningwear. You can have your order custom made or choose off-the-rack if time is short.

Mary Adams: 138 Ludlow Street between Stanton and Rivington Streets. Tel 212-473 0237, www.maryadamsthedress.com. Subway F, J, M, Z at Delancey Street/Essex Street.
A fascinating shop bursting with dresses full of lace, ruffles, satin and feathers. You'll feel like you've stepped into the Moulin Rouge wardrobe and you can even get your own custom-made creation to wow your friends back home.

Piccione: 116 East 57th Street (2nd floor) between Park and Lexington Avenues. Tel 212-421 2828. Subway 4, 5, 6 to Lexington Avenue/59th Street.
The Italian master of tailoring will make made-to-measure suits for men and women using the finest cloths from the best mills in the world. Be warned, prices start from around $3,000 and deliveries can take five weeks.

Ripplu: 575 5th Avenue between 46th and 47th Streets. Tel 212-599 2223, www.rippllu.com. Subway S, 4, 5, 6, 7 to 42nd Street/5th Avenue.
Nip and tuck too scary and expensive? Never fear, your prayers for a better bod have been answered courtesy of Ripplu, the New York women's secret lingerie store. Their custom made bras and pants miraculously lift and reshape those wobbly bits; they even offer free alterations.

WEST VILLAGE

Darling: 1 Horatio Street at 8th Avenue. Tel 646-336 6966. Subway A, C, E to 14th Street.
Ann French Emonts fills this small boutique with her own designs plus choice pieces from other top-notch womens wear designers. Thursday nights are popular as the store stays open until 10pm and customers are offered champagne while they browse.

Girlshop: 819 Washington Street between Little West 12th and Gansevoort Streets. Tel 212-255 4985, www.girlshop.com. Subway A, C, E to 14th Street.
Fun, stylish clothes and accessories from lesser-known designers.

Lulu Guinness: 394 Bleecker Street between 11th and Perry Streets. Tel 212-367 2120, www.luluguinness.com. Subway A, C, E to 14th Street; L to 8th Avenue; 1, 2 to Christopher Street.
Our own home-grown Brit girl Lulu, who started out in Notting Hill, West London, has established herself in the Big Apple. Her vintage-inspired accessories include embroidered and appliquéd bags and purses.

If you think you can get it all in the UK, think again – Lulu's produced some fab bags just for New Yorkers.

VINTAGE FASHION

EAST VILLAGE

Cronick Valentine: 324 East 9th Street between 1st and 2nd Avenue. Tel 212-228 7767, www.cronickvalentine.com. Subway L to 1st Avenue.
Vintage T-shirts rush out of this store, along with accessories like luggage and ties. As an added extra, you can bring in your old T-shirts and have them made into a handbag, cuff, iPod holder or even a duvet cover, from $50 to $150.

★★★★★ BRIT TIP ★★★★
★ For the complete lowdown on what ★
★ New York has to offer shoppers, log ★
★ on to www.newyorkmetro.com/ ★
★ shopping which gives comprehensive ★
★ listings by neighbourhood or ★
★ store type. ★
★★★★★★★★★★★★★★★★★★★★★★★★★

Love Saves The Day: 119 2nd Avenue at East 7th Street. Tel 212-228 3802. Subway 6 to Astor Place.
Currently in the process of moving the store, so be sure to ring up before you make your way to check out the objects of real retro desire such as biker jackets last worn by fans of Evil Knievel or Barry Sheene. As well as clothes, there are gems such as 1950s' *Playboy* magazines and hardback manuals of John Travolta's work-out routines for *Saturday Night Fever*.

Tokio: 7 East 7th Street between 1st and 2nd Avenues. Tel 212-353 8443, www.tokio7.com. Subway 6 to Astor Place; N, R to 8th Street.
Plenty of vintage and downtown designer gear to choose from here. Particularly good collection of Japanese designers.

Tokyo Joe: 334 East 11th Street between 1st and 2nd Avenues. Tel 212-473 0724. Subway 6 to Astor Place.
The pre-worn designer offerings are advertised on a blackboard outside the shop every day.

Village Scandal: 19 East 7th Street between 2nd and 3rd Avenues. Tel 212-460 9358. Subway 6 to Astor Place.
A must-visit for vintage addicts as this retro store is packed full of cool hats and accessories from floppy Bianca Jagger-esque designs to trendy bucket caps. It's open until midnight.

GREENWICH VILLAGE

Stella Dallas: 218 Thompson Street between Bleecker and West 3rd Streets. Tel 212-674 0447. Subway A, C, E, F, V, S to West 4th Street.
An amazing vintage shop full of girly chiffon and other items.

MEATPACKING DISTRICT

Cherry: 19 Eighth Avenue between West 12th and Jane Streets. Tel 212-924 1410. Subway A, C, E to 14th Street.
A cool vintage shop, which stocks all manner of goodies and shoes dating back as far as the 1940s. It's popular for it's one-of-a-kind pieces such as a cute Pucci top or Versace gown. You'll also find lots of fab accessories here, from sunglasses to headscarves. Be sure to leave at least a couple of hours free, for serious shoppers have been known to disappear for an afternoon in this vintage Mecca.

NOLITA

Screaming Mimi: 382 Lafayette Street between 4th and Great Jones Streets. Tel 212-677 6464, www.screaming mimis.com. Subway N, R to NYU 8th Street.
Everything from polyester dresses to denim shirts and tropical prints from the 1960s. There are also jewellery, sunglasses and other accessories, plus a home department upstairs in which to browse.

★ If you need shoe repairs while you're
★ in NY, go to Angelo Shoe Repair at
★ 666 5th Avenue (lower level) at
★ 53rd Street. Tel 212-757 6364, open
★ 7am–6.30pm.

SOHO

Transfer International: 594 Broadway, Suite 1002, between Prince and Houston Streets. Tel 212-941 5472, www.trans ferny.com. Subway N, R to Prince Street.
Specialises in Gucci, Prada, Chanel and Hermès – one of the best places to buy post-worn designer clothes and accessories. They also carry agnès b and Betsey Johnson.

TRIBECA

Geminola: 41 Perry Street near 7th Avenue. Tel 212-675 1994, www.geminola.com. Subway 1, 9 to Christopher Street.
Owner Lorraine Kirke travels the world for vintage fabrics, then reworks and dyes them to create gorgeous and unique clothing. Skirts from $165 and accessories and belts from Afghanistan and handbags from India at around $295.

★ The Americans still measure in
★ feet and inches – good news for
★ older Brits.

UNION SQUARE

Cheap Jack's: 303 5th Avenue at East 31st Street. Tel 212-777 9564, www.cheapjacks.com. Subway N, R, W to 28th/34th Streets.
A huge selection, but on the pricey side despite the name!

JEWELLERY

Want a true sparkler? Then look no further than the 47th Street Diamond District where the little gems are traded, cut and set. More than 2,600 independent businesses are to be found in a single block between 5th Avenue and the Avenue of the Americas (6th Avenue). Many have booths in jewellery exchanges such as the World's Largest Jewellery Exchange at 55 West 47th Street (tel 212-719 5235, www.jewelry55exchange.com). Jack of Diamonds (52 West 47th Street, tel 212-869 7272, www.jackofdiamondsintl.com) has everything from loose diamonds and strings of pearls to watches.

Chelsea

DVVS: 263A 19th Street near 8th Avenue. Tel 212-366 4888, www.dvvs.com. Subway C, E to 23rd Street.
Modern, unusual jewellery from contemporary designers. Prices range from around $1,000 to $2,000.

Lower East Side

Daniel Espinosa: 250 Elizabeth Street near Houston Street. Tel 212-966 4999, www.danielespinosa.com. Subway F, V to 2nd Avenue.
Individual, handmade pieces that range from $80 to $2,000.

Midtown

Agatha: 611 Madison Avenue at 58th Street. Tel 212-758 4301, www.agatha.fr. Subway 4, 5, 6 to 59th Street.
Affordable, fashionable trinkets, $200 or less, like charm bracelets and chunky necklaces.

Asprey: 723 5th Avenue at 56th. Tel 212-688 1811, www.asprey.com. Subway N, R to 5th Avenue.
Pricey, bling-bling jewellery beloved of stars, not least because boho Brit Jade Jagger now has a hand in its designs.

Graff: 721 Madison Avenue near 64th Street. Tel 212-355 9292, www.graffdiamonds.com. Subway 6 to 68th Street.
Some of the best diamonds that you're ever likely to come across are here, to suit every type of price range, from tiny 1-carat to 100-carat yellow diamonds.

H Stern: 645 5th Avenue near 51st Avenue. Tel 212-688 0300, www.hstern.net. Subway E, V to 5th Avenue.
One of New York's most prestigious jewellers.

Tiffany & Co: 727 5th Avenue. Tel 212-755 8000, www.tiffany.com. Subway N, R to 5th Avenue.
Few can resist popping in to sneak a look at the store that featured so highly in the classic film *Breakfast at Tiffany's* starring Audrey Hepburn. If you can't afford the $2,000-plus diamond necklaces and bracelets, you can always fork out for a $100 keyring.

SoHo

Fragments: 116 Prince Street between Greene and Wooster Streets. Tel 212-334 9588, www.fragments.com. Subway A, C, E to Spring Street.
A hit with the fashion crowd keen to snap up the works of between 60 and 100 designers that are on sale at any one time.

Lulu Guinness

UPPER EAST SIDE

Gentlemen's Resale: 322 East 81st Street between 1st and 2nd Avenues. Tel 212-734 2739, www.resaleclothing.net. Subway 6 to 77th Street.
Top-notch designer suits at a fraction of the original price.

BEAUTY STORES AND SPAS

Everyone knows New York is the place to find fabulous fashion bargains, but not so well known are the great beauty buys to be had, too. In the first instance, most make-up – particularly the gorgeous American brands such as Philosophy, Hard Candy, Benefit and Laura Mercier – is a lot cheaper in the Big Apple. The exceptions are the 'prestige' French brands such as Décleor, Christian Dior and Chanel, which are generally cheaper in the UK (they have to be imported to America).

Most brands have dedicated stores in Manhattan, the majority around SoHo and its environs of NoLiTa, north SoHo and West Village.

BEAUTY

MIDTOWN

Mary Quant Colour Concept Store: 520 Madison Avenue at 53rd Street. Tel 212-980 7577, www.maryquant.co.uk/ny.htm. Subway 6 to 51st Street.
Groovy cosmetics brand from the queen of 1960s' cool. It's cheap and cheerful and comes in daisy-plastered packaging.

Sephora: 597 5th Avenue between East 48th and 49th Streets. Tel 212-980 6534, www.sephora.com. Subway B, D F, V to 47th–50th Streets/Rockefeller Center.
The Rockefeller Center is home to the flagship Manhattan Sephora store packed with beauty products and smelling like a perfumerie.

SOHO

To get to SoHo use either the N, R subway lines to Prince Street or the 6, C, E to Spring Street.

Aveda: 233 Spring Street between 6th Avenue and Varick Street. Tel 212-807 1492, www.aveda.com.
As befits the beauty line entirely based on the gentle and nurturing Ayurvedic system, this is a tranquil setting in which to choose your favourite hair and skincare products.

★ Stores in SoHo tend to open some time between 10am and noon and stay open until 7pm Monday to Saturday, while most open from noon to 6pm on Sundays.

Made from natural plant and flower extracts, Aveda's holistic approach is carried through all products including the make-up ranges and massage oils

5S: 98 Prince Street between Greene and Mercer Streets. Tel 212-925 7880.
A make-up and skincare line by Japanese company Shiseido, the products reflect the ancient philosophies of the islands and are organised into five senses of well being including energising and nurturing.

Face Stockholm: 110 Prince Street at Greene Street. Tel 212-966 9110, www.facestockholm.com.
Fans of the cosmetic company can go mad in this glittery emporium, filled as it is with the full range of colours and brushes. You can have your make-up done here or take a lesson. Phone for an appointment or just drop in.

★ Tracie Martyn is considered by many to be the best facialist in New York, using a massage technique that some – including Liv Tyler and Kate Winslet - say can leave you looking 10 years younger. Tel 212-206 9333, www.traciemartyn.com.

Fresh: 57 Spring Street between Lafayette and Mulberry. Tel 212-925 0099, www.fresh.com.
Soaps, lotions and potions with lovely fragrances based on natural ingredients from the Boston-based company. It even has a Memoirs of a Geisha collection, inspired by the film.

Kiehl's: 109 3rd Avenue between 13th and 14th Streets. Tel 212-677 3171, www.kiehls.com.
One of New York's most famous establishments, the crowds still flock to this

Kiehl's

emporium in the Union Square area for its luxurious moisturisers and lip balms.

MAC: 113 Spring Street between Greene and Mercer Streets. Tel 212-334 4641, www.maccosmetics.com.
As with many of the beauty boutiques in SoHo, the wonder of this flagship store for MAC is as much in the architecture, lighting and displays as in the products. In fact, it's such a wonderful place, it has become a big favourite with celebs such as Britney Spears, Gwyneth Paltrow, kd lang and Alanis Morissette.

It sells all MAC products including the MAC Pro range used by make-up artists on fashion shows and movie shoots, which are available in only a few of their outlets around the globe.

During your visit, you can either plump for a 45-minute makeover for $40, complete with useful tips, or turn up with nothing but foundation on your face and let the artists finish off your make-up for free.

Make-Up Forever: 409 West Broadway between Prince and Spring Streets. Tel 212-941 9337, www.makeupforever.com.
A French line specialising in ultra-bright colours thanks to the triple pigment formula used in all its lipsticks and eyeshadows. This is a funky little shop decked out to look like the make-up area of a film set. The well-trained staff are happy to advise on colours and products, while a $50 makeover is redeemable against purchases including the company's best-selling silicon-based foundation.

SCO: 5th Floor, 584 Broadway near Prince Street. Tel 212-966 3011, www.scocare.com. Subway N, R to Prince Street.
Stands for Skin-Care Options, of which there are many. Lots of custom-blended concoctions including face products and sun blocks.

Sephora: 555 Broadway between Prince and Spring Streets. Tel 212-625 1309, www.sephora.com.
One of many New York outlets of this pristine, clean French beauty chain, which has become a sure-fire hit thanks to its incredibly broad range, sparkling presentations and low-key staff who can provide plenty of help and advice when requested. This is the best place to get your favourite American brands such as Benefit, Hard Candy, Nars and Philosophy.

Shu Uemura: 121 Greene Street between Prince and Houston Streets. Tel 212-979 5500, www.shuuemura-usa.com.
Like MAC, Shu Uemura is another make-up range much loved by industry professionals thanks to its quality and texture. The Japanese cosmetics company, based on Eastern philosophies, is famous for its colour and tools – this is the place to come for everything to do with make-up from brushes to eyelash curlers.

A quiet space, the boutique has an open, friendly atmosphere that makes browsing here a delight. You can also get a free 30-minute make-up lesson from one of the professional make-up artists on Thursdays and Fridays 11am–5pm or on Saturdays 11am–1.30pm. The Saturday lessons are very popular, though – they are usually booked up a month in advance – so go in the week.

UPPER EAST SIDE

Face Stockholm: 687 Madison Avenue at 62nd Street. Tel 212-207 8833, www.facestockholm.com. Subway 4, 5, 6 to 68th Street.
Another outlet of the fab beauty company. You'll also find another one of these boutiques on the Upper West Side at 226 Columbus Avenue between 70th and 71st Streets (tel 212-769 1420).

Fresh: 922 Madison Avenue between 73rd and 74th Streets. Tel 212-396 4545, www.fresh.com. Subway 6 to 68th Street.
A Boston-based company specialising in beauty products made from natural ingredients such as honey, milk, soy, sugar and even Umbrian clay. Other branches can be found at 388 Bleecker Street in West Village (tel 917-408 1850), 1367 Third Avenue (tel 212-585 3400) and 872 Broadway (tel 212-477 1100).

L'Occitane: 1046 Madison Avenue at 80th Street. Tel 212-639 9185, www.loccitane.com. Subway 6 to 77th Street.
Ultra-luxurious bath and beauty products from the famous French company. Also branches at 510 Madison at 52nd Street and 1288 Madison at 92nd Street.

WEST VILLAGE

Aedes de Venustas: 9 Christopher Street near 6th Avenue. Tel 212-206 8674, www.aedes.com. Subway 1, 9 to Christopher Street.
Sublime emporium where you can pick up almost impossible-to-find skincare products.

HANDS AND FEET

MIDTOWN
Pinky Nail Fifty Six Corp: 240 East 56th Street. Tel 212-446 9553.
A fab chain of nail salons where manicures start at $10 and pedicures at $20. This location is particularly well known for its cleanliness and friendliness.

SOHO
Jin Soon Natural Hand & Foot Spa: 56 East 4th Street between Bowery and Second Avenue. Tel 212-473 2047. Subway F, V to Lower East Side/Second Avenue.
When in town, actress Julianne Moore always books a full foot treatment with Jin Soon Choi. Expect rose petals and botanicals with the ultra pampering $30 pedicure – a basic manicure costs just $15. The tiny NoLiTa spa became such a mecca for celebs and those wanting perfect hands and feet that a second, larger, Jin Soon Spa has been established in the West Village at 23 Jones Street between Bleecker and West 4th Streets. Tel 212-229 1070. Check out the 'floating room' where gorgeous orange silk hangs over a small pond.

★★★★ **BRIT TIP** ★★★★

For excellent manicures with no frills for just $5, head to the East Village where a plethora of salons dot the streets of Marks Place and 2nd Avenue. Generally New Yorkers pay around $25 for a manicure or a pedicure.

Rescue Nail Spa: 21 Cleveland Place between Kenmare and Spring Streets. Tel 212-431 3805, www.rescuebeauty.com. Subway 6 to Spring Street.
Famous for intensive treatments, this nail specialist also has an outlet in NoLiTa at 8 Centre Market Place between Grand and Broome Streets (tel 212-431 0449) and 2nd Floor, 32 Gansevoort Street, between Greenwich and Hudson Streets (tel 212-206 6409).

UPPER EAST SIDE
Bloomie Nail Corp: 1320 Madison Avenue at 92nd Street. Tel 212-426 5566. Subway 6 to 96th Street.
Another city-wide nail chain where no appointments are necessary (see also Pinky's), here you can have anything from your basic manicures to paraffin pedicures and massages.

HAIR

MIDTOWN
Borjo Colour Studios: 118 57th Street near Park Avenue. Tel 212-308 3232. Subway 4, 5, 6 to 59th Street.
Excellent cuts, highlights and colours as well as a good reputation for eyebrow shaping. Treat yourself to a consultation over a glass of wine.

The Ouidad Salon: Fourth Floor, 37 West 57th Street between 5th and 6th Avenues. Tel 212-888 3288, www.ouidad.com.
Named after the owner, this hair salon specialises in cutting and styling curly hair. In fact, they take curly hair so seriously you won't be allowed in without it! The dedicated team spends up to four hours styling and taming your locks and the salon has its own range of products. This new premises has the feel of a Soho loft, with faux snakeskin couches to boot.

★★★★ **BRIT TIP** ★★★★

For the best shave a man can have in New York take a seat and join the queue in one of three The Art of Shaving Barber shops (Tel 305-593 0667, www.theartofshaving.com) located around the city. You can get every type of shave imaginable, including a hot, straight-edged Royal Shave, at these Victorian-style outlets.

SOHO
To get to SoHo use either the N, R subway lines to Prince Street or the 6, C, E to Spring Street.

Devachan: 2nd Floor, 558 Broadway between Prince and Spring Streets. Tel 212-274 8686, www.devachansalon.com.
Small salon where celebs come to get perfect locks and an amazing scalp massage. It also doubles as a spa.

Prive: The Soho Grand, 310 West Broadway between Canal and Grand Streets. Tel 212-274 8888.
Home of Laurent D, who looks after Gwyneth's hair when she's in town. His haircuts start at around $200.

WEST VILLAGE
Gemini Salon & Spa: 547 Hudson Street between Perry and Charles Street. Tel 212-675 4546. Subway 1, 9 to Christopher Street. If you have wild, untameable hair or you just want your locks to be sleeker, then book an appointment to test out this salon's patented Opti-smooth straightening treatment for yourself.

PERFUMES

MIDTOWN
Bond No 9 New York: 680 Madison Avenue at 61st Street. Tel 212-838 2780. Subway 4, 5, 6 to 59th Street.
Delicious scents with witty names like Chelsea Flowers, Gramercy Park and Madison Soirée. Or you can have your own custom blended. Branches also at 897 Madison Avenue (tel 212-794 4480) and 9 Bond Street (tel 212-228 1940).

Caswell-Massey: 518 Lexington Avenue at East 48th Street. Tel 212-755 2254, www.caswellmassey.com. Subway 6 to 51st Street.
An apothecary founded in 1752, which once provided perfumes for George Washington and Dolly Madison. Today it continues to make a glorious range of floral scents such as freesia, lilac and rose. You can buy gift sets or individual bottles.

UPPER EAST SIDE
Caron: 675 Madison Avenue near 61st Street. Tel 212-319 4888. Subway 4, 5, 6 to 59th Street.
The complete range of glitzy, crystal-bottled Caron fragrances, from $80 upwards, can be bought here.

SPAS

CHELSEA
Nickel: 77 8th Avenue at 14th Street. Tel 212-242 3203, www.nickelspanyc.com. Subway A, 9, A , C, E to 19th Street.
One of the only men-only spas in the city – in a chic, two-storey haven – which offers a wide range of treatments from massages (from $60) to facials and waxing. Book at least four weeks in advance.

Sam-C Spa and Margolin Wellness Center: 2nd Floor, 166 5th Avenue at 21st Street. Tel 212-675 9355.
A doctor-meets-spa centre in Chelsea, owned and run by chiropractor Dr Margolin and celebrated masseur Sam-C. Famous treatments include the hydrotherapy tub in which you are immersed in a large, very hot tub of pulsating water while a therapist massages your head and applies cold compresses, and the Sam-C Massage, a unique, intensive body massage. Other treatments include chiropractic, reflexology, acupuncture, body scrubs, steam shower and mud wraps.

MIDTOWN
Affinia Wellness Spa: 125 East 50th Street at Lexington Avenue (The Benjamin Hotel). Tel 212-715 2517, www.affinia.com. Subway 6, 5 to 51st Street.
A tiny but perfect spa where you can have candlelit massages, hot-salt body scrubs and self-tanning treatments. Also at Oasis Day Spa, Affinia Dumont, 150 East 34th Street. Tel 212-545 5254.

Avon Center Spa: 6th Floor, Trump Tower, 725 5th Avenue between 56th and 57th Streets. Tel 212-755 2866.
An incredible space and a wonderful opportunity to enter the spanking Trump Tower for a face and body treatment. Eliza Petrescu is famous for her eyebrow waxings, so book early.

Bliss 57: 3rd floor, 19 East 57th Street between 5th and Madison Avenues. Tel 212-219 8970, www.blissworld.com. Subway N, R to 59th Street.
Sarah Jessica Parker's favourite spa, which also sells its own skincare range, BlissLabs. Hangover herbie anyone?

Elizabeth Arden Red Door Salon & Spa: 691 5th Avenue at 54th Street. Tel 212-546 0200, www.reddoorspas.com. Subway E, V to 5th Avenue/53rd Street.
For the ultimate beautifier nothing beats the Pomegranate Warm Stone Facial, which promises to firm up skin and deflect damage-inducing free radicals in a trice with the help of a pomegranate paste.

Georgette Klinger Salon: 501 Madison Ave between 52nd and 53rd Streets. Tel 212-838 3200, www.georgetteklinger.com. Subway 6 to 51st Street; E, V to 5th Avenue/53rd Street.
Georgette is one of New York's most famous facialists and the foundation of her work is purification. Each facial is comprehensive and tailor-made for individual needs, starting with a thorough skin analysis. Deep cleansing and steaming rid the skin of underlying impurities, a gentle massage adds skin tone and individualised face

masks finish off the refining process.

Green Tea Nail & Spa: 141 West 35th Street between Broadway and 7th Avenue. Tel 212-564 6971. Subway A, C, E to 34th Street/Penn Station.
Nestled in the 34th Street district right next to Macy's is this large Japanese spa in which you are served antioxidant-rich green tea in a clean, minimalist environment. Treatments include waxing, facials, manicures, pedicures and massages. For the perfect pick-me-up-in-an-instant opt for the 10-minute neck massage for $10.

J Sisters International: 35 West 57th Street at 6th Avenue. Tel 212-750 2485, www.jsisters.com. Subway N, Q, R, W to 57th Street.
Family-run beauty centre famous for its extremely thorough Brazilian waxes. You can also have your make-up, nails and hair done here.

La Prairie Spa: The Ritz Carlton Hotel, 50 Central Park South at 6th Avenue. Tel 212-521 6135, www.ritzcarlton.com. Subway F, N, R, Q, W to 57th Street.
An extremely high-end spa beloved by celebrities. The Caviar Firming Facial is the signature treatment and rings in at around $260 a go.

Physical Advantage: Penthouse, 139 East 57th Street at Lexington Avenue. Tel 212-460 1879. Subway 4, 5, 6 to 59th Street.
This isn't the type of spa where you're going to get reiki and reflexology; it's a no-nonsense massage centre often patronised by professional athletes and dancers. The ideal place if you want a treatment without the frills.

SOHO
To get to SoHo use either the N, R subway lines to Prince Street or the 6, C, E to Spring Street.

Acqua Beauty Bar: 7 East 14th Street between 5th Avenue and Union Square West. Tel 212-620 4329, www.acquabeautybar.com.
This hip beauty parlour in the ultra trendy Union Square area offers a full menu of nail, body and face treatments from just $12 for a manicure and $60 for a Bye Bye Eye Bags facial – or splash out on the works for $150!

Amore Pacific: 114 Spring Street between Mercer and Greene Streets. Tel 212-966 0400, www.amorepacific.com.

A Feng Shui influenced spa that uses Korean AP products and where you can have a massage according to your elemental disposition – wood, metal, earth, water or fire.

Bliss Soho: 2nd Floor, 568 Broadway between Houston and Prince Streets. Tel 212-219 8970, www.blissworld.com.
One of New York's most famous spas, this is the place where you can get it all and in the fastest possible time. You can have a manicure at the same time as your facial and even an underarm wax too. Therein lies its down side though – for some, it can seem too swift and impersonal.

Inspiration – a Rose Alcido Day Spa: Suite 1116, 1133 Broadway between 25th and 26th Streets. Tel 212-243 0432, www.rosealcido.com.
A teeny space that's become famous for Rose's signature Golden-Spoon facial. Following a full facial, two hot spoons are used to massage the face, giving an intense, penetrating treatment.

★★★★ BRIT TIP ★★★★
★ The best anti-aging facial in the Big ★
★ Apple is the Intense Pulsed Light ★
★ treatment at Shizuka spa in ★
★ Midtown East (7 West 51st Street, ★
★ 6th Floor. Tel 212-644 7400, ★
★ www.shizukany.com). ★

John Masters Organic Spa: 77 Sullivan Street between Spring and Broome Streets. Tel 212-343 9590, www.johnmasters.com.
Outstanding full-body massages and facials for those who like to ensure all aspects of their life are organic.

Ling Skin Care: 191 Prince Street at Sullivan Street. Tel 212-982 8833, www.lingskincare.com.
Not big on pampering, so don't expect scented candles, white fluffy robes and Feng

Sephora

Shui, but extremely good facials from $115 that are considered the best in town by some New Yorkers, including the salon's celebrity clientele.

Maximus Soho: 15 Mercer Street between Grand and Canal Streets. Tel 516-333 4083. Subway A, C, E, N, Q, R, W to Canal Street. Treatment rooms that change colour every few seconds for mood enhancement is just one of the reason's to visit this lovely, watercentric spa.

The Mezzanine Spa at Soho Integrative Health Centre: 62 Crosby Street between Broome and Spring Streets. Tel 212-431 1600, www.mezzaninespa.com. Dr Laurie Polis founded this tiny spa at her office. Body treatments include volcanic mud therapy, while the Diamond Peel involves suction and microcrystals to exfoliate the face.

Monique K Skin Care: 345 East 9th Street between Avenues A and D. Tel 212-673 2041, www.moniquek.com/facials. For an excellent deal on superb facials, head to this East Village hideaway. Owned by Monique K, once head facialist at the famous Georgette Klinger Salon (page 106), you get the same quality facials at much better prices.

Oasis Day Spa: 2nd Floor, 108 East 16th Street between Irving Place and Union Square East. Tel 212-254 7722, www.oasisdayspanyc.com. Subway L, N, Q, R, W, 4, 5, 6 to Union Square/14th Street. Get off the beaten track for a truly relaxing experience at one of New York's best-kept secrets. Here you'll escape all elements of hustle and bustle in a sweet-smelling space where you are given your own massage slippers and a comfy robe. Fab therapies

TOP FIVE SPAS FOR MINOR COSMETIC SURGERY

You're visiting one of the leading cities in the world for beauty treatments, including minor cosmetic surgeries such as laser eye treatment or Botox. Many tourists even combine a long weekend of shopping with a trip to a clinic so that they can return to the UK looking 10 years younger!

If you're considering a minor treatment, make sure that the spa or beauty centre is registered, book well in advance as they tend to get booked up quickly, and be sure to have a consultation prior to any treatment so that you understand exactly what you're getting. Below are five highly rated spas regularly used by New Yorkers, from celebrities to Upper East Side ladies who lunch.

Midtown

Skinklinic: 800B 5th Avenue at 61st Street. Tel 212-521 3100, www.skinklinic.com. Subway 4, 5, 6 to 59th Street.
Nurses, practitioners and dermatologists are on hand at this no-nonsense clinic to treat a wide variety of skin issues, from wrinkles to spots. Treatments include glycolic peels, botox, microdermabrasion, beta for acne, and laser hair removal.

Smooth Synergy: 686 Lexington Avenue at East 57th Street. Tel 212-397 0111, www.smoothsynergy.com. Subway 4, 5, 6 to 59th Street.
Laser hair removal, microdermabrasion, botox, vein therapy and glycolic peels are just some of the many treatments on offer at this highly regarded spa.

Upper East Side

Ajune: 1294 3rd Avenue at 74th Street. Tel 212-628 0044, www.ajune.com. Subway 6 to 77th Street.
Experts in laser wrinkle reduction, collagen implants and Botox, all administered in a tranquil setting with slate floors and wooden features.

Dr Ronald Sherman/Trish McEvoy Skincare Centre: 4th Floor, 800A 5th Avenue at 61st Street. Tel 212-758 7790. Subway N, R to 5th Avenue.
Laser hair removal, botox and skin cancer examinations can be had at the make-up guru and top dermatologist's skincare mecca.

Howard Sobel Skin & Spa: 960 Park Avenue at 82nd Street. Tel 212-288 0060, www.drsobel.com. Subway 4, 5, 6 to 86th Street.
Award-winning specialists in botox treatments.

include a deep-penetrating Lava Stone Massage for $100, or an exquisite facial with customised face mask and warm hand mitts for $95.

Prema Nolita: 252 Elizabeth Street between Houston and Prince Streets. Tel 212-226 3972. Subway 6 to Spring Street. Thought to be the smallest spa in town, Celeste Induddi and her two partners have just one treatment room, but sell their own Prema line plus celeb faves Jurlique and Anne Semonin.

SoHo Sanctuary: 3rd Floor, 119 Mercer Street at Princes Street. Tel 212-334 5550, www.sohosanctuary.com. Fabulous massages in this mellow favourite of the fashion pack. There are also yoga and Pilates classes plus a steam room.

ANTIQUES AND FLEA MARKETS

In balmy weather, nothing beats strolling through the treasure trove of antiques, collectables and one-off pieces at any of New York's outdoor markets or in some of the unusual individual shops.

CHELSEA
Adrian Ruehl: 9th Avenue at Gansevoort Street. Tel 212-242 2576, www.adrianruehl.com (currently under construction). Subway 1, 2, 3, A, C, E to 14th Street; L to 8th Avenue. Packed full of 19th-century European antiques from chandeliers to candlesticks.

Chelsea Antiques Building: 110 West 25th Street between 6th and 7th Avenues. Tel 212-929 0909. Subway F, V to 23rd Street. This 12-storey building houses 90 galleries of antiques and collectables with merchandise ranging from Japanese textiles to vintage phonographs and radios.

The Garage: 112 West 25th Street between 6th and 7th Avenues. Tel 212-647 0707. Subway F, V to 23rd Street. The Garage is exactly that – a two-storey parking garage that transforms into another bustling venue at the weekend.

The Showplace: 40 West 25th Street. Tel 212-741 8520. Subway F, V to 23rd Street. An indoor extension of the outdoor market (open at weekends only), with a small café downstairs.

EAST VILLAGE
Irreplaceable Artefacts: 216 East 125th Street between 2nd and 3rd Avenues. Tel

212-777 2900. An excellent selection of actual architectural bits and bobs.

GREENWICH VILLAGE
Alan Moss: 436 Lafayette Street near Astor Place. Tel 212-473 1310, www.alan mossny.com. Subway 6 to Astor Place. Glass gems and interesting lighting from the mid-20th century.

HELL'S KITCHEN
Annex/Hell's Kitchen Flea Market: 39th Street between 9th and 10th Avenues. Tel 212-243 5343, www.hellskitchenfleamarket.com. Subway A, C, E or 1, 2, 3, 9 to 34th/42nd Streets. Now includes The Annex, America's most famous outdoor market, where celebrities browse through vintage clothing, furniture, pottery, glassware, jewellery and art. Get there early for the best finds. Weekends only.

MADISON SQUARE
Old Print Shop: 150 Lexington Avenue between East 29th and East 30th Streets. Tel 212-683 3950, www.oldprintshop.com. Subway 6 to 33rd Street. This is the place to search out Americana up to the 1950s.

MIDTOWN EAST
Lillian Nassau: 220 East 57th Street between 2nd and 3rd Avenues. Tel 212-759 6062, www.lilliannassau.com. Subway 4, 5, 6 to 59th Street. Come here for art nouveau lamps and glassware, especially original Tiffanys.

★ ★ ★ ★ **BRIT TIP** ★ ★ ★ ★
★   ★
★   Check out www.fleamarket   ★
★   guide.com for a list of flea markets,   ★
★   what they sell and special fairs and   ★
★   events around the city.   ★
★ ★

Manhattan Arts & Antiques Center: 1050 2nd Avenue between East 55th and East 56th Streets. Tel 212-355 4400, www.the-maac.com. Subway 4, 5, 6, to 59th Street, F, N, R, W to Lexington Avenue.

SOHO
Coconut Company: 131 Greene Street near Prince Street. Tel 212-539 1940. Subway N, R to Prince Street. A fascinating, eclectic mix of 19th- and

SHOPPING AND BEAUTY

20th-century antiques, from photographs and books to coffee tables.

The SoHo Antiques Fair: Broadway and Grand Street.
Antiques and collectables all year round.

TRIBECA

Antiqueria Tribeca: 129 Duane Street near Broadway. Tel 212-227 7500, www.antiqueria.com. Subway 1, 2, 3, 9, A, C to Chambers Street.
Filled with French Art Deco pieces, from furniture to accessories. Often some lovely Lalique and Murano glass items to be found.

Burden & Izett Ltd: 180 Duane Street near Houston Street. Tel 212-941 8247, www.burdenandizett.net. Subway 1, 2, 3, 9, A, C to Chambers Street.
Extremely pricey, high-end, one-of-a-kind pieces of furniture to gaze at in awe.

UPPER EAST AND WEST SIDES

Green Flea Market: Greenwich Avenue at Charles Street between West 10th and 11th Streets on Saturdays 10am–5.30pm and Columbus Avenue between West 76th and 77th Streets on Sundays 10am–5.30pm. Tel 212-239 3025, www.greenfleamarkets.com. Subway 1, 9 to 79th Street; B, C to 77th/81st Street.
Antiques, collectables, bric-a-brac, handmade pottery and discount clothing in this indoor and outdoor market.

BOOKS

Books are big business in New York and book readings are a popular form of entertainment. For a real slice of the New York lifestyle, there are a number of places that specialise in readings: The Drawing Center (35 Wooster Street between Grand and Broome Streets, tel 212-694 0910, www.drawingcenter.org) gives readings related to the exhibitions; **The Poetry Project** at St Mark's Church (131 East 10th Street,

tel 212-674 0910, www.poetryproject.com) has three evening readings a week, Monday and Wednesday at 8pm, and Friday at 10.30pm.

The 92nd Street Y (1395 Lexington Avenue, tel 212-415 5500, www.92y.org) has a great series of lectures and readings, as does **The Dia Center for the Arts** (548 West 22nd Street, tel 212-989 5566, www.diacenter.org). Also check out **Barnes & Noble** (page 111) and **192 Books** (below) for more.

CHELSEA

192 Books: 192 10th Avenue between 21st and 22nd Streets. Tel 212-255 4022, www.192books.com. Subway C, E to 23rd Street.
A good range of art and literature titles as well as a large children's section. The atmosphere in this bright, airy shop is very comfortable, with reading tables and comfy chairs to help you relax. There are weekly readings here.

EAST VILLAGE

St Mark's Bookshop: 31 3rd Avenue on the corner of 9th Street. Tel 212-260 7853, www.stmarksbookshop.com. Subway 6 to Astor Place.
An excellent bookstore with a broad range of books. The bulletin board in the front gives details of local literary events.

GREENWICH VILLAGE

Shakespeare & Co: 716 Broadway at Washington Place. Tel 212-529 1330, www.shakeandco.com. Subway N, R to 8th Street; 6 to Astor Place.
This is an excellent bookstore. Unlike many a Barnes & Noble, where the staff sometimes don't appear to recognise joined-up writing, all the assistants here are graduates and will be genuinely helpful.

MIDTOWN

Rizzoli: 31 West 57th Street between 5th and 6th Avenues. Tel 212-759 2424, www.rizzoliusa.com. Subway N, R, W to 5th Avenue/59th Street; F to 57th Street.
This trendy store has a good stock of art, fashion and design publications and is popular with those in the media and with design students.

MIDTOWN EAST

Argosy: 116 East 59th between Park and Lexington Avenues. Tel 212-753 4455, www.argosybooks.com. Subway 4, 5, 6, F, N, R to 59th Street.

SoHo street market

The best bookshop in New York if you're looking for rare, hard-to-find books. There are seven storeys of out-of-print publications, antiques, maps, autographs and letters to browse through. Beware though, you can easily lose an afternoon engrossed in here.

Borders Books & Music: 461 Park Avenue at 57th Street. Tel 212-980 6785, www.bordersstores.com. Subway N, R to Lexington Avenue; 4, 5, 6 to 59th Street. Excellent outlets for books, CDs, videos and more obscure books, too. A few other megastores throughout the city.

Urban Centre Books: 457 Madison Avenue, between East 50th and East 51st Streets. Tel 212-935 3595, www.urbancenterbooks.org. Subway 6 to 51st Street; E, F to 5th Avenue. Housed in the pretty Villard Houses, this bookstore is a treasure trove for anyone interested in architecture and buildings.

NOLITA
Tower Books: 383 Lafayette Street at 4th Street. Tel 212-228 5100. Subway B, D, F, Q to Broadway/Lafayette; 6 to Bleecker Street. A wide range of contemporary fiction and a huge magazine section.

WEST VILLAGE
Biography Bookshop: 400 Bleecker Street at West 11th Street. Tel 212-807 8655. Subway 1, 2, 3 to 14th Street. A massive selection of biographies covering all genres.

Bookleaves: 304 West 4th Street near Bank Street. Tel 212-924 5638. Subway 1, 2, 3 or A,C, E or L to 14th Street. Just what you imagine a New York bookstore to be like; dusty, quiet and tucked away in a neighbourhood and offering a fabulous selection of everything from paperbacks to out-of-print pricey tomes.

Three Lives Bookstore: 154 West 10th Street off 7th Avenue. Tel 212-741 2069, www.threelives.com. A delightful shop with a charming ambience, known for attentive staff with encyclopaedic knowledge. Specialises in literary fiction, poetry and design books, as well as memoirs.

UNION SQUARE
Barnes & Noble: 105 5th Avenue at 18th Street. Tel 212-675 5500, www.bnnewyork.com. Subway L, N, R, 4, 5, 6 to 14th Street/Union Square.

This is the original store of one of the largest chains of bookstores in America and, as well as a massive selection of books, it also sells CDs and videos. Barnes & Noble is responsible for putting many independent bookstores out of business, but is well worth a visit. Many branches have coffee shops and seating areas for you to look through books before buying. You'll see branches everywhere.

Strand Book Store: 828 Broadway at 12th Street. Tel 212-473 1452, www.strandbooks.com. Subway L, N, R, Q, W 4, 5, 6 to 14th Street/Union Square. This whole area used to be famous for antiquarian bookshops, but the Strand is the only one left. The store has over two million second-hand and new books on any subject you'd care to name – all at around half the published price.

CAMERAS AND ELECTRONICS
Have a clear idea of what you're looking for before buying – pick up a copy of Tuesday's *New York Times* to check out prices in the science section first. Of course, you can always find electrical items at really cheap prices in the Chinatown stretch of Canal Street, but you won't get a guarantee.

CHELSEA
Adorama: 42 West 18th Street near 6th Avenue. Tel 212-741 0052, www.adorama.com. Subway 1, 9 to 18th Street.
Six floors that cover all your photographic needs, from disposable cameras through to $10,000 professional snappers. In addition, it offers a range of other services including creating digital prints for 20 cents each.

★★★★ ★★★★
★ **National electronics chain Best Buy** ★
★ **(tel 888-237 8289, www.bestbuy.** ★
★ **com) sells a wide variety of gadgets** ★
★ **and gizmos from speakers to stereos** ★
★ **plus games, CDs and computers at** ★
★ **really competitive prices. They can** ★
★ **be found at locations throughout** ★
★ **the city including 60 23rd Street in** ★
★ **Chelsea (tel 212-366 2373) and** ★
★ **1280 Lexington Avenue at 86th** ★
★ **Street, Upper East Side (tel 917–** ★
★ **492 8870).** ★
★★★★★★★★★★★★★★★★★★★★★★★

MADISON SQUARE

Fotografica: 124 West 25th Street between 6th and 7th Avenues. Tel 212-929 6080. Subway F, V to 23rd Street.
A vast stock of used camera equipment at trade prices. Owner Ed Wassel will be happy to order anything not in stock.

MIDTOWN

Datavision Computer Video: 445 5th Avenue near 39th Street. Tel 212-689 1111. Subway 7, B, D, F, V to 42nd Street/5th Avenue.
You'll find whatever teccie treat you desire, from laptops to iPod accessories, in this cramped but comprehensive store.

34TH STREET–PENN STATION

B&H Photo & Video: 420 9th Avenue between West 33rd and West 34th Streets. Tel 212-444 6615, www.bhphotovideo.com. Subway A, C, E to 34th Street/Penn Station.
A massive three-storey, block-long store, which stocks every conceivable piece of electronic imaging, audio, video and photo equipment you've ever heard of. All the staff are professionals in their own right and really know their onions. They're helpful, too, which is why this emporium is an excellent place to go for everyone from novices to professionals.

Willoughby's: 136 West 32nd Street between 6th and 7th Avenues. Tel 212-564 1600, www.willoughbys.com. Subway B, D, F, Q, N, R, V, W, 1, 2, 3 to 34th Street.
Reputedly the world's largest collection of cameras and all things audio, but the service isn't brilliant so make sure you know what you want before you go.

CD AND RECORD STORES

EAST VILLAGE

Downtown Music Gallery: 342 Bowery between East 2nd and East 3rd Streets. Tel 212-473 0043, www.downtownmusic gallery.com. Subway 6 to Astor Place.
Jazz aficionados love this specialist shop with its wide selection of records and CDs to search through. Live performances take place on Sunday nights at 6pm.

Sounds: 20 St Mark's Place between 2nd and 3rd Avenues. Tel 212-677 2727. Subway 6 to Astor Place.
The place to visit if you want to buy the latest popular tracks from well-known artists at very competitive prices.

FINANCIAL DISTRICT

J&R Music World: 33 Park Row between Ann and Beekman Streets. Tel 212-238 9000, www.jr.com. Subway A or C to Broadway/Nassau Street.
Check out the weekly ads in the *New York Post* and *Village Voice* to get an idea of what's on offer. The store also sells jazz, Latin and pop music.

GREENWICH VILLAGE

Bleecker Bob's Golden Oldies Record Shop: 118 West 3rd Street at MacDougal Street. Tel 212-475 9677, www.bleeckerbobs.com. Subway A, B, C, D, E, F, V to West 4th Street.
Whatever sounds you're into, you'll find something to satisfy. Choose from thousands of jazz, rock, punk and R&B vinyls and now CDs and DVDs too.

Tower Records: 692 Broadway at 4th Street. Tel 212-505 1500, www.tower records.com. Subway N, R, W to 8th Street.
An excellent range of CDs and tapes. Around the block on Lafayette Street is the knockdown Tower Clearance shop.

MIDTOWN

Virgin Megastore: 1540 Broadway between 45th and 46th Streets. Tel 212-921 1020, www.virginmega.com. Subway 1, 2, 3, 9, N, Q, R, S, W to 42nd Street.
Just like the ones in the UK, only this is even bigger and better, with an even wider variety of CDs, records, DVDs, games, T-shirts and posters. It's always worth checking out the website before you visit the city, as the store often has high-profile pop stars performing there to promote a new release.

UPPER WEST SIDE

Tower Records: 1961 Broadway at 66th Street. Tel 212-799 2500, www.towerrecords.com. Subway 1, 9 to 66th Street/Lincoln Center.
The Lincoln Center branch also has an excellent range of CDs and tapes.

CHILDREN

MIDTOWN

The Disney Store: 711 5th Avenue between 55th and 5th Streets. Tel 212-702 0702, www.worldofdisney.com. Subway E, F to 5th Avenue. Also at 218 West 42nd Street. Tel 212-302 0595. Subway 1, 2, 3, 9, N, R to Times Square/42nd Street.
If it comes with a pair of ears, then you'll find it here!

FAO Schwarz: 767 5th Avenue at 58th Street. Tel 212-644 9400 ext. 4242, www.fao.com. Subway N, R to 5th Avenue. The most famous children's store in the world, it's not only huge but is also an entertainment centre in its own right with oversized displays that take your breath away, plus every conceivable toy your child could want.

★ **If you stay at the Ritz-Carlton Hotel**
★ **in Battery Park City, you'll be**
★ **entitled to a 10 per cent discount at**
★ **FAO Schwarz.**

Hershey's Times Square: 48th Street and Broadway. Tel 212-581 9100, www.hersheys.com/discover/timessquare. Subway N, R, S, 1, 2, 3, 7, 9, A, C, E to 42nd Street/Times Square.
The Cadbury's of America now has a massive chocolate haven in Times Square. Enter (at your peril) under the 65m (215ft) tall, 18m (60ft) wide giant Hershey bar to find every kind of Hershey sweet under the sun, as well as clothing, toys and giant chocolate greetings cards.

Toys R Us: 1514 Broadway between 44th and 45th Streets. Tel 212-225 8392, www.toysrus.com. Subway N, Q, R, S, W, 1, 2, 3, 7 to Times Square.
In the heart of the rejuvenated Times Square district, this three-storey, glass-enclosed building is home to an 18m (60ft) Ferris wheel, a giant roaring dinosaur and a life-size Barbie townhouse. If you are here with kids, it's a must-see.

WEST VILLAGE
Gepetto's Toy Box: 10 Christopher Street between Gay Street and Greenwich Avenue. Tel 212-620 7511. Subway 1, 9 to Christopher Street.
A great antithesis to the bright, brash modern toy stores. Here you'll find beautiful, traditional handmade toys, such as rocking horses and mobiles.

FOOD

CHELSEA
Chelsea Market: 75 9th Avenue between 15th and 16th Streets. Tel 212-243 6005, www.chelseamarket.com. Subway A, C, E, L to14th Street and 8th Avenue.

You'll find everything you need here for a gourmet feast, from fishmongers and bakers to wine merchants, and even florists for table decorations. Check out Buon Italia for great cheeses, sauces and all manner of Italian fodder and Amy's for breads you never dreamed of. An instant picnic!

GREENWICH VILLAGE
Take the subway A, C, E, F, V, S to West 4th Street for a whole area of foodie shops.

Aphrodisia: 264 Bleecker Street between 6th and 7th Avenues. Tel 212-989 6440. A huge selection of bulk herbs, spices, teas and pot-pourris.

★ **If you'd like a taste of the foods**
★ **sold in some of the shops in**
★ **Greenwich Village, go on the Foods**
★ **of New York tour, which also**
★ **introduces you to great restaurants**
★ **in the area (page 80).**

Balducci's: 155A West 66th Street, near the Lincoln Center just west of Broadway. Tel 212-653 8320, www.suttongourmet.com. One of the most famous gourmet food emporiums in New York. You can find everything from fresh vegetables and fruit to edible flowers and hung game.

Faicco's Sausage Store: 260 Bleecker Street between 6th and 7th Avenues. Tel 212-243 1974.
A landmark Italian speciality food shop established in 1900, it is known for its own sausages that are made daily (and sold to many of the neighbouring restaurants), its home-made Mozzarella cheese, again made daily, plus rice balls made with three cheeses and rolled in breadcrumbs. Other specialities include prosciutto balls, potato croquettes, fried ravioli and stuffed breads.

Murray's Cheese Shop: 254 Bleecker Street between 6th and 7th Avenues. Tel 212-243 3289, www.murrayscheese.com. The owner travels all over the world to bring back a fascinating selection of more than 350 cheeses with amazing names such as Wabash Cannonball, Crocodile Tears, Mutton Buttons and Cardinal Sin, a British cow's milk cheese. They also sell olives, chorizos, pâtés and breads and you may even catch a cookery class.

Pasticceria Bruno: 245 Bleecker Street between 6th and 7th Avenues. Tel 212-242 4959, www.brunobakery.com.
An Italian-French bakery run by one of the top 10 pastry chefs in New York. It does miniature and large fruit tarts, mousses, cookies, sorbets, ice-cream cakes and home-made chocolates, and you can sit down to try any of them with a nice cup of tea or coffee.

Rocco's: 243 Bleecker Street between 6th and 7th Avenues. Tel 212-242 6031, www.roccospastry.com.
Famous for its fresh cannolis (an Italian pastry filled with cream), it sells large and small sizes of everything from Italian cheesecakes to chocolate, hazelnut and lemon cakes. You can eat in, too, with a cup of delicious coffee.

LITTLE ITALY
Di Palo's: 206 Grand Street at Mott Street. Tel: 212-226 1033. Subway J, M, N, Q, R, W, Z, 6 to Canal Street.
One of the last remaining Italian speciality food stores in Little Italy, it was founded 80 years ago and is particularly famous for its Mozzarella and Italian sausages and salami. It even has its own ageing room for cheeses.

LOWER EAST SIDE
Russ & Daughters: 179 East Houston Street between Allen and Orchard Streets. Tel 212-475 4880, www.russanddaughters.com. Subway F to 2nd Avenue.
Along with Katz's Deli (page 165), this is one of the most famous outlets in the Lower East Side. Established in 1914, it sells every possible kind of fish, caviar, pickled vegetables and bagels.

SOHO
Dean & Deluca: 560 Broadway at Prince Street. Tel 212-226 6800. Subway N, R, Q, W to Prince Street.
Gourmets love the fresh bread, cheese, coffee beans and other delicious foods on sale at this SoHo secret.

Times Square Toys 'R Us

34TH STREET
Cucina & Co: In the Cellar at Macy's (page 89), 151 West 34th Street, 6th Avenue and Broadway. Tel 212-868 2388, www.rapatina.com/cucinaCoMacys. Subway B, D, F, N, Q, R, V, W to 34th Street.
One of the most fabulous grocer's markets in New York, now famous for its supplies of lobster and caviar.

UPPER EAST SIDE/YORKVILLE
Martine's Chocolates: 400 82nd Street off 1st Avenue. Tel 212-744 6289, www.martineschocolates.com. Subway 6 to 86th Street.
If you're not on a diet, drool over the rich Belgian choccies which take up to three days to make. Chocolate heaven.

The Vinegar Factory: 431 East 91st Street between York and 1st Avenues. Tel 212-987 0885. Subway 4, 5, 6 to 86th Street.
One of the most famous markets in the city. Here you'll find stacks of cheeses, meats, breads, salads and cakes – in fact, everything you need to create a perfect picnic.

UPPER WEST SIDE
Zabar's: 2245 Broadway at 80th Street. Tel 212-787 2000, www.zabars.com. Subway 1, 2 to 79th Street.
Just about the most famous food store in New York and also considered to be one of the finest. It has a tremendous range of cheeses, fresh fruit and veg, meats, fish and bagels. In fact it's so famous it's even been featured in *Friends*.

DRINK

CHELSEA
Chelsea Wine Vault: 75 9th Avenue at Chelsea Market. Tel 212-462 4244, www.chelseawinevault.com. Subway A, C, E to 14th Street.
More than 3,000 labels to choose from. Take advantage of the fun free tastings – mainly at weekends (see website).

★ ★ ★ ★ **BRIT TIP** ★ ★ ★ ★
Don't be fooled by the bottles of wine you may see in food shops in New York. They are either non-alcoholic or low alcohol as it is illegal for food stores to sell wine. However, this rule doesn't apply to beer.

EAST VILLAGE

Astor Wines & Spirits: 399 Lafayette Street at 4th Street at the corner of Astor Place. Tel 212-674 7500, www.astorwines.com. Subway 6 to Astor Place; R, W to 8th Street.
Has a wide range of wines and spirits.

LOWER EAST SIDE

Schapiro's Winery: 120 Essex Street, The Essex Street Market, www.schapiro-wine.com. Subway J, M, Z, F to Essex/Delancey Street.
The Schapiro family has been running this winery since 1899 and it's decorated with old casks and bottles. It's the city's only kosher wine and spirits warehouse and sweet wine is made on the premises. There is a free tasting tour at 2pm on Sundays.

MIDTOWN EAST

Park Avenue Liquor Shop: 292 Madison Avenue between 40th and 41st Streets. Tel 212-685 2442, www.parkaveliquor.com. Subway 4, 5, 6, 7 to Grand Central/42nd Street.
Specialises in Californian wines and European bottles. Discounts are given with bulk purchases.

Schumer's Wine & Liquor: 59 East 54th Street between Park and Madison Avenues. Tel 212-355 0940. Subway E, F to Lexington Avenue; 6 to 51st Street.
With a great range of American and European wines, it also stocks a good selection of spirits and champagne.

SOHO

Vintage New York: 482 Broome Street at the corner of Wooster and SoHo Streets. Tel 212-226 9463, www.vintagenewyork.com. Subway 6 to Spring Street.
SoHo is home to a complete first in New York City – a shop that can sell both wine and food. And the reason why is because it is owned by a vineyard from New York State, which means it can open on Sundays and sell alcoholic wine and food together – both of which are otherwise illegal in New York. All the wines come from New York State vineyards and five tastes cost just $5. It also houses a wine bar open in the evening with over 200 wines by the glass and a creative, delicious menu.

UNION SQUARE

Union Square Wine and Spirits: 33 Union Square West between 16th and 17th Streets. Tel 212-675 8100, www.wine access.com/store/unionsquarewines. Subway 4, 5, 6, L, N, Q, R, W to Union Square.
More than 4,000 wines, good prices and the staff know their wines.

UPPER EAST SIDE/YORKVILLE

Best Cellars: 1291 Lexington Avenue at 87th Street. Tel 212-426 4200, www.bestcellars.com. Subway 4, 5, 6 to 86th Street.
One of the best-value stores in the city for fine wines under $10. Free tastings every weekday 5–8pm and Saturday 2–4pm paired with food from top new chefs are even better value!

Sherry–Lehmann: 679 Madison Avenue between 61st and 62nd Streets. Tel 212-838 7500, www.sherry-lehmann.com. Subway 4, 5, 6 to 59th Street.
The most famous wine shop in New York. A huge selection and well situated for that Central Park picnic.

UPPER WEST SIDE

Acker, Merrall & Condit Wine Merchants: 160 West 72nd Street between Broadway and Columbus. Tel 212-787 1700, www.ackerstore.com. Subway 1, 2, 3, 9 to 72nd Street.
America's oldest wine store – it opened in 1820 – is well worth a visit for its vast selection of wines from around the world which range in price from a couple of dollars to more than $20,000.

★ ★ ★ ★ **BRIT TIP** ★ ★ ★ ★
★ ★
★ **You can only buy wine and spirits** ★
★ **from liquor stores, which do not sell** ★
★ **mixers or even beer!** ★
★ ★

Tea and Sympathy

HOMEWARE

MIDTOWN

Crate & Barrel: 650 Madison Avenue at 59th Street. Tel 212-308 0011, www.crateandbarrel.com. Subway 4, 5, 6 to 59th Street.

Fashionable, funky furniture, accessories, kitchen and tableware for incredibly low prices. There's also another branch in SoHo at 611 Broadway at Houston Street.

SOHO

Anthropologie: 375 West Broadway at Spring Street. Tel 212-343 7070, www.anthropologie.com. Subway C, E to Spring Street.

One of our favourite shops selling gorgeous boudoir items, such as silk quilts, Venetian-style mirrors and night stands, in an airy loft-like space. There's also a collection of stylish women's clothes on sale with the same thrift-store, trendy feel.

Broadway Panhandler: 477 Broome Street between Greene and Wooster Streets. Tel 212-966 3434, www.broadwaypanhandler.com. Subway N, R, W to Prince Street.

All things for the kitchen, from the latest gadgets to classic pieces such as steel saucepans and Alessi toasters. There are hundreds of items to choose from and it's a must-visit for any domestic gods or goddesses when in town. Famous chefs often give in-store demonstrations.

UPPER EAST SIDE

Laytner's Linen and Home: 237 East 86th Street at 2nd Avenue. Tel 212-996 4439, www.laytners.com. Subway 4, 5, 6 to 86th Street.

Come here to buy some luxurious high thread-count linen to take home.

UPPER WEST SIDE

Avventura: 463 Amsterdam Avenue at 82nd Street. Tel 212-769 2510. Subway A, 9 to 79th Street.

Contemporary tableware, from cocktail and champagne glasses to Deruta dishes.

SPECIALITY AND GIFT SHOPS

CHELSEA

IS: 136 West 17th Street between 6th and 7th Avenues. Tel 212-620 0300. Subway A, C, E, 1, 9 to 14th Street.

A designer stationery store with a distinctly hip edge.

GREENWICH VILLAGE

Village Comics: 214 Sullivan Street between West 3rd and Bleecker Streets. Tel 212-777 2770, www.villagecomics.com. Subway C, E to West 4th Street.

If comics are the name of the game for you, then there's a good chance you'll find a back issue of what you're looking for. A mail order and online service is available.

UPPER EAST SIDE

E.A.T. Gifts: 1062 Madison Avenue at 80th Street. Tel 212-861 2544. Subway 6 to 77th Street.

You can hardly move for the shelves that are tightly packed with every conceivable gift, from gadgets to trinkets, a lot of it fun stuff for kids.

WEST VILLAGE

Flight 001: 96 Greenwich Avenue between Jane and West 12th Streets. Tel 212-691 1001, www.flight001.com. Subway 1, 2, 3, 9 to 14th Street.

A travel accessories shop that looks like a sleek 1960s' airport lounge, it stocks fabulously cool carry-on items such as digital cameras, spray-on vitamins and WAP-activated global travel guides. It also has practical but funky luggage.

MXYPLYZYK: 125 Greenwich Avenue at West 13th Street. Tel 212-989 4300, www.mxyplyzyk.com. Subway 1, 2, 3, 9 to 14th Street.

Kitschy-cool gifts and whatnots including Devil Ducks (with horns – glow-in-the-dark or plain red) and tractor-seat stools for when you're tired of serious shopping.

Tea and Sympathy: 110 Greenwich Avenue between 12th and 13th Streets. Tel 212-989 9735, www.teaandsympathynewyork.com. Subway 1, 2, 3, 9 to 14th Street.

Filled with all things the Brit abroad loves, this is a combination of a shop and café offering sausage rolls, fish and chips and 'proper' tea. Liz Hurley orders food for her fashion shoots, David Bowie had his 50th birthday bash here and Kate Moss and Rupert Everett are regulars.

SMOKER'S CORNER

Amazingly enough, the best shop to buy your ciggies from is a chain of chemists called Duane Reade – the New York equivalent of our Boots! Check www.duanereade.com for locations.

CHAPTER 6

Museums and Galleries

New York has some of the best-known museums and galleries in the world, so it's little wonder that some tourists visit the Big Apple just to visit these major attractions. Among the names that you are most likely to be familiar with are the Metropolitan Museum of Art (the Met), the Solomon R Guggenheim Museum, Whitney Museum of Modern Art and the Museum of Modern Art (MoMA).

Most of the major museums are located around a specific area of the city called the Museum Mile, which stretches along 5th Avenue on the Upper East Side north to 89th Street.

As befits a city that is famed for regenerating itself, none of the museums sits on its laurels. There is a constant wave of refurbishment and renewal that inspires people to keep returning. Recently, for instance, the American Museum of Natural History has finished a $25-million programme to update its Hall of Ocean Life using state-of-the-art technology, and MoMA has re-opened after a multimillion dollar refurbishment and expansion, when exhibitions were moved out to Queens. The Museum of Jewish Heritage and the Morgan Library both re-opened in 2006 after extensive refurbishment.

On top of this a raft of new museums have opened, including the American Folk Art Museum, the Chelsea Art Museum and the Annette Green Museum dedicated to the history of perfumes. The new Jewish Children's Museum in Brooklyn and The National Sports Museum added to these in 2006. Be one of the first to visit the National Cartoon Museum (formerly the International Museum of Cartoon Art), which opens in 2007 in the Empire State Building as the largest museum of cartoon art in the world.

Of course, it does mean there is a lot to choose from and, especially if you're on your first visit to New York, you'll want to ensure you don't waste any time. For this reason, we've given you our Top Five first, which includes the major institutions and covers everything from art to natural history. It should also be noted that many cultural institutions in New York go to great lengths to make themselves accessible to children and details of events and programmes for youngsters and families can be found in Chapter 9, New York for Families.

TOP FIVE MUSEUMS

No matter how long you intend to stay in New York, it's useful to plan exactly what you want to see. As you get to know the city, you'll form your own opinions but, in the meantime, here are the Brit's Guide favourites. They cover a broad spectrum, from the history of New York City to art and the world's amazing natural history, and each is a true delight in itself.

AMERICAN MUSEUM OF NATURAL HISTORY
Upper West Side
✉ Central Park West at 79th Street
☎ 212-769 5100
🖳 www.amnh.org
🚇 Subway B, C to 81st Street/Museum of Natural History; 1, 9 to 79th Street
🕐 10am–5.45pm daily.
$ Suggested price $14 adults, $10 students and seniors, $8 under 13s. The most comprehensive package, which includes the space shows, IMAX films and special exhibitions, costs $30 adults, $22 seniors and students and $19 children.

Like the Metropolitan, this is an epic of a museum, best seen in parts rather than attempting the whole (although you'll save money if you do!). It provides an amazingly detailed yet comprehensive overview of life on Earth and beyond and has undergone an enormous amount of growth and redevelopment over the last few years.

One of its most famous permanent exhibitions is the **Milstein Hall of Ocean Life**, which has recently been given a $25-million redesign using the latest marine technology and a $15-million donation by museum trustee Irma Milstein and her husband Paul (hence the new name). Using the hall's massive blue whale as its centrepiece, lights, video and sound effects create the illusion of being immersed in the ocean to provide a dynamic and breathtaking view of life under the sea.

Other permanent exhibits include the dinosaur collection, the $50-million gem collection including the famous Star of India blue sapphire, the Native American section and the seven continents. Along the way, much fun is to be had using the many interactive computer exhibits, for instance, to travel back in time in order to trace the roots of evolution.

In addition to the main museum, there is the **Rose Center for Earth and Space** – a spectacular museum within a museum, which incorporates the newly revamped **Hayden Planetarium** as its centrepiece. This is the place to come to learn about both the inner workings of Earth and the outer reaches of the universe. The **Big Bang Theater** gives a dramatic recreation of the first minutes of the origins of the universe and is found inside a 26.5m (87ft) wide sphere that appears to float in a glass-walled ceiling.

Here you will also find the **Space Theater**, billed as the most technologically advanced in the world, which shows incredibly realistic views of outer space. The two films are *Passport to the Universe*, in which Tom Hanks narrates an amazing journey from Earth to the edge of the universe, and *The Search For Life: Are We Alone?* Narrated by Hollywood star Harrison Ford, this film takes you on an incredible journey in a search of the answers.

The **IMAX Theater** also shows a wonderful range of breathtaking movies examining different aspects of life on earth.

And don't miss the **Butterfly Conservatory**, full of stunning tropical butterflies, which is open every year from

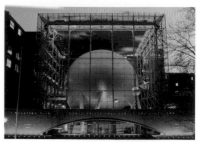

Rose Center for Earth and Space

the beginning of October to the end of May. Walk among the lush vegetation and flowering plants to see some of the 500 free-living butterflies, but do remember it's 27°C (80°F) inside, so leave your coat in the cloakroom.

For more information on family programmes, see page 209.

★ ★ ★ ★ **BRIT TIP** ★ ★ ★ ★

★ If you take the B or C train to 81st
★ Street you can go straight into the
★ American Museum of Natural
★ History from the subway. Just follow
★ the tiled signs in the mosaic wall to
★ avoid the crowds, heat or cold.

INTREPID SEA-AIR-SPACE MUSEUM
Clinton

✉ USS *Intrepid*, Pier 86, west end of 46th Street at the Hudson River
☎ 212-245 0072
🖰 www.intrepidmuseum.org
🚌 Subway A, C, E to 42nd Street, then the M42 bus to 12th Avenue
🕐 1 Apr–30 Sept Mon–Fri 10am–5pm, Sat, Sun and holidays 10am–6pm. 1 Oct–31 Mar Tue–Sun 10am–5pm. Last admission 1 hour before closing
$ $16.50 adults, $12.50 seniors and students, $11.50 children (6–17), $4.50 children (2–5), under 2s free

A thoroughly enjoyable museum, which appeals to all ages. All the staff are very friendly and there are former members of the crew around the ship who are happy to give an insight into its history and life on board. *Intrepid* was one of 24 Second World War US aircraft carriers and, despite incidents of serious damage to these ships,

Intrepid Sea-Air-Space Museum

Starry Night at the MoMA

none of them was ever sunk. *Intrepid*'s worst moment came on 25 November 1944, when two kamikaze pilots hit the ship 5 minutes apart, killing 69 men and seriously injuring 85 others.

★ The only way to see the submarine at *Intrepid* is on a tour and long queues build up very quickly, so get there early and see it before anything else.

The second plane exploded on the hangar deck and the ship burned for about 6 hours, but *Intrepid* made it back to America for repairs and returned to the war. Stories of life on board are told by veterans at film screenings throughout the ship and there are also plenty of hands-on exhibits to keep children happy. One of the best exhibits is the F-18 navy jet flight simulator, which costs an extra $5 but is great fun.

METROPOLITAN MUSEUM OF ART

Upper East Side
✉ 1000 5th Avenue at 82nd Street
☎ 212-535 7710
🖰 www.metmuseum.org
🚇 Subway 4, 5, 6 to 86th Street
◷ Tues–Thurs, Sun 9.30am–5.30pm, Fri, Sat 9.30am–9pm. Closed Mon.
$ Suggested price $12 adults, $7 students and seniors, under 12s free with an adult. Same-day entrance to The Cloisters (page 122) is included in the price

New York is filled with fine museums, yet this really is the mother of them all and you could easily spend a well-paced day here. But with 5,000 years of art spread over 139,500 sq m (1.5 million sq ft), it's best to admit that you won't be able to see it all in one visit. And therein lies your perfect excuse to return to the city! If you can, visit the website in advance to get a good feel for the layout. Think about what you really want to see and write out a list of priorities, allowing a reasonable amount of time to absorb what each gallery has to offer.

★ Don't miss the Metropolitan's fabulous outdoor café on the second floor for stunning views of Central Park. It's generally open from May to early September.

A good place to start is with an aspect of American culture, which you will find in the **American Wing** where there is a wonderful collection of Tiffanys along with US arts and crafts and glorious neo-classical sculptures in the garden court. It's one of the Met's most popular areas, with three floors and 25 rooms filled with more than 1,000 paintings by American artists, 600 sculptures and 2,500 drawings. The two real musts are the **Egyptian Art** exhibits and the **Temple of Dendur**, which was built by Egypt to thank the American people after the US helped rescue monuments threatened by the Aswan Dam. Other greats include the **Greek** and **Roman** displays, the **Japanese** and **Chinese** exhibits and the **medieval** art.

The wonderful thing about this museum is that you can wander around by yourself, hire an audio guide for the day ($6 adults, $4 under 12s), which you can use in any order you choose, or take advantage of a plethora of free tours, talks and lectures.

The hour-long tours leave from the front hall at 10.15am, 11.15am, 1.15pm, 2.15pm and 3.15pm. Check the calendar on the website in advance for information on the

Metropolitan Museum of Art

1-hour gallery talks or lectures, which focus on either a special exhibition or one of the permanent collections. The free lectures tend to be held at 6pm on a Friday or 3pm on a Sunday, while free films tend to be held from Tuesday to Friday at 2pm (plus 7.30pm on Friday) and on Saturday at 1.15pm. You do not need to make reservations except for the Saturday afternoon film.

For comprehensive information on family programmes, see page 210.

MUSEUM OF MODERN ART (MOMA)
Midtown
- ✉ 11 West 53rd Street between 5th and 6th Avenues
- ☎ 212-708 9400
- ⊕ www.moma.org
- 🚇 Subway E, V to 5th Avenue/53rd Street
- ⏲ Sat, Sun, Mon, Weds, Thurs 10.30am–5.30pm, Fri 10.30am–8pm; closed Tues
- $ $20 adults, $16 seniors, $12 students, under 16s free with an adult; on Fri 4.30–8pm, you can pay what you wish

Founded in 1929 by three private citizens, including Abby Rockefeller, this was the first museum to devote its entire collection to the modern movement. Since then it has retained its pioneering sense of the new, and was the first museum to see architecture, design, photography and film as art forms. The museum's collection, which started with a gift of eight prints and one drawing, dates from the 1880s to the present day and now encompasses more than 100,000 works.

The museum was shut for two years from 2002 for a major, multi-million dollar refurbishment and building work, and the new-look MoMA re-opened in November 2004 in time to celebrate its 75th anniversary. The new building, designed by Yoshio Taniguchi, has received much praise and occupies over 58,000 sq m (630,000 sq ft).

Many of the icons of modern and contemporary art are here, including Van Gogh's The Starry Night, Monet's Water Lilies, Picasso's Les Demoiselles and Andy Warhol's Gold Marilyn Monroe. The collection includes paintings, sculptures, drawings, photographs, films, film stills and videos. Films are screened daily in the two cinemas (cost included in the entrance fee, though you need to get a special ticket to reserve your place). Free gallery talks are given at 1pm and 3pm every day except

Wednesdays and on Fridays at 6pm and 7pm, or for $4 you can take a personalised audio self-guided tour.

For more information on family events, see page 211.

SOLOMON R GUGGENHEIM MUSEUM
Upper East Side
- ✉ 1071 5th Avenue at 89th Street
- ☎ 212-423 3500
- ⊕ www.guggenheim.org
- 🚇 Subway 4, 5, 6 to 86th Street
- ⏲ Mon, Wed, Sat, Sun 10am-5.45pm; Fri 10am-8pm; closed Thurs
- $ $15 adults, $10 students and senior citizens, under 12s free

The Guggenheim Museum in New York is probably best known for its beautiful building, which was designed by Frank Lloyd Wright and is now one of the youngest buildings in the city to be designated a New York City landmark. It houses one of the world's largest collections of Kandinsky, as well as works by Chagall, Klee, Picasso, Cézanne, Degas, Gauguin and Manet. It also has Peggy Guggenheim's entire collection of cubist, surrealist and abstract expressionist art. Tours are free. For information on family events, see page 211.

THE INSIDE STORY
If you haven't much time, try a 1-hour tour of museums. From January to March and July to September, the **Insider's Hour** gives you a quick peek around the most diverse art collections and interactive exhibits. Participating institutions include the Metropolitan Museum of Art (page 119), Lower East Side Tenement Museum (page 126), Intrepid Sea-Air-Space Museum (page 118), American Museum of Natural History (page 117), Museum of Modern Art (above), Museum of Jewish Heritage (page 129) and National Museum of the American Indian (page 130).

★ Check out the Guggenheim's sculpture gallery for some of the best views of Central Park. ★

A-Z OF THE REST

AMERICAN FOLK ART MUSEUM
Midtown
- ✉ 45 West 53rd Street between 5th and 6th Avenues
- ☎ 212-265 1040
- 🖥 www.folkartmuseum.org
- 🚇 Subway E, V to 5th Avenue/53rd Street
- ⏰ Tues–Sun 10.30am–5.30pm, except Fri 10.30am–7.30pm; closed Mon
- $ $9 adults, $7 students and seniors, under 12s and members free

The first entirely new museum building in New York since 1966, the museum's $18 million structure was designed by award-winning architects Tod Williams and Billy Tsien. From a punter's point of view, this new museum provides an excellent opportunity to get to grips with American folk art. It also gives an insight into America's history and cultural heritage from the perspective of these arts.

AMERICAN MUSEUM OF THE MOVING IMAGE
Queens
It's only a short trip to Queens and worth a visit here if you are into films. See page 121.

ANNETTE GREEN FRAGRANCE MUSEUM
Murray Hill
- ✉ 145 East 32nd Street between Lexington and 3rd Avenues
- ☎ 212-725 2755
- 🖥 www.fragrance.org
- 🚇 Subway 6 to 33rd Street
- ⏰ Open by appointment only Mon–Fri 10am–noon and 1–4pm
- $ $5 adults, $2.50 students and seniors

America's first ever perfume museum is owned and run by the Fragrance Foundation and aims to give an insight into the importance of scent in our lives. Exhibits include the Lure and Lore of Perfume Classics, which explains our continuing love affair with traditional fragrances such as Chanel No 5 and Obsession.

ASIA SOCIETY
Midtown East
- ✉ 725 Park Avenue at 70th Street
- ☎ 212-288 6400
- 🖥 www.asiasociety.org
- 🚇 Subway 6 to 68th Street
- ⏰ Tues–Sun 11am–6pm, Fri 11am–9pm
- $ $10 adults, $7 students and seniors, members and under 16s free; Fri 6–9pm

Founded in 1956 by John D Rockefeller III with his collection of Asian art, the society celebrated its 50th birthday in 2006. It aims to build an awareness of the 30 Pan Asian countries, which include Japan, New Zealand, Australia and the Pacific Islands. To this end it runs films, lectures and seminars in conjunction with its exhibitions and even has a regular schedule of Asian musicians who play at the museum.

BROOKLYN CHILDREN'S MUSEUM
New York's first children's museum, it has a great programme of events and workshops and is particularly worth the trip if you are on a family holiday. See page 216.

BROOKLYN MUSEUM OF ART
One of the largest museums in the world and has recently undergone a facelift. It is easy to reach in Brooklyn if you have the time to plan it into your schedule. See page 262.

CARNEGIE HALL/ROSE MUSEUM
Midtown
- ✉ 2nd Floor, 154 West 57th Street
- ☎ 212-903 9629
- 🖥 www.carnegiehall.org
- 🚇 Subway C, E to 23rd Street
- ⏰ Daily 11am–4.30pm
- $ Free

In 1991, the Rose Museum opened as part of Carnegie Hall's 100th anniversary celebrations. Located on the First Tier level of Carnegie Hall, the museum houses special temporary exhibitions as well as a permanent collection of a century's worth of photographs, letters, musical quotes and Carnegie Hall archival material, from programmes to unique memorabilia.

CHELSEA ART MUSEUM
Chelsea
- ✉ 556 West 22nd Street at 11th Avenue
- ☎ 212-255 0719
- 🖥 www.chelseaartmuseum.org
- 🚇 Subway C, E to 23rd Street
- ⏰ Tues–Sat noon–6pm, except Thurs noon–8pm; closed Sun and Mon
- $ $6 adults, $3 seniors and students; $3 for everyone Thurs 6–8pm

In the heart of Chelsea's new gallery district, this new medium-sized, three-storey museum provides a venue for abstract work by artists who have not been exhibited in

★ ★ ★ ★ BRIT TIP ★ ★ ★ ★
★ ★
★ Be prepared to prove you're a ★
★ student if you want to make the ★
★ most of discounted admissions to ★
★ the museums. ★
★ ★
★★★★★★★★★★★★★★★★★★★★★★★★★★

New York before and for mid-size travelling shows from Europe and smaller American museums. It is also the new home of the Miotte Foundation, which is dedicated to the conservation of Informal Art (abstract) works by Jean Miotte, who has had a studio in SoHo since 1978.

CHILDREN'S MUSEUM OF ART
Little Italy
A wonderful children's museum, see page 208.

CHILDREN'S MUSEUM OF MANHATTAN
Upper West Side
Dedicated to children under the age of 10 and their families. See page 208.

THE CLOISTERS
Washington Heights
✉ Fort Tyron Park, Fort Washington Avenue at Margaret Corbin Plaza
☎ 212-923 3700
🖱 www.metmuseum.org
🚇 Subway A to 190th Street
🕐 Mar–Oct Tues–Sun 9.30am– 5.15pm, Nov–Feb Tues–Sun 9.30am–4.45pm
$ Suggested donation $15 adults (includes free same-day admission to the Metropolitan Museum of Art (page 119), $10 seniors and students, under 12s free with an adult

Rockefeller cash allowed the Metropolitan Museum to buy this beautiful red-tiled Romanesque building 70 years ago. Now it is used purely to display examples of medieval art and architecture, including five

The Cloisters Arcade

cloisters – hence the name – from ruined French monasteries dating from the 12th to the 15th century. It is stunning to look at and houses some really exciting exhibits. For details about family events, see page 210.

★ ★ ★ ★ BRIT TIP ★ ★ ★ ★
★ ★
★ It's a long way north to The ★
★ Cloisters, so make the most of your ★
★ time by combining it with a walking ★
★ tour of Harlem (page 83). ★
★ ★
★★★★★★★★★★★★★★★★★★★★★★★★★★

COOPER–HEWITT NATIONAL DESIGN MUSEUM
Upper East Side
✉ 2 East 91st Street at 5th Avenue
☎ 212-849 8400
🖱 www.cooperhewitt.org
🚇 Subway 4, 5, 6 to 86th Street
🕐 Tues–Thurs 10am–5pm, Fri 10am–9pm, Sat 10am–6pm, Sun noon–6pm
$ $10 adults, $7 students and seniors; under 12s free

The only American museum devoted entirely to historic and contemporary design, the Cooper-Hewitt covers everything from applied arts and industrial design to drawings, prints, textiles and wall coverings. Take time to look at the exterior of the building itself, which was designed in a Georgian style for tycoon Andrew Carnegie.

American Museum of Natural History

The Frick Collection

DAHESH MUSEUM OF ART
Midtown East
- ✉ 580 Madison Avenue between 56th and 57th Streets
- ☎ 212-759 0606
- ⌁ www.daheshmuseum.org
- 🚇 Subway 4, 5, 6 to 59th Street
- ⏱ Tues–Sun 11am–6pm; open until 9pm on first Thurs of each month; closed Mon
- $ $10 adults, $6 students, $8 seniors, free children under 12 and first Thurs of month 6–9pm

Established in 1995, Dahesh is the only museum in America solely dedicated to 19th- and 20th-century European art. It occupies three storeys of architect Edward Larrabee Barnes's black granite IBM building. Dahesh was a Lebanese writer and philosopher, known as Salim Achi, and his collection of more than 3,000 works of art was moved to the US in 1975 from Beirut because of unrest.

★★★★ **BRIT TIP** ★★★★
★ ★
★ ★
★ **The mezzanine, overlooking Madison** ★
★ **Avenue, in the Danesh Museum of** ★
★ **Art is a good place for a snack with** ★
★ **city views.** ★
★ ★
★★★★★★★★★★★★★★★★★★★★★★★★

EDWYNN HOUK GALLERY
- ✉ 4th Floor, 745 5th Avenue between 57th and 58th Streets
- ☎ 212-750 7070
- ⌁ www.houkgallery.com
- 🚇 Subway N, R, W to 5th Avenue/59th Street
- ⏱ Sept–July Tues–Sat 11am–6pm
- $ Free admission

A delightful gallery for photography enthusiasts with both vintage and contemporary prints on display and for sale

from the likes of May Ray, Dorothea Lange and Annie Leibovitz.

EL MUSEO DEL BARRIO
Spanish Harlem
- ✉ 1230 5th Avenue at 104th Street
- ☎ 212-831 7272
- ⌁ www.elmuseo.org
- 🚇 Subway 6 to 103rd Street
- ⏱ Wed–Sun 11am–5pm
- $ Suggested donation $5 adults, $3 students and seniors, under 12s free with an adult

Opened in 1969 by a group of Puerto Rican parents, teachers and artists, it houses 8,000 objects of Caribbean and Latin American art from pre-Colombian times to date. Exhibits include musical instruments, miniature houses, dolls and masks.

ELLIS ISLAND IMMIGRATION MUSEUM
Battery Park
See page 60.

FORBES MAGAZINE GALLERIES
Financial District
- ✉ 62 5th Avenue at 12th Street
- ☎ 212-206 5548
- ⌁ www.forbesgalleries.com
- 🚇 Subway F, L, N, V to 14th Street
- ⏱ Tues–Sat 10am–4pm
- $ Free

The Forbes Magazine Galleries at the magazine's headquarters showcase The Forbes Collection™ of home and business furnishings, decorative accessories, gifts, jewellery, books, toy boats, miniature soldiers, presidential manuscripts and fine art.

Fraunces Tavern Museum

GETTING IN FREE

No charge is made for admission to the following museums so they make a great addition to your itinerary:

Carnegie Hall/Rose Museum: (page 121)

Forbes Magazine Galleries: (page 123)

National Museum of the American Indian: (page 130)

Schomburg Center for Research In Black Culture: (page 133)

Whitney Museum of American Art at Philip Morris: (page 134)

In addition to this, many museums offer times – usually on a Friday or Tuesday evening – when you can gain access free or pay a voluntary donation of whatever you wish:

American Folk Art Museum: 6–9pm Friday (page 121)

Asia Society: 6–9pm Friday (page 121)

Frick Collection: after 6pm on certain Fridays (below)

International Center of Photography: 5–8pm Friday (below)

Jewish Museum: 5–8pm Thursday (page 126)

FRAUNCES TAVERN MUSEUM
Financial District

- ✉ 54 Pearl Street at Broad Street, 1st and 2nd floors
- ☎ 212-425 1778
- 🖱 www.frauncestavernmuseum.org
- 🚇 Subway J, M, Z to Broad Street; 4, 5 to Bowling Green; 1, 2 to Wall Street
- ⏲ Tues–Fri 12am–5pm, Sat 10am–5pm
- $ $4 adults, $3 children and seniors, under 6s free

When New York was (briefly) capital of America, the Fraunces Tavern housed the Departments of Foreign Affairs, Treasury and War and was where George Washington delivered his famous farewell speech to his officers. Now, nestled among the skyscrapers of the Financial District, this 18th-century Georgian building, along with four adjacent 19th-century buildings, houses a fine museum dedicated to the study of early American history and culture. Although well preserved, an awful lot of restoration work has been done to keep its 1783 façade.

★ ★ ★ ★ **BRIT TIP** ★ ★ ★ ★

Don't miss the cosy restaurant at the Fraunces Tavern Museum – it serves lovely food in a stately tourist environment.

FRICK COLLECTION
Midtown East

- ✉ 1 East 70th Street at 5th Avenue
- ☎ 212-288 0700
- 🖱 www.frick.org
- 🚇 Subway 4, 5, 6 to 68th Street
- ⏲ Tues–Sat 10am–6pm, Sun 11am–5pm; closed Mon
- $ $15 adults, $10 seniors, $5 students; pay what you wish on Sundays; admission includes ArtPhone audio guide

Henry Clay Frick (1849–1919) was a fascinating man who, obsessed with making money, built up a massive fortune with the Carnegie Steel Company. His sole interest outside the business was art and, as his wealth grew, so did his fabulous collection of European art, which he hung in his palatial mansion on 5th Avenue. Despite having a reputation as an ungenerous man, he bequeathed both the pictures and the mansion to the public when he died.

There are 16 galleries and, unusually, the pictures aren't displayed by period or style, but in the way that Frick would have hung them in his home. The Fragonard Room shows the large Fragonard paintings as well as 18th-century furniture and porcelain. Paintings by Holbein, El Greco, Titian and Bellini are in the Living Room, while in the West Gallery you'll find landscapes by Constable and portraits by Rembrandt.

INTERNATIONAL CENTER OF PHOTOGRAPHY
Midtown

- ✉ 1133 Avenue of the Americas at 43rd Street
- ☎ 212-857 0000
- 🖱 www.icp.org
- 🚇 Subway B, D, F to 42nd Street
- ⏲ Tues–Thurs 10am–6pm, Fri 10am–8pm Sat and Sun 10am–6pm; closed Mon
- $ $10 adults, $7 students and seniors, under 12s free. Voluntary contribution Friday 5–8pm

The ICP is a school and a museum. It houses

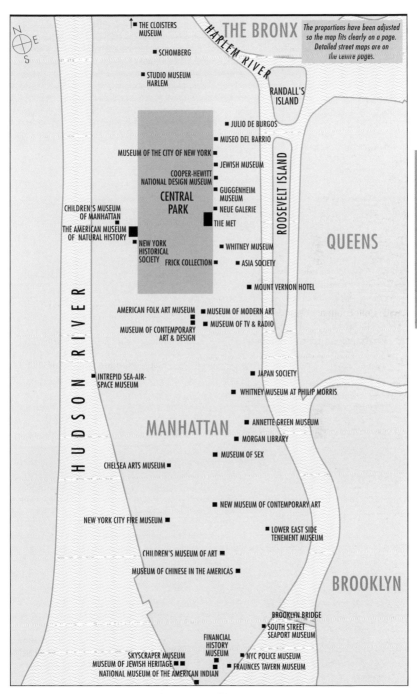

Museums in Manhattan

some excellent exhibitions, such as legendary photographer Larry Clark's work, as well as a permanent collection, which consists of more than 60,000 photographs spanning decades including some original prints by Weegee, who photographed crime scenes and New York nightlife in the 1930s and 1940s.

ISAMU NOGUCHI GARDEN MUSEUM

The Japanese sculptor's art can be seen at this museum in Queens. See page 269.

JAPAN SOCIETY
Midtown East
- ✉ 333 East 47th Street between 1st and 2nd Avenues
- ☎ 212-832 1155
- 🖰 www.japansociety.org
- 🚇 Subway E, V to Lexington Avenue/53rd Street; 6 to 51st Street
- ☉ Tues–Thurs 11am–6pm, Fri 11am–9pm, Sat and Sun 11am–5pm
- $ $12 adults, $10 students and seniors, under 16s free

The perfect place to feed your yearnings for all things Japanese from textiles and modern photography to historical ceramics, paintings, glass and metalworks. The ideal combination of Zen and now.

JEWISH MUSEUM
Upper East Side
- ✉ 1109 5th Avenue at 92nd Street
- ☎ 212-423 3200
- 🖰 www.thejewishmuseum.org
- 🚇 Subway 4, 5, 6 to 96th Street
- ☉ Sun–Wed 11am–5.45pm, Thurs 11am–8pm, Fri 11am–3pm; closed Sat and major Jewish holidays
- $ $10 adults, $7.50 students and seniors, children under 12 free. Voluntary contribution Thurs 5–8pm

Impressive annual exhibitions. The core exhibit is called The Jewish Journey and sets out how the Jewish people have survived

The Jewish Museum

Museum of Chinese in the Americas

through the centuries and explores the essence of Jewish identity. Many of the objects were actually rescued from European synagogues before the Second World War. It covers 4,000 years of history with an emphasis on art and culture both ancient and modern.

★ ★ ★ ★ **BRIT TIP** ★ ★ ★ ★
★   ★
★ Treat yourself to delicious kosher ★
★ cuisine at the Jewish Museum's ★
★ trendy Café Weissman. Closed ★
★ on Fridays. ★
★ ★

LOWER EAST SIDE TENEMENT MUSEUM
Lower East Side
- ✉ 108 Orchard Street between Broome and Delancey Streets
- ☎ 212-431 0233
- 🖰 www.tenement.org
- 🚇 Subway F to Delancey Street; B, D, Q to Grand Street; J, M, Z to Essex Street
- ☉ Visitor Center open Mon 11am-5.30pm; Tues–Fri 11am–6pm; Sat and Sun 10.45am–5.30pm. However, the museum can only be visited via a tour – best to book in advance.
- $ $15 adults, $11 students and seniors for 1-hour tour; 2 Ticket Combo: $23 adults, $16 students and seniors; 3 Ticket Combo: $32 adults, $22 students and seniors. Under 5s free.

★ ★ ★ ★ **BRIT TIP** ★ ★ ★ ★
★   ★
★ Before you take one of the walking ★
★ tours at the Lower East Side ★
★ Tenement Museum, it is well worth ★
★ watching the slide show and film. ★
★ ★

TOP FIVE GALLERIES FOR MODERN ART

New York is a hotbed of artistic talent so if you want to pick up some original work while you're there, or just look at some, here's five places to head for.

Andrew Kreps Gallery: Chelsea
✉ 516A West 20th Street between 10th and 11th Avenues.
☎ 212-741 8849
🖰 www.andrewkreps.com.
🚇 Subway 23rd Street
🕐 Tues–Sat 10am–6pm
An innovative band of work on display from artists including Ruth Root and Roe Ethridge.

Deitch Projects: SoHo
✉ 18 Wooster Street between Canal and Grand Streets
☎ 212-343 7300
🚇 Subway N, R, W to Prince Street; B, D, F, V to Broadway/Lafayette Street
🕐 Tues–Sat noon–6pm
$ Free
Jeffrey Deitch's gallery is worth a peep if you're in SoHo. Focusing on large-scale installations, and sometimes live spectacles, by contemporary artists (including Yoko Ono) working in all kinds of media, it's not as scary as it sounds.

Gagosian Gallery: Chelsea
✉ 555 West 24th Street between 10th and 11th Avenues
☎ 212-741 1111
🖰 www.gagosian.com

🕐 Sept–May Tues–Sat 10am–6pm; Jun–Aug Mon–Fri 10am–6pm.
$ Free
An excellent, vast gallery that opened in 1999 and has featured exhibitions of work by the likes of Damien Hirst.

Maccarone Inc: Lower East Side
✉ 45 Canal Street between Ludlow and Orchard Streets
☎ 212-431 4977
🚇 Subway F to East Broadway/Delancey Street
🕐 Wed–Sun noon–6pm
$ Free
Spread over four floors, this cool gallery run by Michele Maccarone features work by up-and-coming local and European artists.

Projectile Gallery: 57th Street
✉ 3rd floor, 37 West 57th Street between 5th and 6th Avenues
☎ 212-688 4673
🚇 Subway F to 57th Street. N, R, W to 5th Avenue/59th Street.
🕐 Sept–Jun Tues–Sat noon–6pm. Call for summer times.
$ Free
A darling of the art world since it opened in 1998, it features work by hotter than hot young artists.

After they had gone through Ellis Island, what happened to many of those millions of immigrants? They ended up in tenements on the Lower East Side of New York and this is the museum that tells their poignant stories. You'll get the chance to see four re-created apartments in a typical, five-storey tenement, giving a good insight into the living conditions of the seekers of the American Dream.

The museum consists of several tenement houses – essentially America's first public housing, predating almost every housing law in the US – that are accessible only via the tours. These houses contain several apartments, faithfully restored and complete with furniture and clothes. It's a must-see in order to understand not only this neighbourhood, which continues to function as a launching pad for fresh generations of artists and retailers, but also the American success story.

The tour Piecing It Together: Immigrants in the Garment Industry examines the life of the Polish Levine family, who ran a garment shop in their apartment in the

Morgan Library

early 1900s, plus the stories of other immigrants involved in the garment industry from the 1930s to the present day. The tour Getting By: Weathering the Great Depressions of 1873 and 1929 focuses on the German-Jewish Gumpertz family in the 1870s and the Sicilian-Catholic Baldizzi family in the 1930s and how they forged new lives for themselves in America.

For information on family activities at the museum, see page 210.

MERCHANT'S HOUSE MUSEUM
East Village

- ✉ 29 East 4th Street between Lafayette and Bowery Streets
- ☎ 212-777 1089
- ⌂ www.merchantshouse.com
- 🚗 Subway 6 to Astor Place
- ◷ Thurs–Mon 12pm–5pm; regular tours Mon, Thurs, Fri and 1pm Sat and Sun.
- $ $8 adults, $5 students and seniors, children free

Built in 1832, this was home to prosperous merchant Seabury Tredwell and his family for over 100 years and is the city's only preserved 19th-century home – complete with original furnishings and decor.

MORGAN LIBRARY
Midtown East

- ✉ 29 East 36th Street between Madison and Park Avenues
- ☎ 212-590 0300
- ⌂ www.morganlibrary.org
- 🚗 Subway 6 to 33rd Street

The Morgan re-opened in Spring 2006 after a 3-year $102 million major expansion and renovation. This doubles the exhibition space for its fabulous collection, which includes medieval and Renaissance manuscripts; drawings and prints from the 14th century onwards, including works by Rubens, Degas, Blake and Pollock; ancient Middle Eastern seals and tablets; and original handwritten music manuscripts by Bach, Beethoven, Brahms and Schubert. It also has a new reading room and a central court in the style of an Italian Piazza.

MOUNT VERNON HOTEL MUSEUM AND GARDEN
Upper East Side

- ✉ 421 East 61st Street between 1st and York Avenues
- ☎ 212-838 6878
- ⌂ www.mvhm.org
- 🚇 Subway 4, 5, 6 to 59th Street
- ◷ Tues–Sun 11am–4pm; Tues 6-9pm in summer; closed Aug and some holidays
- $ $8 adults, $7 students and seniors, under 12s free

An amazing structure that dates back to the colonial era, this was once the coach house of the daughter of America's second president, John Adams. An early 18th-century building, it has been lovingly restored by the Colonial Dames of America who will sometimes be on hand to talk about the furnishings in the house and the park at the back.

MUSEUM OF AMERICAN FINANCE
Lower Manhattan

- ✉ 48 Wall Street
- ☎ 212-908 4110
- ⌂ www.financialhistory.org
- 🚗 Subway 4, 5 to Bowling Green; N, R to Rector Street
- ◷ Tues–Sat 10am–4pm
- $ Suggested donation $2

Founded in 1998, this museum, which moved into the former headquarters of the Bank of New York on Wall Street in late 2006, traces the growth of the world's largest financial superpower. It has the largest public museum archive of financial documents in the world and exhibits include rare $100,000 bills. Wow!

MUSEUM OF ART AND DESIGN
Midtown

- ✉ 40 West 53rd Street between 5th and 6th Avenues
- ☎ 212-956 3535
- ⌂ www.madmuseum.org
- 🚗 Subway E, V to 5th Avenue
- ◷ Daily 10am–6pm, Thurs 10am–8pm
- $ $9 adults, $7 students and seniors, under 12s free; pay what you wish Thurs 6-8pm

Along with the neighbouring American Folk Art Museum, this museum, formerly known as the American Craft Museum, gives a perfect insight into American arts and crafts. It has everything from wood and metal to clay, glass and fibre. In 2006, it revealed plans for a $60 million renovation of the building at 2 Columbus Circle that will be its new home in 2008, complete with floor-to-ceiling windows on the ground floor and zigzagged windows on the upper floors.

MUSEUM OF CHINESE IN THE AMERICAS
Chinatown
- ✉ 2nd floor, 70 Mulberry Street on the corner of Bayard Street
- ☎ 212-619 4785
- ⌂ www.moca-nyc.org
- 🚇 Subway N, R, 6 to Canal Street
- ⏰ Tues–Sun noon–6pm, Fri until 7pm.
- $ $3 adults, $1 seniors and children, under 12s free

A fascinating little museum tucked away on the first floor of the community centre. It contains photographs and personal belongings and talks are given on the history of Chinese immigrants to both North and South America.

MUSEUM OF THE CITY OF NEW YORK
Spanish Harlem
- ✉ 1220 5th Avenue at 103rd Street
- ☎ 212-534 1672
- ⌂ www.mcny.org
- 🚇 Subway 6 to 103rd Street
- ⏰ Tue–Sun 10am–5pm; closed Mon
- $ Suggested donation $20 families, $9 adults, $5 seniors, students and children; under 12s free

★ ★ ★ ★ **BRIT TIP** ★ ★ ★ ★

The Museum of the City of New York is very relaxed about defining your family. Groups can buy a family ticket here even if they are not related.

★ ★

The entire breadth of New York's history and the people who played parts in its development are celebrated in this fascinating museum. Prints, photographs, paintings and sculptures and even clothing and decorative household objects are used to tell the story of New York City. The museum is particularly noted for its Broadway memorabilia.

MUSEUM OF JEWISH HERITAGE: A LIVING MEMORIAL TO THE HOLOCAUST
Battery Park City
- ✉ 36 Battery Place, Battery Park City
- ☎ 646-437 4200 info; 212-437 4200 tickets in advance
- ⌂ www.mjhnyc.org

- 🚗 Subway 1 to South Ferry; R, W to Whitehall Street; 4, 5 to Bowling Green
- ⏰ Sun–Tues, Thurs 10am–5.45pm, Wed 10am–8pm, Fri and eve of Jewish holidays 10am–5pm. Sat and Jewish holidays closed
- $ $10 adults, $7 seniors, $5 students, under 12s free; free for all Wed from 4pm

★ ★ ★ ★ **BRIT TIP** ★ ★ ★ ★

Before entering the Museum of Jewish Heritage, take a look at the six-sided shape of the tiered roof, a symbolic reminder of the six million who died in the Holocaust and of the Star of David.

★ ★

Joy, tradition, tragedy and unspeakable horror are the powerful themes of this museum, which tells the moving story of 20th-century Jewish life from the perspective of those who lived it. Created as a living memorial to the Holocaust, it puts the tragedy into the larger context of modern Jewish history and includes 24 original films that feature testimonies from Steven Spielberg's Survivors of the Shoah Visual History Foundation, as well as the museum's own video archive.

★ ★ ★ ★ **BRIT TIP** ★ ★ ★ ★

It is worth renting an audio guide at the Museum of Jewish Heritage, narrated by Meryl Streep and Itzhak Perlman, cost $5.

★ ★

MUSEUM OF SEX
Madison Square Park
- ✉ 233 5th Avenue at 27th Street
- ☎ 212-689 6337
- ⌂ www.museumofsex.org
- 🚇 Subway 6, N, R, W to 28th Street
- ⏰ Sun–Fri 11am–6.30pm, Sat 11am–8pm
- $ $14.50 adults, $13.50 students and seniors. Minimum age 18 and IDs will be checked

Times Square may have been cleaned up, but the prostitutes are back in Manhattan in force at New York's most audacious museum. Not for the fainthearted, the inaugural exhibition examined how New York City transformed sex in America by

MUSEUMS AND GALLERIES

exploring the histories of prostitution, burlesque, birth control, obscenity and fetish. This and other exhibitions use selections from private and public collections never shown before and if you're in any doubt as to whether this is the museum for you, just bear in mind that some of the material was once confiscated and classified as obscene.

★★★★ **BRIT TIP** ★★★★

★ Special package holiday breaks that
★ include a ticket to this museum are
★ available for guests staying at the
★ nearby Gershwin Hotel. Check out
★ www.gershwinhotel.com for details.

The main collections of the museum include serious works of art by contemporary artists and a massive collection of film, videos, magazines, books and artefacts acquired over 20 years by Ralph Whittington, the former curator of the Library of Congress. Blow-up dolls never had it so good! Clearly the entrance fee is designed to put off casual thrill-seekers and the museum strictly enforces the minimum age requirement. Despite the subject matter, it is a serious institution with an important message about past and present sexual subcultures and our modern attitudes to sex and sexuality.

MUSEUM OF TELEVISION AND RADIO
Midtown
✉ 25 West 52nd Street between 5th and 6th Avenues
☎ 212-621 6600
🖰 www.mtr.org
🚇 Subway E, V to 5th Avenue/53rd Street; B, D, F, V to 47th–50th Streets/Rockefeller Center
🕐 Tues–Sun noon–6pm, Thurs noon–8pm, Fri theatre programmes until 9pm; closed Mon

Museum of Jewish Heritage

$ $10 adults, $8 students and seniors, $5 under 14s

In addition to the exhibits, the museum also has a daily programme of screenings in two cinemas and two presentation rooms. Pick up a copy of the schedules in the lobby on your way in. You can also make an appointment with the library to check out the museum's collection of over 100,000 radio and TV programmes before accessing them on the custom-designed database.

NATIONAL ACADEMY OF DESIGN
Midtown
✉ 1083 5th Avenue
☎ 212-369 4880
🖰 www.nationalacademy.org
🚇 Subway 4, 5, 6 to 86th Street
🕐 Weds, Thurs noon–5pm,; Fri–Sun 11am–6pm
$ $10 adults, $5 students and seniors, children free

Both a museum and a design school of fine art, with the largest collection of 19th- and 20th-century American art in the country, comprising more than 5,000 works. Museum tours every Friday at 2pm ($5 per person).

NATIONAL CARTOON MUSEUM
Midtown
✉ Empire State Building, 350 5th Avenue between 33rd and 34th Streets
🖰 www.cartoon.org

Opened in 2006, the former International Museum of Cartoon Art is now housed where you simply can't miss it. With over 200,000 original cartoons, 10,000 books and 1,000 hours of animation, it is the largest collection in the world. Check the website for up-to-date information on visiting.

NATIONAL MUSEUM OF THE AMERICAN INDIAN
Bowling Green/Financial District
✉ George Gustav Heye Center, US Custom House, 1 Bowling Green between State and Whitehall Streets
☎ 212-514 3700
🖰 www.americanindian.si.edu
🚇 Subway 4, 5 to Bowling Green; 1, 9 to South Ferry
🕐 Daily 10am–5pm, Thurs 10am–8pm
$ Free

The first museum dedicated entirely to Native American history, art, performing art and culture. The collection includes fabulous leather clothing, intricately beaded headdresses, sashes, hats and shoes, explaining the white man's influence on

Indian culture, as well as their own centuries-old traditions. Despite the size and grandness of the beautiful building, it has only 500 pieces on display and thus seems quite small. However, it is very well laid out and the explanations of each piece have usually been given by Native Americans.

NATIONAL SPORTS MUSEUM
Lower Manhattan

✉ 26 Broadway at the base of the Canyon of Heroes, at the starting point for the ferry to the Statue of Liberty and Ellis Island
☎ 212-837 7950
⌐ www.thesportsmuseum.com

Just opened in late 2006, this is the first ever dedicated sports museum, with interactive exhibitions on sports across the ages and throughout the world. Check the website for up-to-date information.

NEUE GALERIE MUSEUM FOR GERMAN AND AUSTRIAN ART
Upper East Side

✉ 1048 5th Avenue at 86th Street
☎ 212-628 6200
⌐ www.neuegalerie.org
🚇 Subway 4, 5, 6 to 86th Street at Lexington Avenue; B, C to 86th Street at Central Park West
⊙ Sat, Sun, Mon, Thurs 11am–6pm, Fri 11am–9pm; closed Tues and Wed
$ $15 adults, $10 students and seniors. Under 12s not permitted, under 16s only with an adult

Founded by the late German Expressionist art dealer Serge Sabarsky and chairman of the MoMA board Ronald S Lauder, this museum exhibits fine and decorative arts of Germany and Austria from the first half of the 20th century. A real bonus is the building itself – a wonderful Louis XIII-style Beaux Art landmark.

★ ★ ★ ★ **BRIT TIP** ★ ★ ★ ★

While you're on the Museum Mile, take a pit stop at the fabulous Sabarsky Café in the Neue Galerie, which is open every day except Tuesday. Catch a classical music performance on Wed and Thurs afternoons or Friday evenings.

NEW MUSEUM OF CONTEMPORARY ART
Chelsea

✉ 556 West 22nd Street at 11th Avenue
☎ 212-219 1222
⌐ www.newmuseum.org
🚇 Subway
⊙ Tues–Sat noon–6pm, Thurs noon–8pm; closed Sun, Mon
$ $6 adults, $3 students, under 18s free; $3 Thurs 6–8pm

When they say 'contemporary', they really mean it. All the works exhibited are by living artists, often looking at social issues through modern media and machinery.

This will open in late 2007 at 235 The Bowery, Lower East Side. Designed by cutting-edge Japanese architects, SANAA, their stunning seven-storey white tower was named one of the top architectural projects of the year in 2003. It will house a theatre, library, learning center and café, as well as rooftop terraces where you can gaze out on the New York skyline.

NEW YORK CITY FIRE MUSEUM
West SoHo

✉ 278 Spring Street between Varick and Houston Streets
☎ 212-691 1303
⌐ www.nycfiremuseum.org
🚇 Subway 1, 9 to Houston Street; C, E to Spring Street
⊙ Tues–Sat 10am–5pm, Sun 10am–4pm
$ $5 adults, $2 students and seniors, $1 under 12s

Technically not a children's museum, though the bright shiny engines are an undoubted hit with youngsters and the young at heart.

South Street Seaport Museum

BRIT'S GUIDE MUSEUM AWARDS

Most unmissable museum:
Metropolitan Museum of Art (page 119)

Most hands-on museums:
American Museum of Natural History (page 117)
Intrepid Sea-Air-Space Museum (page 118)
Children's Museum of Manhattan (page 208)

Most audacious museum:
Museum of Sex (page 129)

Most amazing museum building:
Solomon R Guggenheim (page 120)

Most unattractive museum building:
Whitney Museum of American Art (page 134)

Most fun bijou museum:
Museum of the City of New York (page 129)

Most tear-jerking museums:
Lower East Side Tenement Museum (page 126)
Museum of Jewish Heritage (page 129)

★★★★ **BRIT TIP** ★★★★

★ At the beginning of June, don't miss
  the wonderful Museum Mile
  Festival. On the first Tuesday of the
  month all nine museums along 5th
  Avenue – including the Met – are
  free to the public. The road is closed
  and the traffic is replaced by live
  bands, street entertainers and
  outdoor art activities for children.

Housed in the old quarters of Engine 30, here you will find artefacts and fire engines depicting 200 years of city firefighting.

NEW YORK CITY POLICE MUSEUM
Bowling Green/Financial District
✉ 100 Old Slip between South and Water Streets
☎ 212-480 3100
🖥 www.nycpolicemuseum.org
🚇 Subway 4, 5 to Bowling Green; 2, 3 to Wall Street; 1, 9 to South Ferry/Whitehall

🕐 Tues–Sat 10am–5pm, Sun 11am–5pm
$ Suggested donation $5 adults, $3 seniors, $2 age 6–18, under 6s free

Having opened in January 2000, this is one of the very latest attractions in the Downtown area and it's a little corker. It is now permanently housed in the former 1st Precinct building – the oldest cop shop in New York. Highlights include the Mounted Unit – one of the oldest and most prestigious within the NYPD – and the K-9 dog unit. In addition to the police memorabilia – a line-up of guns, uniforms and badges – there's even the Tommy gun with its original violin case that was used to kill mobster Frankie Yale. Plus, you can have a go at playing detective yourself in the interactive crime scene area. View the NYPD Hall of Heroes, which now has a memorial to the 23 policemen and women who lost their lives in the attack on the World Trade Center in 2001.

NEW YORK CITY TRANSIT MUSEUM
Brooklyn Heights
A great little museum that is particularly popular with children. See page 264.

NEW YORK HALL OF SCIENCE
Queens
A great science museum with demos. See page 269.

NEW YORK HISTORICAL SOCIETY
Upper West Side
✉ 170 Central Park West between 76th and 77th Streets
☎ 212-873 3400
🖥 www.nyhistory.org
🚇 Subway B, C to 81st Street; 1 to 79th Street
🕐 Tues–Sun 10am–6pm
$ $10 adults, $5 students and seniors, under 12s free

When this jewel was formed in 1804 it was the only art museum in the city until the opening of the Metropolitan Museum of Art in 1872. The Historical Society was founded to chronicle New York's history and is home to the world's largest collection of Tiffany stained-glass shades and lamps, two million manuscripts, including letters sent by George Washington during the War of Independence, and a lock of his hair.

P.S. 1 CONTEMPORARY ART CENTER
Long Island City, Queens
A ground-breaking modern art museum.
See page 269.

QUEENS COUNTY FARM MUSEUM
Floral Park, Queens
A fun, working historical farm with hayrides.
See page 270.

SCHOMBURG CENTER FOR RESEARCH IN BLACK CULTURE
Harlem
✉ 515 Malcolm X Boulevard at 135th Street
☎ 212-491 2200
🖱 www.schomburgcenter.org
🚇 Subway 2, 3 to 135th Street
🕐 Tues, Wed noon–8pm; Thurs, Fri noon–6pm; Sat 10am–6pm; closed Sun
$ Free. Tours by appointment

Established in 1926 by Arthur Schomburg, the museum has more than five million items including books, photographs, manuscripts, art works, films, videos and sound recordings that document the historical and cultural development of black people in the United States, the Caribbean, the Americas, Africa, Europe and Asia.

★★★★ **BRIT TIP** ★★★★

★ To see the Schomburg Center at its ★
★ best, phone or check out the ★
★ website in advance to find out ★
★ about film screenings and jazz ★
★ concerts. ★

★★★★★★★★★★★★★★★★★★★★★★★★★★★

The research unit is open to anyone, while there are exhibitions on art dating back to the 17th century that include masks, paintings and sculptures. Incidentally, the corner of Malcolm X Boulevard, where the Schomburg sits, was once home to Harlem's Speaker's Corner where people used to come and talk about their political beliefs and organisations.

SKYSCRAPER MUSEUM
Battery Park
✉ 39 Battery Place
☎ 212-968 1961
🖱 www.skyscraper.org
🚇 Subway 4, 5 to Bowling Green; 1, R, W to South Ferry/Whitehall Street

🕐 Wed–Sun 12–6pm
$ $5 adults, $2.50 seniors and students

In a new home since 2004, this is one of New York's most apt museums, celebrating as it does the city's rich architectural heritage and examining what historic forces and which individuals shaped the different skylines of its past. Through exhibitions, programmes and publications, the museum offers a fascinating insight into how individual buildings were created, complete with detailed information about how the contractors bid for the work, what was involved and how the building work was executed, all with comprehensive photographic illustrations.

Since 1997, the museum has presented exhibitions in temporary spaces – two vacant banking halls on Wall Street in the heart of New York's historic Financial District – including Downtown New York, Building The Empire State and Big Buildings. The exhibitions are surprisingly moving as they manage to convey the very real human sacrifices and energy put into creating these incredible edifices. Most moving of all was its recent homage to the Twin Towers, which marked the entire 30-year history of the World Trade Center. In its current space is a Ground Zero Viewing Wall.

SOUTH STREET SEAPORT MUSEUM
Financial District
✉ 12 Fulton Street at South Street
☎ 212-748 8600
🖱 www.southstseaport.org
🚇 Subway A, C to Broadway/Nassau Street; 2, 3, 4, 5, J, Z, M to Fulton Street
🕐 Summer (Apr–Sept) Tues–Sun 10am–5pm, winter (Nov–Mar) Fri–Mon 10am–5pm.
$ $8 adults, $6 seniors and students, $4 children (5–12) including all tours, films, galleries and museum-owned ships.
Discounted entrance on winter Mondays.

A sprawling mass of galleries, 19th-century buildings, a visitors' centre and a selection of ships, all of which give an insight into life in the olden days of New York. The museum is also the venue for a series of free outdoor summer concerts held almost nightly. A new exhibition launched in 2006 shows how important the port once was to New York's livelihood.

STUDIO MUSEUM IN HARLEM
Harlem
- ✉ 144 West 125th Street between 7th and Lenox Avenues
- ☎ 212-864 4500
- 🖰 www.studiomuseum.org
- 🚇 Subway A, B, C, D, 2, 3, 4, 5, 6 to 125th Street
- ◷ Wed–Fri 10am–6pm, Sat 10am–6pm, Sun noon–6pm; closed Mon–Tues
- $ $7 adults, $3 students and seniors, under 12s free

Works of art by African-American, African and Caribbean artists.

THE TALLER BORICUA AT THE JULIA DE BURGOS LATINO CULTURAL CENTER
Spanish Harlem
- ✉ 1680 Lexington Avenue at 106th Street
- ☎ 212-831 4333
- 🚇 Subway 6 to 110th Street
- ◷ Tues–Sat noon–6pm, Thurs 1–7pm
- $ Free

Another excellent location to see works by Latino artists. Around the museum, look out for pavement artwork by James de la Vega, a young local artist.

VAN CORTLANDT HOUSE MUSEUM
The Bronx
Fascinating former family plantation estate-turned museum. See page 266.

WHITNEY MUSEUM OF AMERICAN ART
Upper East Side
- ✉ 945 Madison Avenue at 75th Street
- ☎ 212-570 3676 or 1-800-WHITNEY
- 🖰 www.whitney.org
- 🚇 Subway 6 to 77th Street
- ◷ Wed, Thurs 11am–6pm; Fri 1–9pm; Sat, Sun 11am–6pm; closed Mon, Tues

Whitney Museum

- $ $12 adults, $9.50 students, under 12s free; first Friday of every month 6–9pm pay what you wish, plus musical performances

The Whitney may be housed in one of the most ghastly looking buildings in the world – a series of grey, granite cubes designed by Marcel Breuer – but it has a world-class collection of 20th-century art. Yet it all came about almost by accident. Gertrude Vanderbilt Whitney offered her entire collection to the Metropolitan but was turned down, so she decided to set up her own museum. As a result, in 1931, the Whitney was founded with a core group of 700 art objects.

Subsequently, the museum's holdings have been greatly enriched by other purchases and the gifts of other major collectors. It now has a permanent collection of 12,000 works including paintings, sculptures, drawings, prints, photographs and multimedia installations and is still growing.

As well as the wide range of artists in its collection, the Whitney has huge bodies of works by artists such as Alexander Calder, Edward Hopper, Georgia O'Keefe, Gaston Lachaise and Agnes Martin.

Although the Midtown branch (below) is known for exhibitions of works by contemporary artists, the main museum still likes to mount cutting-edge exhibitions. To make the most of your visit, you can take an audio tour.

The shop in the basement, next to the restaurant, is filled with funky and colourful gifts. There's some great stuff for kids including soap crayons that will wash off baths and tiles and colourful blocks of soap that can be moulded into sculptures.

WHITNEY MUSEUM OF AMERICAN ART AT PHILIP MORRIS
Midtown
- ✉ 120 Park Avenue at 42nd Street
- ☎ 212-878 2550
- 🚇 Subway S, 4, 5, 6, 7 to 42nd Street/ Grand Central
- ◷ Mon–Fri 11am–6pm, Thurs 11am–7.30pm. The Sculpture Court is open Mon–Sat 7.30am–9.30pm, Sun 11am–7pm
- $ Free

The Midtown branch of the Whitney is devoted to exhibitions of the work of individual contemporary artists.

CHAPTER 7

Restaurants

New York is a city of extremes when it comes to dining out. There are nearly 18,000 restaurants to choose from, at one end are the classics, such as Union Square Café, that seem to transcend fashion and continually turn out delicious cuisine to cross the Atlantic for. At the other end of the spectrum are eateries that are so hip they're practically going out of fashion before they've even served up their first plate of fusion food.

Brit's Guide aims to help you to experience the must-eat-at places that have been around for years and those achingly hip joints that are as much about whom you're going to spot air kissing whom as the food. We also include a smattering of restaurants that sit between the established and the new that are just plain good value – or unusual.

One of the great things about New York restaurants is that they're usually excellent value for money when compared with eating out in the UK, particularly London. You can get a first-class breakfast for under $10 and a slap-up dinner for less than $40. It's well worth heading off the beaten track to find some of your own delectable diners in the city's coolest neighbourhoods, but we have plenty of suggestions for you if you don't fancy chancing it. The chapter starts with a selection of our favourite restaurants for fine dining, romance and views, categories that cover the majority of enquiries we receive from Brits keen to sample the culinary delights of Manhattan in a wonderful environment.

DINING PRICE GUIDE

It's clear from the outset what price categories many Big Apple eateries fall into. Crisp white tablecloths, wine glasses the size of goldfish bowls and waiters in designer garb indicate a blow-the-budget $100-plus bill. Dark, dingy diners with formica table tops and a waitress with a name tag suggest that you're going to be paying cash, and not much of it. However, there are some restaurants where the tariff doesn't match the decor or the standard of food the façade, so we have compiled a price guide to help you make your dining decisions with confidence.

$	Cheap and cheerful
$$	Good value
$$$	Posh meal out
$$$$	Blow the budget

TOP FIVE NEW OPENINGS

The last 12 months has proved an exciting time for the dining capital of the world, with openings of new restaurants adding around 5,000 more restaurant seats to a city that already boasts over a million. Here are the five that have been creating the most buzz in the gourmet world.

The Four Seasons

NOBU 57 $$$$
Japanese-Peruvian
Midtown
- ✉ 40th West 57 Street between 5th and 6th Avenues
- ☎ 212-757 3000
- ⌂ www.noburestaurants.com
- 🚇 Subway F to 57th Street

Opened in 2005, the newest Nobu to hit the scene serves the same food in must-be-seen-to-be-believed surroundings according to Zagat, who describe it as a 'triumph of theatrical Feng Shui'. It is tipped to be as hot for people-watching as the original.

GORDON RAMSAY AT LONDON NYC HOTEL $$$$
British fusion
Midtown
- ✉ 151 West 54th Street at 7th Avenue
- ☎ 212-307 5000
- ⌂ www.thelondonnyc.com
- 🚇 Subway B, D, E to 7th Avenue

London's most notorious Michelin three-star chef hit the Big Apple in style in autumn 2006 at the former Righa Royal Hotel which, after a $50m refurbishment and name change, is now the new darling of the dining and bar scene.

COLORS RESTAURANT $$-$$$
International
Theater district
- ✉ 417 Lafayette Street at Astor Place
- ☎ 212-777 8443
- ⌂ www.colors-nyc.com
- 🚇 Subway 6 to Astor Place

Colors made the headlines in 2006 as the restaurant where dozens of surviving workers from Windows on the World, the restaurant that was atop the World Trade Center, have regrouped. And they not only work there but also have a financial say and stake in it. It's a co-operative venture, owned and run by its waiters and waitresses, bus boys and cooks. The menu is as global as you can get, from Eastern spring rolls with shellfish to Caribbean goat stew, or American rib-eye steak and seared scallops.

BUDDAKAN $$$-$$$$
Pan-Asian
Chelsea
- ✉ 75 9th Avenue at 16th Street
- ☎ 212-989 6699
- ⌂ www.buddakan.com
- 🚇 Subway 1, 2, 3, 9 to 14th Street

A Pan-Asian import from the successful restaurant of the same name in

Philadelphia. It was introduced to New York by Stephen Starr and is watched over by consultant Angelo Sosa, formerly of Yumcha. Expect seriously beautiful people and food.

DEL POSTO $$$
Italian
Meatpacking District
- ✉ 85 10th Avenue at 16th Street
- ☎ 212-497 8090
- 🚇 Subway A, C, E to 14th Street

This new restaurant from Mario Batali and the Bastianich family is posh Italian nosh, which has left the New York restaurant critics split. The surroundings are super-plush – think old-style gentleman's club – with a live pianist, and the food fancy; lobster risotto for two at $60.

TOP FIVE FOR FINE DINING

Considering how many thousands of eating establishments there are in New York and how many of them serve up wonderful food in delightful environments, it's difficult to narrow them down to a top five. Yet all the restaurants listed below have earned their stripes for getting all the elements of fine dining and hospitality right: consistently excellent and innovative cuisine, attentive service and an enjoyable ambience in a wonderful setting. They obviously have prices to match, but for a once-in-a-holiday treat they won't disappoint.

UNION SQUARE CAFE $$-$$$
American–Italian
Midtown East
- ✉ 21 East 16 Street between 5th Avenue and Union Square
- ☎ 212-243 4020
- ⌂ www.unionsquarecafe.com
- 🚇 Subway 4, 5, 6, L, N, R to Union Square.

One of America's most popular restaurants, Danny Meyer's Union Square Cafe serves robustly flavoured, seasonal American cuisine in a relaxed setting of casual elegance. It's worth noting that, despite the proliferation of fashionable eateries that regularly open in New York, it's this restaurant that the city's movers and shakers still flock to, to flex the company credit card. There are three dining areas: balcony seating and a cluster of tables on the lower level, both offshoots of the long mahogany bar, and an adjacent main dining room. The decor is simple but effective – think polished cherrywood floors, oversized pussy willows and colourful artwork on the walls. There's a full lunch and dinner menu with daily specials in the dining room and the bar.

Union Square Cafe is as famous for its impeccable, friendly service as it is for its unusual but fabulous food. Top Chef Michael Romano's Tuscan-influenced menu includes delicacies such as grilled lamb chops with potato-Gruyère gratin and sautéed insalata tricolore, pan-roasted salmon with plum tomatoes, almonds, olives and bottarga, wild striped bass Barigoule, with a savoury artichoke-spring onion broth. Weekly specials include a lobster shepherd's pie and roast suckling pig. And don't forget to order the famous home-made garlic potato chips.

★ Restaurant mogul Danny Meyer, the brains behind the Union Square Cafe, has opened swish new restaurant The Modern at the Musuem of Modern Art (tel 212-333 1220, www.themodernnyc.com). ★

BABBO $$$$
Italian
Greenwich Village
✉ 110 Waverly Place between MacDougal and 6th Avenues
☎ 212-777 0303
🖥 www.babbonyc.com
🚇 Subway A, B, C, D, E, F, Q to Washington Square

The crown jewel of Greenwich Village restaurants is unmatched for the quality and quantity of its Italian dishes;

★ Order one of the fabulous tasting menus at Babbo for a really great choice of dishes. The pasta tasting menu is particularly mouth-watering, including black tagliatelle with parsnips and pancetta, garganelli with funghi trifolatia and pappardelle Bolognese. It's also a cheaper option than choosing individual dishes as the menus ring in at around $64 per person. ★

forewarned is forearmed so make sure you wear a skirt or trousers with an elasticated waist, because we're talking large, rich portions here. Everything in Mario Batali's restaurant is delightful, from the simple split-level dining room that seats 90 to the stunning bar area. However, it's the imaginative food that pushes this restaurant into the top five fine dining experiences. How about goats' cheese tortelloni dusted in dried orange and wild fennel pollen? Or 'mint love letters' with spicy lamb sausage? Yum.

NOBU $$$$
Japanese-Peruvian
TriBeCa
✉ 105 Hudson Street at Franklin Street
☎ 212-219 0500
🖥 www.myriadrestaurantgroup.com
🚇 Subway 1, 9 to Hudson Street

It's been around for 13 years now (ancient for a fashionable New York restaurant) but this TriBeCa Mecca is still without a doubt the best Japanese restaurant in the US, serving excellent fresh cuisine that will find 'tastebuds you never knew you had' according to the restaurant researchers at Zagat. The decor, by architect David Rockwell, is East meets West, with birch trees, wood floors, seaweed mats and subdued lighting. The multi-award-winning menu includes lots of cooked and raw delicacies, the black cod with miso continues to be a favourite and the new style sashimi lightly cooked with garlic is also amazing.

★ If you can't get into the celeb-jammed Nobu, try Nobu Next Door (212-334 4445), which only takes walk ins and is, unsurprisingly, located next door to the main restaurant. It is a more reasonably priced outlet for mere mortals who would rather wait for an hour than a month to sample some of the food everyone is raving about. ★

The only downside of this hip joint, part-owned by Robert De Niro, is that it's mostly celebrities and the rich and ravishing that get to experience it. Your best bet is to book weeks ahead to get a chance of a table, or go at lunchtime.

RESTAURANTS

LE CIRQUE $$$–$$$$
French–American
Midtown East

✉ One Beacon Court, The Bloomberg Building, 151 58th Street at Lexington Avenue

☎ 212-759 5000

Sirio Maccioni's family-run restaurant has been the toast of the city for 30 years. After shutting the doors on Le Cirque 2000 at the New York Palace Hotel, it has taken over a year for the master restaurateur to find a suitable place to re-open. And he has, in the shape of the shining new Bloomberg Tower, or One Beacon Court as it's officially known, which will also house luxury condominiums. Le Cirque, which has regular patrons from the political, financial, music and film worlds, including Robert De Niro, Oprah Winfrey, Bill Clinton and The Rolling Stones, re-opened to a glittering party in May 2006. The 16,000 sq ft restaurant features a main dining room, separate bar area and private mezzanine for those who want to see but not be seen. Expect lots of jaw-dropping sights such as a soaring wine tower that connects the mezzanine to the first floor, an all-glass bar and giant abstract Big Top light shade. Foodies will salivate at the prospect of sampling the menu of executive chef Pierre Schaedelin, who began his career with Le Cirque in 1999 and mentored top chef Alain Ducasse.

★ ★ ★ ★ **BRIT TIP** ★ ★ ★ ★
★ If you're a real foodie, visit New York ★
★ during Winter Restaurant Week ★
★ 23-27 Jan and 30 Jan-3 Feb, when ★
★ more than 100 of the city's best ★
★ restaurants offer three-course prix- ★
★ fixe meals for a bargain $24 for ★
★ lunch and $35 for dinner. (Tel 212- ★
★ 484 1222, www.nycvisit.com.) ★
★ ★

Battery Gardens

LE BERNARDIN $$$$
Seafood
Midtown West

✉ 155 West 51st Street between 6th and 7th Avenues

☎ 212-554 1515
Fax 212-554 1100

🖰 www.le-bernardin.com

🚇 Subway V, F, B, D to Rockefeller Center

This is a truly marvellous restaurant. It's very pricey, the prix-fixe lunch alone is $51, with dinner from $96 per person, but it's more than worth it as the mouth-watering dishes are sublime. Chef Eric Ripert's cuisine is regarded by NY gourmets as very inventive. He provides an almost raw menu, which has featured delicacies such as lemon-splashed scallops with olive oil and chives. From the cooked menu, tasty treats include celeriac open ravioli with lobster and shrimp with fois gras truffle sauce, or baked snapper in spicy sour broth. The dining room itself is also a pleasure to experience, featuring crisp white linen, rich furnishings and a wood-panelled bar with smart blue-and-gold striped chairs for lounging in pre- and post-dinner.

★ ★ ★ ★ **BRIT TIP** ★ ★ ★ ★
★ If you want to experience ★
★ Le Bernardin but aren't keen on ★
★ seafood, you can put in a request ★
★ with a waiter for pasta or ★
★ lamb dishes. ★
★ ★

TOP FIVE RESTAURANTS WITH A VIEW

BATTERY GARDENS $$$$
Gourmet American
Battery Park

✉ South-west corner of Battery Park (State Street) by the river

☎ 212-809 5508

🚇 Subway 1, 9 to South Ferry

🖰 www.batterygardens.com

A superb American restaurant in an elegant, glass building that shows off the spectacular views of the Hudson and East Rivers and the Statue of Liberty from every table. In good weather you can eat outside on the terrace. Sumptuous American dishes with an Asian inflection may include miso-glazed Chilean sea bass with jasmine rice, shitake mushrooms and haricots vert or Amish chicken breast with roasted chestnuts, broccoli flan and sherry mushroom sauce.

★★★★ **BRIT TIP** ★★★★

★ Don't be too put off by the prices of ★
★ these landmark restaurants – many ★
★ offer fixed price menus and the ★
★ cheapest is for lunch, when it's ★
★ also easier to get a table. Go on, ★
★ treat yourself! ★

RAINBOW ROOM $$$-$$$$
Continental
Midtown
✉ 65th Floor, 30 Rockefeller Plaza – entrance on 49th Street between 5th and 6th Avenues
☎ 212-632 5100
Fax 212-632 5105
🖱 www.rainbowroom.com
🚇 Subway B, D, F, V to 47th–50th Streets/ Rockefeller Plaza

This legendary Art Deco landmark makes a fantastic location for dinner – complete with delicious Continental food. The opulent interior is matched only by the views and – get this – you can experience it all at a reasonable price if you opt for the fixed-price theatre menu served from 5.30pm. For a slice of real Hollywood glamour, find out when the Ballroom is open to the public for dinner dances.

THE VIEW $$$-$$$$
Continental
Theater District
✉ Top floor, Marriott Marquis Hotel, 1535 Broadway at 45th Street
☎ 212-704 8900
🖱 www.nymarriottmarquis.com
🚇 Subway N, R, S, 1, 2, 3, 7, 9 to Times Square/42nd Street

New York's recently spruced-up revolving restaurant attracts lovebirds and tourists in droves but serves up a high standard of Continental cuisine. As expected, the views over Manhattan are spectacular – particularly at sunset.

WATER CLUB $-$$$
Seafood
Midtown East
✉ 500 East 30th Street at East River – entrance on East 23rd Street
☎ 212-683 3333
🖱 www.thewaterclub.com
🚇 Subway 6 to 28th Street, near Madison Square

Another delightful and special venue from the owner of the River Café (page 141), this nautical restaurant, set on an East River barge, also specialises in seafood. The Crow's Nest, seasonal outdoor patio, sits atop the main dining room and features a moderately priced menu and fun drinks from mid-May through to late September and offers fab views of the East River. Although on the pricey side, it's well worth splashing out for the fine cuisine and, if you're counting the pennies, the weekend brunch option at a prix-fixe is an excellent way to sample some delicious dishes while gazing at that view.

WORLD YACHT DINNER CRUISES $$$
Gourmet American
Midtown West
✉ Pier 81, West 41st Street at Hudson River
☎ 212-630 8100
🖱 www.worldyacht.com
🚇 Subway A, C, East to 42nd Street

If there's one thing that you do before you leave the city, it's to book a four-course dining experience with World Yacht. This seasonal cruise down the river and around the bay offers without doubt the best views

The View

uf Midtown and Lower Manhattan plus the Statue of Liberty. You can chow down on delicacies like steak and lobster skewer, filet mignon, sevruga caviar and mustard-marinated organic chicken cooked while gazing at the city spread out before you. The chefs are some of the finest in New York, yet the prix-fixe meals are pretty reasonable – including a 3-hour cruise and live music for dancing – $82.50 from Sunday to Thursday and $101.25 Friday and Saturday from 1 April to 30 December, and $75 off-season on Friday and Saturday.

TOP FIVE ROMANTIC RESTAURANTS

There are many restaurants in New York that can deliver on the food front, but don't quite get it right with the ambience. The venues listed below are the top places in town if you really want to inject a bit of romance into your dining experience, from tactile furnishings and soft lighting to sensuous food, they're a must-visit for lovers that are also food lovers.

DANIEL $$$$
French
Upper East Side
- ✉ 60 East 65th Street between Park and Madison Avenues
- ☎ 212-288 0033
- ⌁ www.danielnyc.com
- 🚇 Subway 6 to 68th Street; F to Lexington Avenue/63rd Street

This is the place to 'dazzle a date' according to hip website www.gonyc.about.com. It's a grand, elegant place with soaring ceilings, gilded columns, plush wall hangings and upholstery, plus fine art and mosaics – a wonderful backdrop to a romantic interlude. It is the perfect setting for celebrity chef Daniel Boulud's sumptuous haute cuisine. Classic dishes have included the signature potato-wrapped paupiette of sea bass with leeks and red wine sauce; tuna tartare with caviar and a lemon coulis; and seared foie gras with sliced kumquats. Best of all though are the amazing, award-winning desserts; the chocolate bombe is indeed the bomb. It's fine dining with excellent service that will transport you as close to heaven as a mortal can get! A jacket is required to start the journey.

PARK VIEW AT THE
BOATHOUSE $$-$$$
American–seafood
Central Park
- ✉ Central Park Lake, Park Drive North at East 72nd Street
- ☎ 212-517 2233
  Fax 212-744 3949
- ⌁ www.thecentralparkboathouse.com
- 🚇 Subway 6 to 68th Street/Hunter College

This picture-book restaurant boasts one of the most wonderfully romantic locations in New York. Set right by a lake dotted with blue rowing boats in the heart of Central Park, circled by the famous high-rise skyline, the outside terrace provides a particularly gorgeous place to bag a seat at sunset. After dark, the restaurant's sparkling lights add to the romantic atmosphere. The mainly seafood menu isn't what you'd call adventurous, but it's delicious and well cooked and Zagat recommends the tasting menu. There is also a roaring open fireplace in the bar for those wintry days, when you can almost feel as if you really were deep in the countryside. Be sure to book well in advance in the summer.

AUREOLE $$$$
French
Upper East Side
- ✉ 34 East 61st Street between Madison and Park Avenues
- ☎ 212-319 1660
- ⌁ www.charliepalmer.com
- 🚇 Subway 4, 5, 6 to 59th Street; N, R to Lexington Avenue

The courtyard garden of this superb restaurant is what makes it so especially romantic. One of New York's best-kept secrets is tucked behind the brownstone that houses Aureole, and makes an idyllic spot for outdoor dining and is always incredibly romantic in candlelight. Inside is a curvaceous balcony, elegant decor and hot-house flower arrangements. Celebrity chef Charlie Palmer – considered the king of New York chefs – frequently changes the menu, but delicious concoctions have included sesame-seared Atlantic salmon with orange-miso vinaigrette and sticky rice croquettes, and foie gras with port-glazed Bing cherries and young onions. Expensive, but worth it to experience dining in one of the best restaurants in town. Closed on Sundays.

JEAN GEORGES $$$$
French
Midtown West
- ✉ Trump International Hotel, 1 Central Park West between 60th and 61st Streets
- ☎ 212-299 3900
- 🖰 www.jean-georges.com
- 🚇 Subway A, B, C, D, 1, 9 to 59th Street/Columbus Circle

Celebrity chef Jean-Georges Vongerichten's exquisite French dishes are served in an elegant and visually stunning landmark restaurant that is both romantic and relaxed. 'Prepare to sit open mouthed – when you're not eating, that is' declares a *New York Metro* review of this Adam Tihany-designed contemporary Art Deco-style restaurant. The upscale crowd that frequents it also gets to enjoy superb views of Central Park, while in good weather it's possible to sit outside. An advantage of this is the bargain $20 prix-fixe lunches on the terrace, also served in the Nougatine Room. Dish highlights on a continually changing menu have included asparagus with rich morel mushrooms, Arctic char baked with wood sorrel, and Muscovy duck steaks with sweet and sour jus. It's an unbeatable combination, so plan ahead, book your table and get your partner to treat you!

RIVER CAFE $$$
Gourmet American
Brooklyn
- ✉ 1 Water Street under the Brooklyn Bridge
- ☎ 718-522 5200
  Fax 212-875 0037
- 🖰 www.rivercafe.com
- 🚇 Subway A, C to High Street/Brooklyn Bridge

If a panoramic view of the Manhattan skyline makes you feel romantic, and it does for the majority of us, then the River Café on Brooklyn's waterfront is for you. Even better, the food matches up to the location

★ Wine is incredibly expensive in New ★
★ York. Do as New Yorkers do, have a ★
★ glass of wine or cocktail before you ★
★ go out and drink beer with your ★
★ meal or just stick to the one glass ★
★ of wine. ★

– in fact it's worth leaving Manhattan for. Superb dishes that include braised Maine lobster, crisp black sea bass, seared diver sea scallops, grilled aged prime sirloin steak, and rabbit and ravioli are served up by attentive, friendly staff.

A–Z AREA-BY-AREA GUIDE TO RESTAURANTS

BATTERY PARK AND BATTERY PARK CITY

2 WEST $-$$$
American fusion
- ✉ 2 West Street between Battery Place and West End
- ☎ 212-344 0800
- 🖰 www.ritzcarlton.com
- 🚇 Subway 1, 9 to Rector Street

The lobby-level restaurant of the Ritz-Carlton has fabulous views of the Hudson River and Statue of Liberty, plus outdoor seating for al fresco dining in the warmer months. A French-American steakhouse, the menu offers a choice of American classics plus some global fusions such as duo of ahi tuna carpaccio and tuna tartare and, of course, numerous dishes involving certified prime Angus beef. The lunch menu also offers quick and easy Bento Boxes with Italian and Spanish themes.

BATTERY GARDENS
See Top Five Restaurants with a View, page 138.

GIGINO AT WAGNER PARK $
Italian
- ✉ 20 Battery Place at Hudson River
- ☎ 212-528 2228
- 🖰 www.gigino-wagnerpark.com
- 🚇 Subway 1, 9 to South Ferry

Great little café/diner near the Museum of Jewish Heritage in the relatively new Robert Wagner Junior Park. Good for a coffee and sarnie pit stop with great views of the harbour and Statue of Liberty.

★ If you want an even cheaper pit ★
★ stop than Gigino while in Battery ★
★ Park City, opt for items from the ★
★ well-priced snack cart in ★
★ Wagner Park. ★

BROOKLYN

GRIMALDI'S $
Italian
- ✉ 19 Old Fulton Street between Front and Water Streets
- ☎ 718-858 4300
- ⌂ www.grimaldis.com
- 🚕 Subway A, C to High Street/Brooklyn Bridge

Considered the best place in New York to get a delicious pizza at a great price.

NOODLE PUDDING $$
Italian
- ✉ 38 Henry Street between Cranberry and Middagh Streets
- ☎ 218-625 3737
- 🚕 Subway A, C to High Street/ Brooklyn Bridge

Despite its name, this is a dedicated Italian rather than an Asian eatery, and it's very good. Traditional dishes such as osso buco (veal knuckle) and penne arrabiata ensure that it attracts an Italian-American crowd and is constantly packed. It is also praised for its fine pizza.

RIVER CAFE $$$
See Top Five Romantic Restaurants, page 141.

CENTRAL PARK

TAVERN ON THE GREEN $$$
Gourmet American
- ✉ Central Park at West 67th Street
- ☎ 212-873 3200
  Fax 212-580 4265
- ⌂ www.tavernonthegreen.com
- 🚕 Subway B, C to 72nd Street

Looking at the glitzy razzmatazz that is the Tavern, it's hard to imagine this building started life in 1870 as a house for the sheep that roamed Central Park. By the early

Tavern on the Green

1930s, Parks Commissioner Robert Moses had spotted its potential as a restaurant. He banished the sheep to Brooklyn's Prospect Park and, in 1934, opened what was known as The Restaurant with a coachman in full regalia at the door and the blessing of Mayor Fiorello LaGuardia.

★ ★ ★ ★ **BRIT TIP** ★ ★ ★ ★

★ **You don't have to eat at the Tavern**
★ **to enjoy its fabulous garden. From**
★ **May to October you can sip a**
★ **cocktail in the garden bar.**

In the 1970s, famous restaurateur Warner LeRoy spent $10 million turning it into a spectacle in its own right, creating the Crystal and Terrace Rooms with his lavish use of brass, stained glass, etched mirrors, antique paintings and prints and chandeliers – including genuine Baccarat crystal and stained-glass Tiffanys. The Tavern on the Green took the city by storm when it opened in 1976. Celebrities, politicians and anyone who was anyone flocked to it to see and to be seen here.

Now the Tavern pulls in out-of-towners, who've all been told by their friends to visit this unique site, and the restaurant has a staggering turnover of around $34 million a year! And what a riot of colours and textures its clients are greeted with. The food is classic gourmet American with typical main courses including cedar-planked salmon, herb-roasted chicken and prime rib.

CHELSEA

BONGO $$$–$$$$
Seafood
- ✉ 299 10th Avenue between 27th and 28th streets
- ☎ 212-947 3654
- 🚕 Subway C, E to 23rd Street; 1, 9 to 28th Street

A swish oyster bar where Chelsea gallery types sip champagne and slip down oysters for $3 a pop. If you're not a fan, there are other delicacies like smoked trout salad, lobster roll and cod cakes.

BOTTINO $$
Italian
- ✉ 246 10th Avenue between 24th and 25th Streets

RESTAURANTS

☎ 212-206 6766
🖰 www.bottinonyc.com
🚗 Subway C, E to 23rd Street
This is the place to go if you want to see the chic art dealers in recreational mode. You can tuck into the delicious Tuscan cuisine, such as roast rack of lamb with rosemary, in either the minimalist dining room or the back garden. If you don't have time to stop and eat, grab a sarnie to take away from the next-door Bottino to Go.

BRIGHT FOOD SHOP $
Asian–Mexican
✉ 216 8th Avenue at West 21st Street
☎ 212-243 4433
🖰 www.kitchenmarket.com
🚗 Subway C, E to 23rd Street
A classic neighbourhood diner with a twist – it serves south-western and Asian versions of American classics like five-spice roast pork loin with pineapple salsa.

CAFETERIA $
American diner
✉ 119 7th Avenue at 17th Street
☎ 212-414 1717
🚗 Subway 1, 9 to 18th Street
Another diner comfort-food experience, only this time filled with the beautiful people who use the 24-hour joint before and after hitting the local clubs.

★ ★ ★ ★ BRIT TIP ★ ★ ★ ★
★ ★
★ Bottles of water can cost $10 at ★
★ some of the pricier restaurants. ★
★ Save your money! New York has ★
★ access to the finest and cleanest tap ★
★ water, direct from the Catskill ★
★ Mountains upstate. ★
★ ★

THE PARK $$$
Mediterranean
✉ 118 10th Avenue at 18th Street
☎ 212-352 3313
Fax 212-352 9139
🖰 www.theparknyc.com
🚗 Subway C, E to 23rd Street
Once a mechanic's garage, this is one of the 'in' spots for film-industry executives. It's a huge industrial bar-cum-restaurant space with a kind of African safari camp interior serving Mediterranean food.

THE RED CAT $$
Mediterranean–American
✉ 227 10th Avenue between 23rd and 24th Streets
☎ 212-242 1122
🖰 www.theredcat.com
🚗 Subway C, E to 23rd Street
One of the earlier arrivals in Chelsea, along with the original galleries, this is a real staple with the art pack. It serves up Mediterranean-influenced American food, but you can just go for a cocktail.

CHINATOWN
Hundreds of tiny restaurants line the Chinatown streets, mostly serving good-value food from various regions in China. Here is our Top Five to get you started.

BIG WONG $
Cantonese
✉ 67 Mott Street between Bayard and Canal Streets
☎ 212-964 0540
🚗 Subway J, M, N, Q, R, W, A, Z, 6 to Canal Street
Cheap, tasty food – particularly the duck, shrimp and chicken noodles, and congee. Don't expect much of the decor but the service is good and lots of Chinese eat here, which is always a good sign. The wonton noodle soup, full of fun noodles, is a bargain at $3.

★ ★ ★ ★ BRIT TIP ★ ★ ★ ★
★ ★
★ Well-priced steaming hot food is ★
★ the trademark of the restaurants in ★
★ Chinatown. But don't expect ★
★ elegance in the decor or any ★
★ politeness from the waiters – ★
★ it simply isn't available! ★
★ ★

DIM SUM GO GO $
Chinese–vegetarian
✉ 5 East Broadway between Catherine Street and Chatham Square
☎ 212-732 0797

Dim Sum Go Go

RESTAURANTS

🚇 Subway J, M, Z, 6 to Canal Street; F to East Broadway

One of the more popular restaurants in the area, thanks to its delicious dim sum, and fantastically priced; dim sum platter, $8.95 for ten pieces; roast chicken with fried garlic stems, $11.95; hamburger in a steamed bun with ginger sauce, $8.95.

JOE'S SHANGHAI $
Chinese–Shanghai
✉ 9 Pell St between Bowery and Mott Street
☎ 212-233 8888
🖰 www.joesshanghai.com
🚇 Subway J, M, N, R, Z, 6 to Canal Street

A Chinese restaurant known for creating the most fabulous soup dumplings in New York. 'Lots of food for little money' according to the Zagat survey.

NEW GREEN BO $–$$
Chinese–Shanghai
✉ 66 Bayard Street between Elizabeth and Mott Streets
☎ 212-625 2359
🚇 Subway J, M, Z, N, Q, R, W, 6 to Canal Street

Up until recently Joe's Shanghai had little in the way of competition for delicious dim sum and dumplings at great prices, then along came this place, giving New Yorkers another place to rave about. There is a famous teahouse of the same name in Shanghai, and it feels like you could be there. The dumplings are extremely fresh, hot and succulent and their fish fillet in wine sauce is excellent.

GARDEN DINING

Aureole: French, Upper East Side, $$$$ (page 140)

Barbetta: Northern Italian, Midtown West, $$$$ (page 171)

Bottino: Italian, Chelsea, $$$ (page 142)

Remi: Italian, Midtown, $$$$ (page 168)

Provence: French, SoHo, $$ (page 173)

Tavern on the Green: Gourmet American, Central Park West, $$$ (page 142)

NEW YORK NOODLE TOWN $
Hong Kong-style noodle house
✉ 28½ Bowery at Bayard Street
☎ 212-349 0923
🚇 Subway J, M, Z, N, Q, R, W, 6 to Canal Street

Noodles, of course, are a speciality here and come in fragrant broths with dumplings or stir-fried with vegetables, meat or seafood. And, according to the New York Metro, it's the city's best spot for delicious, succulent Chinese barbecue.

EAST VILLAGE

There are dozens of great places to dine in the East Village. It's a very safe part of town so, if you have the time, it's well worth taking a wander around at night and having a look at all of the various options before you make your choice.

ANGELICA KITCHEN $
Vegetarian–vegan
✉ 300 East 12th Street between 1st and 2nd Avenues
☎ 212-228 2909
🖰 www.angelicakitchen.com
🚇 Subway L, N, Q, R, W, 4, 5, 6 to 14th Street/Union Square

A shock for anyone who thinks veggie food is boring. This cool spot serves up very tasty soups, chilli and noodle dishes like butternut squash and tempeh made from soya beans. Macrobiotic heaven? No alcohol.

FRANK $
Italian
✉ 88 2nd Avenue between 5th and 6th Streets
☎ 212-420 0202
🖰 www.frankrestaurant.com
🚇 Subway 6 to Astor Place

A tiny Italian restaurant with a real parlour feel. No matter the hour, Frank is full of hungry hipsters looking to fill up on Grandma Carmela's slow-cooked ragu.

★ ★ ★ ★ **BRIT TIP** ★ ★ ★ ★

★ There are more restaurants for the
★ Village and Chelsea in Chapter 10,
★ Gay New York, plus many of the
★ bars referred to in Chapter 8 serve
★ meals, too.

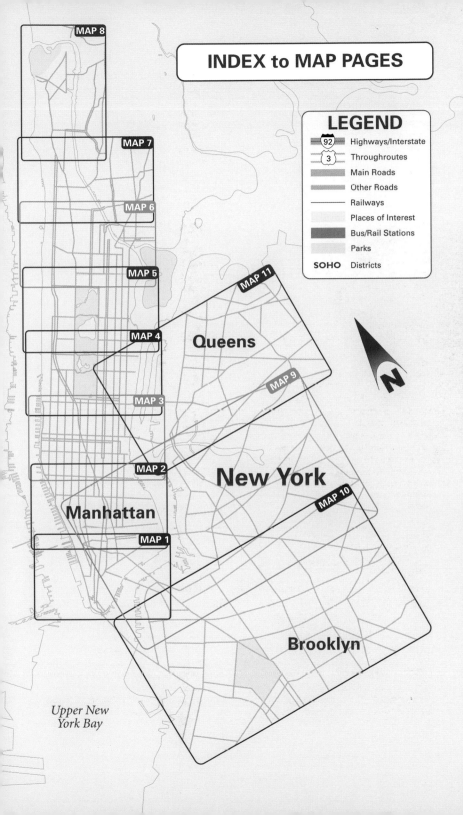

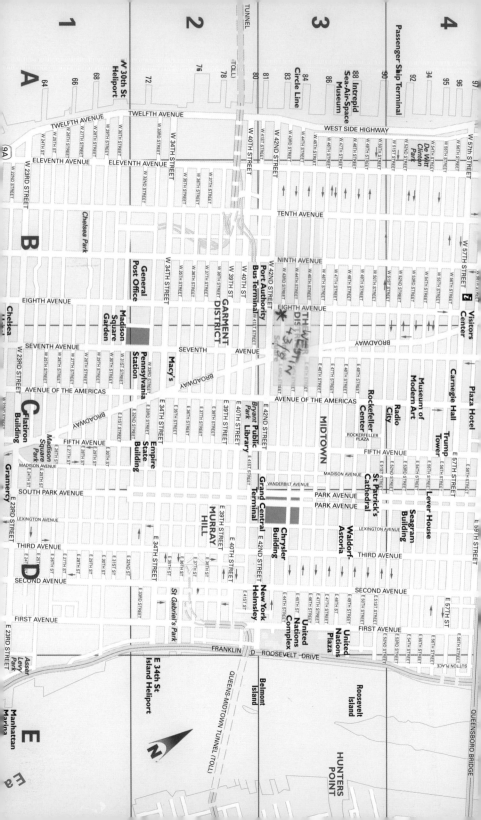

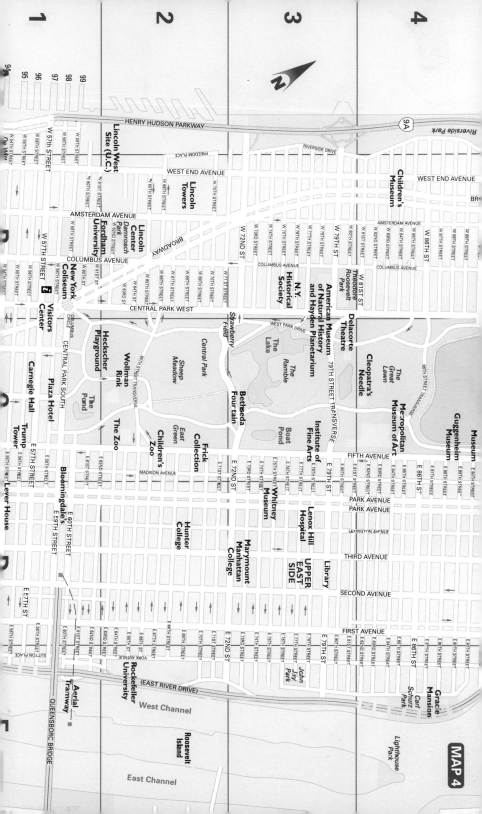

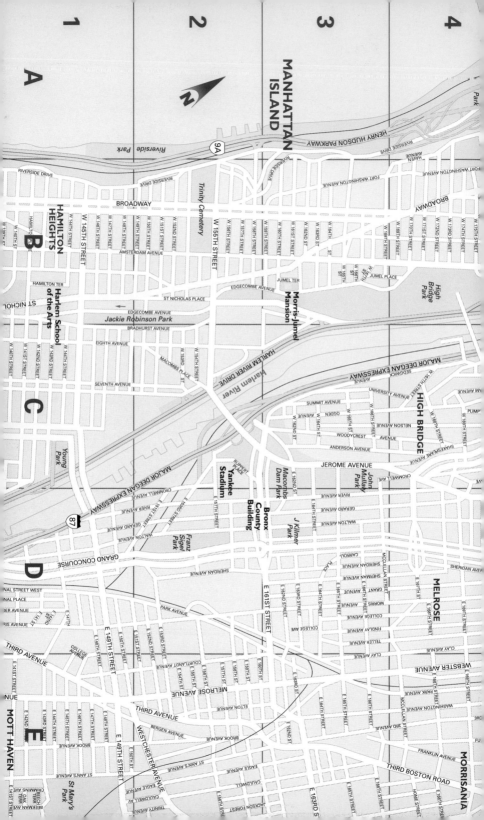

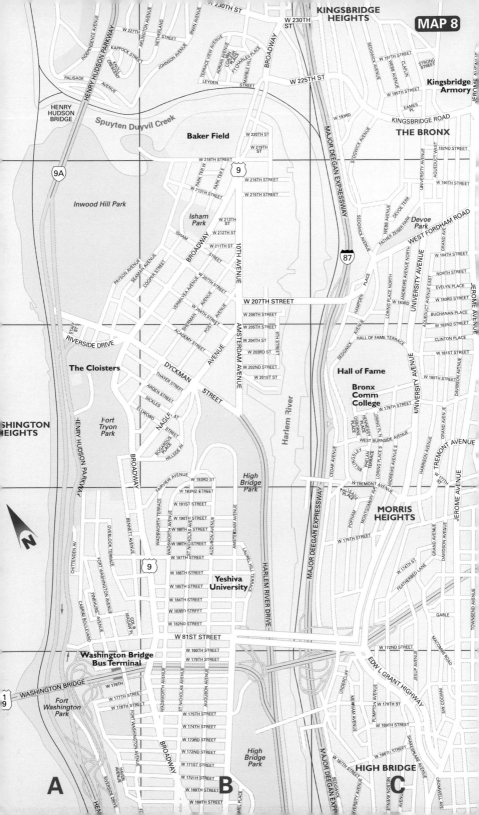

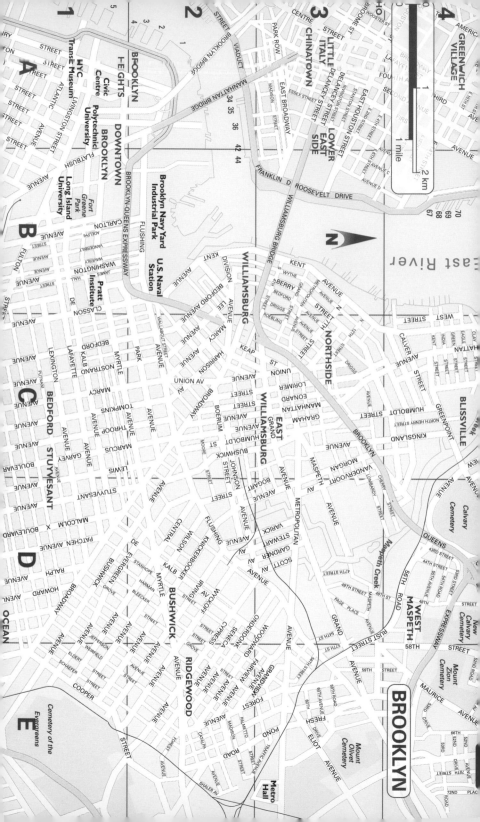

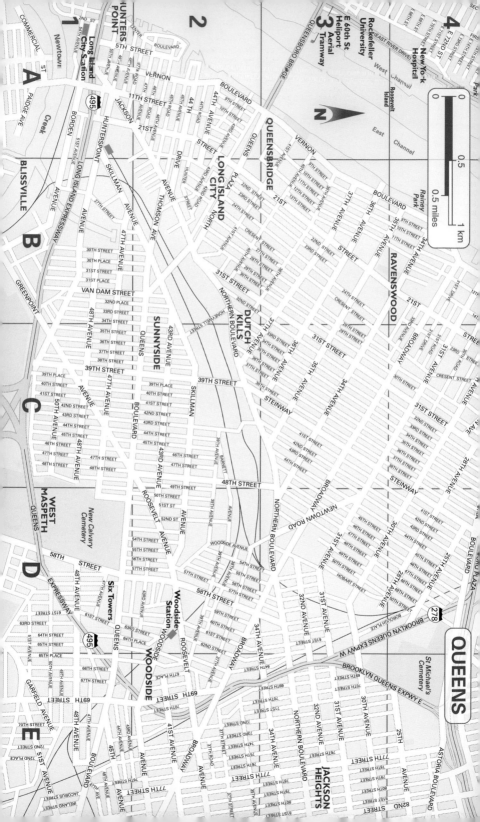

MANHATTAN STREET INDEX

Single bold number refers to map number

Alpha numerics refer to those within specified map

LA PALAPA $$
Mexican
- ✉ 77 St Mark's Place between 1st and 2nd Avenues
- ☎ 212-777 2537
  Fax 212-777 9730
- ⌐ www.lapalapa.com
- 🚇 Subway E, V to Lexington Avenue/53rd Street

Superb Mexican cuisine with shrimp dishes and barbecued cod with chile guajillo and achiote rub. Rices are flavoured with tomato, saffron and tomatillo; moles concocted from sesame seeds, pumpkin seeds and guajillo chillies. The restaurant is dark and sultry and serves refreshing fresh fruit margaritas.

THE ELEPHANT $$
French–Thai fusion
- ✉ 58 East 1st Street between 1st and 2nd Avenues
- ☎ 212-505 7739
- ⌐ www.elephantrestaurant.com
- 🚇 Subway F, V to 2nd Avenue

The food is tasty Thai with a dash of French, but the dark, loud, crowded red and gold interior is most definitely more of a French scene. A fun place to enjoy a cocktail or two; the cool crowd often end up spilling out on to the sidewalk.

YAFFA CAFÉ $
American diner
- ✉ 97 St Mark's Place between 1st and Avenue A
- ☎ 212-674 9302
- ⌐ www.yaffacafe.com
- 🚇 Subway 6 to Astor Place

A classic American diner with a grungy East Village twist. Open 24 hours.

FINANCIAL DISTRICT AND SOUTH STREET SEAPORT

KOODO SUSHI $$
Japanese
- ✉ 129 Front Street on the lower level of Seaport Suites Hotel between Pine and Wall Streets
- ☎ 212-425 2890
- ⌐ www.koodoosushi.com
- 🚇 Subway 1, 2, 4, 5 to Wall Street

This place doesn't look like much, but it has one of the best sushi chefs in town. The fish is impeccable, but the chef really shines in his daily specials - take hostess Michelle's advice on this.

MARKJOSEPH STEAKHOUSE $$
Steakhouse
- ✉ 261 Water Street between Peck Slip and Dover Street
- ☎ 212-277 0020
  Fax 212-277 0033
- ⌐ www.markjosephsteakhouse.com
- 🚇 Subway 1, 2, 4, 5, A, C, J, M, Z to Fulton Street/Broadway Nassau

This restaurant has made its mark as one of the best steakhouses in the city. The porterhouse steak is so tender some people have said it 'could be eaten through a straw'. Team it with the delicious hash browns. Wearing a jacket is advisable.

★★★★ **BRIT TIP** ★★★★
Sometimes the only way to get into a very popular restaurant is to go very early or very late in the evening. Ask what times are available when you book.

QUARTINO $$
Italian
- ✉ 21-23 Peck Slip at Water Street
- ☎ 212-349 4433
- 🚇 Subway 1, 2, 4, 5, A, C, J, M, Z to Fulton Street/Broadway Nassau

A little slice of Italy tucked away in a very charming, high-ceilinged, wooden-tabled restaurant. The small menu includes delicious and well-priced thin-crust pizzas and just one or two daily specials. Everything is organic and very fresh and wholesome; nothing is fried. Again, like MarkJoseph's, it's just a stone's throw from the main tourist drag of Fulton Street, but is remarkably unexplored by anyone other than locals.

GRAMERCY PARK

ELEVEN MADISON PARK $$$$
French–American
- ✉ 11 Madison Avenue (the corner) at 24th Street
- ☎ 212-889 0905
- ⌐ www.elevenmadisonpark.com
- 🚇 Subway 6, N, R to 23rd Street

With a soaring ceiling, marble floors and French-influenced dishes, this is one of New York's hottest restaurants. It's expensive but not snooty and the service is attentive, as seen in *Sex And The City*.

GRAMERCY TAVERN $$$
Gourmet American
- ✉ 42 East 20th Street between Broadway and Park Avenue South
- ☎ 212-477 0777
- ⌂ www.gramercytavern.com
- 🚗 Subway N, R to 23rd Street

Another real winner and again always highly ranked by the Zagat survey – an excellent American restaurant.

PORCAO CHURRASCARIA $$$
Brazilian
- ✉ 360 Park Avenue at 26th Street
- ☎ 212-252 7080
- 🚗 Subway 6 to 28th Street

Hot from Rio de Janeiro is this new South American churrascaria where dozens of styles of meat are served up tableside in the 1,020 sq m (11,000 sq ft) space. There's also an ample salad bar with a bewildering array of options.

TAMARIND $$
Indian
- ✉ 41–43 East 22nd Street between Broadway and Park Avenue South
- ☎ 212-674 7400
- ⌂ www.tamarinde22.com
- 🚗 Subway N, R to 23rd Street

Lovely modern decor that defies the normal Indian dining room cliché of flocked wallpaper. The cuisine is equally contemporary, with lots of fruit-infused dishes such as fritters with spinach, banana and home-made cheese. If you want a cheaper, lighter snack try their tea room next door.

VERITAS $$$$
Gourmet American
- ✉ 43 East 20th Street between Broadway and Park Avenue South
- ☎ 212-353 3700
- ⌂ www.veritas-nyc.com
- 🚗 Subway N, R to 23rd Street

The city's largest wine list can be found here – an impressive 2,700-plus bottles to choose

---

Cornelia Street Café

TOP FIVE RESTAURANTS TO BRING A BOTTLE TO

If you're on a budget, you can save a fortune on your NY dining experiences by picking restaurants that allow you to bring your own bottle of vino or beer to the table. There are liquor stores all over the city, giving you the opportunity to select a really good wine without the hefty price tag to accompany your meal. Be warned however, some restaurants will charge you for corkage (opening the wine on their premises) which can vary from under $10 to $25 plus. Here's our top five:

Angelica Kitchen (page 000). Great organic vegetarian and vegan cuisine. No corkage fee.

Lamarca (161 East 22nd Street at corner of 3rd Avenue; tel 212-674 6363). Filling Italian fodder. No corkage fee.

Les Sans Culottes (329 West 51st Street; tel 212-581 1283). Hearty bistro food. Corkage $8.

Morrells Restaurant (900 Broadway; tel 212-253 0900). Monday night is bring your own special bottle night. No corkage fee.

Ottomanelli's Cafe 86 (1626 York Avenue at 86th Street; tel 212-772 7722). Italian specialities. No corkage fee.

---

from. The cuisine is as impressive, think tender braised ribs with parsnip purée and porcini mushrooms or scallops with a black truffle vinaigrette. The prix-fixe dinner is $76.

GREENWICH & WEST VILLAGES

CAFE DE BRUXELLES $$
Belgian
- ✉ 118 Greenwich Avenue at West 13th Street
- ☎ 212-206 1830
- 🚗 Subway A, C east to 14th Street

Another friendly Belgian bistro serving great grub, like moules for $15.75 and waterzooi de poulet, a creamy chicken dish, for $16.75. There's also a great selection of Belgian beers to wash it all down with.

CORNELIA STREET CAFE $$
Eclectic
- ✉ 29 Cornelia Street between Bleecker and West 4th Streets
- ☎ 212-989 9319

Fax 212-243 4207
🖰 www.corneliastreetcafe.com
A fabulous neighbourhood restaurant, which serves lunch and dinner seven days a week. Specials include butternut squash risotto, sesame-crusted salmon, lobster ravioli and Thai bouillabaisse. Local artists' work hangs on the walls, good service and a small downstairs performance space for readings and acoustic performances, in particular its jazz club, which begins at 9pm and costs from $6 for the whole evening plus a house drink (page 193).

GARAGE RESTAURANT & CAFÉ $
American
✉ 99 7th Avenue South between Barrow and Grove Streets
☎ 212-645 0600
🖰 www.garagerest.com
🚇 Subway 1, 2, 3, 9 to Christopher Street
A friendly spot for contemporary American food in a great location; it also has live jazz and some cool people-watching.

GOTHAM BAR AND GRILL $$$
Gourmet American
✉ 12 East 12th Street between 5th Avenue and University Place
☎ 212-620 4020
🖰 www.gothambarandgrill.com
🚇 Subway L, N, R, 4, 5, 6 to Union Square/14th Street
Always highly rated by Zagat, the excellent American cuisine is served up in a superb environment to a stylish crowd. It costs $25 for the lunch prix-fixe.

JOHN'S PIZZERIA $
Italian
✉ 278 Bleecker Street between 6th and 7th Avenues
☎ 212-243 1680
🚇 Subway A, B, C, D, E, F, V to West 4th Street
A great place for brick-oven pizzas.

PHILIP MARIE $$
American
✉ 569 Hudson Street at West 11th Street
☎ 212-242 6200
Fax 212-242 1278
🖰 www.philipmarie.com
🚇 Subway 1, 9 to Christopher Street
Hearty American fare. Try the newcomer's parsley salad with country ham, dried tomatoes and Wisconsin cheese.

TOMOE SUSHI $$
Japanese
✉ 172 Thompson Street between Bleecker and West Houston Streets
☎ 212-777 9346
🚇 Subway 6 to Bleecker Street
This place looks pretty grotty but there is usually an incredible queue outside and not without reason. You can get the best sushi in New York here for about a tenth of the price it would cost you at Nobu.

HARLEM

GEORGE & GINA'S RESTAURANT $$
Puerto Rican
✉ 169 East 106th Street between Lexington and 3rd Avenues
☎ 212-410 7292
🚇 Subway 6 to 103rd Street
A Puerto Rican restaurant with a casual ambiance, deep in the heart of Spanish Harlem.

RAO'S $
Italian
✉ 455 East 114th Street at Pleasant Avenue
☎ 212-722 6709
🖰 www.raos.com
🚇 Subway 6 to 116th Street
An institution that you'll get into only if you come across the handful of people who actually have access to this eight-table Italian restaurant! Famous for its sauces,

★ ★ ★ ★ **BRIT TIP** ★ ★ ★ ★
★ ★
★ ★
★ If you can't get in to Rao's, you can ★
★ still taste their fabulous sauces, by ★
★ buying them either direct from the ★
★ restaurant or from Faicco's Sausage ★
★ Store in Bleecker Street, Greenwich ★
★ Village (page 113). ★
★ ★ ★ ★ ★ ★ ★ ★ ★ ★ ★ ★ ★ ★ ★ ★ ★ ★

which Sinatra used to have flown to him around the world. Now the jukebox plays all the crooner's favourites.

Katz's Deli

SYLVIA'S $

Southern soul food

✉ 328 Lenox Avenue between 126th and 127th Streets

☎ 212-996 0660

🖰 www.sylviassoulfood.com

🚇 Subway 2, 3 to 125th Street

Southern home-style cooking – aka soul food. Sylvia's place is a New York institution and famous for its Sunday gospel brunch, but you need to book a few weeks ahead as it's always very busy.

★★★★ **BRIT TIP** ★★★★
★ ★
★ If you need a break around 110th ★
★ Street, drop in for a cuppa and a ★
★ delicious cake at Make My Cake, ★
★ 103 West 110th Street at Lenox ★
★ Avenue/Malcom X Boulevard. ★
★ Tel 212-932 0833. ★
★★★★★★★★★★★★★★★★★★★★★★★★★★

LITTLE ITALY

Mulberry Street from Hester to Kenmare Street and along Grand Street to Mott Street is all that remains of a once thriving Italian community. Thankfully, though – especially for anyone who feels relieved to have escaped the madness and mayhem of Chinatown – the tiny area is incredibly vibrant and filled with ambient pizzerias and trattorias, many with pavement tables and some even having gardens at the back.

Of course, the area gets packed with tourists, but locals also eat here so the food is 100 per cent authentic. The restaurants all have plenty in common – fading decor, if any, large portions of piping hot Italian classics, friendly service and great value for money. If you're really on a budget, stick to the excellent fixed-price menus, then just sit back and watch the world go by.

BREAD $$

Italian

✉ 20 Spring Street between Elizabeth and Mott Streets

☎ 212-334 1015

🚇 Subway 6 to Spring Street

A lovely little café serving up delicious panini, soup and various salads and great fresh bread. There's also a good choice of wine, many of which are sold by the glass. There's an equally good Bread in TriBeCa www.breadtribeca.com.

BEST OF LITTLE ITALY

It's hard to go wrong with any of the restaurants in Little Italy, but here is a round-up of six of the best, moving northwards along Mulberry from Hester to Grand Street: **Il Fornaio** (132a Mulberry, tel 212-226 8306); **Pellegrino's** (138 Mulberry, tel 212-226 3177); **Angelo's** (146 Mulberry, tel 212-966 1277, www.angelomulberry.com); **Taormina** (147 Mulberry, tel 212-219 1007); **Il Palazzo** (151 Mulberry, tel 212-343 7000); and **Da Nico** (164 Mulberry, tel 212-343 1212). By the way, Taormina was once the local hangout of former Mafia boss 'Teflon Don' John Gotti (page 46).

To get to Little Italy, take subway 6 to Spring or Bleecker Streets.

CAFE GITANE $

French–North African

✉ 242 Mott Street at Prince Street

☎ 212-334 9552

🚇 Subway 6 to Spring Street

Great value Moroccan-style dining; think couscous and tajines. Tables and chairs are put out on the sidewalk in the summer, but they are in a hot spot so you're more likely to end up in the noisy but nice dining room.

FERRARA $

Italian café

✉ 195 Grand Street between Mulberry and Mott Streets

☎ 212-226 6150

🖰 www.ferraracafe.com

🚇 Subway S to Grand Street

This is the oldest surviving pastry joint in an area that was once teeming with cannoli caverns. A spacious area, it serves up delicious drinks and cakes and provides plenty of entertaining people-watching.

★★★★ **BRIT TIP** ★★★★
★ ★
★ If you've been wandering around ★
★ Chinatown for a while and don't ★
★ want a meal but do need a WC, ★
★ Ferrara's has a lovely clean one on ★
★ the first floor (up the stairs at the ★
★ back). Keep the owners happy, ★
★ though, by at least buying ★
★ something to take away. ★
★★★★★★★★★★★★★★★★★★★★★★★★★★

SAL ANTHONY'S SPQR $$-$$$
Italian
- ✉ 133 Mulberry Street between Hern and Grand Streets
- ☎ 212-925 3120
- ✎ www.salanthonys.com
- 🚇 Subway 6 to Spring Street

An authentic Italian that's big on fresh ingredients – the Mozzarella is made twice a day on the premises to ensure it's perfect. There are lots of regional dishes like trout with garlic and rosemary and fusilli pasta with prosciutto and tomato, all served in elegant, wood-panelled surroundings at prices far below what you'd expect to pay uptown for similar fare. There's also a three-course fixed-price menu served 4–6.30pm for $25.50.

LOWER EAST SIDE

ALIAS $
American
- ✉ 76 Clinton Street at Rivington Street
- ☎ 212-505 5011
- 🚇 Subway F to Lower East Side/2nd Avenue

This 'cool bodega' has lower lighting, tablecloths and a small but serious wine list, yet remains funky with laid-back clients and staff. Chef Scott Ehrlich turns out some pretty big tastes from his mini kitchen but at far less than Midtown pricing.

BEREKET $
Turkish
- ✉ 187 East Houston Street at Orchard Street
- ☎ 212-475 7700
- 🚇 Subway F to 2nd Avenue

A good place to pop into if you've got the munchies after a big night out as it's open 24/7 and the food is filling but fresh. The hummus, stuffed vine leaves and lamb shawarma sandwich are recommended.

KATZ'S DELICATESSEN $
American–Jewish
- ✉ 205 East Houston Street at Ludlow Street
- ☎ 212-254 2246
  Fax 212-674 3270
- ✎ www.katzdeli.com
- 🚇 Subway F to 2nd Avenue

A real institution, this deli has been here since 1888. The sandwiches may sound pricey at around $9, but I defy you to finish one. Luckily, there are plenty of brown paper bags around to take your leftovers away with you (as everybody else does). Stick to the sandwiches though – the soups are a bit disappointing. You take a ticket on the way in, order your food at the counter and have your ticket filled out, then you pay for it all as you leave.

★★★★ **BRIT TIP** ★★★★
★ If the canteen-style seating at Katz's seems familiar to you, it's because that sex scene with Meg Ryan and Billy Crystal in *When Harry Met Sally* was filmed here. ★
★★★★★★★★★★★★★★★★★★★★★★★★★★★

MADISON SQUARE/FLATIRON

METRONOME $$$
Mediterranean
- ✉ 915 Broadway at 21st Street
- ☎ 212-505 7400
- ✎ www.metronomenyc.com
- 🚇 Subway N, R to 23rd Street

The cheaper alternative to the Supper Club (page 176), it serves Mediterranean food in a beautiful candlelit setting and has great jazz from Wednesday to Saturday.

TABLA $$$$
American Indian
- ✉ 11 Madison Avenue at 25th Street
- ☎ 212-889 0667
- ✎ www.tablany.com
- 🚇 Subway N, R to 23rd Street

Danny Meyer's bi-level restaurant serving American Indian cuisine is a big hit and attracts a trendy crowd. Downstairs is cheaper, you'll be pleased to know.

MEATPACKING DISTRICT

Manhattan's Meatpacking District, between Chelsea and the West Village on the lower west side of Manhattan, used to be a no-go area for diners. Now it has become a style magnet for the kind of restaurants that you want to brag to your friends about. If you don't want to splash out in the chic venues however, there are some groovy little coffee and cake shops that will take the weight off your feet but not your wallet.

RESTAURANTS

FLORENT $

French

✉ 69 Gansevoort Street between
Greenwich and Washington Streets
☎ 212-989 5779
🕙 www.restaurantflorent.com
🚇 Subway A, C, East to 14th Street

This is the Meatpacking District's original 24-hour hangout with fine coffee at the Formica counter or steak frites served by a transsexual waitress.

MARKT $$

Belgian

✉ 401 West 14th Street at 9th Avenue
☎ 212-727 3314
🕙 www.marktrestaurant.com
🚇 Subway L to 8th Avenue; A, C east to 14th Street

A stylish Belgian brasserie with a popular bar. Great mussels and good beer selection.

MEET $$

Mediterranean

✉ 71-73 Gansevoort Street at Washington Street
☎ 212-242 0990
🕙 www.the-meet.com
🚇 Subway A, C east to 14th Street

This chilled little restaurant used to be a meat freezer in a former life, but it has now been Feng Shui-ed and you can enjoy delicious Mediterranean cuisine to music from live DJs.

OLD HOMESTEAD $$

American

✉ 56 9th Avenue between 14th and 15th Streets
☎ 212-242 9040
🕙 www.theoldhomesteadsteakhouse.com
🚇 Subway L, A, C, E to 14th Street/8th Avenue

An original chophouse joint complete with tacky cow sculpture outside that opened in 1868 and is still serving massive portions of good ol' steak and chips today.

Meet

21 CLUB $-$$$

Gourmet American

✉ 21 West 52nd Street between 5th and 6th Avenues
☎ 212-582 7200
🕙 www.21club.com
🚇 Subway F to 5th Avenue

Despite its name, this landmark restaurant has never been a club, but during Prohibition it was a speakeasy, starting life in Greenwich Village before moving to its Midtown location in 1929. West 52nd Street between 5th and 6th Avenues was known then as the 'wettest block in Manhattan' because there were at least 38 speakeasies.

One of the most discreet was the 21 Club, which purposefully remained a tiny, clandestine retreat behind the iron gate of its townhouse façade, to avoid both the gangsters and police raids. Its success depended on an employee who was assigned to spot gangsters, policemen and revenue agents through the peephole – and who was so skilful that 21 escaped most raids and troubles except for one in 1930. After that the owners had a new security system designed to create false stairways and walls to hide its 2,000 cases of fine wines. It involved the building of a 2-tonne door to the secret cellar, made out of the original bricks to look like a wall. The cellar is still going strong and now houses $1.5 millions-worth of wine, much of which is owned by the celebrities and power brokers who call the 21 Club their own. Actress Liz Taylor and former President Gerald Ford still keep their bottles here.

Once Prohibition ended in 1932, many of the former speakeasies went out of business, but the 21 turned itself into a fine dining establishment that has been attracting celebrities and movers and shakers ever since. Patrons have included Joe DiMaggio, Aristotle Onassis, Franklin D Roosevelt, Humphrey Bogart, Ernest Hemingway and Jackie Gleason. The night before Brit's Guide enjoyed lunch here, Margaret Thatcher had been at a private function and Joan Collins had dined in the main restaurant.

44 $$$

Gourmet American

✉ Royalton Hotel, 44 West 44th Street between 5th and 6th Avenues
☎ 212-944 8844

Diwan

⊕ www.royaltonhotel.com
🚇 Subway B, D, F, Q to 42nd Street
A très trendy joint in the Philippe Starck-designed Royalton Hotel, serving new American cuisine. A favourite with posh magazine editors.

ACQUA PAZZA $$$
Italian
⊠ 36 West 52nd Street between 5th and 6th Avenues
☎ 212-582 6900
⊕ www.acquapazzanyc.com
🚇 Subway F to 5th Avenue
Its name means Crazy Water, but it is in fact a very chic little restaurant with tasteful cream and beige decor, crisp white tablecloths and a pricey menu; think octopus, crab and grilled swordfish. Pasta and some delicious desserts are also on offer to widen the waistline.

AQUAVIT $$$$
Scandinavian
⊠ 65 East 55th Street between Madison and Park Avenues
☎ 212-307 7311
⊕ www.acquavit.org
🚇 Subway E, V to 53rd Street/Fifth Avenue
Swedish chef Marcus Samuelsson won the Best Chef in New York City award four years ago, but the menu is still as varied and imaginative today. Seafood stew and brioche-wrapped salmon are mouth-watering, while the tasting menus, including a vegetarian one, are a great idea and comprise seven-course Aqua Bite meals.

BG $$$-$$$$
American nouveau
⊠ 754 Fifth Avenue at 58th Street
☎ 212-872 8977
⊕ www.bergdorfgoodman.com
🚇 Subway N, R, W to Fifth Avenue/59th Street

The new restaurant at Bergdorf Goodman department store makes a posh place to stop for a long lunch during a shopping spree. Or head here for an early dinner, as the restaurant shuts at 8pm. You can also go for the afternoon tea option – which is fabulous, darling.

CHINA GRILL $$
Chinese
⊠ CBS Building, 60 West 53rd Street between 5th and 6th Avenues
☎ 212-333 7788
⊕ www.chinagrillmgt.com
🚇 Subway B, D, F, V to 47th–50th Streets/Rockefeller Center
Classy establishment serving eclectic food in a fairly noisy setting. Has a bar that gets pretty crowded.

DB BISTRO MODERNE $$$
French–American
⊠ City Club Hotel, 55 West 44th Street between 5th and 6th Avenues
☎ 212-391 2400
Fax 212-391 1188
⊕ www.danielnyc.com/dbbistro
🚇 Subway B, D, F, V, S, 4, 5, 6, 7 to 42nd Street
The latest showcase for one of New York's superstar chefs, Daniel Boulud. It got lots of press for the $29 hamburger, and became an instant scene. Located in the very star-chic City Club Hotel, this is one of the few really good places to eat close to the Theater District.

DIWAN $$
Indian
⊠ Helmsley Middletowne,148 East 48th Street between Lexington and 3rd Avenues
☎ 212-593 5425
⊕ www.diwanrestaurant.com
🚇 Subway 6 to 51st Street
An upmarket Indian with more unusual dishes than your average vindaloo or tandoori – papad stuffed lamb crabmeat, for example.

Aquavit

RESTAURANTS

GENKI SUSHI $$
Japanese
✉ 9 East 46th Street
☎ 212-983 5018
Fax 212-983 5018
🖰 www.genkisushi.com.sg
🚇 Subway 6 to 51st Street
Watch your fresh fish whizz around on a metal conveyor belt at this great value, colourful dining spot. Plates, including sashimi, are colour coded according to price.

HARD ROCK CAFE $
American
✉ 1501 Broadway at 43rd Street
☎ 212-343 3355
🖰 www.hardrock.com
🚇 Subway N, Q, R, S, W, 1, 2, 3, 7, 9 to Times Square/42nd Street
Classic burger and chips 'cuisine' in a noisy, rock 'n' roll environment.

HARLEY DAVIDSON CAFE $
American
✉ 1370 6th Avenue at 56th Street
☎ 212-245 6000
🚇 Subway B, Q to 57th Street
Home-style American comfort food like meatloaf and chicken pot pie. Memorabilia includes a huge floor map of Route 66.

NORMA'S $–$$
American
✉ Le Parker Meridien Hotel, 118 West 57th Street between 6th and 7th Avenues
☎ 212-708 7460
🖰 www.parkermeridien.com
🚇 Subway B, D, E to 7th Avenue
This award-winning all-day breakfast joint is très chi-chi, beautifully decorated and serves some of the most inventive 'breakfast' food going! Specialities include molten chocolate French toast with pineapple chutney, caramelised onion corned beef hash with poached eggs, and a serious stack of strawberry and rhubarb pancakes. Also desserts and fruit smoothies.

OPIA $$
French
✉ 130 East 57th Street at Lexington Avenue
☎ 212-688 3939
🖰 www.opiarestaurant.com
🚇 Subway 4, 5, 6, N, R, W to 59th Street/ Lexington Avenue
Antoine Blech, formerly of the great neighbourhood bistro Orienta, is the very welcoming host at this nifty and trendy hideaway for beautiful people in the Habitat Hotel. The French-inspired cuisine is absolutely delicious.

RAINBOW ROOM $$$–$$$$
See Top Five Restaurants with a View, page 139.

REMI $$$
Italian
✉ 145 West 53rd Street between 6th and 7th Avenues
☎ 212-581 4242
🚇 Subway N, R to 49th Street; B, D east to 7th Avenue
To New Yorkers, this special restaurant is like a taste of Venice with its enchanting Atrium Garden that offers foreign films and live music to accompany dinner al fresco. It also has rotating art exhibitions all year long in the Rialto Room. The food is delicious and you can even get Remi takeaways.

ROCK CENTER CAFE $$
American
✉ Rockefeller Center, 20 West 50th Street between 5th and 6th Avenues
☎ 212-332 7620
🖰 www.restaurantassociates.com
🚇 Subway B, D, F, Q to 47th–50th Streets/ Rockefeller Plaza
A Mecca for tourists, thanks to the scenic setting, though the American dishes are a little disappointing.

SEAGRILL $$$$
Seafood
✉ Rockefeller Center, 19 West 49th Street between 5th and 6th Avenues
☎ 212-332 7610
🖰 www.theseagrillnyc.com
🚇 Subway B, D, F, Q to 47th–50th Streets/ Rockefeller Centre
Surrounded by lush greenery, the outdoor tables topped with striped umbrellas in summer are replaced in winter by the famous skating rink. The seafood specialities include Australian barramundi with wilted aragula, poached lobster with truffled potato and herb-crusted skate. Note that the refurbished restaurant's dress code has changed to exclude jeans, shorts and trainers.

SEPPI'S $$
French–Italian–Turkish
✉ 123 West 56th Street between 6th and 7th Avenues
☎ 212-708 7444
🖰 www.parkermeridien.com
🚇 Subway B, D, E to 7th Street

Perfect for Carnegie Hall goers and open until 2am. A French bistro, eclectic dishes range from escargots in garlic butter to beef carpaccio with baby arugula and Parmesan and crawfish ravioli with lobster bisque, which are served in an informal, laid-back environment.

TOWN $$$
Gourmet American
- ☒ Chambers Hotel, 15 West 56th Street between 5th and 6th Avenues
- ☎ 212-582 4445
- ⌂ www.townnyc.com
- ☛ Subway F to 5th Avenue

A fashionista's favourite that's attached to an über trendy hotel. The menu changes each season but some recurring favourites include softshell crab in summer and white asparagus in spring.

UPSTAIRS AT 21 $$
Gourmet American
- ☒ 21 West 52nd Street between 5th and 6th Avenues
- ☎ 212-582 7200
- ⌂ www.21club.com
- ☛ Subway F to 5th Avenue

Here you can get many of the 21 Club's classic dishes in a less formal but equally well-serviced restaurant – and see out of windows into the bargain! It has quickly become a favourite with the trendy jet set.

MIDTOWN EAST

ASIA DE CUBA $$$
Asian–Cuban
- ☒ Morgan's Hotel, 237 Madison Avenue between 37th and 38th Streets
- ☎ 212-726 7755
- ⌂ www.chinagrillmanagement.com
- ☛ Subway 6 to 33rd Street; 4, 5, 6, 7 to Grand Central/42nd Street

The Philippe Starck interior guarantees a trendy crowd for the fusion Asian and Cuban food.

BULL & BEAR $$$–$$$$
Steakhouse
- ☒ The Waldorf Hotel entrance on Lexington Avenue at 49th Street
- ☎ 212-872 4900
- ⌂ www.waldorfastoria.com
- ☛ Subway 6 to 51st Street

A landmark restaurant renowned for its excellent hospitality and unashamedly masculine decor that pays homage to the stock market bull and bear symbols. This is the number one restaurant in New York for delicious, melt-in-the-mouth, prime, aged Black Angus beef dishes, yet has plenty to offer the less carnivorously inclined.

Chef Eric Kaplan has introduced a range of eclectic, mouth-watering dishes that include yellowfin tuna mignon and shrimp Creole with andouille sausage and rice. For something lighter opt for one of the salads such as lobster salad with mango, avocado and corn.

CAVIAR RUSSE $$$$
Caviar
- ☒ 2nd floor, 538 Madison Avenue, between 54th and 55th Streets
- ☎ 212-980 5908
- ⌂ www.caviarrusse.com
- ☛ Subway F to 5th Avenue

Posh caviar and cigar lounge where you can see how the other half lives.

CHIN CHIN $$
Chinese
- ☒ 216 East 49th Street between 2nd and 3rd Avenues
- ☎ 212-888 4555
- ⌂ www.chinchinny.com
- ☛ Subway 6 to 51st Street

One of New York's finest Chinese restaurants, it frequently plays host to the city's power crowd.

DOCKS OYSTER BAR $$$
Seafood
- ☒ 633 3rd Avenue at 40th Street
- ☎ 212-986 8080
- ⌂ www.docksoysterbar.com
- ☛ Subway 4, 5, 6, 7 to Grand Central/42nd Street

This raw fish and seafood speciality restaurant also has a popular bar.

EUROPA GRILL $$
Mediterranean
- ☒ 599 Lexington Avenue at 53rd Street
- ☎ 212-755 6622
- Fax 212-755 1044
- ☛ Subway E, F to Lexington/3rd Avenue

A welcoming restaurant, which has been designed in natural elements of wood, stone and earth tones to create a soothing and tranquil environment. Lincoln Engstrom, formerly of the River Café (page 141), is the chef and he has created delicious and stylish Mediterranean dishes. They include poussin stuffed with Ricotta salata and courgette, peppers and sage, pomegranate-marinated lamb with crispy panisse and fresh mint, and lemon-cured pork loin served with soft polenta.

FOUR SEASONS $$$$
Continental
✉ 99 East 52nd Street between Lexington and Park Avenues
☎ 212-754 9494
🖰 www.fourseasonsrestaurant.com
🚗 Subway 6 to 51st Street; E, F to Lexington/3rd Avenue

You have a choice between the Grill Room or the Pool Room at this landmark restaurant, and whichever you opt for will make you feel like one of New York's movers and shakers – this is where they come for their power lunches. The Continental dishes are exquisite, the setting elegant and the service impeccable. Pricey? You bet.

ISTANA $$
Mediterranean
✉ NY Palace Hotel, 455 Madison Avenue at 51st Street
☎ 212-303 6032
🚗 Subway 6 to 51st Street

A little-known but excellent restaurant serving Mediterranean cuisine in the incredibly beautiful environs of the former Villard Houses that are also home to Le Cirque (page 138).

LA GRENOUILLE $$$
French
✉ 3 East 52nd Street between 5th and Madison Avenues
☎ 212-752 1495
🖰 www.la-grenouille.com
🚗 Subway 6 to 51st Street

A sophisticated temple for Francophiles, the exquisite French food is well worth its price. If money's no object, go for dinner: otherwise go for a more economical lunch.

Café Habana

LE CIRQUE $$–$$$
See Top Five Fine Dining Restaurants, page 138.

MAMA MEXICO $$
Mexican
✉ 214 East 49th Street between 2nd and 3rd Avenues
☎ 212-935 1316
🖰 www.mamamexico.com
🚗 Subway 6 to 51st Street

A proper Mexican restaurant with bright colours, pulsating mariachi music and a festive crowd enjoying the extensive menu, which includes 20-plus appetisers and great main courses like grilled rack of lamb with chilli and pineapple sauce. The margaritas and over forty types of tequila will help put you in the party mood.

OYSTER BAR $$
Seafood
✉ Grand Central Station, lower level, between 42nd Street and Vanderbilt Avenue
☎ 212-490 6650
🖰 www.oysterbarny.com
🚗 Subway 4, 5, 6, 7 to Grand Central/42nd Street

It seems only appropriate to have a landmark restaurant like this in the landmark that is Grand Central Station. Its fame stems from the generations of connoisseurs who have consumed 1,000 dozen oysters every day at the counters of this atmospheric saloon.

PALM $$
Seafood–steakhouse
✉ 837 2nd Avenue between 44th and 45th Streets
☎ 212-687 2953
🖰 www.thepalm.com
🚗 Subway 4, 5, 6, 7 to Grand Central/42nd Street

A family-run business and now the heart of a multi-million pound empire of Palm restaurants the length and breadth of North America, this establishment celebrated its 80th anniversary in 2006. Thanks to the double steak speciality, it had earned its reputation as one of New York's greatest steakhouses by the 1930s. In the 1940s, lobster was introduced, setting the seal on the surf-and-turf trend.

Palm continues to be a Mecca for celebrities and the wheelers and dealers of Manhattan, who come not only for the giant steaks and jumbo Maine lobsters but also for the Italian classics and wide choice of dishes. Palm Two across the road (840 2nd Avenue, tel 212-697 5198) was opened to take the overspill and now has its own loyal customers.

VONG $$$
Thai–French
- ✉ 200 East 54th Street at 3rd Avenue
- ☎ 212-486 9592
- 🖰 www.jean-georges.com
- 🚇 Subway E, F to Lexington/3rd Avenue

Another of Jean-Georges Vongerichten's masterpieces, this Thai–French restaurant has sunken tables and deep booths that keep the trendy crowd happy.

WATER CLUB $-$$$
See Top Five Restaurants with a View, page 139.

MIDTOWN WEST

BARBETTA $$$
Italian
- ✉ 321 West 46th Street between 8th and 9th Avenues
- ☎ 212-246 9171
- 🖰 www.barbettarestaurant.com
- 🚇 Subway A, C east to 42nd Street

During the summer, the rather special Barbetta garden is one of the city's most sought-after sites for dining, with its century-old trees and the scented blooms of magnolia, wisteria, jasmine and gardenia. Having celebrated its 100th birthday in 2006, Barbetta is the oldest Italian restaurant in New York and features cuisine from Piedmont in the north-west region of Italy.

NOHO

FIVE POINTS $$
American
- ✉ 31 Great Jones Street between Lafayette Street and Bowery
- ☎ 212-253 5700
- 🖰 www.fivepointsrestaurant.com
- 🚇 Subway B, V, S to Broadway/Lafayette; 6 to Bleecker Street

Named after the once infamous gangland area, this is a popular neighbourhood restaurant with a friendly bar, so now there's no need to worry. For a good, tasty meal, try out the Maine scallop with apple cider sauce or the home-made sweet potato ravioli.

INDOCHINE $$$
Vietnamese–French
- ✉ 430 Lafayette Street between Astor Place and East 4th Street
- ☎ 212-505 5111
- 🚇 Subway 6 to Astor Place

This celebrity haunt serves delicious Vietnamese–French dishes, such as spring rolls and sole fish wrapped in banana leaf, in tiny portions.

NOLITA

CAFE HABANA $
Cuban
- ✉ 17 Prince Street at Elizabeth Street
- ☎ 212-625 2001
- 🚇 Subway N, R to Prince Street; 6 to Spring Street

A hot little restaurant filled with beautiful people eating spicy Cuban food – think chicken tacos with coriander and tomato salsa. Delish!

★ ★ ★ ★ BRIT TIP ★ ★ ★ ★
★ Weird but true: some of the smaller ★
★ restaurants don't take credit cards. ★
★ Check in advance. ★
★ ★

EIGHT MILE CREEK $$
Australian
- ✉ 240 Mulberry Street between Prince and Spring Streets
- ☎ 212-431 4635
- 🖰 www.eightmilecreek.com
- 🚇 Subway N, R to Prince Street; 6 to Spring Street

Just a few steps north of Little Italy, the laid-back Aussies have arrived serving up cuisine from Down Under. Good Aussie food is both deliciously exotic and pricey – and this tiny restaurant is no exception.

Zoe in SoHo

SOHO

SoHo is a great place to head for when eating out, day or night. Its diverse range of restaurants, at all different price points, means that you're pretty much guaranteed to find something to appeal to even the most picky of dining partners.

BALTHAZAR $$
Bistro
✉ 80 Spring Street between Broadway and Crosby Streets
☎ 212-965 1414
🖥 www.balthazarny.com
🚇 Subway N, R to Prince Street
A classy French brasserie, with a genuinely French ambience, serving up good food to a trendy crowd. Great oysters.

BLUE RIBBON $$$
Seafood
✉ 97 Sullivan Street between Prince and Spring Streets
☎ 212-274 0404
🖥 www.blueribbonrestaurants.com
🚇 Subway C east to Spring Street
This restaurant gets packed at any time of the day or night so don't decide to come here if you are on a tight schedule. If you're not, the eclectic seafood dishes, like sweet and spicy catfish, sushi and paella, are definitely worth the wait.

DANI $$-$$$
Mediterranean
✉ 333 Hudson Street at King Street
☎ 212-633 9333
🚇 Subway N, R to Prince Street
Chef Don Pintabona, who worked for years at the Tribeca Grill, has gone out on his own with this new eatery on the edge of SoHo that takes inspiration from his Sicilian roots. Expect delicious dishes such as chick pea fried calamari or rabbit cacciatore, all served up in trendy warehouse surroundings with wood floor and concrete columns.

FANELLI CAFE $
American
✉ 94 Prince Street at Mercer Street
☎ 212-226 9412
🚇 Subway N, R to Prince Street
Contemporary crowds pack this former speakeasy, which is now an old saloon-style bar and dining room serving American food. It does an excellent selection of sandwiches for lunch.

FIAMMA OSTERIA $$
Italian
✉ 206 Spring Street between 6th Avenue and Sullivan Street
☎ 212-653 0100
🖥 www.brguestrestaurants.com
🚇 Subway C, E to Spring Street
A bi-level restaurant which is very fancy, in a Hollywood type of way. The food is very good – think risotto with creamy arborio rice, wild mushrooms, seared scallops and shaved black truffles or sautéed red snapper, manila clam, Italian sausage and broccoli rabe.

KITTICHAI $$
American
✉ 60 Thompson Street between Spring and Broome Streets
☎ 212-219 2000
🖥 www.kittichairestaurant.com
🚇 Subway C, E to Spring Street
Based in trendy SoHo hotel 60 Thompson, this is a fashionable restaurant in its own right and serves up delicious American cuisine at reasonable prices.

L'ECOLE $$
French
✉ 462 Broadway
☎ 212-219 3300
🖥 www.frenchculinary.com/lecole
🚇 Subway 6, J, M, Z, N, Q, W to Canal Street; 6 to Spring Street.
This is the place to come if you want haute cuisine for café prices, as the chefs of this bright, airy restaurant are students of the French Culinary Institute who try out their cooking skills on willing customers. Just think, you could be eating poached sole with shrimp and mussels made by a star chef of the future.

LUCKY STRIKE $$
French
✉ 59 Grand Street between West Broadway and Wooster Street
☎ 212-941 0772
Fax 212-274 9365

🖰 www.luckystrikeny.com
🚇 Subway A, C, E, 1, 9, N, A, 6 to Canal
Street
Restaurateur Keith McNally's hot spot has
become a watering hole for models,
celebrities and club kids as well as SoHo's
art crowd. Ask for the cocktail list and
marvel at the many martinis, including
chocolate and espresso.

MERCER KITCHEN $$$
French–eclectic
✉ Mercer Hotel, 99 Prince Street at
Mercer Street
☎ 212-966 5454
🖰 www.jean-georges.com
Jean-Georges Vongerichten (he of Jean-
Georges fame) oversees the eclectic French-
inspired cuisine that is served to a trendy
crowd in a chic environment.

PROVENCE $$
French
✉ 38 MacDougal Street at Prince Street
☎ 212-475 7500
Fax 212-602 9772
🖰 www.provence-soho.com
🚇 Subway 1, 9 to West Houston Street; C,
E to Spring Street; A, C, E, B, D, Q, V, F
to 4th Street
One of the hidden gems of SoHo, this is a
beautifully rustic restaurant with a fountain
in the garden. The food is country-style
French cooking; order the pommes frites
with everything as they're delicious. Try the
prix-fixe brunch for $19.50 or make a
reservation for about 6.30pm to get a table
in the garden.

ZOE $$$
Californian
✉ 90 Prince Street between Broadway and
Mercer Street
☎ 212-966 6722
Fax 212-966 6718
🖰 www.zoerestaurant.com
🚇 Subway N, R to Prince Street; B. D, F, Q
to Broadway–Lafayette; G to Spring
Street.
Fabulous Californian-style American food in
a beautiful environment. Dishes include
seared arctic char with truffle-whipped
potatoes, black trumpet mushrooms and
caramelized shallots, or rotisserie Long
Island duck breast with wheatberry salad
with apricots and almonds and
pomegranate vinaigrette. The amazing
range of breads include everything from
soda to focaccia and come with butter that

includes sesame seeds, poppy seeds, salt and
pepper and garlic, plus their own spread
made with white beans. The award-winning
All American wine list is pretty special too.

THEATER DISTRICT (BROADWAY)
From 6th Avenue in the east to 9th Avenue
in the west and from West 40th Street to
West 53rd Street, the Theater District is as
good a place as any to get a pre-theatre
meal. As well as the many theatres, there
are hundreds of restaurants and you'd be
hard-pressed to go wrong.

★ ★ ★ ★ BRIT TIP ★ ★ ★ ★
★   ★
★   The main drag for eating in the   ★
★   Theater District is between 8th and ★
★   9th Avenues on West 46th Street   ★
★   and is known as Restaurant Row.   ★
★   ★
★ ★

BLUE FIN $$
Seafood
✉ W Times Square Hotel, 1567 Broadway
at 47th Street
☎ 212-918 1400
🖰 www.brquestrestaurants.com
🚇 Subway N, R, W to 49th Street
The Blue Fin made a big splash when it
opened in 2000. It serves up fresh fish in
theatrical surroundings. Sushi is available on
the first floor.

FIREBIRD $$
Caviar–Russian
✉ 365 West 46th Street between 8th and
9th Avenues
☎ 212-586 0244
🖰 www.firebirdrestaurant.com
🚇 Subway A, C east to 42nd Street
The opulent Russian decor creates a
fabulous setting for tucking into the caviar
and blinis. The prix-fixe pre-theatre dinner
used to be good value, but prices have
crept up.

★ ★ ★ ★ BRIT TIP ★ ★ ★ ★
★   ★
★ Due to the law that bans smoking in ★
★   all indoor public spaces, it is no   ★
★   longer possible to smoke even at a   ★
★   restaurant's bar. Some restaurants   ★
★   with outdoor seating are able to set ★
★   aside tables for smoking, though.   ★
★ ★

FRANKIE AND JOHNNIE'S STEAKHOUSE $$
Steakhouse
- ✉ 269 West 45th Street between Broadway and 8th Avenue
- ☎ 212-997 9494
- 🕆 www.frankieandjohnnies.com
- 🚗 Subway A, C, E, N, R to 42nd Street

This is considered to be one of the longest-running shows on Broadway, having first opened as a speakeasy in 1926. Now it still retains its intimate hideaway aura and archetypal New York reputation as a classic steakhouse that has become renowned for its generous portions.

HUDSON CAFETERIA $$
Asian
- ✉ The Hudson Hotel, 356 West 58th Street between 8th and 9th Avenues
- ☎ 212-554 6000
- 🕆 www.chinagrillmgt.com
- 🚗 Subway A, B, C, D, 1, 2 to 59th Street/ Columbus Circle

The restaurant at Ian Schrager's hotel is a haven for people- and celeb-watching and you'll enjoy the Asian cuisine.

JEAN GEORGES $$$$
See Top Five Fine Dining Restaurants, page 141.

LE BERNARDIN $$$$
See Top Five Romantic Restaurants, page 138.

MARS 2112 $
American
- ✉ 1633 Broadway at 51st Street
- ☎ 212-582 2112
- 🕆 www.mars2112.com
- 🚗 Subway 1, 9 to 51st Street

This theme restaurant offering will take you out of this world to Mars via the space

Hudson Cafeteria

TOP FIVE RESTAURANTS TO SPOT A CELEBRITY
Blue Water Grill: Union Square (page 177)
Lucky Strike: SoHo (page 172)
Mark's: Upper East Side (page 179)
Nobu: TriBeCa (page 137)
TriBeCa Grill: TriBeCa (page 177)

shuttle. Fortunately, the food is pretty American Earthbound so you won't be eating little green men. Of course, it comes with the ubiquitous shop where you can buy your own Martian doll.

PALM NEW YORK WEST SIDE $$-$$$
Seafood-steakhouse
- ✉ 250 West 50th Street between Broadway and 8th Avenue
- ☎ 212-333 7256
- 🕆 www.thepalm.com
- 🚗 Subway 1, 9 to 50th Street

A sister restaurant to the incredibly successful Palm restaurant (page 170), this has very quickly become a hot spot for celebrities, theatre-goers and tourists.

PETROSSIAN $$$
Caviar-Russian
- ✉ 182 West 58th Street at 7th Avenue
- ☎ 212-245 2214
- 🕆 www.petrossian.com
- 🚗 Subway N, R to 57th Street

Take advantage of the $37 prix-fixe theatre menu to enjoy caviar, foie gras and smoked salmon.

PLANET HOLLYWOOD $
American
- ✉ 1540 Broadway at West 45th Street
- ☎ 212-333 7827
- 🕆 www.planethollywood.com
- 🚗 Subway N, Q, R, S, W, 1, 2, 3, 7 to Times Square

Brilliant Hollywood memorabilia with the standard American burger fare.

RENE PUJOL $$
Bistro
- ✉ 321 West 51st Street between 8th and 9th Avenues
- ☎ 212-246 3023
- 🕆 www.renepujol.com
- 🚗 Subway C east to 50th Street

A great French bistro serving delicious food in a delightful setting.

Dining al fresco in SoHo

SUPPER CLUB $$$
Gourmet American
- ✉ 240 West 47th Street between Broadway and 8th Avenue
- ☎ 212-921 1940
- 🖰 www.thesupperclub.com
- 🚇 Subway 1, 9 to 50th Street

At this special place you'll find fine dining combined with swing dancing and a cabaret – the show is a mix of Cab Calloway, the Blues Brothers and other swing acts. The food is also delicious, particularly the lobster and steak, and I defy anyone not to like the New York cheesecake – so much lighter than European cheesecake, it just melts in your mouth. Stupendous!

THE VIEW $$$–$$$$
See Top Five Restaurants with a View, page 139.

WORLD YACHT DINNER CRUISES $$$
See Top Five Restaurants with a View, page 139.

TRIBECA

66 $$$–$$$$
Chinese
- ✉ 241 Church Street at Leonard Street
- ☎ 212-925 0202
- 🖰 www.jean-georges.com
- 🚇 Subway 1, 9 to Franklin Street

Expensive but worth it is the general consensus on this very chic Chinese restaurant. Its trendy interior – lots of minimalist metallic silver and sparkling white plus some fish tanks – makes it a hit

with the fashionable city crowd. Its dishes, such as steamed cod and Peking duck, are exceptionally good and the bar's cocktails are pleasant to sip while you wait for your table.

ACAPPELLA $$$–$$$$
Italian
- ✉ 1 Hudson Street at Chambers Street
- ☎ 212-240 0163
- 🖰 www.acappella-restaurant.com
- 🚇 Subway 1, 9 to Franklin Street

You can chow down on rabbit, wild boar, quail and venison at this lovely restaurant specialising in northern Italian cuisine. The decor is as impressive as the menu, with 5m (16ft) high beamed ceilings and Italian tapestries on the walls, plus huge windows offering views over TriBeCa.

CHANTERELLE $$$
French
- ✉ 2 Harrison Street at Hudson Street
- ☎ 212-966 6960
- 🖰 www.chanterellenyc.com
- 🚇 Subway 1, 9 to Franklin Street

'If this restaurant were any more romantic it would be illegal', gushes one of the entries in New York's Zagat survey. A 'first class trip' to 'heaven on earth' says another. It's true that it's a premier spot in the city for a romantic night out, and the great food matches the ambience. The $42 prix-fixe lunch is one of the best bargains in NY and includes dishes such as striped bass sauté with red wine and sage.

Blue Water Grill

BEST FOR DINING AND DANCING

Cornelia Street Café: Greenwich Village (page 162)

Metronome: Madison Square (page 165)

Rainbow Room: Rockefeller Plaza (page 139)

Supper Club: Times Square (page 175)

Swing 46 Jazz & Supper Club: Times Square (page 193)

The View: Times Square (page 139)

World Yacht Dinner Cruises: from Midtown West (page 139)

HARRISON $$
Continental

✉ 355 Greenwich Street at Harrison Street
☎ 212-274 9310
🖰 www.theharrison.com

🚇 Subway 1, 2 to Franklin Street
Created by the owners of the hip Red Cat in Chelsea (page 143), this chic restaurant serves up delicious Continental cuisine in an elegant setting.

LE ZINC $
Bistro

✉ 139 Duane Street between West Broadway and Church Street
☎ 212-513 0001
🖰 www.lezincnyc.com
🚇 Subway A, C, 1, 2 to Chambers Street
A casual, well-priced bistro. Here you'll get French food infused with Asian and Hungarian influences. Delicious stuff.

MONTRACHET $$$–$$$$
Bistro

✉ 239 West Broadway between Walker and White Streets
☎ 212-219 2777
🖰 www.myriadrestaurantgroup.com
🚇 Subway 1, 2 to Franklin Street

NEW YORK FOODS AND FOOD TERMS

Arugula: The American name for rocket, used in salads.

Bagels: As opposed to bialys, these are the delicious Jewish creations, which are at their very best when filled with smoked salmon and cream cheese.

Bialy: A cousin of the bagel, it originates from Bialystock in Eastern Europe and is kosher Jewish food. The dough is not as chewy as a bagel and there is no hole in the middle, just a depression in which garlic and onions are put. Without any tasty extras such as cream cheese, this is truly boring food.

Cannoli: Tubular-shaped biscuit bells with fresh cream on the inside, these come from Italy and are truly delicious.

Cilantro: American name for the fresh leaves of coriander.

Cobbler: A fruit pie topped with a biscuit-style crust.

Grits: Corn kernels.

Halva: Sweetened, crushed sesame paste. It originates from the Mediterranean, Turkey and Arabia.

Konja: A Chinese dessert, which you can buy in bags – they are individual mouth-size pots of lychee jelly.

Lox: Thinly sliced pieces of smoked salmon, generally sold with a 'schmear' of cream cheese. It tastes the same as a smoked salmon and cream cheese bagel but works out much cheaper.

Morels: Deliciously meaty mushrooms from Oregon.

Pie: Used to refer to an entire pizza. Most are much larger than the ones we eat in the UK, so people tend to buy by the slice or share a whole 'pie'.

Scallion: Spring onion.

Schmear: A spreading of cream cheese on a bagel.

Sub: An extra large, long roll, named for its submarine-like shape.

You can find a list of more general US foods and food terms on page 20.

One of the best French bistros in the city and well known for excellent service. Decor is tired but charming. Go on a Friday for a $20 prix-fixe lunch.

NOBU $$$$
See Top Five Fine Dining Restaurants, page 137.

ODEON $$
American–French
- ✉ 145 West Broadway between Duane and Thomas Streets
- ☎ 212-233 0507
- ⌂ www.theodeonrestaurant.com
- 🚗 Subway 1, 9 to Chambers Street

A très hip hangout that still attracts celebrities for its cool atmosphere and American–French cuisine. You'll need to book ahead. A great late night stop as it stays open until 2am.

TRIBECA GRILL $$$
American
- ✉ 375 Greenwich Street at Franklin Street
- ☎ 212-941 3900
- ⌂ www.tribecagrill.com
- 🚗 Subway 1, 9 to Franklin Street

Robert De Niro and Drew Nieporent's popular American restaurant opened in 1990 and is one of the main reasons why TriBeCa has become such a hip hangout in recent years. It's located on the first two floors of the TriBeCa Film Center where De Niro has his film production company, so it's a good place to try to spot a celeb or two. Dishes like braised short ribs with foie gras ravioli are rich and filling. The $24.07 prix-fixe lunch attracts major crowds, and in winter the prix-fixe dinner is $35.

UNION SQUARE

BLUE WATER GRILL $$$$
Seafood
- ✉ 31 Union Square West at 16th Street
- ☎ 212-675 9500
- ⌂ www.brguestrestaurants.com
- 🚗 Subway L, N, Q, R, W, 4, 5, 6 to Union Square

Voted seventh most popular restaurant in New York in Zagat's 2006 survey, this place is not only brilliant for people- and celeb-watching, it is also a Mecca for all those who love their seafood. Dishes include lobster-glazed mahi mahi with mango coulis, ginger-crusted big eye tuna with shiitake mushrooms, and blackened swordfish with sweet potato-crabmeat

hash. It also has an oyster bar and a 150-seat jazz club for nightly entertainment and dining. Or you can go on Sundays for the wonderful jazz brunch, which is served from 10.30am.

CHAT 'N' CHEW $
American diner
- ✉ 10 East 16th Street between 5th Avenue and Union Square West
- ☎ 212-243 1616
  Fax 212-243 2895
- ⌂ www.chatnchewnyc.com
- 🚗 Subway L, N, R, 4, 5, 6 to Union Square/ 14th Street

Classic 1950s' American diner with huge servings of meatloaf etc. Regulars know to order the crispy-topped macaroni and cheese, with chicken or bacon added.

MESA GRILL $$
South-western
- ✉ 102 5th Avenue between 15th and 16th Streets near Union Square
- ☎ 212-807 7400
  Fax 212-989 0034
- ⌂ www.mesagrill.com
- 🚗 Subway L, N, R, 4, 5, 6 to Union Square/ 14th Street

Delicious and inventive south-western cuisine from chef Bobby Flay. A real winner, so give it a try if you are in the area.

REPUBLIC $
Asian
- ✉ 37 Union Square West between 16th and 17th Streets
- ☎ 212-627 7172
- ⌂ www.thinknoodles.com
- 🚗 Subway L, N, R, 4, 5, 6 to Union Square/ 14th Street

Specialists in excellent, quick, noodle-based pan-Asian dishes in a canteen-style environment. There is also a branch in Upper West Side.

STRIP HOUSE $$
American
- ✉ 13 East 12th Street between 5th Avenue and University Place
- ☎ 212-328 0000
- ⌂ www.theglaziergroup.com
- 🚗 Subway L, N, Q, R, W, 4, 5, 6 to 14th Street/Union Square

You can eat succulent beef here, especially, of course, the New York 'strip'. Lots of other cuts are available as well as some fish, all served in the glorious surroundings of leather banquettes and velvet.

RESTAURANTS

Mesa Grill

UPPER EAST SIDE

ATLANTIC GRILL $$-$$$
Seafood
- ✉ 1341 3rd Avenue between 76th and 77th Streets
- ☎ 212-988 9200
- ⌖ www.brguestrestaurants.com
- 🚇 Subway 77th Street

A long-standing popular restaurant with the fussy Upper East Side set. It's all very chic, from the polished wood floors and artwork to the well-prepared, very fresh fish. There's also an excellent wine list.

AUREOLE $$$$
See Top Five Fine Dining Restaurants, page 140.

Manhattan skyline

BLUE GROTTO $
Mediterranean
- ✉ 1576 3rd Avenue between 88th and 89th Streets
- ☎ 212-426 3200
- 🚇 Subway 4, 5, 6 to 86th Street

This is more Yorkville than 'silk stocking' Upper East Side, which is reflected in the reasonable prices. It's popular with the locals and serves Italian and Mediterranean-style cuisine in a lounge-like space.

Ithaka

CAFE SABARSKY $
Bistro
- ✉ 1048 5th Avenue at 86th Street
- ☎ 212-288 0665
  Fax 212-645 7127
- ⌖ www.wallse.com
- 🚇 Subway 4, 5, 6 to 86th Street

This is not just in a fabulous location – all but opposite the Metropolitan Museum of Art, yet quietly tucked away in the new Neue Galerie Museum for German and Austrian Art (page 131) – but is a wonderful pit stop for light breakfasts, lunches and afternoon tea. You'll also love its elegant decor to match the Austrian-German art theme of the museum itself.

CANDLE 79 $-$$
Vegetarian
- ✉ 154 East 79th Street near Lexington Avenue
- ☎ 212-537 7179
- ⌖ www.candlecafe.com
- 🚇 Subway 6 to 77th Street

An unusual place in this swish neighbourhood as it's veggie – though undoubtedly upscale. The menu is well thought out and attracts plenty of meat eaters because it's so tasty, such as the delicious mushroom and squash risotto.

Food is 24/7 in New York

There's organic wine on offer, along with fresh juices and smoothies.

CARLYLE $$$
French

✉ Carlyle Hotel, 35 East 76th Street at Madison Avenue
☎ 212-744 1600
    Fax 212-717 4682
🖰 www.thecarlyle.com
🚇 Subway 6 to 77th Street

An old establishment that attracts an older 'silk stocking' clientele but, if you want to see how the other half lives, try the fine French cuisine for breakfast or a delicious brunch. Divine.

DANIEL $$$$

See Top Five Romantic Restaurants, page 140.

ITHAKA $$
Greek

✉ 308 East 86th Street between 1st and 2nd Avenues
☎ 212-628 9100
🖰 www.ithakarestaurant.com
🚇 Subway 4, 5, 6 to 86th Street

A superb Greek restaurant with exposed brick walls painted white, stone floor and recessed lighting filtered through white fabric. It's known for its large portions, a real locals' favourite with the added benefit of a guitar player Wednesday to Saturday.

MARK'S $$$
French–American

✉ The Mark, 25 East 77th Street at Madison Avenue
☎ 212-879 1864
🖰 www.mandarinoriental.com/themark
🚇 Subway 6 to 77th Street

Excellent French–American cuisine. The prix-fixe lunch and pre-theatre deals are great value – just make sure you give yourself time to soak up the ambience.

ROSA MEXICANO $$
Mexican

✉ 1063 1st Avenue at 58th Street
☎ 212-753 7407
🖰 www.rosamexicano.com
🚇 Subway 4, 5, 6 to 59th Street

Extremely popular Mexican eatery that is known as much for its margaritas as for its delicious food. Its signature dish is its gaucamole mashed right beside your table.

Yellow cabs are a great way to get around

RESTAURANT REFERENCE GUIDE

Name	Area	Style	Price range	Page
Ithaka	Upper East Side	Greek	$$	179
Jean Georges	Midtown West	French	$$$$	141
Joe's Shanghai	Chinatown	Chinese-Shanghai	$	144
John's Pizzeria	Greenwich Village	pizza	$	163
Jones Diner	NoLiTa	diner	$	184
Katz's Delicatessen	Lower East Side	American-Jewish	$	165
Kittichai	SoHo	American	$$$	172
Koodo Sushi	Financial District	Japanese	$$	161
La Grenouille	Midtown East	French	$$$	170
La Palapa	East Village	Mexican	$$	161
Le Bernardin	Midtown West	seafood	$$$$	138
L'Ecole	SoHo	French	$$	172
Le Cirque	Midtown East	French-American	$$$-$$$$	138
Le Zinc	TriBeCa	bistro	$	176
Lucky Strike	SoHo	French	$$	172
M&G Soul Food Diner	Harlem	diner	$	184
Mama Mexico	Midtown East	Mexican	$$	170
Market Diner	Midtown West	diner	$	184
MarkJoseph Steakhouse	South Street Seaport	steakhouse	$$	161
Mark's	Upper East Side	French-American	$$$	179
Markt	Meatpacking District	Belgian	$$	166
Mars 2112	Theater District	American	$	174
Meet	Meatpacking District	Mediterranean	$$	166
Mercer Kitchen	SoHo	French-eclectic	$$$	173
Mesa Grill	Union Square	south-western	$$	177
Metronome	Madison Square	Mediterranean	$$$	165
Montrachet	TriBeCa	bistro	$$$-$$$$	176
Moondance	SoHo	diner	$	184
New Green Bo	Chinatown	Chinese-Shanghai	$-$$	144
New York Noodle Town	Chinatown	Hong Kong-style noodle house	$	144
Nobu	TriBeCa	Japanese-Peruvian	$$$$	137
Nobu 57	Midtown	Japanese-Peruvian	$$$$	136
Nobu Next Door	TriBeCa	Japanese	$$	137
Noodle Pudding	Brooklyn	Italian	$$	142
Norma's	Midtown	American	$-$$	168
Odeon	TriBeCa	American-French	$$	177
Old Homestead	Meatpacking District	American	$$	166
Opia	Midtown	French	$$	168
Ouest	Upper West Side	French-American	$$	182
Oyster Bar	Midtown East	seafood	$$	170
Palm	Midtown East	seafood-steakhouse	$$	170
Palm New York West Side	Theater District	seafood-steakhouse	$$-$$$	174
Park View at the Boathouse	Central Park	American-seafood	$$-$$$	140
Pasha	Upper West Side	Turkish	$$	182
Pellegrino's	Little Italy	Italian	$	164
Petrossian	Theater District	caviar-Russian	$$$	174
Philip Marie	West Village	American	$$	163
Picholine	Upper West Side	Mediterranean	$$$	183
Pizzeria Uno	Upper West Side	Italian	$	183
Planet Hollywood	Theater District	American	$$	174
Porcao Churrascaria	Gramercy Park	Brazilian	$$$	162
Provence	SoHo	French	$$	173
Quartino	South Street Seaport	Italian	$$	161
Rainbow Room	Midtown	Continental	$$$-$$$$	139
Rao's	Harlem	Italian	$	163
Remi	Midtown	Italian	$$$	168
René Pujol	Theater District	bistro	$$	174
Republic	Union Square	Asian	$$	177
River Café	Brooklyn	gourmet American	$$$	141
Rock Center Café	Midtown	American	$$	168
Rosa Mexicana	Upper East Side	Mexican	$$	179
Ruby Foo's	Upper West Side	Asian	$$	183
Sal Anthony's SPQR	Little Italy	Italian	$$-$$$	165
Seagrill	Midtown	seafood	$$$$	168
Seppi's	Midtown	French-Italian-Turkish	$$	168
Serafina Fabulous Grill	Upper East Side	Italian	$$$	182
Spazzia	Upper West Side	Mediterranean	$$	183
Strip House	Union Square	American	$$	177
Supper Club	Theater District	gourmet American	$$$	175
Sylvia's	Harlem	southern soul food	$$	164
Tabla	Madison Square	American Indian	$$$$	165
Tamarind	Gramercy Park	Indian	$$	162
Taormina	Little Italy	Italian	$	164
Tavern on the Green	Central Park	gourmet American	$$$	142
The Elephant	East Village	French-Thai fusion	$$	161
The Park	Chelsea	Mediterranean	$$$	143
The Red Cat	Chelsea	Mediterranean-American	$$$	143
The View	Theater District	Continental	$$$-$$$$	139
Tomoe Sushi	Greenwich Village	Japanese	$$	163
Tom's Restaurant	Morningside Heights	diner	$	184
Town	Midtown	gourmet American	$$$	169
TriBeCa Grill	TriBeCa	American	$$$	177
Union Square Cafe	Midtown East	American-Italian	$$-$$$	136
Upstairs at 21	Midtown	gourmet American	$$	169
Veritas	Gramercy Park	gourmet American	$$$$	162
Vong	Midtown East	Thai-French	$$$	171
Water Club	Midtown East	seafood	$-$$$	139
World Yacht Dinner Cruises	Midtown West	gourmet American	$$$	139
Yaffa Café	East Village	American diner	$	161
Zoe	SoHo	Californian	$$$	173

SERAFINA FABULOUS GRILL $$$
Italian

✉ 393 Lafayette Street at 4th Street or 2nd floor, 1022 Madison Avenue at 79th Street

☎ 212-702 9595/212-734 2676

🖰 www.serafinarestaurant.com

🚗 Subway 4, 5, 6 to 59th Street

Famous for thin-crust pizzas that have been voted the best in the world by gourmets, this is a haunt of both Prince Albert of Monaco and Ivana Trump. Toppings include Al Porcini with porcini mushrooms, fontina cheese and Mozzarella and Al Caviale with salmon caviar, potatoes and crème fraîche. The signature focaccias – two layers of stuffed dough with delicious fillings – range from a delicious Scottish smoked salmon, asparagus and Italian Robiola cheese to truffle oil and Robiola.

UPPER WEST SIDE

ALOUETTE $$$
Bistro

✉ 2588 Broadway between 97th and 98th Streets

☎ 212-222 6808

🚗 Subway 1, 2, 3, 9 to 96th Street

This French bistro attracts the crowds despite having a very simple menu.

Serafina Fabulous Grill

Ruby Foo's

CAFE DES ARTISTES $$
French

✉ 1 West 67th Street between Columbus Avenue and Central Park West

☎ 212-877 3500

🖰 www.cafenyc.com

🚗 Subway 1, 9 to 66th Street

A reasonably priced, fine dining establishment that serves up wonderful French cuisine in a romantic setting.

EL MALECON II $
Dominican Caribbean

✉ 764 Amsterdam Avenue between 97th and 98th Streets

☎ 212-864 5648

🚗 Subway 1, 9 to 66th Street

Great value for money. Locals pop in for the fried chicken, plantain, rice, peas and steak. The dining room is pretty mediocre, but who cares when the food is this tasty and $6 for the best roasted chicken outside the Caribbean. You can eat in or take out.

OUEST $$
French–American

✉ 2315 Broadway between 83rd and 84th Streets

☎ 212-580 8700

🖰 www.ouestny.com

🚗 Subway 1, 2 to 86th Street

Once you can get your tongue around the restaurant's name – it's simply pronounced West! – you'll be ready to enjoy the French–American cuisine created by Valenti.

PASHA $$
Turkish

✉ 70 West 71st Street between Columbus Avenue and Central Park West

☎ 212-579 8751

🖰 www.pashanewyork.com

🚗 Subway 1, 2 to 86th Street

A delightfully sumptuous restaurant that looks like part of a palace; think deep reds

Tom's Restaurant

and yellows, luxurious fabrics and tapestries hanging on the walls. You can order lots of Turkish delights, from stuffed vine leaves to kebabs.

PICHOLINE $$$
Mediterranean
⊠ 35 West 64th Street between Broadway and Central Park West
☎ 212-724 8585
🚇 Subway 1, 9 to 66th Street/Lincoln Center

A beautiful restaurant serving exquisite Mediterranean dishes in a refined and elegant setting. Opt to make it one of your 'special' treats while in the city so you can sample the amazing cheese trolley – yes trolley, not board. Each day more than 50 different cheeses, out of a total of 70 varieties, are on offer and, if you don't know which to choose, all the waiters are well versed in what cheeses go well with what wines and for what kind of palates. Take advantage of their considerable knowledge. A tradition to be savoured.

PIZZERIA UNO $
Italian
⊠ Columbus Avenue at 81st Street
☎ 212-595 4700
🖰 www.unos.com
🚇 Subway B, C to 81st Street

Okay, so this is a chain restaurant, but it actually provides good-quality food for those wanting a simple, but tasty, meal at a very good price. This one is a great little

neighbourhood joint offering an excellent range of family-friendly dishes just around the corner from the American Museum of Natural History (page 117). There is an excellently priced children's menu, plus crayons. What more could you ask after tramping round dinosaur exhibits?

RUBY FOO'S $$
Asian
⊠ 2182 Broadway at 77th Street
☎ 212-724 6700
🖰 www.brguestrestaurants.com
🚇 Subway 1, 9 to 79th Street

Beautiful Asian decor combined with delicious Asian food. Dim sum is a speciality of the house.

SPAZZIA $$
Mediterranean
⊠ 366 Columbus Avenue at West 77th Street
☎ 212-799 0150
🚇 Subway 1, 9 to 79th Street

This restaurant serves delicious Mediterranean food just a stone's throw away from the American Museum of Natural History (page 117).

Comfort Diner, East 45th Street

THE AMERICAN DINER

We don't have a real equivalent of an American diner in the UK but the closest is probably a cross between a transport café and a Garfunkels. In a nutshell, diners are relatively cheap, have a homey feel to them but are a lot smarter than your average café. They specialise in American comfort food – pancakes, waffles, crispy bacon, eggs, grill foods, meatloaf – the kind of things that we would choose for a brunch. Go to just about any American city or town and you'll find a good smattering of diners. The one exception is Manhattan, where they are very thin on the ground. Some of the few diners in New York include:

Chelsea
Empire Diner: 210 10th Avenue at 22nd Street. Tel 212-243 2736. A real New York institution and a great pitstop for clubbers as it's open 24 hours a day. The interior is fabulous with its Art Deco style and the people are pretty gorgeous, too.

Garment District
Cheyenne Diner: 411 9th Avenue at 33rd Street. Tel 212-465 8750. In the heart of the Garment District and just around the corner from Penn Street Station, this is a great place to fill up.

Harlem
M&G Soul Food Diner: 383 West 125th Street at Morningside Avenue. Tel 212-864 7326. This is the southern soul food version of a diner and a great venue for a meal in Harlem. You'll also enjoy the background soul music.

Midtown East
Comfort Diner: 214 East 45th Street between 2nd and 3rd Avenues. Tel 212-867 4555. A classic retro diner known for its friendliness and also its wholesome staples of meatloaf and fried chicken.

Midtown West
Market Diner: 572 11th Avenue at West 43rd Street. Tel 212-695 0415. One of the most famous diners in Manhattan, this is where clubbers go to get breakfast or fill up before the evening run.

Morningside Heights
Tom's Restaurant: 2880 Broadway at 112th Street. Tel 212-864 6137. The exterior was made famous by its use in *Seinfeld*. If you come here you'll be sharing the space with Columbia University students, who enjoy the cheap comfort food.

NoLiTa
Jones Diner: 371 Lafayette Street at Great Jones Street. Tel 212-673 3577. Pretty dingy-looking from the outside, this is one of the cheapest and best places in the area to get very basic grills and sarnies.

SoHo
Moondance: 80 6th Avenue between Grand and Canal Streets. Tel 212-226 1191, fax 212-226 1169. A cracking spot for a cheap meal, it gets packed at the weekends when it's open all night.

Theater District
Ellen's Stardust Diner: 1650 Broadway at 51st Street. Tel 212-956 5151, fax 212-956 5834. Tourists and children love this 1950s-style diner thanks to its kitsch-retro decor and the singing waitresses. It's great fun, but you wouldn't want to eat here too often – think burgers, chips and anything else that's greasy!

Upper East Side
Comfort Diner: 142 East 86th Street at Lexington Avenue. Tel 212-369 8628. The Upper East Side/Yorkville branch of the friendly diner.

Upper West Side
EJ's Luncheonette: 447 Amsterdam Avenue between 81st and 82nd streets. Tel 212-873 3444. A traditional American diner that serves a mean cup of coffee.

CHAPTER 8

Shows, Bars and Clubs

New York is synonymous with shopping, shows and exciting nightlife. After a day of shopping and sightseeing, it's time to hit the streets at night and discover exactly what makes the Big Apple one of the top cities in the world for partying.

A glance at any of the listings pages in the press will confirm that there is an amazing amount of evening entertainment to choose from. Any night of the week you'll find comedy shows with stand-up routines from some of the best in the business, award-winning Broadway musicals and live music from the hottest bands. And the bar scene in NYC is particularly exciting: whether it's soaking up some cool jazz in the West Village, partying into the small hours in the hip Meatpacking District or sipping apple martinis in a sophisticated Upper East Side joint, there's a bar or lounge to suit every type of person.

BROADWAY SHOWS

One of the first things you discover about Broadway, as we Brits think of it, is that it is just one tiny stretch of almost the longest thoroughfare on Manhattan. The Theater District, as it is known, is a congregation of theatres between Broadway and 8th Avenue from about 44th to 52nd Streets (take the N, R, Q, W, 1, 2, 3, 7, 9, S lines to 42nd Street/Times Square). This is Broadway. You'll also see and hear the terms 'Off Broadway' and 'Off-Off Broadway' (yes, really), which refer to uptown and downtown theatres, particularly in Greenwich Village, East Village and SoHo. These theatres are well worth a visit, as they may be offering rarely seen revivals, the innovative work of new playwrights, or productions featuring hilarious, off-the-wall humour. But they do change frequently, so we have included only a sample selection.

Of course, Broadway productions are changing all the time, but many of the big shows – the ones that many Brits want to see – do stay around a little longer. We have

included reviews of those shows we believe will be available for the next couple of years, but for a completely up-to-date guide to what's on at the theatre, look in the *New York Times*, which has comprehensive listings of dance, classical music, opera, Broadway, Off Broadway and Off-Off Broadway every day. Other papers and magazines that you can check out include the *New Yorker*, *Village Voice*, *New York Metro* and *New York Press*. If you want to find out what's on before you go, visit the Keith Prowse or Theatre Direct websites given below.

★ ★ ★ ★ **BRIT TIP** ★ ★ ★ ★

Look for discount coupons for Broadway shows at neighbourhood information stands and barrows throughout Manhattan.

BOOKING YOUR TICKETS

You can book tickets in advance in the UK through either your travel agent or Keith Prowse (tel UK 0870 840 1111 or US 800-669 8687, www.keithprowse.com). An alternative is to use the TicketMaster website at www.ticketmaster.com.

If booking in New York, try Theater Mania (tel 212-352 0255, www.theatermania.com); Americana Tickets & Travel (tel 212-581 6660, www.americanatickets.com); and Prime Tickets and Tours (tel 305-661 8646, www.primetickets.com).

For cheaper tickets, go to the **Theater Development Fund/TKTS** booths (tel 212-221 0013, www.tdf.org). The less crowded (but less convenient) downtown booth is at 108 Front Street at John Street, open Mon-Fri 11am-6pm, Sat 11am-7pm, Sun 11am-3pm; matinee tickets bought here are for the following day's performance. The booth in the middle of Times Square at 47th Street is open Mon-Sat 3-8pm, Wed and Sat 10am-2pm for matinee tickets and Sun 11am-2pm for matinees, 3-7pm for evening performances. It gets very busy so arrive early for the best selection, then spend the day in Midtown (see Chapter 3, The New York Neighbourhoods).

Discounts range from 25–50 per cent but bear in mind that the booths only accept cash or travellers' cheques. Have plenty of options ready in case there are no tickets for your first show choice. If you are flexible about what you would like to see, you can decide to go to a show at the very last minute, since TKTS Midtown is open right until showtime.

Bookings for ALL of the shows and performances below can be made with Theater Direct (tel 800-541 8457, www.broadway.com).

★★★★ **BRIT TIP** ★★★★
★ ★
★ Watch out for ticket touts – an ★
★ increasing number of the tickets ★
★ they sell are fakes. ★
★★★★★★★★★★★★★★★★★★★★★★★★

MUSICALS

All the Broadway and Off Broadway shows listed here have one interval. The suggested ages given are for guidance only.

ALL SHOOK UP

✉ Palace Theater, 1564 Broadway at 47th Street
🕐 Tues 7pm, Wed–Sat 8pm; matinees Wed, Sat 2pm, Sun 3pm

All Shook Up tells the story of a square little town in the middle of a square state in the middle of a square decade where a lonely young girl dreams of hitting the open road. Into her life rides a guitar-playin' roustabout who changes everything and kick-starts a hip-swivelin', lip-curlin' musical

Taxis in Times Square

The Lincoln Center

fantasy that will have you jumpin' out of your blue suede shoes and singing along to classics such as Heartbreak Hotel, Burning Love, Jailhouse Rock, Blue Suede Shoes and Don't Be Cruel.
Length of show: 2 hours 15 minutes
Age: 12 and over

AVENUE Q

✉ John Golden Theater, 252 West 45th Street between Broadway and 8th Avenue
🖰 www.avenueq.com
🕐 Tues–Fri 8pm, Sat 2pm, 8pm, Sun 2pm, 7pm

A bright and entertaining show with people and puppets about the struggles with life when you're straight out of college. Funny and urbane. Has been called a mix of *Sesame Street, The Simpsons* and *Sex And The City.*
Awards: Several Tony Awards in 2004, including Best Musical
Length of show: 2 hours 15 minutes
Age: 18 and over (don't let the puppets fool you)

★★★★ **BRIT TIP** ★★★★
★ ★
★ The Hit Show Club (630 9th Avenue ★
★ at 45th Street, 8th Floor, tel 212- ★
★ 581 4211, www.hitshowclub.com) ★
★ and Broadway Bucks (226 West ★
★ 47th Street between Broadway and ★
★ 8th Avenue, l0th floor, tel 212-398 ★
★ 8383, www.bestofbroadway.com) ★
★ distribute coupons that can be ★
★ redeemed at the box office for one- ★
★ third or more off regular ticket ★
★ prices. If you don't see them in your ★
★ hotel, pick them up from the offices. ★
★★★★★★★★★★★★★★★★★★★★★★★★

Metropolitan Opera House

BEAUTY AND THE BEAST

✉ Lunt-Fontanne Theater, 205 West 46th Street between Broadway and 8th Avenue

🖰 www.disneyonbroadway.com

🕔 Tues–Thurs 7pm, Fri, Sat 8pm, Sun 7.30pm; matinees Sat, Sun 2pm; subject to change so check website

The wonderful, award-winning Disney version with music by Alan Menken and lyrics by Tim Rice and the late Howard Ashman. It tells the age-old story of how a young woman falls in love with a stubborn but charming beast.

Awards: 1 Tony Award 1994
Length of show: 2 hours 30 minutes
Age: From the very young to the very old

★★★★ **BRIT TIP** ★★★★

Many theatres have started scheduling Tuesday performances at 7pm, an hour earlier than customary, to accommodate those who have to travel far or want to dine afterwards.

CHICAGO

✉ Ambassador Theater, 219 West 49th Street between Broadway and 8th Avenue

🖰 www.chicagothemusical.com

🕔 Tues 7pm, Wed, Thurs, Fri, Sat 8pm, Sun 6.30pm; matinees Wed, Thurs 2pm

This great musical with wonderful dancing is the winner of six Tony Awards and has other productions throughout the world, but many still consider this one to be the best. *Chicago* tells the story of a chorus girl who kills her lover and then escapes the noose and prison with the help of a conniving lawyer. If greed, corruption, murder and treachery are your bag, then this is the musical for you.

Awards: 6 Tony Awards 1997
Length of show: 2 hours 30 minutes
Age: 12 and over (parental guidance)

CHITTY CHITTY BANG BANG

✉ Hilton Theater, 214 West 43rd Street between Broadway and 7th Avenue

🕔 Tues–Thurs 7pm, Fri, Sat 8pm; matinees Wed, Sat 2pm, Sun 3pm

Based on the film and Ian Fleming's timeless original story, *Chitty Chitty Bang Bang* features a beloved score, including memorable classics such as 'Truly Scrumptious', 'Toot Sweets', 'Hushabye Mountain' and the Oscar-nominated title song 'Chitty Chitty Bang Bang'.

Length of show: 2 hours 45 minutes
Age: All ages

DIRTY ROTTEN SCOUNDRELS

✉ Imperial Theater, 249 West 45th Street between Broadway and 8th Avenue

🕔 Tues 7pm, Wed–Sat 8pm; matinees Wed, Sat 2pm, Sun 3pm

Dirty Rotten Scoundrels reunites members of the creative team – composer/lyricist David Yazbek, director Jack O'Brien and choreographer Jerry Mitchell – who brought the comedy *The Full Monty* to Broadway a few seasons back with such stunning results. Throw in a company led by twice Tony winner John Lithgow and featuring favourites like Norbert Leo Butz, Sherie Rene Scott, Joanna Gleason and Gregory Jbara and you've got a Broadway hit.

Length of show: 2 hours 40 minutes
Age: All ages

Times Square

HAIRSPRAY

✉ Neil Simon Theater, 250 West 52nd Street between Broadway and 8th Avenue

⌂ www.hairsprayonbroadway.com

☉ Tues 7pm, Fr, Sat 8pm, Tues, Thurs 7pm, Sun 6.30pm; matinees Wed, Sat 2pm, Sun 1.30pm

A fabulous production based on John Waters's cult 1988 movie, it tells the story of how a bumbling Baltimore teenager is turned from social outcast to star when she gets the chance to dance on the popular Corny Collina Show (well, it is set in 1962!). But then her troubles really start. Hilarious – and the girls have hair that Marge Simpson would be proud of!

Length of show: 2 hours 40 minutes
Age: 12 and over

THE LION KING

✉ Minskoff Theater, 200 West 45th Street between Broadway and 8th Avenue

⌂ www.disneyonbroadway.com

☉ Tues–Sat 8pm, Sun 6.30pm; matinees Wed, Sat, Sun 2pm

With the original music from Elton John and Tim Rice (which won them Oscar and Grammy awards) combined with new music from Hans Zimmer and Lebo M, Disney tells the story of Simba, a lion cub who struggles to accept the responsibilities of adulthood and his destined role as king.

Awards: 6 Tony Awards 1998
Length of show: 2 hours 45 minutes
Age: From the very young to the very old

★ ★ ★ ★ BRIT TIP ★ ★ ★ ★
★ ★
★ Visit www.disneyonbroadway.com for ★
★ details of *Mary Poppins* and *Tarzan*, ★
★ both showing on Broadway. ★
★ ★
★ ★

LITTLE WOMEN

✉ Virginia Theater, 245 West 52nd Street at Broadway

☉ Tues 7pm, Wed–Sat 8pm, Sun 6.30pm; matinees Wed, Sat 2pm, Sun 1pm

The classic story set to music of the March sisters – Jo, Meg, Beth and Amy – coming of age in Civil War-torn New England. Rising star Sutton Foster, who won the 2002 Tony Award for Thoroughly Modern Millie, is taking on the role of talented tomboy Jo, who dreams of becoming a writer and discovers unexpected love.

Length of show: 2 hours 30 minutes
Age: From the very young to the very old

THE MAMBO KINGS

✉ Broadway Theater, 1681 Broadway at 53rd Street

☉ Tues 7pm, Wed–Sat 8pm, Sun 7 pm; matinees Wed, Sat 2pm, Sun 3pm

Brand new musical (opening 16 August) based on the Pulitzer Prize-winning novel, *The Mambo Kings Play Songs of Love*, and Oscar-nominated film of the same name, *The Mambo Kings* takes you from Havana to New York with two brothers, inspired by their Cuban past and bound together by their American dream. As they set out to conquer the glamorous nightclub world of 1950s Manhattan, every encounter is a reason to dance, and every step brings them closer to their destiny.

Age: 5 and over

MAMMA MIA!

✉ Cadillac Winter Garden Theater, 1634 Broadway at 50th Street

⌂ www.mamma-mia.com

☉ Wed–Sat 8pm, Sun 7 pm; matinees Wed, Sat , Sun 2pm

If you haven't had a chance to see this fabulously uplifting musical in London, then why not try it in New York? Set on a mythical Greek island, it tells the story of a single mum and her daughter on the eve of her daughter's wedding – and comes with 22 cracking ABBA songs.

Length of show: 2 hours 30 minutes
Age: 5 and over

MONTY PYTHON'S SPAMALOT

✉ Shubert Theater, 225 West 44th Street between Broadway and 8th Avenue

⌂ www.montypythonspamalot.com

☉ Tues 7pm, Wed–Sat 8pm, Sun 3pm.

Eric Idle, co-founder of Monty Python, is behind this musical adaptation of *Monty Python and the Holy Grail*.

Awards: Tony Award for Best Musical 2005
Age: 12 and over

THE PHANTOM OF THE OPERA

✉ Majestic Theater, 247 West 44th Street between Broadway and 8th Avenue

⌂ www.thephantomoftheopera.com

☉ Tues 7pm, Mon, Wed–Sat 8pm; matinees Wed, Sat 2pm

Set in 19th-century Paris, this is Andrew Lloyd Webber's famous musical of Gaston Leroux's novel. It tells the timeless story of a mysterious spectre who haunts the Paris opera house, spooking the owners and

falling in love with a beautiful singer.
Awards: 7 Tony Awards 1998
Length of show: 2 hours 30 minutes
Age: 5 and over, depending on whether
your child may be scared of the mask.

★ ★ ★ ★ **BRIT TIP** ★ ★ ★ ★
★ ★
★ For fantastic views of Times Square, ★
★ treat yourself to a drink at the ★
★ Broadway Lounge on the eighth ★
★ floor lobby level of the Marriott ★
★ Marquis Hotel at 1535 Broadway ★
★ (www.nymarriottmarquis.com). ★
★ ★

THE PRODUCERS
✉ St James Theater, 246 West 44th Street
between Broadway and 8th Avenue
🖰 www.producersonbroadway.com
🕐 Tues 7pm, Wed-Sat 8pm; matinees
Wed, Sat 2pm, Sun 3pm
Based on Mel Brooks's zany 1968 movie,
this tells the story of a down-on-his-luck
theatre producer who hatches a plot to
raise cash from a Broadway flop scam.
Awards: 11 Tony Awards 2001
Length of show: 2 hours 50 minutes
Age: 12 and over

RENT
✉ Nederlander Theater, 208 West 41st
Street between 7th and 8th Avenues
🖰 www.siteforrent.com
🕐 Mon-Sat (except Wed) 8pm, Sun 7pm;
matinees Sat, Sun 2pm
The Tony Award- and Pulitzer Prize-winning
musical is based on Puccini's opera La
Bohème, but is set in New York's East
Village. It tells the story of struggling young
artists who are living on the edge in the
search for glory.
Awards: 4 Tony Awards 1996
Length of show: 2 hours 45 minutes
Age: 16 and over due to adult themes

TOP JUST-OPENED BROADWAY MUSICALS

MARY POPPINS
✉ New Amsterdam Theater, 214 West
42nd Street
🖰 www.broadway.com
🕐 No schedule at time of going to press
Mary Poppins flew into Broadway in
October 2006 high on the success of being
a box office hit in the West End in London.
Based on the Oscar-winning 1964 Walt

Disney film, it's the perfect musical for
families.

RING OF FIRE: THE JOHNNY CASH MUSICAL EXPERIENCE
✉ Barrymore Theater, 243 West 47th
Street between Broadway and Eighth
Avenue
🖰 www.ringoffirethemusical.com
🕐 Tues 7pm, Wed-Sat 8pm; matinees
Wed, Sat 2pm, Sun 3pm
The songs of folk legend Johnny Cash can
be enjoyed in this musical extravaganza,
which has been a real success with critics
since it opened in spring 2006. You'll get to
hear 38 tunes of the Man in Black's classics,
including Ring of Fire and A Thing Called
Love.

TARZAN
✉ Richard Rodgers Theater, 226 West 46th
Street
🖰 www.broadwayworld.com
🕐 No schedule at time of going to press
Disney Theatrical Productions brings the
classic story of a boy raised by wild animals
to the Broadway stage. Based on the film of
the same name, expect great songs, high
jinks and lots of fun. Opened May 2006.

THE THREEPENNY OPERA
✉ Studio 54, 254 West 54th Street
🖰 www.broadwayworld.com
🕐 Tue, Thur, Fri 8pm; Wed, Sat 2pm, 8pm,
Sun 2pm
Serving up deliciously dark satire with
dashing thieves and lingering melodies.
Based on Elizabeth Hauptmann's German
translation of the 18th century Beggar's
Opera, this fabulous musical shows the
audience a glimpse of the seedy underworld
of Mack the Knife and his love affair with
Polly Peachum.

BROADWAY PLAYS

THE ODD COUPLE
✉ Brooks Atkinson Theater, 256 West 47th
Street between 8th Avenue and
Broadway
🕐 Tues-Sat 8pm; matinees Wed, Sat 2pm,
Sun 3pm.
Starring Matthew Broderick (Sarah Jessica
Parker's hubby) and Nathan Lane playing a
pair of mismatched room mates. Debuted
on Broadway in 1965, re-opened 4 October
2005.
Length of show: 2 hours 10 minutes
Age: Adults

OFF BROADWAY

BLUE MAN GROUP: TUBES
✉ Astor Place Theater, 434 Lafayette
Street at Astor Place
🖰 www.blueman.com
🕐 Mon–Thurs, Sun 8pm, Fri, Sat 7pm,
10pm; matinees Sat 4pm, Sun 2pm,
5pm

One of the most successful Off Broadway
shows. Take a trio of post-modern clowns,
cover them in blue rubber and allow them
to be outrageous with sound and art and
you have this wonderful avant-garde
extravaganza that is both hilarious and
challenging to watch.
Length of show: 2 hours
Age: 15 and over

I LOVE YOU, YOU'RE PERFECT, NOW CHANGE
✉ Westside Theater Upstairs, 407 West
43rd Street between 8th and 9th
Avenues
🖰 www.loveperfectchange.com
🕐 Mon, Tues, Sun 7pm, Fri, Sat 8pm;
matinees Wed 2.30pm, Sat 4pm, Sun
3pm

For a thoroughly modern take on the whole
notion of dating and romance, you can't go

Broadway

Times Square TKTS stand

wrong with this comedy. It's a kind of
Seinfeld set to music.
Length of show: 2 hours
Age: Adult

JEWTOPIA
✉ Westside Theater, 407 West 43rd Street
between 8th and 9th Avenues
🖰 www.jewtopiaplay.com
🕐 Tues–Sat 8pm; matinees Wed, Sat 2pm,
Sun 3pm

The story of two 30-year-old single men,
Chris O'Connell and Adam Lipschitz. Chris, a
gentile, wants to marry a nice Jewish girl so
he'll never have to make another decision.
After forming a secret pact, Adam promises
to help Chris shed his gentile-ness and bring
him undercover into the Jewish world.
Length of show: 2 hours
Age: 11 and over

The Lion King, Times Square

STOMP
✉ Orpheum Theater, 126 2nd Avenue between 2nd and 1st Avenues
🖱 www.stomponline.com
🕐 Tues–Fri 8pm, Sat 7pm, 10.30pm, Sun 7pm; matinees Wed 2pm, Sun 3pm

A very unusual show now in its 12th year. Dancers make their own music by using everyday objects such as dustbin lids, brooms and sticks. The rhythmic beats are infectious and the performers' stamina amazing.

Length of show: 1 hour 45 minutes
Age: All ages (although tots may not like the noise)

LIVE MUSIC

THE TOP FIVE CLASSIC VENUES

APOLLO THEATER
Harlem
✉ 253 West 125th Street between Adam Clayton Powell Jnr and Frederick Douglas Boulevards
🖱 212-531 5300 info; 212-531 5301 events hotline
🖱 www.apollotheater.com
🚗 Subway A, B, C, D, 2, 3 to 125th Street

This venue started life as a burlesque house for whites only when Harlem was actually a white neighbourhood, but it very quickly changed and became a theatre for blacks with live entertainment. The Amateur Night has been a launching pad for Stevie Wonder and James Brown. When Ella Fitzgerald came here she planned to dance, but at the last moment she decided to sing and, as the saying goes, a star was born. Wednesday's Amateur Night is still going strong and is shown on NBC at 1am on Saturday night/ Sunday morning.

CARNEGIE HALL
Midtown West
✉ 154 West 57th Street at 7th Avenue
🖱 212-247 7800
🖱 www.carnegiehall.org
🚗 Subway B, D, E, N, R, Q, W to 57th Street

Built in the Beaux Arts style under the patronage of Andrew Carnegie, this is perhaps one of the most famous classical concert venues in New York and a real landmark. Check the listings sections of newspapers or *Time Out* for details of visiting artists or take a guided tour Monday to Friday at 11.30am, 2pm and 3pm.

Carnegie Hall

★★★★ **BRIT TIP** ★★★★
★ ★
★ ★
★ Pace yourself during the day so ★
★ you've enough juice left to enjoy ★
★ one of the many theatre productions ★
★ in the evening. ★
★★★★★★★★★★★★★★★★★★★★★★★★★

LINCOLN CENTER
Upper West Side
✉ 65th Street at Columbus Avenue
☎ 212-875 5400
⌖ www.lincolncenter.org
🚗 Subway 1, 9 to 66th Street/Lincoln Center

The major venue for classical music in New York, the Lincoln Center, a collection of buildings that includes the home of the Metropolitan Opera, was built on slums that were featured in the film *West Side Story*. The Alice Tully Hall (tel 212-875 5050) houses the Chamber Music Society of Lincoln Center; the Avery Fisher Hall (tel 212-875 5030) is home to the New York Philharmonic; the Metropolitan Opera House (tel 212-362 6000); the New York State Theater (tel 212-870 5570) is the base of New York City Opera; and the Walter Reade Theater (tel 212-875 5600) is home to the Film Society of Lincoln Center. Jazz at Lincoln Center is at the AOL Time Warner Center (page 193).

You can take a behind-the-scenes tour of the Lincoln Center, which is really the only way to see beyond the ornate lobbies of the buildings, unless you're paying big bucks for a performance. The tours are fabulous and give a really good insight into the workings of the various venues. Options include a 1-hour Lincoln Center tour, Tours with a Bite – at Café Vienna, the Piano Forte tour which takes you to Klavierhouse, a piano restoration museum, and Starry Nights, the full treatment including a performance and, if in a group, meeting the artists. The tours are very popular so it's best to book in advance on 212-875 5350.

★★★★ **BRIT TIP** ★★★★
★ ★
★ Standing room tickets to the Met go ★
★ on sale on the day of the ★
★ performance for $20. ★
★★★★★★★★★★★★★★★★★★★★★★★★★

In addition to the tours, you can enjoy the Lincoln Center environment with a series of jazz and folk bands that entertain the crowds for free during the summer. The Autumn Crafts Fair is held in the first week of September.

MADISON SQUARE GARDEN
34th Street
✉ 4 Pennsylvania Plaza at 33rd Street and 7th Avenue
☎ 212-465 MSG1 info
⌖ www.thegarden.com
🚗 Subway A, C, E, 1, 2, 3, 9, B, D, F, N, Q, R, V, W to 34th Street/Penn Street Station

New York's biggest and most famous rock venue, which doubles up as a sports stadium. Also the Theater at Madison Square Garden, which is underneath, plays host to big-name stars who want to share some intimacy with their audience.

RADIO CITY MUSIC HALL
Midtown
✉ 1260 6th Avenue at 50th Street
☎ 212-247 4777
⌖ www.radiocity.com
Ô Subway B, D, F, V to 47th–50th Street/Rockefeller Centre

Recently renovated, this home to the Rockettes in its Art Deco splendour also plays host to some big-name stars.

★★★★ **BRIT TIP** ★★★★
★ ★
★ For the lowdown on what's ★
★ happening on the jazz scene in New ★
★ York, from shopping to tours to ★
★ clubs, click on to ★
★ www.bigapplejazz.com. ★
★★★★★★★★★★★★★★★★★★★★★★★★★

GIGS

KNITTING FACTORY
TriBeCa
✉ 74 Leonard Street between Broadway and Church Street
☎ 212-219 3132
⌖ www.knittingfactory.com
🚗 Subway 2, 3, 9 to Franklin Street

A funky performance venue run by The Knitting Factory Record Label that's well known for avant-garde live bands spanning all types of music, from heavy rock to a choir. There are three spaces, Main Space,

ALL THAT JAZZ

A visit to New York City wouldn't be complete without an evening at one of the various jazz venues, but it can get very expensive, so it's good to know your way around. At all the main venues it'll cost you around $25 to hear one set which lasts only 1–1½ hours. It's worth it if you're happy with the music, but the idea of having to move on after only one set is a bit strange to us Brits, so be warned!

The most important new venue is **Jazz at Lincoln Center**'s recent $128-million home at the AOL Time Warner Centre at Columbus Circle, with three performance spaces – two large and one intimate. Visit www.jalc.org to find out about events or call the JazzTix hotline, 212-258 9800.

THE MAIN CLUBS

One of the best jazz clubs is the **Iridium** (1650 Broadway at 51st Street, tel 212-582 2121, www.iridiumjazzclub.com). It's not too touristy, is smaller than many clubs and has a nice intimate feel. Try it for Sunday brunch! The entrance fee varies but there's a $10 minimum. **The Village Vanguard** (178 7th Avenue South at Perry Street, tel 212-255 4037, www.villagevanguard.com), probably the most famous club of all, always hosts great talent and sets last the full 1½ hours. Another famous Greenwich Village venue is the **Blue Note** (131 West 3rd Street between MacDougal and 6th Avenue, tel 212-475 8592, www.bluenote.net), but this is more touristy, very expensive and has a Las Vegas-style interior. **Swing 46 Jazz and Supper Club** (349 West 46th Street between 8th and 9th Avenues, tel 212-262 9554, www.swing46.com) offers big bands and small combos to suit hip downtown loungers and traditional uptown swingers – it's rapidly becoming an institution.

Other good venues include **Birdland** (315 West 44th Street between 8th and 9th Avenues, tel 212-581 3080, www.birdlandjazz.com) in Midtown West; the **Jazz Standard** (116 East 27th Street between Park and Lexington Avenues, tel 212-576 2232, www.jazzstandard.com) near Madison Square; **Sweet Rhythm** (88 7th Avenue South between Bleecker and Grove Streets, tel 212-255-3626, www.sweetrhythmny.com) in the Village; **Bubble Lounge** (228 West Broadway at White Street, tel 212-431 3433, www.bubblelounge.com) in TriBeCa, which has live music every Monday and Tuesday; closed Sunday. **55 Bar** (55 Christopher Street, tel 212-929 9883, www.55bar.com) has been a West Village institution since 1919 and has shows all week from 6/7pm and late shows 9.30/10pm; open until 4am. **Smoke** (2751 Broadway, tel 212-864 6662, www.smokejazz.com) is an intimate club with low-hanging chandeliers, red velvet curtains and seating for 70. Open until 4am. Finally, book early for Monday nights at Hotel Carlyle (page 203) where Woody Allen and friends play a set.

CHEAP AND CHEERFUL

One of the best off-the-beaten-track jazz venues is in the heart of Greenwich Village at the **Cornelia Street Café** (29 Cornelia Street, tel 212-989 9319, http://corneliastreetcafe. com), a haunt of the locals. Prix-fixe dinner is $21 and is served from 5.30pm. The jazz starts at 8.30pm and costs from $6 to $15, with many evenings $10 and a drink thrown in. They don't have big names, but they do have a lot of New York talent. **Zinc Bar** (90 West Houston Street between Thompson Street and LaGuardia Place, tel 212-477 8337, www.zincbar.com) is one of the most intimate places in town to enjoy live jazz, open until 4am weekends and it's only $5 to get in.

The cheapest jazz clubs tend to be in Harlem, Queens and Brooklyn, but because they can't afford to advertise you really don't hear about them. Furthermore, most don't even have names on the door. Good places to look for venues are the *New York Times* weekend edition and the *Village Voice*. The latter is a lot better and it's free, visit www.villagevoice.com.

lap Bar and Old Office, the last of which is the most intimate and where there are sometimes poetry readings and film screenings as well as music. Check out the website to see who'll be playing when you're in town. Open until 4am.

TONIC
Lower East Side
✉ 107 Norfolk Street between Rivington and Delancey Streets
☎ 212-358 7501
🖰 www.tonic107.com
🚇 Subway F to Delancey Street
A very wide range of live bands performs every night from 7.30pm keeping indie kids through to electronica fans and jazz funk afficianados content. Downstairs, DJs work their magic at Subtonic.

COMEDY CLUBS

FLATIRON DISTRICT
Gotham Comedy Club: 34 West 22nd Street between 5th and 6th Avenues. Tel 212-367 9000, www.gothamcomedy club.com.
This club opened in 1996 and was an instant success. It's elegant and sophisticated with a solid oak bar and a chandelier. The line-ups are equally dazzling, from surprise guests to comedians who have appeared on *Saturday Night Live* and *The Tonight Show*.

MIDTOWN
Caroline's Comedy Club: 1626 Broadway between 49th and 50th Streets. Tel 212-757 4100, www.carolines.com.
It opened in 1981 as a small club in Chelsea but proved such a hit it moved uptown, where it offers live comedy every night of the year, including big names such as Jerry Seinfeld and Rosie O'Donnell.

Caroline's Comedy Club

The Knitting Factory

WEST VILLAGE
The Comedy Cellar: 117 MacDougal Street between West 3rd Street and Minetta Lane. Tel 212-254 3480, www.comedycellar.com. This club has been a starting ground for many famous faces for more than 20 years. It's basic, with brick walls and cramped seating, and in a basement so it's not a glam night out in New York, but it will certainly be a funny one. The cover charge is $10 Sunday to Thursday and $15 Friday and Saturday.

★★★★ BRIT TIP ★★★★
★   ★
★   Phone 212-777-FILM or visit   ★
★ www.moviefone.com for accurate ★
★ movie show times and, to make sure ★
★   you don't miss out, buy tickets in   ★
★   advance.   ★
★   ★
★★★★★★★★★★★★★★★★★★★★★★★★★

BARS & LOUNGES

Here's a selection of bars to drop into while you are out and about in the city, including some of the hotel bars that stand out from the crowd and lounges that stay open into the early hours. Lounges are very much an integral part of the New York nightlife scene. Placed somewhere between a plush bar and a club, they're somewhere for you to stay late, listen to DJs and sip cocktails, but most don't have dance floors.

CHELSEA
Kanvas: 219 9th Avenue between 23rd and 24th Streets. Tel 212-727 2616, www.kanvasnyc.com.
The latest favourite Chelsea hang-out is owned by two firefighters, who have furnished a couple of giant loft rooms with comfy banquettes, subtle lighting and a chilled line in music. There's also gallery space on both floors so you can snap up some art while you're sipping your sour apple Martini, the bar's speciality.

CINEMAS

Catch some great blockbuster movies! For complete listings of movies and cinemas near your hotel, check *Time Out* or the free *Village Voice* and *New York Press*.

AMC Empire 25: 234 West 42nd Street between 7th and 8th Avenues, tel 212-398 3939, www.amctheatres.com. This has 25 screens on five levels and has devoted seven screens on the top floor, known as the Top of the Empire, to repertory classics and independent films. You can catch a pre-show snack – pizza to ribs – in the 42nd Street Food Court.

Film Forum: 209 Houston Street between 6th and 7th Avenues, tel 212-727 8110, www.filmforum.com. A three-theatre venue showing independent and vintage films. There are seasons, such as a run of films dedicated to Audrey Hepburn, and talks given by directors plus film merchandise on sale.

Loews 42nd Street E Walk: 243 West 42nd Street between 7th and 8th Avenues, tel 212-840 7761, www.amctheatres.com. The recent Loews E Walk, with 13 screens and all-stadium seating, is billed as a modern-day movie palace. A one-storey high, hand-painted mural honours the local landmarks of Broadway and Times Square.

The Angelika Film Center: 18 West Houston Street, tel 212-995 2000, www.angelikafilmcenter.com. A good selection of the latest art films is shown here, as well as at the Lincoln Plaza Cinemas, 1886 Broadway at 62nd Street, tel 212-757 2280, http://lincolnplaza.moviefone.com. The Angelika has a café and the Lincoln Plaza Cinemas sell sandwiches and pastries.

EAST VILLAGE

Angel's Share: 8 Stuyvesant Street between East 9th and East 10th Streets. Tel 212-777 5415.
Dedicated to the art of mixology, this little gem of a bar will rustle up any cocktail you desire. Part of its charm is the fact that it's so hard to find, you'll feel as if you've stumbled across a city secret. Take the stairs to the second floor and veer left past the restaurant to the door at the rear. Inside you'll find a dark, intimate bar where classy city dwellers take their first dates.

Beauty Bar: 231 East 14th Street between 2nd and 3rd Avenues. Tel 212-539 1389, www.beautybar.com.
Deb Parker's theme bar is equipped with 1960s-style hairdryers and chairs, real manicurists, great drinks and a heavy dose of the hip and beautiful.

Buddha Lounge: 29 East 3rd Street between 2nd Avenue and Bowery. Tel 212-505 7344.
A new laid-back, non-showy bar with exposed brick walls that is popular mid-week and at weekends.

CBGC: 315 Bowery between 1st and 2nd Streets. Tel 212-982 4052, www.cbgc.com. Subway 6, F to Bleecker Street.
Legendary underground club that's been the toast of the hip New York rock scene for more than 27 years. The likes of Guns 'n

Roses and The Ramones have graced the stage and you're sure to catch an exciting new band if you drop by.

KGB: 85 East 4th Street between 2nd and 3rd Avenues. Tel 212-505 3360, www.kgbbar.com.
Decorated with deep-red walls, portraits of Lenin and Brezhnev, propaganda posters and an oak bar from when it was a front for the Communist party. The crowd is a mix of actors, writers and drunks who love the private-parlour feel. Up-and-coming writers and successful authors often do free readings, so call to see who's on.

Korova Milk Bar: 200 Avenue A between 12th and 13th Streets. Tel 212-254 8838, www.korovamilkbar.com.
Wacky retro-futuristic style that pays homage to Stanley Kubrick's *A Clockwork Orange*. It attracts a sci-fi crowd who love its surreal quality and the ice-cream drinks.

Iridium jazz club

TOP FIVE BARS FOR ALFRESCO DRINKING

Brooklyn
Gowanus Yacht Club: 323 Smith Street, tel 718-246 1321. You'll feel you've really got off the tourist trail at this small outside bar close to the lovely Carroll Gardens. It attracts a chilled crowd of locals who sip beer and wine beneath the fairylight-bedecked trees before and after sunset. Bar food is also available.

Chelsea
Glass: 287 10th Avenue, tel 212-904 1580. 'Cool' is usually the reaction staff get when people see the bamboo-filled patio in this very, very hip bar for the first time. It's a place to see and be seen in, so if you don't mind rubber necking alongside models and aspiring actors, you'll fit right in.

Lower East Side
Barramundi: 147 Ludlow Street, tel 212-529 6900. A gorgeous walled garden covered with twinkling fairylights is très romantic or cool depending on whether you're with a partner or friends. Attracts a mixed crowd of internationals.

Upper East Side
Rooftop at the Met: 1000 5th Avenue at 82nd Street, tel 212-535 7710. The terrace (open in the summer) at the Metropolitan Museum of Art offers stunning views of the city, particularly at sunset. It's also known as a great singles pick-up joint.

West Village
B-Bar & Grill: 40 East 4th Street, tel 212-475 2220, www.bbarandgrill.com. The large outside patio here, with bar, chic furniture and trees, is a magnet for fashionable West and East Villagers.

Sutra: 16 1st Avenue at East 1st Street. Tel 212-677 9477.
Red velvet and lots and lots of candles create an intimate atmosphere in this sumptuous new lounge bar.

GARMENT DISTRICT

Stitch: 247 West 37th Street between 7th and 8th Avenues. Tel 212-852 4826, www.stitchnyc.com.
A good name for a new bar in the heart of the clothing district. Cocktails, such as the Stiletto, are just as well named.

GREENWICH VILLAGE

Cafe Wha?: 115 MacDougal Street between West 3rd and Bleecker Streets. Tel 212-254 3706, www.cafewha.com.
Village hangout since the beginning of time. There is something fun and exciting on every night of the week here, including live Brazilian dance parties on Mondays, funk on Tuesdays and comedy nights on Saturdays. Best of all, the bill for drinks and snacks won't inhale the entire contents of your wallet. Get there before 10pm if you want to get a table.

Madame X: 94 West Houston Street between Thompson Street and La Guardia Place. Tel 212-539 0808, www.madamexnyc.com.

There's a real London Soho den-of-iniquity feel to this joint, bathed as it is in red and lit by the glow of lanterns. Known for serving pretty potent cocktails and rare imported beers. In summer, head for the black door at the rear and you'll find the new outdoor alcove, where red lights above the benches bring the boudoir theme outside. Best of all, you'll probably be able to find a free corner.

LOWER EAST SIDE

Boss Tweed's: 115 Essex Street between Rivington and Delancey Streets. Tel 212-475 9997, www.bosstweeds.com.
Previously on the site of Smithfields bar, this is the closest you'll get to a local in Manhattan. The glass-bricked bar offers everything from pints of Guinness to vodka shots, each served up with a great story by bartender and co-owner Stuart Delves. Very entertaining.

Dark Room: 165 Ludlow Street between Stanton and Houston Streets. Tel 212-353 0536.
A new bar that draws a rock-loving clientele. It occupies a bunker-like basement, with low ceilings and dim lighting, and a horsehoe-shaped bar serves a great selection of beers to a decidedly unposey crowd.

SHOWS, BARS AND CLUBS 197

TOP FIVE BARS TO ENJOY A CIGARETTE IN

We're not encouraging you to smoke, but the reality is there are lots of Brits who like to indulge and are pretty shocked when they arrive in New York only to discover they can't light up anywhere. Just to keep all readers happy, we've tracked down five places where you won't be chucked out for smoking.
Circa Tabac: 32 Watts Street at Thompson Street
Hudson Bar & Books: 626 Hudson Street between Horatio and Jane Streets
Karma: 51 First Avenue between 3rd and 4th Streets
Lexington Bar & Books: 1020 Lexington Avenue between 72nd and 73rd Streets
Shebeen: 202 Mott Street between Princes and Spring Street

Good World: 3 Orchard Street between Canal and Hester Streets. Tel 212-925 9975.
A mellow bar with a semi-regular DJ and an attractive young crowd. Stars that have been spotted here include Keanu Reeves, Djork, Courtney Love and Matt Dillon. Best time to go is Sunday to Thursday and order the Scandinavian-style Good World, an elderberry-infused caipirinha.

Inoteca: 98 Rivington Street at Ludlow Street. Tel 212 614-0473.
The staff at this wine bar are ingratiating and knowledgeable. The crowd is a mixture of neighbourhood denizens and drop-ins from uptown, creating a good atmosphere.

Kush: 191 Chrystie Street between Rivington and Stanton Streets. Tel 212-677 7328, www.kushlounge.com.
Get a taste of paradise by sipping a few cocktails and nibbling on tasty bar snacks like mixed olives and salted almonds in this Moroccan oasis. The decor is fab, with wonderful tiling and whitewashed walls lit by candles.

Lansky Lounge: 104 Norfolk Street between Delancey and Rivington Streets. Tel 212-677 9489.
Once the former boardroom of infamous 1920s' gangster Meyer Lansky, the Jewish genius who masterminded many of Bugsy Siegal's and Lucky Luciano's biggest moves, the Lansky Lounge has a real speakeasy vibe. Swing, Latin and lounge music nights draw good crowds, and don't forget to sample the superb flavoured martinis – the Diplomat is a favourite. The prices can be a bit steep, though, and in observance of the Jewish Sabbath it is closed on Friday.

Orchard Bar: 200 Orchard Street between Houston and Stanton Streets. Tel 212-673 5350.
One of the best lounges on the Lower East Side, the decor at the Orchard Bar is very different (think rocks for seats and bamboo shoots hanging from the walls). Cutting-edge DJs, cheapish drinks and a trendy crowd of artists and musicians mean it gets packed at the weekends so, if you want to try it out, you'll need to plan ahead.

BRIT TIP

Many of the hip bars get packed out on Friday and Saturday nights with the people who live outside Manhattan. If you want to experience the scene without tourists, choose another night.

MEATPACKING DISTRICT
APT: 419 West 13th Street at 10th Avenue. Tel 212-414 4245, www.aptwebsite.com.
A real hit with trendy New Yorkers since the day it opened, this intimate bar/club makes you feel you are somewhere extra special. The dark, candlelit first floor is furnished like an apartment, complete with bed, dining table and chairs and sofas, offering comfortable lounging. Charming staff serve up tasty cocktails, such as Moscow Mules and Appletinis, for around $10. The wood-walled room downstairs has a more modern vibe, and punters propping up the long bar

BRIT TIP

If you're a smoker who enjoys a cigarette with a drink, you'll rejoice at the new Aer Lounge (409 West 13th Street near 9th Avenue, tel 646-989 0100, www.aerlounge.com) in the Meatpacking District. It has opened the first smoking section – a heated veranda glassed off from the main bar – since the smoking in public places ban began in 2001.

SHOWS, BARS AND CLUBS

TOP FIVE BARS TO SPOT STARS

Alphabet City–East Village
2A: 25 Avenue A. Tel 212-505 2466. A real musos hangout. Band of the moment The Strokes is just one of the combos that you may find enjoying the New Wave and punk 1970s' music in this supercool bar and lounge.

Meatpacking District
Lotus: 409 West 14th Street between 9th and 10th Avenues. Tel 212-243 4420. Three storeys devoted to nightlife, including a bar, restaurant and club. Jennifer Lopez, Bruce Willis and Britney Spears have been seen here, but the celeb scene has hardly cooled off since it opened in 2000. Avoid the weekend crush by going midweek. Try their Tartini – a Cosmo with Chambord.

Midtown East
Wet Bar at W New York, The Court Hotel: 130 East 39th Street between 5th and Madison Avenues. Tel 212-592 8844, www.starwoodhotels.com. George Clooney, Whoopi Goldberg and D'Angelo Marc Anthony have all been spotted in this sleek and uncluttered setting, which plays host to professionals and hotel guests. Try their apple martini.

NoHo
Joe's Pub: 425 Lafayette Street between 4th Street and Astor Place. Tel 212-539 8770, www.web.joespub.com/web_joes. This newish cabaret continues to be a real hot spot. An extension of the Public Theater, Joe's brings you live music, spoken-word performances and a crowd jam-packed with trendy types. Stars spotted here include Ethan Hawke, Minnie Driver, Janeane Garofalo and Camryn Manheim. The drink to order is the Lady Macbeth – 115ml (4 fl oz) of champagne and 115ml (4 fl oz) of ruby port. Strong stuff!

Upper East Side
Mark's Bar at the Mark Hotel: 25 East 77th Street at Madison Avenue. Tel 212-744 4300, www.themarkhotel.com. This bar has been described as a cosy tearoom that feels like a luxury train carriage. It never gets too noisy and patrons, who perch on forest-green sofas and floral slipper chairs, are treated like guests in an elegant private home. Julia Roberts and Kate Moss have both been spotted here in the past. The bar attracts a youngish fashion set, but the crowd can be diverse, depending on the evening.

often end up strutting their stuff to the DJ's hip tunes. Book in advance for the weekend.

Earth NYC: 116A 10th Avenue at 17th Street. Tel 212-337 0016, www.earth-nyc.com.
Two floors covered in plush red sofas and a wall lined with hundreds of candles makes for a romantic, laid-back setting in this Karma Sutra-inspired new lounge. The Indian tapas are delicious.

Mark's Restaurant

Hogs & Heifers: 859 Washington Street at West 13th Street. Tel 212-929 0655, www.hogsandheifers.com.
The hogs are the motorcyclists and the heifers are the dames, who are known for hanging their bras on the ceiling. There's no longer bar dancing here, so there'll be no repeats of Drew Barrymore's performance.

MIDTOWN

Campbell Apartment Bar: Gallery Level, Grand Central Station. Tel 212-953 0409.
This apartment used to be the office/salon of the 1920s' tycoon John W Campbell. The beamed ceiling, huge leaded-glass window and the massive stone fireplace make a unique, almost castle-like space. But the dark wood, couches and club armchairs create an intimate place for a drink.

Russian Vodka Room: 265 West 52nd Street between Broadway and 8th Avenue. Tel 212-307 5835, www.russianvodkaroom.com.
A brilliant vodka bar that doesn't require

5th Avenue

you to take out a second mortgage. There are cheap smoked fish platters, delicious cocktails and marvellous vodka infusions. It tends to attract the publishing crowd.

SOHO AND TRIBECA

Botanica: 47 East Houston Street between Mott and Mulberry Streets. Tel 212-343 7251.
Serving drinks at decent prices in très chic SoHo, this dark and rather grungy basement bar is a watering hole for artists and locals.

Brandy Library: 25 North Moore Street at Varwick Street. Tel 212-226 5545, www.brandylibrary.com.
As its name suggests, this new bar is dedicated to the finest brandys, plus there are more than 100 cocktails on the menu. Waitresses climb ladders to pick out your chosen tipple from the brandy-lined shelves. A lovely place to end a sophisticated evening as it stays open until 4am.

Café Noir: 32 Grand Street at Thompson Street. Tel 212-431 7910.
Moroccan comfort food meets Spanish tapas in this little urban oasis. Think tagines, stews and pitchers of sangria. There's also an extensive wine list and the occasional live jazz session.

Dekk: 134 Reade Street between Hudson and Greenwich Streets. Tel 212-941 9401, www.thedekk.com.
A new TriBeCa haunt, which has modelled itself on a traditional Parisian wine bar. It also has a cool screening room that shows old movies.

Merc Bar: 151 Mercer Street between Prince and Houston Streets. Tel 212-966 2727, www.mercbar.com.
A long-time fixture on the SoHo scene, this cool bar draws an attractive crowd to its luxuriously deep sofas. It's at its best in summer when worn leather chairs get an airing on the sidewalk – a great place to sit

and people-watch. Be warned: the drinks are pricey at $10-plus.

Velvet Restaurant and Lounge: 223 Mulberry Street between Prince and Spring Streets. Tel 212-965 0439, www.velvetnyc.com.
A truly discreet lounge bar that takes darkness to new depths. The giant sofas and adjoining parlour where you can play games of chess and backgammon add to the chilling-out factor.

UPPER WEST SIDE

Kama: 380 Columbus Avenue at 78th Street. Tel 212-724 2363.
An exotic place for a romantic evening. This new lounge has sari drapes, beds and private tents and a rose-petal wading pool to get you in the mood for love; if the furnishings don't the orgy cocktails may.

WEST VILLAGE

Chumley's: 86 Bedford Street between Grove and Barrow Streets. Tel 212-675 4449.
A former literary speakeasy, it's still a great place to drink and have a spot of shepherd's pie while you look over the book jackets that line the wall. Yes, they were all donated by the authors who used to frequent the establishment such as Jack Kerouac and F Scott Fitzgerald. You'll find their signatures imprinted on some of the older tables. There's even a roaring fire giving a cosy atmosphere in winter.

BROOKLYN

Bar Below: 209 Smith Street at Baltic Street. Tel 718-694 2277.
A funky basement bar that stays open until 4am where you'll find hip-hop kids at the extremely long bar. Head to the back for chilled-out sounds from the DJ. Chocolate lovers should definitely try the delicious Snickers martini.

Fiftyseven Fiftyseven

HOTEL BARS

Hotel bars have always been a popular place to meet for New Yorkers. From sinking into leather sofas in legendary hangouts, propping up the bars in some of Midtown's trendy hotels where the fashionable crowds gather, they make an ideal place to start, or end, a big night out.

BATTERY PARK

Rise at the Ritz-Carlton Hotel: 2 West Street between Battery Place and West End. Tel 212-344 0800, www.ritzcarlton.com. Subway 1, 9 to Rector Street; 4, 5 to Bowling Green.

A big hit with both visitors and the Wall Street crowd is this 14th floor bar. They go for the comfy, plush chairs with fabulous views of the harbour, Statue of Liberty and amazing sunsets. The bar specialises in a series of colourful martinis served in gorgeous corkscrew-stemmed glassware and 710ml (25 fl oz) margaritas, sangrias and mojitos, which are a perfect size for sharing. If you fancy a nibble, then either go for the dim sum or signature 'tiers' – platters of food for up to four people. They include the Pacific Union with sesame chicken, cured salmon and seared beef with dipping sauces. You can sit inside or outside and, best of all, the service is excellent.

★★★★ **BRIT TIP** ★★★★
★ ★
★ If you can, visit Plunge (see box on ★
★ page 201) on a Monday night when ★
★ it's much quieter so you're ★
★ guaranteed a space and you'll be ★
★ able to hear what the person next ★
★ to you is saying. ★
★★★★★★★★★★★★★★★★★★★★★★★★★

GREENWICH VILLAGE

North Square at the Washington Square Hotel: 103 Waverly Place at MacDougal Street. Tel 212-254 1200, www.wshotel.com. Subway A, B, C, D, E, F, V to West 4th Street/Washington Square.

The small, cosy basement space's classic bar and luxurious leather chairs are a reminder of another era, while beautifully stencilled windows offer a glimpse of the current street scene. It attracts a large European crowd, who find it the perfect spot to pore over a map and a martini, but locals – as well as the occasional celeb – can also be found enjoying the laid-back atmosphere.

MIDTOWN

Cellar Bar at the Bryant Park Hotel: 40 West 40th Street between 5th and 6th Avenues. Tel 212-869 0100, www.bryantparkhotel.com. Subway B, D, F, V, 7 to 42nd Street/Bryant Park.

A must-do for any fashionista, because this new boutique hotel on the block has been adopted by the fashion pack. Expect to see models, designers and magazine editors propping up the bar, but don't even think about dropping in during fashion week- you won't be able to move for the wafer-thin clientele.

Fiftyseven Fiftyseven at the Four Seasons Hotel: 57 East 57th Street between 5th and Park Avenues. Tel 212-758 5700, www.fourseasons.com/newyork. Subway N, R, Q, W to 5th Avenue.

The Four Seasons is dynamic in early evening when celebs rub shoulders with power-broking businessmen and hip hotel guests, while a pianist provides the background music. Be sure to sample some of the 15 types of martini on offer.

Sky Bar at La Quinta Manhattan: 17 West 32nd Street between Broadway and 5th Avenue. Tel 212-736 1600, www.applecorehotels.com. Subway N, R, W to 28th Street.

A cross between a backyard deck and a funky beach bar, this partially enclosed rooftop watering hole is packed year-round with international visitors who appreciate the casual atmosphere and towering views of the Empire State Building.

MIDTOWN EAST

Gilt at the New York Palace Hotel: 455 Madison Avenue between 50th and 51st Streets. Tel 212-888 7000, www.newyorkpalace.com. Subway E, V to 5th Avenue; 6 to 51st Street.

Located inside the Madison Avenue courtyard gates of the Palace Hotel's historic Villard Mansion, this new restaurant and bar has been pulling in the city's most glamorous movers and shakers since it opened. You'll be wowed by the gilded walls, cathedral ceilings, funky lighting and amazing food whipped up by super chef Paul Liebrandt (that's if you can get a table).

Oasis at W New York: 541 Lexington Avenue at 49th Street. Tel 212-755 1200, www.starwoodhotels.com. Subway 6 to 51st Street.

TOP FIVE HIPPEST HOTEL BARS

Chelsea
Cabana at the Maritime Hotel: 88 9th Avenue between 16th and 17th Streets. Tel 212-242 4300, www.themaritimehotel.com. Subway A, C, E to 14th Street.
So hot it's practically on fire, this plant-filled rooftop retreat is the perfect place to sip a martini in winter as it has patio heaters. Sean Penn and Paris Hilton are recent celeb visitors.

Plunge at Hotel Gansevoort: 18 9th Avenue at 13th Street. Tel 877-426 7386/212-206 6700, www.hotelgansevoort.com. Subway A, C, E to 14th Street.
Take the lift to the penthouse on the 15th floor and you'll arrive at one of NYC's most happening bars of the moment. On a dry day it's open-air: if it's rainy or cold there's a glass cover, so you still get the views. The only downside of Plunge is that, despite its name, you're not allowed in the rooftop swimming pool unless you're a guest and it's absolutely packed for most of the week.

Midtown
Morgans Bar at the Morgans Hotel: 237 Madison Avenue between 37th and 38th Streets. Tel 212-726 7755, www.morganshotel.com. Subway 4, 5, 6, 7 to 42nd Street/Grand Central.
Heaving with an attitude-heavy Upper East crowd, it's a sleeker, more sophisticated version of the bar that opened in London's St Martin's Lane Hotel and should be at the top of your must-go-there list. If you like your drinks deliciously expensive and served in punchbowl-size glasses, you'll love it.

SoHo
The Grand Bar and Salon at the SoHo Grand Hotel: 310 West Broadway between Grand and Canal Streets. Tel 212-965 3000, www.sohogrand.com. Subway A, C, E to Canal Street.
A chic gathering place that has attracted the rich and famous such as Matt Damon and Venus Williams since its opening in the mid-90s. It was at the forefront of the lounge-as-living-room trend and is filled with a mix of comfy, retro chic furnishings that serve as great perches for drinking and watching the multi-lingual crowd – mostly dressed in classic New York black. Sit back, nibble on the snacks and feel the energetic we're-at-the-centre-of-the-universe buzz.

Thom's Bar at the 60 Thompson Hotel: 60 Thompson Street between Broome and Spring Streets. Tel 212-219 2000, www.60thompson.com. Subway 6, C, E to Spring Street.
A sophisticated decor of dark wood, soft violet seats, brown leather club chairs and white Venetian plaster walls make for pleasant surroundings. The entertainment is provided by the chic crowd who know that this boutique hotel is the only place to be seen in midweek. Drinks are surprisingly cheap, like flavoured vodka for $7.50.

An oasis of tranquillity, the bar heats up when the fashion, art and music crowd descends for cocktails before dinner at the hotel's Heartbeat restaurant. The ambience is Californian and casual with clever touches that include a waterfall and backgammon tables disguised as tree stumps. Also at the hotel is the Whiskey Blue, overseen by Randy Gerber, otherwise known as Cindy Crawford's husband. The hip clientele enjoy cosy sofas that are great for people-watching and a top-notch sound system that plays until the wee small hours.

MIDTOWN WEST

Hotel Metro Rooftop Bar: 45 West 35th Street between 5th and 6th Avenues. Tel 212-279 3535, www.hotelmetronyc.com. Subway B, D, F, N, Q, R, V, W to 34th Street. The views of the Empire State Building from this compact rooftop retreat are one reason why this is well worth a visit. The cheap beer and laid-back vibe created by the DJ are two others.

Hudson Hotel Bar at the Hudson Hotel: 356 West 58th Street between 8th and 9th Avenues. Tel 212-554 6000,

www.hudsonhotel.com. Subway A, B, C, D, I, 9 to 59th Street/Columbus Circle.
This Ian Schrager and Philippe Starck mecca for the in-crowd provides wonderful theatre. There's a glowing glass floor, flashy DJ and dark and enticing Games Room. In the summer, the after-work crowd heads to the Private Park – the hotel garden – and sip cocktails next to giant watering cans. Pure, surreal magic.

King Cole Bar at the St Regis Hotel: 2 East 55th Street. Tel 212-339 6721, www.starwoodhotels.com/stregis. Subway E, V to 5th Avenue at 53rd Street.
The specialities of the (very upscale) house are the Bloody Marys and the mural behind the bar, by noted American illustrator Maxfield Parrish.

Living Room at the W Times Square Hotel: 1567 Broadway at 47th Street. Tel 212-930 7444, www.starwoodhotels.com. Subway 4, 5, 6, L, N, Q, R, W to 14th Street.
Another of the cool W Hotel bar scenes, a magnet for fashion models (many agencies are in the area) and other pretty people.

Lobby Bar at the Royalton: 44 West 44th Street between 5th and 6th Avenues. Tel 212-869 4400, www.royaltonhotel.com. Subway B, D, F, V to 42nd Street; 7 to 5th Avenue.
The first of the Philippe Starck-designed hotels is still holding its own against all newcomers and its long, narrow bar continues to be a place to see and be seen in. The loos are wonderful, too. It's incredibly easy to walk past the Royalton, or '44' as it's known – there is no sign outside, just large wooden doors.

Mobar at the Mandarin Oriental: 59th Street at Columbus Circle. Tel 212-805 8800, www.mandarinoriental.com. Subway A, B, C, D, 1, 9 to Columbus Circle.
In the dazzling new AOL Time Warner Center, the sleek lobby lounge is drawing the crowds. The cocktails are $15 but the spectacular view of Central Park from the 35th floor (not to mention celebrity sightings) is free.

Mobar

Thom Bar at the 60 Thompson

The Oak Room at the Algonquin: 59 West 44th Street between 5th and 6th Avenues. Tel 212-840 6800, www.algonquinhotel.com. Subway B, D, F, V to 42nd Street; 7 to 5th Avenue.
Once world-famous as the New York literary set's salon of choice, this handsome room provides an intimate and civilised setting for some of the country's leading jazz and cabaret artists, who are usually booked for extended runs. The clientele is clubby and patrician, but anyone can buy dinner or drinks here.

Pen-Top Bar at the Peninsula Hotel: 700 5th Avenue, 23rd Floor. Tel 212-956 2888, www.newyork.peninsula.com. Subway E, V to 5th Avenue/53rd Street; N, R, W to 5th Avenue/59th Street.
The view is breathtaking and the prices can be, too, but in beautiful weather you'll feel you're at the centre of the universe – like the power brokers who surround you.

Town at the Chambers Hotel: 15 West 56th Street between 5th and 6th Avenues. Tel 212-974 5656, www.chambershotel.com. Subway F to 57th Street.
A very sophisticated place to drink, or dine (page 234), with lush leather sofas, one of the city's largest cocktail menus and wonderful, attentive staff.

TRIBECA
Church Lounge at TriBeCa Grand Hotel: 2 6th Avenue at White Street. Tel 212-519 6600, www.tribecagrand.com. Subway A, C, E to Canal Street.
The Wall Street crowd has made this upscale bar an after-work hangout. It's meant to look like a living room – if your living room was full of beautiful people. Sanctum Lounge with DJs, open Thursday to Sunday only, is the even more exclusive adjunct.

Marquee

UPPER EAST SIDE

Café Carlyle at the Carlyle Hotel: 35 East 76th Street at Madison and Park Avenues. Tel 212-744 1600, www.rosewood hotels.com/www.thecarlyle.com. Subway 6 to 77th Street.
A highly glamorous bar and restaurant that specialises in cabaret. Woody Allen still plays clarinet with The Eddie Davis New Orleans Jazz Band on Monday nights and Bobby Short, a New York favourite, plays piano during spring and autumn. $75 per person cover charge.

NIGHTCLUBS

This category includes live music venues and late-night lounges as well as dance clubs. The club scene in New York literally changes by the week. Venues are constantly opening, closing and relaunching so we've picked out the best of the well-established clubs, plus a scattering of new or smaller places that are currently creating a stir. By the way, while many of the clubs stay open until 4am, hours do vary so check out the listings in the *Village Voice, Paper, New York Press* and *New Yorker*.

CHELSEA

Bungalow 8: 515 West 27th Street between 10th and 11th Avenues. Tel 212-675 1567, www.bungalow8.com. Subway C, E to 122nd Street.
Here's where the hippest post-premiere parties are held and the gossip columnists get all their material. Cool decor and lots of attitude: it's an A-list kind of place.

Crobar: 530 West 28th Street between 10th and 11th Avenues. Tel 212-629 9000, www.crobar.com. Subway C, E to 23rd Street.
A New York import from Chicago and Miami, it's a paradox: a wild and crazy spot that's very well run, and a venue that evokes the huge clubs of the past.

Marquee: 289 10th Avenue at 26th Street. Tel 645-473 0202, www.marqueeny.com. Subway C, E to 23rd Street.
One of the coolest clubs in the city, or so the hype would have you believe, so there's always a massive queue. We can confirm that once inside it's worth the wait; intimate banquettes around the edge of the room with chandeliers overhead and models making some moves on the dance floor.

CHINATOWN

Happy Endings: 302 Broome Street at Forsyth Street. Tel 212-334 9676, www.happyendinglounge.com. Subway 6, N, R to Canal Street.
A brothel-turned-bar with a DJ in the basement dance room and a mixed lounge scene that attracts hip young things.

EAST VILLAGE

Bowery Ballroom: 6 Delancey Street between Bowery and Christie Street. Tel 212-533 2111, www.boweryballroom.com. Subway F, V to 2nd Avenue.
If you have one chance to visit the live music scene in Manhattan, this might be the place to go. A multi-level concert hall, the Bowery has lots of bars, good sight lines and a realistic admission price.

Lit: 93 2nd Avenue between 5th and 6th Streets. Tel 212-777 7987. Subway 6 to Astor Place; F, V to Lower East Side/2nd Avenue.
If you've always wanted to see a hot bartender in action, this art-meets-celebs joint is the place to come. A haven for indie filmsters, it has an art gallery – The Fuse – and a cellar-like dance room downstairs.

Webster Hall: 125 East 11th Street between 3rd and 4th Avenues. Tel 212-353 1600, www.webster-hall.com. Subway L, N,Q, R, W, 4, 5, 6 to 14th Street/Union Square.
There are lots of different rooms with different sounds, so you're bound to find something you enjoy. The best area is the main dance floor in the huge, ornate ballroom. It attracts a fairly straight crowd from the suburbs, but is a fun night out.

Crobar

TOP FIVE CLUBBING TIPS

On Friday and Saturday nights, the clubs are packed with crowds from boroughs outside Manhattan. For a quieter night, go on Thursday. Sunday is the big night for Manhattanites, so you'll get the real vibe then, along with the crowds.

Call ahead early in the evening to find out if there's a cover charge, when to arrive and how to dress. Also find out if there's a party theme on the night that you plan to go. Clubs can change nightly – for example, catering to straights one night, gays the next.

The real nightlife doesn't get going until after midnight, so get some zeds in before you go out.

Carry some ID with you just in case – it would be terrible if you couldn't get a drink when you're over 21.

Large groups of men don't stand much hope of getting into straight clubs – they'll have more chance if they are with a woman.

FLATIRON

40/40 Club: 6 West 25th Street between Broadway and 6th Avenue. Tel 212-832 4040, www.the4040club.com.
If you want some serious bling, and a possible celebrity sighting, then look no further than rapper Jay-Z's lavish two-level club. It's like being on an MTV set; seven cream-coloured leather swing chairs are suspended from the ceiling; sleek Italian marble shines on the floor, and a collection of LCD flat-screen televisions (including three 60-inch plasmas) display ESPN. There's also a cigar lounge and two VIP rooms are tucked away on the second level. After you've watched the game on the screens, the DJ blasts R&B and hip-hop. The club stays open until 4am.

★ ★ ★ ★ **BRIT TIP** ★ ★ ★ ★
★ As clubs and club nights change so ★
★ frequently, log on to websites ★
★ www.papermag.com and ★
★ www.clubnyc.com to find out ★
★ what's on where. ★

GREENWICH VILLAGE

Roxy: 515 West 18th Street between 10th and 11th Avenues. Tel 212-645 5156, www.roxynyc.com. Subway A, C, E to 14th Street; L to 8th Avenue.
A huge venue with plenty of different themes such as Roller Disco Wednesday, Old School Friday, and Hunky Gay Saturday.

SOBs: 204 Varick Street at Houston Street. Tel 212-243 4940, www.sobs.com. Subway 1, 9 to Houston Street.
The name stands for Sounds Of Brazil, which says it all. It's the place to come for the last word in Latin music from salsa to samba and even reggae. DJ Rekha's new monthly Bhangra Basement party has got New Yorkers in a spin.

LOWER EAST SIDE

Pianos: 158 Ludlow Street between Rivington and Stanton Streets. Tel 212-505 3733, www.pianosnyc.com. Subway F, J, M, Z to Delancey Street/Essex Street.
A former piano shop turned clean, whitewashed bar space that attracts trendy fashionistas plus the NYU students from the area. Local and national up-and-coming rock bands play in the somewhat dingy back room, while there's also a more intimate lounge upstairs.

Sapphire Lounge: 249 Eldridge Street between Houston and Stanton Streets. Tel 212-777 5153, www.sapphirenyc.com. Subway F to 2nd Avenue.
Pretension and attitude are left at the door in this tiny dance club that plays a great mix of hip-hop, reggae, acid jazz, R&B and disco classics. Opens at 7pm.

Slipper Room: 167 Orchard Street between Rivington and Stanton Streets. Tel 212-253 7246, www.slipperroom.com. Subway F, M, J, Z to Delancey Street/Essex Street.
Adding some real showbiz panache to the Lower East Side, this glitzy retro lounge is the venue for genuinely good cabaret as well as some far out, gender-bending burlesque. A great evening out.

MADISON SQUARE

Cheetah: 12 West 21st Street between 5th and 6th Avenues. Tel 212-206 7770. Subway F, N, R to 23rd Street.
An intimate venue with attractive animal-print decor and snuggly booths. Attracts a great mix, ranging from ghetto fabulous to the supercool.

MEATPACKING DISTRICT

Cielo: 18 Little West 12th Street between 9th Avenue and Washington Street. Tel 212-645 5700, www.cieloclub.com. Subway A, C, E to 14th Street; L to 8th Avenue.
The dance floor is sunken but the fabulous sound system hits the heights. This is one of the hottest spots in the city, and the good news and bad news is that it draws the big crowds.

One: 1 Little West 12th Street at 9th Avenue. Tel 212-255 9717. Subway A, C to 14th Street; L to 8th Avenue.
It's big (465 sq m/5,000 sq ft), it's bi-level and there's lots of action on the dance floor. A popular spot with the college crowd – though it helps if they're on big allowances!

Passerby: 436 West 15th Street at Washington Street. Tel 212-206 7321. Subway A, C, E, 1, 2 3, 9 to 14th Street; L to 8th Avenue.
Hurry before everyone else discovers this place: plenty already have. Tiny but with an awesome dance floor.

PM: 50 Gansevoort Street. Tel 212-255 6676, http://pmloungenyc.com. Subway A, C to 14th Street; L to 8th Avenue.
Half a dozen doormen enforce the beautiful-person policy that's considered the most brutal in the area. But if you get in, you'll experience Hawaiian island decor with big booths, big signs prohibiting dancing, and a big tab. The bottle service doesn't come cheap, but the attitude is laid back and the place gets really hot well past midnight.

MIDTOWN EAST

Light: 125 East 54th Street between Park and Lexington Avenues. Tel 212-583 1333, www.lightnyc.com. Subway 6 to 51st Street; E, V to Lexington Avenue/53rd Street.
This has had a good run with young professionals and glamorous *Sex And The City* types. Sip a Cosmo and tuck into the Asian-inspired appetisers while DJs spin a wide range of lounge music from Wednesday to Saturday.

Vue: 151 East 59th Street between Lexington and 3rd Avenues. Tel 212-753 1144. Subway 6 to 51st Street; E, V to Lexington Avenue.
Is it the visuals projected on a planetarium-

TOP FIVE HOT CLUBS

Chelsea

Cain: 544 West 27th Street between 10th and 11th Avenues. Tel 212-947 8000, www.cainnyc.com. Based around a safari theme– elephant-trunk door handles, zebra-hide bar and game lodge style wood pillars – it's caught the imagination of young Manhattanites, including film star Lindsay Lohan who's been spotted here.

Ruby Falls: 609 West 29th Street between 11th and 12th Avenues. Tel 212-643 6464. Subway A, C, E to 34th Penn Station. You can buy the art on the walls of this Chelsea club, which is appropriate as the vast warehouse space it is housed in is a bit like a gallery. The music veers between hip-hop and techno and it's attracting a fashionable crowd.

Lower East Side

Libation: 137 Ludlow Street between Stanton and Rivington Streets. Tel 212-529 2153, www.libationnyc.com. Subway F to Delancey Street. DJs play from Wednesday to Saturday at this sleek new club that attracts a good mix of people. It also boasts a seasonal cocktail and tapas menu to help keep you going through the night.

Meatpacking District

Glo: 431 West 16th Street between 9th and 10th Avenues. Tel 212-229 9119. Subway A, C, E to 14th Street; L to 8th Avenue. Divided into three levels, this chic, white, modern club has more than enough room for dancers, divas, people-watchers and any other trendy types who want to enjoy the district's latest place to be. The main bar is lit by neon tubing and the dance floor has white speakers hovering above it.

Murray Hill

Vapor: 143 Madison Avenue between 31st and 32nd Streets. Tel 212-686 6999, www.vapornyc.com. Subway 5 to 23rd Street. Drinkers get misted with air-purifying vapour in the back room of this new two-storey cocktail bar. DJs provide the sounds to the eager just-out-of-work crowd.

type dome or is it the great sound and big club feeling? Whatever... this is still one of the most popular clubs in the city.

MIDTOWN WEST

Copacabana: 617 West 57th Street between 11th and 12th Avenues. Tel 212-582 2672, www.copacabanany.com. Subway A, C, B, D, 1, 9 to Columbus Circle/59th Street.
A mostly Latin clientele who go for the live bands playing salsa and merengue. Everyone is fairly well dressed – not casual but not overdone. It's great but it does get packed.

SOHO

Don Hill's: 511 Greenwich Street at Spring Street. Tel 212-219 2850, www.donhills.com. Subway 6, C, E to Spring Street; N, R to Prince Street. Open nightly 9pm–4am.
One of the top rock venues in the city, Don Hill's is a live venue, club and bar all rolled into one, with great effect. It used to attract lots of celebs and the in-crowd; now it's not so showy, there's very little attitude and it's a fun place for a top night out.

NV: 289 Spring Street at Hudson Street. Tel 212-929 NVNV, www.nvbar.com. Subway 6, C, E to Spring Street; N, R to Prince Street. Open Wednesday to Sunday 10pm–4am.
The crowd is trendy and friendly, while the music is a great mix of everything from house and disco to hits from the 1980s. The upstairs has dance-floor energy while the much larger downstairs keeps a mellow lounge atmosphere.

★ ★ ★ ★ **BRIT TIP** ★ ★ ★ ★
★ **Do make an effort to get dressed up** ★
★ **if you are going clubbing. Don't** ★
★ **wear trainers or jeans – you won't** ★
★ **get in.** ★
★ ★

SoHo 323: 323 West Broadway between Grand and Canal Streets. Tel 212-334 2232, www.soho323.com. Subway 6, C, E to Spring

North Square

Street; N, R to Prince Street.
New York party animals who love the South Beach (Florida) scene are flocking to this new spot, opposite the SoHo Grand. Even before its official opening, it hosted post-premiere parties for the TriBeCa Film Festival, and Eva Mendes, David Duchovny, and Robert De Niro were among the first celebrities on site. There's a sleek, clean lounge and a dark, loft-like upstairs bar. The drink to go for is Twos & Threes – champagne and lychee purée with a touch of Chambord.

THEATER DISTRICT

Show: 135 West 41st Street between 6th Street and Broadway. Tel 212-278 0988, www.show-nightclub.com. Subway N, Q, R, S, W, 1, 2, 3, 7, 9 to 42nd Street/Times Square.
A Moulin Rouge-inspired hot spot with scantily clad burlesque dancers, swinging trapeze artists, go-go girls aplenty and a gilded stage for dancing to the mainstream music. Edgier hip-hop is played in the small upstairs lounge.

UNION SQUARE

Underbar at the W Hotel Union Square: 201 Park Avenue South at 17th Street. Tel 212-253 9119, www.starwoodhotels. com/whotels. Subway 4, 5, 6, L, N, Q, R, W to 14th Street/Union Square.
The plush velvet couches, the insistent throb of the music and the curtained-off private nooks all help send a seductive message in a way that some find amusing, others find a touch unsubtle. Still, the crowds – especially Europeans – keep coming.

UPPER WEST SIDE

Shalel Lounge: 65-1/2 West 70th Street between Central Park West and Columbus Avenues. Tel 212-799 9030. Subway B, C to 72nd Street.
Dark and dangerous – in the nicest kind of way. The exotic North African atmosphere transports aficionados directly to Morocco or a similar locale.

WEST VILLAGE

Sullivan Room: 218 Sullivan Street between Bleecker and West 3rd Streets. Tel 212-252 2151, www.sullivanroom.com. Subway A, B, C, D, E, F, V to West 4th Street. An absolutely brilliant, intimate club with no attitude, which is rare in New York. You can dance to soulful house with other friendly types, or just lounge around and chat.

CHAPTER 9

New York for Families

New York is like a giant playground to a child so is a great place to go with the family. Towering skyscrapers, mammoth bridges, vast parks, bright lights and rows of shops packed with enticing kid-friendly products are enough on their own to keep children entertained for a week. But there are plenty of other attractions to hunt out that can make a stay in NYC for the under 16s even more exciting. Central Park, for example, has a wealth of entertainment year-round, while some of the museums offer some real hands-on, fun activities. A word of warning: visiting any of the incredible children's stores with a real-life child in tow is likely to lead to plastic card meltdown!

CIRCUSES

BIG APPLE CIRCUS
Midtown West
- ✉ Damrosch Park, Lincoln Center
- ☎ 212-268 2500
- ⌁ www.bigapplecircus.org
- 🚇 Subway 1, 9 to 66th Street/Lincoln Center
- $ Ticket prices vary

A not-for-profit, totally family-friendly circus that has been operating since the 1970s.

RINGLING BROS AND BARNUM & BAILEY CIRCUS
Midtown West
- ✉ Madison Square Garden, 7th Avenue at 32nd Street
- ☎ 212-465 6741
- ⌁ www.ringling.com
- 🚇 Subway A, C, E, 1, 2, 3, 9 to 34th Street/Penn Station
- $ $12.50 upwards from TicketMaster 212-307 7171 or go through www.ticket master.com for a 10 per cent saving for weekday matinees

An extremely popular circus, America's original and most famous company keeps children and adults glued to their seats with a triple extravaganza of thrilling acts taking place in three rings at once each spring.

UNIVERSOUL CIRCUS
Midtown West
- ✉ Venues vary
- ☎ 800 316 7439 or book through TicketMaster on 212-307 7171, www.ticketmaster.com
- ⌁ www.universoulcircus.com
- $ $13–25

For thrills with a difference, try this African-American troupe, which provides circus standards to hip-hop, R&B and salsa music. Catch them at Brooklyn's Prospect Park in spring.

★ ★ ★ ★ **BRIT TIP** ★ ★ ★ ★
★ Pick up the NY Convention Bureau's ★
★ *Kids Guide to New York City* from ★
★ www.nyc visit.com or, hot off the ★
★ press, *Miffy Loves New York City* ★
★ ($9.99 from the Visitors Information ★
★ Center orbBookshops) where the ★
★ popular bunny takes parents and ★
★ kids around 30 family-friendly sites. ★
★ ★

FILM AND THEATRE

Many of the Broadway musicals are appropriate to take children to (pages 186–189) but there are many other plays, performances and films specifically for youngsters that take place in venues around the city.

Stilt walkers at Universoul Circus

KIDS 'N COMEDY
Midtown

⊠ Gotham Comedy Club, 34 West 22nd Street between 5th and 6th Avenues
☎ 212-877 6115
🖱 www.kidsncomedy.com
🚇 Subway F, N, V, R, W to 23rd Street
$ $15 plus drink. Visit website for schedule

This popular club has a stable of funny kids aged between 9 and 17 who deliver their own stand-up material. Not for tots, but sure to be popular with the over-8s to teenagers in the family.

LOEWS LINCOLN SQUARE 12
Midtown

⊠ 1998 Broadway at 68th Street
☎ 212-336 5000
🖱 www.enjoytheshow.com
🚇 Subway 1, 9 to 66th Street
$ $15 adults, $9 children/seniors at www.moviewatcher.com

The 3D IMAX experience is breathtaking, particularly as the screen is 8 storeys high and the surround-sound fantastic. Anyone aged 6 plus is going to enjoy it; children younger than that may be a little overwhelmed by the scale and sound levels.

NEW VICTORY THEATER
Theater District

⊠ 10th Floor, 229 West 42nd Street between Broadway and 8th Avenue
☎ 626-223 3020
🖱 www.newvictory.org
🚇 Subway 6 to 68th Street
$ $10–30 depending on seat type and show. You can buy online or by calling Telecharge.com on 212-563 2266 (a $14 fee will be added)

New York's first theatre aimed purely at families is very popular in the city, which, combined with the fact that it's an intimate space, means it sells out quickly. Every show is aimed at children aged from 4 to 12, but they are of such high standard, and often with two levels of humour, so that all can enjoy it.

★ ★ ★ ★ **BRIT TIP** ★ ★ ★ ★
★ To inspire kids aged 8 to 12 about ★
★ their trip, get a copy of *Melanie in* ★
★ *Manhattan* by Carol Weston ★
★ (www.melaniemartin.com), a novel ★
★ about a girl and her family ★
★ travelling in the Big Apple. ★

THEATREWORKS NYC
Greenwich Village

⊠ Lucille Lortel Theatre, 121 Christopher Street between Hudson and Bleecker Streets
☎ 212-647 1100
🖱 www.theatreworksusa.org
🚇 Subway 1 to Hudson Street.
$ Prices vary, but from $25 upwards. Order on 212-279 4200, www.ticketcentral.com

A not-for-profit group that puts on classic children's plays and musicals such as The Lion, the Witch and the Wardrobe for children aged 4 and above. Saturday morning shows at 10.30am.

MUSEUMS FOR CHILDREN

New York is brilliant when it comes to providing exciting and engaging museums and museum activities for children. They not only have plenty of dedicated children's museums, but many of the adult ones are genuinely interesting for children, too, while others provide a host of activities.

CHILDREN'S MUSEUM OF ART
Little Italy

⊠ 182 Lafayette Street between Broome and Grand Streets
☎ 212-941 9198
🖱 www.cmany.org
🚇 Subway N, R to Prince Street, B, D, F, Q to Broadway/Lafayette Street; 6 to Spring Street
$ $8, free for infants under 1

Under 7s can have an artistic ball with art computers, an art playground and a giant floor-to-ceiling chalkboard. There are also regular performing arts workshops led by local artists. A visit here is the perfect way to combine a shopping trip to SoHo for you with fun for the kids!

CHILDREN'S MUSEUM OF MANHATTAN
Upper West Side

⊠ The Tisch Building, 212 West 83rd Street between Broadway and Amsterdam Avenue
☎ 212-721 1234
🖱 www.cmom.org
🚇 Subway 1, 9 to 86th Street
🕐 Winter Wed–Fri (and school holidays) 10am–5pm, Sat, Sun 9am–5pm; summer Tues–Sun 10am–5pm
$ $8 adults and children, $5 seniors, infants under 1 free

The CMOM is entirely dedicated to children under the age of 10. This is a fabulous place and almost worth a visit even if you don't have kids. Its mission statement is to inspire children and their families to learn about themselves and our culturally diverse world through a unique environment of interactive exhibits and programmes.

★ After you've explored CMOM, cross the street for a light snack and drinks at Café Lalo (212-496 6031, www.cafelalo.com), which serves up great cakes and is featured in the Meg Ryan and Tom Hanks movie *You've Got Mail*.

And they certainly achieve it with their inspiring exhibits, such as the zany and fun-filled **Body Odyssey**, which shows children just what they're made of. Youngsters aged 5 and over can rush through the blood tunnel, hold their noses and slime around in the digestive tract, or take deep breaths and wind their way down the windpipe. On the way, they will learn about where burps come from, what makes a cut stop bleeding and where shed skin goes.

Other exhibits include **WordPlay** for tots aged 6 months to 4 years. The **Time Warner Media Center** helps children aged 6 and above to get behind the scenes of a professionally equipped TV studio and produce their own show, and the **CMOM Theater** takes children into a magical world of dance, music, theatre and puppetry.

★ Many museums are closed on national holidays, such as Thanksgiving Day on the fourth Thursday of November. Be sure to check first before you make your trip.

MUSEUM ACTIVITIES

Major New York museums put their wealth of resources to great use by offering fabulous events and activities that both entertain and educate children from as young as 4 years old to their teens. Full details of all the following museums appear

in Chapter 6, but here is an outline of what they specifically offer children and families.

AMERICAN MUSEUM OF NATURAL HISTORY
Upper West Side
✉ Central Park West at 79th Street
☎ 212-769 5100
⌨ www.amnh.org
🚇 Subway B, C to 81st Street
🕐 10am-5.45pm daily
$ $14 adults, $8 children (2-12). The most comprehensive package, which includes the space shows, IMAX films and special exhibitions, costs $30 adults, $19 children.

This museum is a mine of entertaining exhibits and interactive displays filled as it is with ever-popular dinosaurs, an amazing new ocean life display, thousands of dollars worth of sparkling gems and a whole array of interactive devices that bring so many aspects of the natural world to life. Each weekend it offers workshops and astronomy programmes for children from 4. And in the Discovery Room, open weekdays 1.30pm-5.15pm and weekends 10:30am-1:30pm and 2:15-5:15pm, children from 5 to 12 can have a hands on, behind the scenes look at science. There's also a **Story Time for Tots** in the Museum Shop 11-11.30am on Sundays, which is free with your admission ticket. Teenagers will be enthralled with SonicVision, a digitally animated alternative music show on Friday and Saturday evenings 7.30pm and 8.30pm.

★ Avoid the restaurants at the American Museum of Natural History and head round the corner to Pizzeria Uno in Columbus Avenue at 81st Street (page 183) where you'll find far more friendly-family fare at excellent prices.

Saturday sessions generally run from noon to 1.30pm and Sunday sessions from 10.30am. Check out the website first to see which activities will be available during your visit to the city.

The museum has a butterfly conservatory and also runs field trips, such as bird watching, bug (insect) hunts or flower inspections in the adjacent Central Park.

THE CLOISTERS
Washington Heights
✉ Fort Tyron Park, Fort Washington Avenue at Margaret Corbin Plaza
☎ 212-923 3700
🕙 www.metmuseum.org
🚗 Subway A to 190th Street then the M4 bus
🕐 Nov–Feb 9.30am–4.45pm, Mar–Oct 9.30am–5.15pm
$ $15 adults, $10 seniors, under 12s free (includes entry to Metropolitan Museum of Art on same day)

The northern Manhattan branch of the Metropolitan Museum, which is devoted to the art and architecture of medieval Europe, also has a series of free workshops for children aged from 4 to 12, usually on a Saturday 1–2pm. Subjects include medieval feasts and celebrations and stories from the Middle Ages. www.metmuseum.org/calendar.

JEWISH CHILDREN'S MUSEUM
Brooklyn
✉ 792 Eastern Parkway at corner of Kingston Avenue, Crown Heights, Brooklyn
☎ 718-467 0600
🕙 www.jcmonline.org
🚗 Subway 3 to Kingston Avenue
🕐 Mon–Thurs 10am–4pm, Sun 10am–6pm; Fri, Sat closed (apart from select evenings).
$ £10 per person; children under 2 free

The first of its kind in the world, opened in 2004 at a cost of $31 million by Jewish Children International, interactive multimedia exhibits entertain, educate and engage children of all backgrounds about Jewish heritage.

Lower East Side Tenement Museum

LOWER EAST SIDE TENEMENT MUSEUM
Lower East Side
✉ 108 Orchard Street between Broome and Delancey Streets
☎ 212-431 0233
🕙 www.tenement.org
🚗 Subway F to Delancey Street
🕐 Mon 11am–5.30pm, Tues–Fri 11am–6pm, Sat–Sun 10.45am–5.30pm. The museum can only be visited via a tour.
$ $15 adults for 1-hour tour, free for under 5s

The best tour for children is the 45-minute **Confino Family Apartment Tour**, which aims to bring history to life. The apartment recreates the life of the Sephardic Jewish Confino family from Kastoria in Greece in 1916. Teenager Victoria Confino welcomes visitors as if they were newly arrived immigrants and she were teaching them how to adapt to life in America. Along the way you can touch any items in the apartment, try on period clothing and foxtrot to music played on an authentic wind-up Victrola.

★ ★ ★ ★ 　 　 　 　 　 ★ ★ ★ ★
★ 　 　 　 　 　 　 　 　 　 　 ★
★ 　 Holiday-time tours at the Lower 　 ★
★ East Side Tenement Museum sell out ★
★ 　 quickly, so book as far in advance 　 ★
★ 　 　 　 　 as possible. 　 　 　 　 ★
★★★★★★★★★★★★★★★★★★★★★★★★★★

METROPOLITAN MUSEUM OF ART
Upper East Side
✉ 1000 5th Avenue at 82nd Street
☎ 212-535 7710
🕙 www.metmuseum.org
🚗 Subway 4, 5, 6 to 86th Street
🕐 Tues–Thurs, Sun 9.30am–5.30pm; late opening Fri, Sat until 9pm. No pushchairs on Sun.
$ $12 adults and children over 12, children under 12 free (includes admission to The Cloisters above)

This magnificent museum uses various means to make its resources as accessible to children as possible – for free – and provides printed gallery guides and museum hunts at the **Uris Information Desk** on the ground floor near the 81st Street entrance. A whole series of workshops and programmes are available both through the week and at weekends. For exact times and dates, check out the calendar section of the website or call. Programmes include:

Art Evening for Families: Conversation and sketching help visitors aged from 6 to 12 to explore the museum's art collection. Sat 6–7pm.

Hello Met!: Children from 5 to 12 and their families are given a stimulating introduction to the Met's encyclopaedia collection through sketching and a short film. Sunday 2–3pm.

Look Again!: The history, meaning and cultural aspects of art in the museum are explored through chats, drawing and, from time to time, performances for children from 5 to 12 (plus an adult) on Sat, Sun, 11am–12.30pm, 2–3.30pm.

Start With Art: Children aged 3 to 7 (plus an adult) meet at the Uris tiered seating area to explore art at the Met through storytelling, sketching and games. Tues, Thurs 2.30–3.30pm, Wed, Fri 3.30–4.30pm.

MUSEUM OF MODERN ART (MOMA)
Midtown

✉ 11 West 53rd Street between 5th and 6th Avenues
☎ 212-708 9400
🖱 www.moma.org
🚗 Subway E, V to 5th Avenue/53rd Street
🕐 Mon, Wed, Thurs, Sat, Sun 10am–5.30pm, Fri 10.30am–8pm
$ Family programmes are free for under 16s (and this includes admission to the museum), adults $20, seniors $16

The Family Programs at the MoMA introduce children and their parents to the world of modern art through guided walks, art workshops, artist talks and film screenings. For a list of scheduled activities, phone or email familyprograms@moma.org.

The Gallery Talks: Saturday morning sessions for children aged 4–10, which offer lively interactive discussions in the museum's galleries before it opens to the public and include:

Family Art Workshops: Children aged 5 to 10 and their parents explore artworks in the museum, then create their own art in a hands-on workshop.

One-at-a-Time: Families can explore the permanent collection and special exhibitions. Tours for Fours is especially designed for 4-year-olds and introduces

BRILLIANT MUSEUMS FOR ALL THE FAMILY

Intrepid Sea-Air-Space Museum (page 118)

Lower East Side Tenement Museum (page 126)

National Cartoon Museum (page 130)

New York City Fire Museum (page 131)

New York City Police Museum (page 132)

New York City Transit Museum, Brooklyn (page 132)

And a brilliant site:
Historic Richmond Town, Staten Island (page 271)

families to painting, sculpture, photography and works on paper.

★ ★ ★ ★ ★ ★ ★ ★
★ Some museums offer free or half ★
★ price entry late afternoon/evenings ★
★ on Fridays. It's worth checking for if ★
★ you're on a budget. ★
★ ★

SOLOMON R GUGGENHEIM MUSEUM
Upper East Side

✉ 1071 5th Avenue at 89th Street
☎ 212-423 3500
🖱 www.guggenheim.org
🚗 Subway 4, 5, 6 to 86th Street
🕐 Mon, Wed, Sat, Sun 10am–5.45pm, Fri 10am–8pm
$ $15 adults, $10 seniors/students, under 12s free

In addition to special free family days, the Guggenheim runs a series of fascinating paid-for workshops. They include **Art and**

Solomon R Guggenheim Museum

Technology workshops, in which 7–13-year-olds get real hands-on experience, **My iMovie**, when they get to use digital cameras to create short animated videos, and **Portraiture in Photoshop**, in which they study paintings in the museum before creating portraits of their family using Photoshop 6.0.

STATEN ISLAND CHILDREN'S MUSEUM

- ✉ 1000 Richmond Terrace, Staten Island
- ☎ 718-273 2060
- 🖱 www.statenislandkids.org
- 🚌 Staten Island Ferry to St George Terminal then S40 bus to Snug Harbor Road
- ☉ Tues–Sun 12pm–5pm
- $ $5; grandparents free on Wed

Interactive exhibitions such as crawling through an ant hill to watch butterflies emerging from the chrysalis and exploring a pirate ship and becoming a sailor. **Great Explorations** takes children from the rainforest canopy to dog sledding and building an igloo and there's a chance to be a fireman, learn dog body language or go to sea on an outdoors boat, weather permitting. **Storytime** and **Feeding the Animals** happen daily and creative workshops include Science Thursday 1.30–4.30pm.

THE WHITNEY MUSEUM
Uptown

- ✉ 945 Madison Avenue at 75th Street
- ☎ 212-570 3676
- 🖱 www.whitney.org
- 🚌 Subway 6 to 77th Street
- ☉ Wed, Thur, Sat, Sun 11am–6pm, Fri 1–9pm
- $ $12 adults, $9.50 seniors/students, under 12s free

The Whitney has worked hard to make itself accessible to young children. Free guides are

---

TOP SHOPS FOR CHILDREN

New York has some fantastic shops dedicated to children (pages 112–113). The two not to be missed are the classic, long-established toy store **FAO Schwarz** and the much newer but equally incredible **Toys R Us** flagship store in Times Square. Other fun places include the **Warner Brothers Studio Store** and, of course, **The Disney Store**.

---

provided for families to introduce children and adults to selected works of art and encourage new ways of learning about art together. The **From the Ground Up!** guide helps families to explore the architecture of the building and includes in-museum and take-home activities. **People, Places and Spaces** is the Whitney's first family audio guide to works from the Whitney's permanent collection and is included with the admission fee.

Every Saturday 2–3.30pm the **Look Out! Families Explore American Art** session for children aged 7 to 11 explores different parts of the museum through sketching activities. It's best to reserve a place by calling. **Family Fun! Workshops** are held Saturdays 9–11am, $8 per family, and feature gallery tours and art projects for children aged 5 to 10 and their families. Registration is necessary.

OTHER INDOOR ACTIVITIES

BUILD-A-BEAR WORKSHOP

- ✉ 565 5th Avenue at 46th Street
- ☎ 212-871 7080
- 🖱 www.buildabear.com
- 🚌 Subway B, D, F, V to 5th Avenue

A recently opened attraction offering kids the chance to make a bear in the world's largest build-a-bear workshop. It's a unique, interactive shopping space where they build and personalise their bears and then get a bite to eat at the Eat With Your Bear Hands Café.

PARKS AND GARDENS

CENTRAL PARK

- ✉ From Central Park South at 59th Street in the Midtown area to 110th Street in Harlem
- 🖱 www.centralparknyc.org

Top of the pile for all-round entertainment, with a small but perfectly formed Wildlife Conservation Center and Children's Petting Zoo, the fun carousel, ice-skating at the Wollman Rink and the Discovery Center at Belvedere Castle, plus a whole host of activities, make for an all-round winner where kids are concerned. For more details on Central Park, see pages 249–250.

Through the Grand Army Plaza at the southern end of the park at 59th Street, you will find the following:

BELVEDERE CASTLE DISCOVERY CENTER

✉ Mid-park at 97th Street
☎ 212-722 0210
🖰 www.centralparknyc.org; click on 'Just for Kids'
🚇 Subway B, C to 79th Street
🕓 Tues–Sun 10am–5pm; closes 4pm in winter
$ Free

Sitting on a Vista Rock, this is the highest point in the park and gives great views in all directions. The Henry Luce Nature Observatory includes exhibits on flowers, trees and birds in the park. The Center is a popular venue and the starting point for many fun events (call 212-772 0210 to register) such as:

Discovery Kits: The Central Park Conservancy lends a backpack with binoculars, guidebook, maps and sketching materials for bird-watching in the Ramble and other locations. For children aged 6 and up, though those under 12 must be with an adult.

Experimental Science and Nature Fun: Learn about botany, geology, weather and animal habitats through science experiments and short demonstrations at various points in the park. Open to all ages.

Woods and Water Exhibit: A colourful, hands-on exhibit sponsored by the Central Park Conservancy that focuses on the rich variety of plants and animals in the park.

SUMMER IN THE CITY

Puppet shows, free storytellings, films and workshops in libraries – these form just a part of what's on offer in the city throughout the summer, so you'll be hard pressed to find a moment's peace! To find out what's going on where and when, pick up a copy of *Events For Children* from any branch of the New York Public Library. Most are free or very good value for money.

Here is an outline of some of the many activities available for children in summer:

Central Park
The park is a year-round winner, but summer time is when it really comes into its own. Specific children's events abound, including those organised by Arts in the Park (tel 212-988 9093), while the whole family can enjoy offerings put on by the **Central Park SummerStage** (tel 212-360 2756, www.summerstage.org) and **Shakespeare in the Park** (tel 212-539 8750, www.publictheater.org).

Bryant Park Summer Film Festival (tel 212-391 4248)
Perfect for adults and children alike, head to Bryant Park on a Monday night and pull up a chair or lay out a rug to enjoy a free outdoor film on the massive screen. Remember to take some snacks and drinks. Children can let off a little steam before or after at the nearby carousel.

New York Philharmonic Young People's Concerts (Avery Fisher Hall, 10 Lincoln Center Plaza, tel 212-875 5656/5030, www.newyorkphilharmonic.org $7–$26)
A series of summer concerts where children get to meet the musicians and try out their instruments for an hour before the concert. You'll also be in the right spot for the Lincoln Center's free Out-of-Doors Festival, with events throughout August (see below). The Lincoln Center also offers a family programme of music and dance afternoons for children.

International Festival of Puppet Theater (tel 212-680 1400, www.hensonfoundation.org)
A biennial puppet festival held at various venues throughout the city in September (next one 2008) produced by the Jim Henson Foundation. Sign up on the website for puppet happenings that may time with your visit.

Lincoln Center Out-of-Doors (Lincoln Center Plaza, Broadway at 65th Street, tel. 212-875 5456, www.lincolncenter.org).
A free festival for all ages running throughout August with specific events for children. They include the **Iced Tea Dance** where children get to dance with professionals, a **Homemade Instrument Day** in which children can make their own musical instruments and play them, and a **Play Day**.

CAROUSEL
- ✉ Mid-park at 64th Street and 5th Avenue
- ☎ 212-879 0244
- 🚇 Subway N, R to 5th Avenue; 6 to 68th Street
- 🕐 10.30am–6pm daily Apr–Nov, Sat, Sun 10am–4.30pm in winter
- $ $1.25 a ride

A carousel has been on this site since 1871 when the original was powered by a blind mule and a horse, which walked a treadmill in an underground pit. Fortunately, no animals have to be put through such torture any more as the current electrical ride was donated by the Michael Friedsam Foundation in 1951. It features some of the largest hand-carved horses in the US.

CHARLES A DANA DISCOVERY CENTER
- ✉ North East Corner at the Harlem Meer/110th Street between 5th and Lenox Avenues
- ☎ 212-860 1370
- 🚇 Subway 2, 3, 6 to 110th Street
- 🕐 Tues–Sun 10am–5pm, closes 4pm in winter
- $ Free

One of Central Park's many visitor centres, it is also its only environmental educational centre with children's workshops year-round. Free to all, the centre sponsors workshops, musical performances and park tours and also loans fishing poles for fishing in the well-stocked Meer. Its catch-and-release fishing programme is open to all ages and gives people the chance to fish for large-mouth bass, catfish, golden shiners and bluegills.

THE DAIRY
- ✉ Mid-park at 65th Street
- ☎ 212-794 6564
- 🚇 Subway N, R to 5th Avenue; 6 to 68th Street
- 🕐 11am–5pm daily, closes 4pm in winter
- $ Free

Family time in Bryant Park

A 19th-century-style building overlooking the Wollman Rink with an interactive touch-screen kiosk giving information about the park. It also houses a reference library and an exhibit about the history and design of the park.

NORTH MEADOW RECREATION CENTER
Central Park
- ✉ Mid-park at 97th Street
- ☎ 212-348 4867
- 🖰 www.centralparknyc.org
- 🚇 Subway B, C, 6 to 96th Street
- 🕐 Summer (end May–Sept) Mon–Fri 10am–8pm, Sat and Sun 10am–6pm; autumn and spring (early Sept–mid-Oct) Mon–Fri 10am–7pm, Sat and Sun 10am–6pm; winter (mid-Oct–mid-Mar) Mon–Fri 10am–6pm, Sat and Sun 10am–4.30pm
- $ Free

Open to all ages, the park's largest open space at 23 acres provides free Field Day Kits that include everything you need to equip a family for a day of fun and games in the park. The kits contain a basketball, ten cones, three bats, horseshoe set, playground ball, football, frisbee, skipping rope and hula-hoops. Call in advance to register. The Center also has a 25ft climbing wall with adventure programmes for children and lends out equipment for the basketball and handball courts.

SWEDISH COTTAGE MARIONETTE THEATER
Central Park West
- ✉ Mid-park at 81st Street
- ☎ 212-988 9093
- 🚇 Subway B, C to 81st Street
- 🕐 Oct–Jun Tues–Fri 10.30am and noon, Sat 1pm; Jul–Aug Mon–Fri 10.30am and noon
- $ $6 adults, $5 children

Formerly a 19th-century Swedish schoolhouse, this cottage was moved to Central Park in 1876 and now holds various

★ ★ ★ ★ **BRIT TIP** ★ ★ ★ ★
★ **If you need a babysitter, contact the** ★
★ **Baby Sitters' Guild for licensed** ★
★ **childcare at 60 East 42nd Street, No** ★
★ **912, tel 212-682 0227, fax 212-** ★
★ **687 4660, www.babysitters** ★
★ **guild.com.** ★
★ ★

TOP FIVE ATTRACTIONS FOR KIDS

Circle Line Sightseeing Cruise (page 75)

Statue of Liberty (page 60)

Empire State Building (page 61)

Times Square (Chapter 8, page 185)

Central Park (pages 212 and 249)

marionette plays for children throughout the year. Book in advance (but note credit cards are not accepted).

NEW YORK BOTANICAL GARDEN
Bronx
- ✉ Bronx River Parkway and Fordham Road
- ☎ 718-817 8700
- 🖰 www.nybg.org
- 🚇 Subway 2, 5 to Bronx Park East. If going direct, take subway C, D or 4 to Bedford Park and then the BX26 bus
- ☉ Closed Mondays. Tues–Sun and Mon on holidays Apr–Oct 10am–6pm, Nov–March 10am–5pm
- $ $13 adults, $5 2-12s, under 2s free; seniors/students $11 (combination ticket allowing children's gardens to be visited)

Fifty gardens and 250 acres to run around in, including an Adventure Garden and a Family Garden with programmes especially for children, make this a great place to visit. There are also puppet shows, dance and music concerts, and other events throughout the year.

THE WOLLMAN RINK
Central Park
- ✉ Central Park, Mid-park at 62nd Street
- ☎ 212-439 6900
- 🖰 www.wollmanskatingrink.com
- 🚇 Subway N, R W to 5th Avenue/59th Street
- ☉ Winter (Oct–Mar) Mon, Tue 10am–2.30pm, Wed, Thur, Sun 10am–9pm, Fri, Sat 10am–11pm
- $ $8.50–11 adults, $4.25–4.50 children; skate rental extra

Skating for beginners and ice dancing are offered on this popular rink An ideal and scenic place to take children and join in the traditional activity of a New York winter.

DON'T MISS...

MADAME TUSSAUD'S
- ✉ 234 West 42nd Street between 7th and 8th Avenues
- ☎ 800-246 8872
- 🖰 www.nycwax.com
- 🚇 Subway A, C, E to 42nd Street/Times Square
- ☉ Daily 10am–10pm
- $ $29 adults, $26 senior, $23 children, under 4s free

The New York version of London's famous waxworks is an enjoyable outing for kids. They'll get to see all their favourite stars from Michael Jordan to Tom Cruise.

SONY WONDER TECHNOLOGY LAB
- ✉ Sony Plaza, East 56th Street between Madison and 5th Avenues
- ☎ 212-833 8100
- 🖰 www.sonywondertechlab.com
- 🚇 Subway E, V to 5th Avenue/53rd Street
- ☉ Tues–Sat 10am–5pm, Sun noon–5pm; closed Mon
- $ Free, but you must book your time in advance

Four floors of interactive exhibits with robots and lots of hi-tech entertainment. Adults will love playing here as much as kids. Reservations only though, so be sure to book well in advance.

BROOKLYN

Brooklyn is a wonderful place to spend time with children. The neighbourhood is not only home to a raft of great museums for adults, it also has its own children's museums, a zoo, a boating lake and wildlife activities in the massive Prospect Park. On top of that, there is the famous Coney Island entertainment centre at the southern end of the borough.

ASTROLAND
Coney Island
- ✉ 1000 Surf Avenue between West 8th Street and Jones Walk
- ☎ 718-372 0275

Coney Island Cyclone

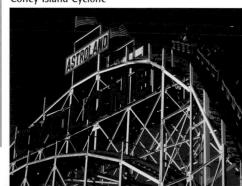

✆ www.astroland.com
🚇 Subway Q, F to West 8th Street/NY Aquarium
🕓 June–Sept daily noon–late evening; Mon–Thurs noon–6pm, 4–10pm; Fri noon–6pm; winter weekends only
$ $22.99 ticket allows you on all rides (Mon–Fri only)
Undoubtedly tacky, Coney Island's amusement park has definitely seen better days, but that doesn't stop children having fun. There are rides for every age.

AUDUBON CENTRE AT THE BOATHOUSE
Prospect Park
✉ Lincoln Road/Ocean Avenue entrance to Prospect Park
☎ 718-287 3400 Audubon Center; 718-965 8999 events hotline
✆ www.prospectpark.org
🚇 Subway Q to Parkside Avenue; S to Prospect Park
🕓 Apr–Dec Thurs–Sun and holidays noon–5pm; Jan–March weekends and school holidays noon–4pm
$ Free admission. $5 13 and over, $3 3–12, children under 3 free on electric boat tour.
The design of this beautiful 1905 Beaux Art boathouse, with its elegant arches, decorative tiles and classical balcony, was based on a 16th-century Venetian library. Now an official Historic New York City Landmark, it is home to the state-of-the-art Audubon Centre, which is dedicated to preserving wildlife and natural education. You can take tours along the new Lullwater Nature Trail or on the Lullwater by electric boat April to October as well as into the surrounding acres of natural habitat, see interactive bird and wildlife exhibits or participate in family activities such as craftwork, music and technology sessions. Nature babies Mondays 9.30–11am is a themed crafts, music and storytelling session for 18 months to 3 year olds (718-287 3400 ext 114).

BROOKLYN CHILDREN'S MUSEUM
Brooklyn
✉ 145 Brooklyn Avenue at St Mark's Avenue, Crown Heights
☎ 718-735 4400
✆ www.bchildmus.org
🚇 Subway 1 to Kingston Avenue
🕓 Summer (July–Aug) Tues–Fri 1–6pm,

Sat and Sun 11am–6pm. Rest of the year closed Mon, Tues.
$ $4, under 1s free
A fabulous place for children, this was the first-ever museum for little ones. They can have a ball here playing with synthesisers, operating water wheels to dam a stream, dancing on the keys of a walk-on piano and playing instruments from around the world. The museum is undergoing a $39 million expansion to open in 2007 as double its size and become New York's first Green Museum. It will feature a kids café and state-of-the-art technology. The new museum is located nearby, at the corner of St Mark's and Brooklyn Avenues, but check the website for up-to-date details, workshops, performances and events and be one of the first to visit!

THE CAROUSEL
Right next door to the zoo and museum is the magnificently carved carousel, which features 51 horses, a lion, giraffe, a deer and two dragon-pulled chariots. It is also one of the few carousels in the world that is wheelchair accessible.

LEFFERTS HOMESTEAD CHILDREN'S MUSEUM
Prospect Park
✉ Children's Corner, Prospect Park, at intersection of Flatbush and Ocean Avenues and Empire Blvd
☎ 718-789 2822
✆ www.prospectpark.org
🚇 Subway Q, S, B to Prospect Park
🕓 Apr–Dec Thurs–Sun 12am–5pm; Dec–March 12am–4pm
$ Free
Right by the main Grand Army Plaza entrance to Prospect Park stands this restored 18th-century farmhouse, once owned by original Dutch settlers in Brooklyn. Children can play with cooking tools, hunt for barnyard implements or play

> ## TOP FIVE HOTELS FOR FAMILIES
> Four Seasons (page 231)
> Le Parker Meridien (page 238)
> Ritz-Carlton at Battery Park (page 230)
> Wellington (page 246)
> Westin New York Times Square (page 248)

with toys from the era. Families can also take part in craft activities such as candle-making, sewing, butter-churning and making fire with a flint and steel. At weekends throughout the summer, stories are told under a tree, plus hoop games to play and gardening to do.

PROSPECT PARK

A massive park brimming with activities for adults and children (see Chapter 14, A Taste of the Outer Boroughs, pages 000–00) where you could easily spend a day enjoying the activities and chilling out.

★ ★ ★ ★ **BRIT TIP** ★ ★ ★ ★

★ The New York Aquarium is just a
★ short stroll away from Astroland
★ amusement park, so if the weather
★ turns bad you can take shelter
★ there.
★ ★

RESTAURANTS

Some restaurants in New York are very well geared up to families, offering excellent value children's menus with plenty of choice and also providing colouring books and crayons to keep little ones occupied. But it is more than that – Americans generally welcome children with pleasure.

The **Pizzeria Uno** chain has good food, great value and friendly service. Some of the city's finest dining establishments such as the **Bull & Bear** at the Waldorf Astoria (page 169), **The View at the Marriott Marquis** (page 139) and the **Ritz-Carlton's Rise** bar and restaurant at **Battery Park** (page 200) have proved welcoming to kids. While these top-notch eateries do not tend to have specific children's menus, they do go to a lot of trouble to accommodate their requests.

The task of eating out can become a little more tricky if your kids aren't yet at the cutlery-holding not-throwing-food stage, which makes your dining choices a little more restricted. Plus, let's admit it, sometimes you just want to hand baby or tot over and enjoy a relaxing lunch (or brunch). If that's the case, read on...

BIG CITY BAR AND GRILL

✉ 1600 3rd Avenue at 90th Street
☎ 212-369 0808
🚇 Subway 4, 5, 6 to 86th Street

PlayDine at this noisy American diner joint is the answer to tourist parents' prayers. There's an in-house play area that's supervised by childcare pros from noon to 4pm. For $10 per child you get to eat with ease from the huge menu. There's a kid's menu too but they will probably be more interested in the play area.

BUBBY'S

✉ 1 Main Street between Plymouth and Water Streets, Brooklyn
☎ 718-222 0666
🖰 www.bubbys.com
🚇 Subway A, C to High Street; F to York Avenue

If you don't want to take your little one on the subway, then enjoy a fun 5-minute water taxi ride from South Street Seaport across to the Fulton Ferry Landing which is close by. There's a well-stocked play area in this famously family-friendly restaurant – there's even crayons and balloons at the table. There's also a branch at 120 Hudson Street at North Moore Street in TriBeCa.

ZOOS

BRONX ZOO AND WILDLIFE CONSERVATION SOCIETY

✉ Bronx River Parkway at Fordham Road
☎ 718-367 1010
🖰 www.bronxzoo.org
🚇 Subway 2, 5 to Bronx Park East
🕐 Apr–Oct Mon–Fri 10am–5pm, Sat and Sun 10am–5.30pm; daily 10am–4.30pm rest of year
$ $12 adults, $9 seniors and children, under 2s free. Suggested donation on Wed. Children under the age of 17 must be accompanied by an adult. Cheaper rates Nov–March. Congo Gorilla Forest, skyfari, zoo shuttle, butterfly garden and monorail Bengali Express $3 each; camel ride $5; bug carousel $2.

The Bronx Zoo is respected worldwide for its tradition of conservation and ecological awareness alongside the naturalistic habitats it provides, such as the African Plains where antelope roam. It is the largest urban zoo in America and houses 4,000 animals and 560 species. The Congo Gorilla Forest is a $43-million, 2.5-hectare (6-acre) rainforest, inhabited by two troops of gorillas. The latest exhibit to open is Tiger Mountain, which takes you a whisker away from the largest member of the cat family.

Disney-style rides include a guided monorail tour through Wild Asia, an aerial safari, camel rides and a zoo shuttle. There is also a children's zoo. Some of the exhibits and all of the rides, apart from the bug carousel, are open only between April and October.

CHILDREN'S ZOO AND WILDLIFE CENTER

- ✉ Mid-park 830 5th Avenue at 64th Street and 5th Avenue
- ☎ 212-439 6500
- ⌚ www.wcs.org
- 🚇 Subway N, R to 5th Avenue; 6 to 68th Street
- ☉ Summer (Apr–Oct) weekdays 10am–5pm, Sat and Sun 10am–5.30pm; winter (Nov–end March) daily 10am–4.30pm. Guided tour 2.30pm.
- $ $8 adults, $4 seniors, $3 3–12, under 3s free

A small but perfectly formed zoo and conservation centre. Exhibits include a polar bear, tamarin monkeys and red pandas, plus other endangered species. Watch the sea lions being fed at 11.30am, 2pm and 4pm, and the penguins at 10.30am and 2.30pm. Close Encounters of the Critter Kind is available for toddlers and a rainforest journey for older children. Call 212-439 6583 to register for programmes. The Leaping Frog Café is kid-friendly and healthy!

Bronz Zoo Congo Gorilla Forest

New York Aquarium

NEW YORK AQUARIUM
Coney Island, Brooklyn

- ✉ 610 Surf Avenue at West 8th Street, Brooklyn
- ☎ 718-265-FISH
- ⌚ www.nyaquarium.com
- 🚇 Subway F, Q to West 8th Street/ NY Aquarium
- ☉ May-Sept Mon–Fri 10am–6pm, Sat, Sun 10am–7pm; Apr–May/Sept-Oct Mon–Fri 10am–5pm, Sat, Sun 10am–5.30pm; Oct–Mar daily 10am–4.30pm
- $ $12 adults, $8 under 13s and seniors, under 2s free

Most famous for its beluga whale family, the aquarium has another unusual exhibit showing the creatures that live in New York's famous East River. Sharks, dolphins and a re-creation of the Pacific coastline also feature.

PROSPECT PARK ZOO

- ✉ Prospect Park, 450 Flatbush Avenue
- ☎ 718-399 7339
- ⌚ nyzoosandaquarium.com
- 🚇 Subway Q, S to Prospect Park
- ☉ Summer (Apr–Oct) Mon–Fri 10am–5pm, weekends and holidays 10am–5.30pm; winter (end Oct–end March) daily 10am–4.30pm
- $ $6 adults, $2.25 seniors, $2 children 3–12; under 3s free

Again close to the Grand Army Plaza entrance to Prospect Park, this is Brooklyn's only zoo. It features nearly 400 animals and more than 80 species in an environment that gives children close-up views of some of the world's most unusual ones. They include prairie dogs, wallabies, tamarin monkeys, baboons, a red panda, plus a vibrant band of birds, reptiles and amphibians. The new interactive Discovery Center is open every weekend 11am to 3pm.

CHAPTER 10

Gay New York

The West Village is traditionally the spiritual home of gays and lesbians in New York, but in today's cosmopolitan city a person's sexual persuasion rarely raises an eyebrow. Gay bars, clubs and restaurants have sprung up all over Manhattan, and Chelsea has become the new 'gaybourhood'. In fact, most restaurants and bars across the Big Apple are open to everyone – whether you're gay or straight.

If you'd like to get to know more about the gay and lesbian culture in New York, Big Onion's tour Before Stonewall: A Gay and Lesbian History Tour gives a good insight into the historical side, tracing the development of Greenwich Village as a community Mecca (see Big Onion Walking Tours, page 82). For a tour of the modern-day Gay New York, try Limotour's Gay Tour of New York, which can be arranged online (www.limotours.com). Check out year-round gay art tours led by Rafael Risemberg PhD, gay studies professor and art critic for gay newspaper the *New York Blade*, at www.nygallerytours.com.

★ ★ ★ ★ **BRIT TIP** ★ ★ ★ ★
★ ★
★ ★
★ **Download a gay map to Manhattan** ★
★ **for free from www.funmaps.com to** ★
★ **find everything from hot nude yoga** ★
★ **to gay-friendly shops.** ★
★ ★
★ ★

INFORMATION

LESBIAN AND GAY COMMUNITY SERVICES CENTER
✉ 208 West 13th Street between 7th and 8th Avenues
☎ 212-620 7310
🖰 www.gaycenter.org
🚗 Subway A, C, E, 1, 2, 3 to 14th Street; L to 8th Avenue

By far the best organisation in New York for information, you'll find millions of leaflets and notices about gay life in the city. There are now around 400 groups that meet here

and it also houses the National Museum and Archive of Lesbian and Gay History.

PUBLICATIONS

The main gay weeklies are *HX* (Homo Xtra) and *HX for Her* (www.hx.com) and *Next* (www.nextmagazine.net), which are available in gay bars, clubs, hotels and cafés. They include listings of bars, dance clubs, sex clubs, restaurants and cultural events. Good newspapers are the *LGNY* (Lesbian and Gay New York), though it's a lot more serious and covers political issues, and *The Blade*.

ACCOMMODATION

Turn to pages 228–229 for some Hotel Tips and booking info. Prices are per room.

CHELSEA PINES INN
Chelsea
✉ 317 West 14th Street between 8th and 9th Avenues
☎ 212-929 1023
🖰 www.chelseapinesinn.org
🚗 Subway A, C East to 14th Street; L to 8th Avenue
$ Rooms $169–209 including breakfast

In an excellent location in Chelsea on the border with the Village this hotel, which is one of the best gay hotels in the city, has recently been given a facelift, and now each room is named after a film star. Yes, there is a Judy Garland. In the morning, guests wake to the aroma of home-made bread and doughnuts. Open to both men and women. You need to book at least six to eight weeks in advance.

Chelsea Savoy Hotel, West 23rd Street

CHELSEA SAVOY HOTEL
Chelsea
- ✉ 204 West 23rd Street
- ☎ 212-929 9353
- ⌁ www.chelseasavoynyc.com
- 🚗 Subway 1, 9, 3 to 23rd Street
- $ Rooms $139-219

This hotel is in a superb location, being close to the Theater District, Financial District, great restaurants, museums and galleries, and SoHo just down the road. The rooms are a good size for NY with all essential amenities such as bathroom and television. Great value too.

COLONIAL HOUSE INN
Chelsea
- ✉ 318 West 22nd Street between 8th and 9th Avenues
- ☎ 212-243 9669
- ⌁ www.colonialhouseinn.com
- 🚗 Subway C east to 23rd Street
- $ Rooms $85-150

A beautiful place to stay and also spotlessly clean. The economy rooms are tiny, but all have cable TV, air con, phone and daily maid service, and smoking is allowed in rooms. The price includes breakfast, which is eaten in the Life Gallery where there are works by gay and lesbian artists. Book as early as you can because this place gets packed with groups coming into town for drag conventions and so on. It's especially popular in the summer months because of its roof deck with a clothing-optional area. The hotel has a 24-hour doorman. Mostly for gay men.

EDISON HOTEL
Theater District
- ✉ 228 West 47th Street between Broadway and 8th Avenue
- ☎ 212-840 5000
- ⌁ www.edisonhotelnyc.com
- 🚗 Subway N, R to 49th Street
- $ Rooms $170, suites from $210

One of New York's great hotel bargains. The Art Deco Edison's 700 rooms have been totally refurbished, and it has a new coffee shop, the Café Edison, considered to be the best place to spot lunching theatre luminaries.

HOTEL WOLCOTT
Midtown
- ✉ 4 West 31st Street between 5th Avenue and Broadway
- ☎ 212-268 2900
- ⌁ www.wolcott.com
- 🚗 Subway N, R to 28th Street
- $ Rooms $160-180

Well, darling, it's location, location, location, for this 300-room hotel. Just three blocks down from 5th Avenue and the Empire State Building, this is a favourite with the serious tourist and budget-minded business traveller. Complimentary coffee, tea and muffins served in the lobby each morning. Call in advance to find out the bargain seasonal, weekend and holiday rates on offer.

INCENTRA VILLAGE HOUSE
West Village
- ✉ 32 8th Avenue between West 12th and Jane Streets
- ☎ 212-206 0007
- ⌁ www.incentravillage.com
- 🚗 Subway A, C east to 14th Street; L to 8th Avenue
- $ Rooms $169-199

A moderately priced guesthouse in two red-brick townhouses from the 1840s (that's old by American standards!). The 12 suites all have kitchens, phones and private bathrooms and some can even accommodate groups of four or five. All the rooms are well decorated with different themes. The Bishop Room is a lovely split-level suite, the Garden Room has a private garden filled with flowers and the Maine Room has a four-poster bed. All rooms are smoker-friendly. A 1939 Steinway piano stands in the parlour and anyone who can is allowed to play.

THE INN AT IRVING PLACE
Gramercy Park
- ✉ 56 Irving Place between 17th and 18th Streets
- ☎ 212-533 4600/ 800-685 1447
- ⌁ www.innatirving.com
- 🚗 Subway L, N, R, 4, 5, 6 to 14th Street/ Union Square
- $ Rooms $325-495

The building is filled with exquisite antique furniture and elegant decor. All 12 rooms have queen-size beds and come with private facilities; some even have study

---

TOP HOTELS

Best location: Hotel Wolcott, Midtown

Best economy: Colonial House Inn, Chelsea

Best luxury: The Inn At Irving Place, Gramercy Park

areas. There is a 24-hour concierge, plus laptops and fax on request, laundry and dry-cleaning, video rentals, a gym within walking distance and 24-hour massage.

THE ROYALTON
Theater District
- ✉ 44 West 44th Street between 5th and 6th Avenues
- ☎ 212-869 4400/ 800 606 6090
- 🖱 www.royaltonhotel.com
- 🚇 Subway 4, 5, 6 to 42nd Street; 7 to 5th Avenue
- $ Rooms $250–500

Ian Schrager's beautiful hotel, designed by Philippe Starck, is now considered to be the best address for gays and lesbians into the power thing. A chic tone is set by the lively fashion and publishing crowd that frequents the lobby bar and restaurant. The modern rooms all have CD players, VCR, mini bar and two phone lines.

CLUBS & LOUNGES FOR HIM

CHELSEA
Barracuda: 275 West 22nd Street between 7th and 8th Avenues. Tel 212-645 8613. Subway C, E, 1, 9 to 23rd Street.
This club attracts a mellow mix of people. Head to the rear lounge, which has a better atmosphere than the dingy front bar and a decent pool table. Monday night is the hilarious Star Search, where drag queens battle it out between each other to reign supreme. Open 4pm–4am every day and a popular two-for-one happy hour 4–9pm during the week.

Centro-Fly: 45 West 21st Street between 5th and 6th Avenues. Tel 212-627 7770, www.centro-fly.com. Subway N, R, F to 23rd Street.
It costs $20–25 just to get in, but boy is it worth it. This is one of the best clubs in the city in terms of music, atmosphere and delicious clientele. GBH on Friday nights is the big one, which has won numerous awards and has been running for four years. Guest DJs have included all the greats including Fatboy Slim, LTJ Bukem and Armand Van Helden. Opens 10pm daily and offers an open bar 3–4am.

Discothèque: 17 West 19th Street between 5th and 6th Avenues. Tel 212-352 9999. Subway F, V, N, R to 23rd Street.
Revamped in 2004, this smallish club attracts up to 400 people on any given

TOP FIVE CLUBS & LOUNGES FOR HIM
g Lounge: Chelsea, below
Roxy: Chelsea, page 222
The Monster: Greenwich Village, page 223
B Bar & Grill: East Village, page 222
The Cock: East Village, page 222

night. Friday nights feature house music and hard bass, giving scantily clad go-go dancers something to bounce about. Saturday nights are for the hip-hop/R&B crowd. The party tends to start well after 1am when club-hoppers begin to make their rounds. Open Thursday to Sunday 10pm–4pm.

Eagle: 554 West 28th Street between 10th and 11th Avenues. Tel 646-473 1866, www.eaglenyc.com. Subway C, E to 23rd Street.
No-expense-spared renovation of the original Eagle, the new incarnation is a spacious watering hole filled with congenial leather-clad S&M New Yorkers. Open Monday to Saturday 10pm–4am, Sunday 5pm–4am.

El Flamingo: 547 West 21st Street between 10th and 11th Avenues. Tel 646-473 1866. Subway C, E to 23rd Street.
If your thing is cross-dressing performers lip-synching along to disco numbers, then The Donkey Show: A Midsummer Night's Disco is for you. It costs $25–30 to get in and you can also dance your ass off until the wee small hours after the show. Open Wednesday to Saturday 10pm–4am. Also known for its hot Latin nights.

g Lounge: 223 West 19th Street between 7th and 8th Avenues. Tel 212-929 1085, www.glounge.com. Subway C, E to 23rd Street; 1, 9 to 18th Street.
A super-popular, sophisticated night spot for gorgeous hunks to see and be seen. Its centrepiece is its oval bar, which the sexy clientele prop up when they're not shimmying to house music. It gets packed later on when the queues build up outside. Open nightly 4pm–4am. Saturday nights are free.

Heaven: 579 6th Avenue between 16th and 17th Streets. Tel 212-243 6100. Subway 1, 2, 3, 9, F to 14th Street; L to 6th Avenue.
Decorated with wall-to-wall white paint

and mirrors, this Chelsea playground offers a divinely gay twist to Dante's vision of the seven layers of hell. A sparkling spectacle that simply must be seen and enjoyed during a trip to NY. Open nightly 5pm–4am. Happy hour 5–7pm.

Kurfew: Tel 212-533 1222, www.kurfew.com. Subway A, C, E, F to 34th Street.
America's youngest all-gay party, with big nights out at different gay clubs around town. Sunday night college fest at Avalon, 47 West 20th Street (212-807 7780) is unmissable. Also has events at SBNY (see SNBY below). Eight beers for $10 anyone?

Rawhide: 212 8th Avenue at 20th Street. Tel 212-242 9332. Subway C, E to 23rd Street.
A darkly lit, leather and Levi's bar in the heart of Chelsea. A great place to start a New York visit, where you can meet friendly down-to-earth locals who will let you in on all the news of what is going on that week in the Big Apple. Famous for its pool tables and beer specials.

Roxy: 515 West 18th Street between 10th and 11th Avenues. Tel 212-645 5157, www.roxynyc.com. Subway A, C east to 14th Street; L to 8th Avenue.
Roxy claims to have 'the only TRULY gay Saturday night of dancing' and it's easy to see why; this mega-popular dance party in a warehouse is designed for maximum Chelsea boy pick-up potential – it even features a sunken dance floor. Go on Friday and Saturday nights for an evening of gorgeous guys, sexy drag queens and brilliant sounds. Or go on Wednesday, put on your blades and have a blast at the roller disco. Open Wednesday 8pm–2am, Friday to Saturday 11pm–4am.

SBNY: 50 West 17th Street between 5th and 6th Avenues. Tel 212-691 0073, www.splashbar.com. Subway L, N, R, W, 4, 5, 6 to 14th Street/Union Square.
Formerly known as Splash, this a popular place to hang out on any night of the week,

B Bar and Grill, East 4th Street

and not just because the handsome bartenders are shirtless. It's done out South Beach style, with a huge dance floor emporium, a downstairs bar for cruising and an adult store in the basement. It's popular with preppy men and those who enjoy attention. Open Sunday to Thursday 4pm–4am, Friday and Saturday 4pm–6am.

EAST VILLAGE

B Bar & Grill: 40 East 4th Street between Lafayette Street and the Bowery. Tel 212-475 2220, www.bbarandgrill.com. Subway B, D, F, Q to Broadway/Lafayette Street; 6 to Bleecker Street.
This is a super-trendy lounge filled with models and gorgeous people. Madonna has been known to drop in. Beige, the weekly A-list gay party, is the place to be on Tuesday night, and it's free. Open Monday 11.30am–1.30am, Tuesday to Friday 11.30am–3am, Saturday and Sunday 10.30am–3am.

The Cock: 29 2nd Avenue at 2nd Street. No phone. Subway F, V to Second/Lower East Side.
'Rock out with your cock out' – their mantra says it all really. The Cock has one of the wildest crowds in the city and has a penchant for irony-laced depravity. The club attracts pretty boys, drag queens, gay celebrities and their friends, and then mixes in lots of alcohol and some serious cruising. Drinks are cheap though there is a cover charge of $5–10. Cash only. Open nightly 9pm–4am.

Dick's Bar: 192 2nd Avenue at 12th Street. Tel 212-475 2071. Subway L to 3rd Avenue. No-frills, theme-free East Village gay bar without the usual cruise-or-die desperation. Dick's is a friendly place that features cheap drinks and a jukebox playing alternative rock and 1970s' music, as well as a disco ball and the occasional pornographic movie. Cash only. Open daily 2pm–4am.

BRIT TIP
★ Check out Travel Gayzette's New
★ York City guide for stores/gyms,
★ accommodation and nightlife at
★ www.travelgayzette.com/newyork.htm.

FLATIRON DISTRICT

Estate@Limelight: 660 6th Avenue at 20th Street. Tel 212-807 7780. Subway F to 23rd Street.
This club has recently undergone a major renovation and holds gay nights on Fridays and Sundays.

GREENWICH VILLAGE

Crazy Nanny's: 21 7th Avenue at Leroy Street. Tel 212-366 6312. Subway 1, 9 to Houston Street.
Great local place to hang out, with a pool table, good juke box and upstairs dance floor. There's a daily happy hour and karaoke on certain nights.

The Monster: 80 Grove Street at Sheridan Square. Tel 212-924 3558, www.manhattanmonster.com. Subway 1, 2, 3, 9 to Christopher Street/Sheridan Square.
Probably the most popular bar in Greenwich Village. Right on Sheridan Square across from the infamous Stonewall. Happy piano bar draws older crowd: downstairs dance floor draws younger hotties. There is a cover charge at weekends, probably the only club with cover in the Village. Open 4pm–4am, party starts at 10pm.

MIDTOWN EAST

Red: 305 East 53rd Street between 1st and 2nd Avenues. Tel 212-688 1294. Subway E, V to Lexington Avenue/53rd Street.
The best time to get dolled up and hit this NY hot spot is Thursday night, which is an anything-goes party that has the added bonus of being free. Inside, you'll be exposed to strippers, rub shoulders with porn stars and be dazzled by lap-dancing go-go boys. The Saturday special is Sinfest, with college-boy videos and other funky stuff, and then Papi Party on Sunday.

MIDTOWN WEST

Chase: 255 West 55th Street between 7th and 8th Avenues. Tel 212-333 3400. Subway B, D, E to 7th Avenue; N, R, Q to 57th Street.
Chase is a sleek, chic, multi-level gay bar in a neighbourhood with a growing gay population. Located 30 blocks north of Chelsea, it manages to avoid much of that area's attitude. Yet, it still provides everything one has come to expect from a gay bar, including attractive bartenders who are clearly not hired for their drinks-making skills. Friday night date crowd. Looking for love? The crowd is diverse enough for there to be someone for almost everyone.

Edelweiss: 137 7th Avenue (south) near 10th Street. Tel 212-929 5155, www.clubedelweiss.com. Subway C, E to 50th Street.
A multi-level dance club for trannies, cross-dressers and their fans.

La Nueva Escuelita: 301 West 39th Street at 8th Avenue. Tel 212-631 0588. Subway A, C east to 42nd Street.
A fantastic latino club famed for its fabulous shows and nights of salsa, merengue and Latin-style drag shows. No shows on Thursday nights, but 2.30am Fridays ($5), 2am Saturdays ($20) and 9pm and 1.30am Sundays ($10).

Xth Avenue Lounge: 642 10th Avenue at 45th Street. Tel 212-245 9088. Subway A, C east to 42nd Street.
Open daily with a happy hour 4–8pm. There is a light menu in the back room, and frozen drinks. Not exclusively for gays.

UPPER EAST SIDE

Pegasus Bar: 119 East 60th Street between Park and Lexington Avenues. Tel 212-888 4702, www.pegasusnyc.com. Subway 4, 5, 6 to 59th Street; N, R to Lexington Avenue.
Gentlemen's piano bar featuring karaoke and cabaret shows on various rotating nights of the week. Friday and Saturday focus on entertainment for Asian gays. It's also the time of the week when the groovy back room opens up to reveal plastic-wrapped, leopard-print benches and intimate lighting. Happy hour 4–8pm every day and a complimentary brunch is served at 1pm on Sundays.

WEST VILLAGE

Dugout: 185 Christopher Street between Washington and West Streets. Tel 212-242 9113, www.thedugoutny.net. Subway L to 6th Avenue.
A great neighbourhood bar and club especially popular for its Sunday afternoon beer busts where 16oz costs just $3. Attracts African-American guys and sometimes an older crowd.

Heaven

Lips: 2 Bank Street at Greenwich Avenue. Tel 212-675 7710. Subway 1, 2, 3, 9 to 14th Street.
This buzzy place is the Hard Rock Café of drag, with supper and shows from 5.30pm until midnight weeknights and until 2am on Friday and Saturday. The Bitchy Bingo Show on Wednesdays – free, open from 8pm – sees Sherry Vine and Yvon Lame preside over the bitchiest bingo game in the world. On Tuesday you can take part in some drag karaoke, and on Sundays a riotous brunch.

HARLEM
Club Chaz: 454 West 128th Street, between Amsterdam Avenue and Convent Avenue. Tel 212-749 8055. Subway 1, 9 at 125th Street.
If you love Latin music, then pop in here on a Friday night to have yourself a sizzling time. If you're more of a hip-hop and house guy, drop in to Industry on a Tuesday. It's $3 before 12pm and $10 after. Open until 5am.

CLUBS & LOUNGES FOR HER

CHELSEA
2i's: 248 West 14th Street between 7th and 8th Avenues. Tel: 212-807 1775. Subway A, C, E to 14th Street; L to 8th Avenue.
The ultra-cool Thursday evening party, G Spot, has weekly themes and music that includes hip-hop, R&B, reggae and house. From 7.30–9pm there are performances by comedians and spoken-word artists while it's happy hour behind the bar. Open Thursday to Saturday 10.30pm–4am.

Heaven: 579 6th Avenue between 16th and 17th Streets. Tel 212-243 6100. Subway 1, 2, 3, 9, F to 14th Street; L to 6th Avenue.
Decorated with wall-to-wall white paint and mirrors, this three-storey club is a sparkling spectacle that simply must be seen and enjoyed during a trip to NY. The long-running Julie's Salsa and Merengue Dance Party comes here for its Wednesday night party, so Latin music lovers really will be in heaven! On Friday night it's the popular Kaleidoscope Party, a massive Girl Club Productions extravaganza with salsa and merengue on two floors. Wet T-shirt contests also feature. Happy hour 5–7pm. Open nightly 5pm–4am.

EAST VILLAGE
Girls Room: 210 Rivington Street between Ridge and Pitt Streets. Tel 212 995 8684.

TOP FIVE CLUBS & LOUNGES FOR HER
Heaven: Chelsea, above
Bluestockings: Lower East Side, below
Cubby Hole: West Village, page 225
Starlight: East Village, below
Chueca: Queens, page 225

A trendy hipster girl club, minus the attitude. Open 7am–4am; happy hour 7–9pm. Open mike on Monday; Thursday is Flirt, networking for female artists; Saturday is Sex for the City Girl. Cosmo/martini specials and dress to impress.

The Slide: 356 Bowery between E 4th and Great Jones Streets. Tel 212-420 8885.
Supertrashy underground dive bar, with go-gos and flesh every night. Connected to The Marquee cabaret house and Marion's Restaurant. Happy hour 5–9pm. First Friday night of the month is Clit Club ladies' night. Open 5pm–4am every night.

Starlight: 167 Avenue A between 10th and 11th Streets. Tel 212-475 2172, www.starlightbarlounge.com. Subway L to 1st Avenue.
A fabulous bar and lounge that has been voted the best gay bar in New York. Starlette, ladies night on Sunday evening, is a popular party with a cool vibe that reflects its trendy East Village location. Open Sunday to Thursday 6pm–3am, Friday and Saturday 6pm–4am.

LOWER EAST SIDE
Bluestockings: 172 Allen Street between Rivington and Stanton Streets. Tel 212-777 6028, www.bluestockings.com. Subway F, V to Lower East Side/2nd Avenue.
A great neighbourhood joint that gives women the opportunity to showcase their talents at open-mike sessions.

MIDTOWN WEST
La Nueva Escuelita: 301 West 39th Street at 8th Avenue. Tel 212-631 0588. Subway A, C east to 42nd Street
Fever on Friday night is a classic venue for a hot night out. Mostly filled with Latin women from the über-feminine to the ultra-butch, there are go-go dancers galore on which to feast the eyes, a drag show at 2am and a lap-dancing lounge.

QUEENS

Chueca: 69–04 Woodside Avenue, Woodside. Tel 718 424 1171, www.chuecabar.com.
A great Latin girl bar and restaurant, famous for gorgeous shot girls. Happy hour 6–8pm Wednesday to Sunday. In December, for example,, there was Girlplay on Wednesdays, Temptation on Thursdays, Hype on Fridays, Adrenaline on Saturdays and Insomnia on Sundays! $10 cover on Saturday night.

THEATER DISTRICT

Cache: 221 West 46th Street between Broadway and 8th Avenue. Tel 212-539 3982. Subway S, 1, 2, 3, 9, 7 to 42nd Street/Times Square; N, Q, R, W to 42nd Street.
Caché, a Girls Club Productions party for women of 23 and over, on Saturday night is definitely a night to go glamorous and enjoy the classics, R&B and pop sounds in an elegant lounge. $10 cover.

WEST VILLAGE

Cubby Hole: 281 West 12th Street between West 4th and West 12th Streets. Tel 212-243 9041. Subway 1, 2, 3, 9 to 14th Street.
It looks as though the owners of this lesbian bar have raided a New Orleans thrift store a few days after Mardi Gras: hundreds of illuminated plastic blowfish, goldfish and Chinese lanterns dangle from the ceiling. Old-timers straggle in long before sunset for half-price drinks (until 7pm Monday to Saturday); after 9pm, younger gals (and a fair number of guys) take centre stage. There's no karaoke here any more, but it almost doesn't matter. Like a pianoless piano bar, Cubby Hole is packed full of regulars who like to belt out tunes along with the jukebox.

Henrietta Hudson's: 438 Hudson Street at Morton Street. Tel 212-924 3347, www.henriettahudson.com. Subway 1, 9 to Houston Street.
A no-nonsense party bar for rocker girls and brainy dykes looking to kick back without pretence. Even when there's no specific party, gals come from far and wide to hang out at this great watering hole. Lush on Sunday is a popular night, with Latin sounds from DJ Culi attracting an exotic crowd. Mamacita is a popular Thursday night dance with R&B, hip-hop and Latin music. If you're into go-go girls, the Back Room Booty Friday night extravaganza is the party for you – and hordes of others, too!

> ### TOP RESTAURANTS FOR GAY PEOPLE
>
> **Primitivo:** Chelsea, page 226
>
> **Florent:** West Village, page 226
>
> **Lips:** West Village, page 227
>
> **Townhouse Restaurant:** Midtown East, page 226

RESTAURANTS

CHELSEA

Better Burger: 178 8th Avenue and 19th Street. Tel 212-989 6688, www.betterburgernyc.com. Subway C, E to 23rd Street.
Low-fat, health-conscience, 100 per cent organic, antibiotic- and hormone-free fare – ostrich, turkey, chicken, soy and vegetarian burgers (and the classic beef) plus other options.

Big Cup: 228 8th Avenue at 22nd Street. Tel 212-206 0059, www.bigcupcoffee.com.
An as-gay-as-it-gets coffee house that is a great place to hang out on a rainy day. It has a local vibe, and even has the movie times for the local cinema chalked on a blackboard so that you won't miss your film.

Eighteenth and 8th: 159 8th Avenue at 18th Street. Tel 212-242 5000.
The gay restaurant of the gay district of New York, it serves healthy American food. But be prepared for a long wait outside as it's tiny inside.

Empire Diner: 210 10th Avenue at 22nd Street. Tel 212-243 2736.
This humble diner has made appearances in countless commercials and movies. It's very low key and a great pit stop for a burger at the end of a heavy night. You'll be rubbing shoulders with all sorts of people, from drag queens to artists in need of a late night snack (page 184).

Lola: 30 West 22nd Street between 5th and 6th Avenues. Tel 212-675 6700.
Famous for its American cuisine with Caribbean and Asian influences, it's packed on Sunday for gospel brunches.

Pad Thai: 114 8th Avenue at 16th Street. Tel 212-691 6226.
Elegant, mellow and seductive noodle lounge with above-average Thai fare.

Primitivo: 202 West 14th Street. Tel 212-255 2060, www.primitivorestaurant.com. Modern authentic Italian fare with the best home-made pasta around, plus seafood, salad and steak. Open 11.30am–11pm daily.

Sapa: 43 West 24th Street between Broadway and 6th Avenue. Tel 212-929 1800, www.sapanyc.com. Gorgeous French-Vietnamese restaurant with a gay lounge night and complimentary cocktails 6–7pm every Sunday.

EAST VILLAGE

Astor Restaurant and Lounge: 316 Bowery at Bleecker Street. Tel 212-253 8644. This Moroccan-style lounge plays host to a gay party on Wednesdays, as well as a French/Mediterranean restaurant.

B Bar & Grill: 40 East 4th Street between Lafayette Street and Bowery. Tel 212-475 2220, www.bbarandgrill.com. Home to Beige on a Tuesday night, this gorgeous bistro serves excellent food.

Benny's Burritos: 93 Avenue, near 6th Street. Tel 212-254 2054, www.harrysburritos.com. This establishment looks as though it has survived from the 1960s: lava lamps, pink walls and Formica tables make up the decor. Serves super-filling burritos and enchiladas, but watch out for the lethal margaritas. (You'll find a larger and more crowded Benny's at 113 Greenwich Ave in the West Village.)

Lucien: 14 1st Avenue at 1st Street. Tel 212-260 6481, www.luciennyc.com. Always packed, this tiny French bistro serves delicious food and is particularly known for its Sunday brunch.

Marion's Continental: 354 Bowery between 4th and Great Jones Streets. Tel 212-475 7621, www.marionsnyc.com. Great, eclectic cuisine and fun, boisterous atmosphere. Now with an XXX Cocktail menu, including concoctions called the Hard Nuts and the Busted Cherry.

Pangea: 178 2nd Avenue between 11th and 12th Streets. Tel 212-995 0900. Known for its wonderful home-made pastas and Mediterranean cuisine.

Yaffa Café: 97 St Marks Place at 1st Avenue. Tel. 212-674 9302, www.yaffacafe.com. This 24-hour hipster hangout serves up hummus, sandwiches, pasta and chicken entrées (page 161). Very inexpensive and with a large garden – and they hand out free condoms to the clientele!

MIDTOWN EAST

Arriba Arriba!: 762 9th Avenue at 51st Street. Tel 212 489 0810. Neighbourhood queens flock to this Mexican-style joint.

Comfort Diner: 214 East 45th Street between 2nd and 3rd Avenues. Tel 212-867 4555. Authentic and delicious American cuisine served in a 1950s-style diner setting with a friendly atmosphere (page 184).

Ida Mae Kitchen-n-Lounge: 111 West 38th Street at Broadway. Tel 212-704 0038, www.idamae.com. Delicious culinary fusion of down-home Southern fare with French influences.

Juice Generation: 644 9th Avenue at 45th Street. Tel. 212-541 5600, www.juicegeneration.com. Delicious fresh juices, smoothies, protein shakes and bakery products served seven days a week.

Maracas: 317 East 53rd Street at 2nd Avenue. Tel 212-593 6600, www.maracasnyc.com. Fiesta time at new Mexican bar and grill from the creators of Lips. Frozen margaritas, explosive visuals, electric ambience. Champagne brunch on Sunday.

Spanky's BBQ: 127 West 43rd Street. Tel 212-575 5848, www.spankysnyc.com. As Spanky's so succinctly puts it: 'Get porked before the show!'

Townhouse Restaurant: 206 East 58th Street between 2nd and 3rd Avenues. Tel 212-826 6241, www.townhouseny.com. This is owned by the same people as The Townhouse Bar, one of the oldest, most upscale and gay-safe haunts – especially among the more mature crowd. It serves delicious food at reasonable prices.

Lips

NOLITA, SOHO AND TRIBECA

Amici Miei: 475 West Broadway at Houston Street. Tel 212-533 1933.
A chic Italian restaurant open for lunch and dinner with outdoor seating.

Basset Café: 123 West Broadway at Duane Street. Tel 212-349 1827.
Tuck into a delicious salad or sandwich, or treat yourself to the home-made cakes at this light and airy haven. Smoking permitted here.

Tenement: 157 Ludlow Street at Rivington Street. Tel 212-598 2130.
Refurbished from a brothel to a parlour, Tenement pays homage to old New York with fine eclectic American fare.

The Pink Pony: 178 Ludow Street at Stanton Street. Tel 212-253 1922.
Young, laid-back, unpretentious crowd enjoying inexpensive comfort food.

THEATER DISTRICT

Coffee Pot: 350 West 49th Street at 9th Avenue. Tel 212-265 3566.
Nice little coffee bar with live music and tarot card readings. Open seven days a week until 11pm.

Mangia East Devi: 800 9th Avenue at 53rd Street. Tel 212-956 3976.
An excellent, popular Italian in the middle of Midtown's gay district.

Revolution: 611 9th Avenue between 43rd and 44th Streets. Tel 212-489 8451.
A club-like restaurant with great food and music videos. It has a DJ every night, a youngish crowd and American menus.

Vintage: 753 9th Avenue at 51st Street. Tel 212-581 4655.
A hip bar/restaurant that serves dinner till midnight and cocktails till 4am.

WEST VILLAGE

Caffe Dell'Artista: 46 Greenwich Avenue between 6th and 7th Avenues. Tel 212-645 4431.
A European-style café serving simple, light meals and desserts.

Cowgirl: 519 Hudson Street at West 10th Street. Tel 212-633 1133, www.cowgirlnyc.com.
This isn't just great for men and women who feel at home surrounded by cowgirl memorabilia, but is also frequented by families. It serves cheap American food – fried onion loaf, huge spare ribs and chicken-fried steak – and is also known for its margaritas. It has a big lesbian following and the people-watching outside the restaurant in summer is a treat.

Florent: 69 Gansevoort Street at Washington Street. Tel 212-989 5779, www.restaurantflorent.com.
Good French food served 24 hours a day at weekends and until 5am weekdays. Busy after the clubs close (page 166).

Garage Restaurant: 99 7th Avenue South at Christopher Street. Tel 212-645 0600, www.garagerest.com.
Serves American cuisine including steaks and a raw bar, with live jazz nightly and a friendly crowd (page 163).

La Ripaille: 605 Hudson Street at West 12th Street. Tel 212-255 4406.
Authentic French country dining since 1980. A small, cosy and romantic restaurant with excellent bistro food. Proudly serving the gay community for more than 20 years.

Lips: 2 Bank Street at Greenwich Avenue. Tel 212-675 7710, www.lipsnyc.com.
Italian menu with dishes named after popular queens; all the waitresses are in drag and plenty of entertainment is provided (page 224).

Nadine's: 99 Bank Street at Greenwich Street. Tel 212-924 3165.
Eclectic and good-value food in a funky but glamorous setting.

Rubyfruit Bar and Grill: 531 Hudson Street at Charles Street. Tel 212-929 3343.
Dedicated lesbian restaurant and bar. Serves good eclectic food both downstairs and in the fun bar upstairs. Live music nightly.

Sacred Chow: Sullivan Street between Bleecker and West 3rd Streets. Tel 212-337 0863, www.sacredchow.com.
Healthy vegan food shop and café.

Stonewall Bistro: 113 7th Avenue at Christopher Street. Tel 917 661 1335.
An elegant and cosy dining experience from the creators of the famous Stonewall; continental cuisine with a French flair. Cabaret every night; dinner and drink specials all week. Thursday networking night.

Sushi Samba: 87 7th Avenue at Barrow Street. Tel 212-691 7885, www.sushisamba.com.
This establishment serves up excellent sushi, ceviches, tiraditos and pratos.

CHAPTER 11

Where to Stay

The beauty of a city as diverse and cosmopolitan as New York is that you can find pretty much any kind of accommodation that you desire. From über-romantic suites in super swish hotels to quirky little downtown boutique retreats, you're guaranteed to find something that meets your taste and budget.

By the end of 2007, there will be more than 75,000 hotel rooms in Manhattan, but less than half of them belong to national or international chains, so the Big Apple is bursting with hotels of character and charm that you're unlikely to find anywhere else.

You may be surprised at the size of some of the rooms in the city, which are on the small side, but remember that Manhattan is a small island where space is at a premium. What rooms lack in size they usually make up for in decor and views; many of the high-rise hotels such as the Four Seasons offer breathtaking panoramic vistas.

If you're visiting the city for the first time, be sure to do some research before you book so that you can decide which area you would like to be based in. This will save you much time and money on getting around. For example, if your prime reason for visiting the city is for theatres and shopping, you're going to want to be staying in Midtown where everything is on your doorstep. It may be that if you intend to stay for a week it would work out best to stay at two hotels – one in Lower Manhattan and one in Midtown, helping you save on travelling time and expensive cab fares.

The most upmarket hotels have always been clustered on the east side of Manhattan from Midtown up to 96th Street. However, in recent years first-class hotels have been popping up all over the place and there are now several in SoHo, Greenwich Village and the Financial District. The best deals tend to be around Herald Square and on the Upper West Side, but if you go for these options check you won't be spending more than you need to on transport. The average rate for a room that can accommodate two people is $200 a night – so if you get something for less (and there are plenty of ways to do this), you will be doing well.

★ ★ ★ ★ **BRIT TIP** ★ ★ ★ ★
★
★
★ If you are planning to take in the ★
★ sights of Lower Manhattan, ★
★ Chinatown, Lower East Side, SoHo ★
★ and the Village, choose a downtown ★
★ hotel. It'll save you loads of time on ★
★ travel and money on cab fares. ★
★ ★

HOTEL TIPS

➡ Demand for hotel rooms at peak times of the year is high, so your best bet for both ensuring a bed and getting the best price is to go in the off-peak times of January to March and July and August.

➡ Most hotels reduce their rates at weekends – including some of the poshest. If you're staying for more than a weekend, negotiate the best rate you can for the rest of your time or switch to a cheaper hotel.

➡ If noise is a particular problem for you, bear in mind that hotels downtown and uptown tend to be quieter than those in Midtown. Also, addresses on streets tend to be quieter than those on avenues, except those nearer the river.

➡ For longer stays, try to choose a hotel room with a kitchenette, then you won't have to eat out all the time.

➡ Smaller hotels tend not to book large groups, so they often have rooms available even during peak periods.

➡ When booking your room, check there isn't going to be a major convention on at the same time. If there is, ask to be put on a different floor.

➡ Ask for a corner room– they are usually bigger and have more windows and, therefore, more light than other rooms and don't always cost more.

➡ Renovation work is often going on in New York hotels so, when making a reservation, ask if any is being done there and, if it is, ask for a room as far away as possible from the work.

➡ The average rate for a hotel room was $212 in 2005.

Below is the Brit's Guide pick of the best hotels in Manhattan, priced by room per night, covering all price brackets. They range from romantic hideaways to the latest hip openings to grand hotels that have been on the map for nearly a century.

$	Less than $100
$$	$100–200
$$$	$200–300
$$$$	$300–400
$$$$$	$400 and over

LANDMARK HOTELS

These hotels aren't simply hotels, they are institutions. Brimming with history, which most hotel staff will be only to willing to tell you about, these grand dames of the New York hotel scene are in a class of their own, and we're not just talking about the high prices.

MIDTOWN EAST

WALDORF ASTORIA $$$–$$$$$

✉ 301 Park Avenue at 50th Street
☎ 212-355 3000
    Fax 212-872 7272
🖰 www.waldorfastoria.com/www.hilton.com
🚇 Subway 6 to 51st Street

A colossus of a hotel in more than one sense, it's an art deco marvel with a wonderful history and has been designated a New York City landmark since 1993. Now is a great time to visit as it's just had a $50 million makeover, which includes a $5.5 million revamp of Peacock Alley, the hotel's top restaurant headed by chef Cedric Tovar.

It all started in 1893 when millionaire William Waldorf Astor opened the 13-storey Waldorf Hotel at 33rd Street. It was the embodiment of Astor's vision of a grand hotel and came with two innovations – electricity throughout and private bathrooms in every guest chamber – and immediately became the place to go for the upper classes. Four years later the Waldorf was joined by the 17-storey Astoria Hotel, built next door by Waldorf Astor's cousin, John Jacob Astor IV. The corridor between

the two became an enduring symbol of the combined Waldorf and Astoria Hotels.

In 1929 it closed, and on its original site now stands another icon of the New York skyline, the Empire State Building. In the meantime, the Waldorf Astoria was rebuilt in Midtown Manhattan, opening its doors in 1931 and immediately dubbed New York's first skyscraper hotel. It rose 42 storeys high, stretched from Park Avenue to Lexington Avenue and contained an astonishing 2,200 rooms. It was such an amazing event, opening as it did in the middle of the Depression, that President Herbert Hoover broadcast a message of congratulations. And ever since, the Waldorf Astoria has had a long association with presidents of countries and corporations.

The art deco aspects of the hotel were brought back into view during a restoration in the 1980s when architects found a huge cache of long-lost treasures, including a magnificent 148,000-piece mosaic depicting the Wheel of Life, by French artist Louis Regal, in the Park Avenue lobby, 13 allegorical murals by the same artist and ornate mouldings on the ceilings. The legendary Starlight Roof nightclub with its retractable roof, which had epitomised glamour and sophistication in the 1930s and 1940s, was restored during the same period.

Another $60-million upgrade in 1998 saw the Park Avenue Cocktail Terrace and Sir Harry's Bar being restored to their full art deco glory. Oscar's, named after the Waldorf Astoria's famous style-setting maître d' Oscar Tschirky, was completely redesigned by Adam Tihany, the hottest restaurant designer in town.

Of course, if you plan to stay here, you'll want to know about the service – excellent – and the standard of the rooms – huge, beautifully decorated and with marble-encased ensuite bathrooms. What more could you ask for?

WALDORF TOWERS $$$$$

✉ 100 East 50th Street
☎ 212-355 3100
  Fax 212-872 7272
🖰 www.waldorf-towers.com/www.hilton.com
🚗 Subway 6 to 51st Street

A boutique hotel occupying the 28th to the 42nd floors of the Waldorf Astoria, this is one of the most exclusive addresses in New York, filled as it is with presidents of countries and global corporations. Thanks to the hotel's security arrangements (it has its own private car parking facilities underground), this is the place where treaties and mergers have been negotiated and signed, momentous peace initiatives have begun and unforgettable music has been made.

The hotel has its own dedicated entrance, lobby, concierge desk, reception and private lifts operated by 'white-gloved' attendants. Guests have included the Duke and Duchess of Windsor, who maintained their New York residence here, Jack and Jackie Kennedy, Frank Sinatra and Cole Porter, who wrote many of his most famous compositions in a room here.

The rooms are not so much rooms or suites, but rather more like apartments. Many come with dining rooms, full kitchens and maids' quarters. Some even have televisions in their bathrooms! Four-footed guests are greeted with a biscuit.

UPPER EAST SIDE

HOTEL CARLYLE $$$$–$$$$$

✉ 35 East 76th Street between Madison and Park Avenues
☎ 212-744 1600
  Fax 212-717 4682
🖰 www.rosewoodhotels.com, www.thecarlyle.com
🚗 Subway 6 to 77th Street

Established in the 1930s, the Carlyle is a timeless classic, patronised by a wide range

The Carlyle

of people from world leaders and top businessmen to It girls and leading lights in entertainment and the arts. Brilliantly positioned on Madison Avenue, it is a true New York landmark. The 180 apartment-style rooms and suites are elegant and very plush – some even have grand pianos and all have whirlpools in the bathrooms. In fact it feels as though you're staying in your elegant Upper East Side pied-à-terre rather than renting a hotel room. If you really want to push the boat out, there's a new, breathtaking Royal Suite on the 22nd floor. It's famous for its impeccable and discreet service but also for its live music in Cafe Carlyle where Woody Allen still plays jazz on Monday nights (page 230).

MODERN LUXURY

A rash of large, new super-stylish hotels have opened in Manhattan in the last couple of years, which have set new standards worldwide for architecture and interiors. We also include a couple of hotels that have been around for a decade that were so ahead of their time they're still attracting a modern crowd. These are the places to check into if you want contemporary rooms with all the trimmings; think fluffy white bathrobes, designer toiletries in the bathroom, plasma screen TVs and a hip cocktail bar or restaurant to spend some time in.

BATTERY PARK CITY

RITZ–CARLTON NEW YORK $$$$$

✉ 2 West Street between Battery Place and West End
☎ 212-344 0800
  Fax 212-344 3804
🖰 www.ritzcarlton.com
🚗 Subway 4, 5 to Bowling Green

A world-class, award-winning hotel with art deco-inspired interiors, incredible views of the Hudson River and Statue of Liberty, state-of-the-art business support services

Ritz Carlton Park View room

Lobby at the Royalton

and unparalleled service. A 39-storey glass-and-brick edifice in Lower Manhattan, it has 298 sumptuous guest rooms, an outdoor waterfront deck and even the Skyscraper Museum (page 133).

The rooms come with the very finest Frette linens, feather beds and goose-down pillows, cotton bathrobes, Ritz-Carlton pyjamas, marble bathtubs and separate marble shower stalls, silk curtains, in-room safe, working desk with two chairs, dual-line cordless phones with voicemail and high-speed internet access. The extensive guest services include a fully equipped health club and spa, massage treatments, limo, complimentary shuttle service in Lower Manhattan and a bath butler! Sheer luxury!

GRAMERCY PARK

GRAMERCY PARK HOTEL $$-$$$$
✉ 2 Lexington Avenue at Gramercy Park North
☎ 212-201 2161
⬦ www.gramercyparkhotel.com
🚇 Subway L, N, R, 4, 5, 6 to 14th Street/ Union Square

Once a famous hotel where the likes of JFK and Humphrey Bogart liked to spend time. It looks set to be on the map again thanks to uber hotelier Ian Schrager getting his hands on it. Expect all of the flair that you usually find in a Schrager creation; think jaw-dropping reception area, quirky bar and super-sexy bedrooms.

MIDTOWN

FLATOTEL $$$-$$$$
✉ 135 West 52nd Street
☎ 212-887 9400
⬦ www.flatotel.com
🚇 Subway B, D, F, Q to 42nd Street

A towering glass complex just around the corner from Radio City Music Hall (page 64) that's home-from-home for rock stars

thanks to the large, light rooms, which have fab marble bathrooms, flatscreen TVs, CD players and huge beds. The view from the floor-to-ceiling windows is awesome.

ROYALTON $$$-$$$$
✉ 44 West 44th Street between 5th and 6th Avenues
☎ 212-869 4400
   Fax 212-869 8965
⬦ www.royaltonhotel.com
🚇 Subway B, D, F, Q to 42nd Street

Still an 'in' place with the magazine and showbiz crowd despite the fact that this hotel, designed by Philippe Starck, first opened in the 1980s. It's theatre-style lobby, which runs the length of an entire block, is worth a visit alone. Each room has a futon, slate fireplace and round bathtub.

> **DIAMOND DISCOUNTS**
> You can cut your room rates significantly by taking advantage of the New York Travel Advisory Bureau's (NYTAB) tie-up with Express Reservations – call 303-440 8481 or visit www.express-res.com. It offers major discounts on more than 25 hotels across most price categories.

MIDTOWN EAST

FOUR SEASONS $$$$-$$$$$
✉ 57 East 57th Street between Madison and Park Avenues
☎ 212-758 5700
   Fax 212-758 5711
⬦ www.fourseasons.com
🚇 Subway 4, 5, 6 to 59th Street

Put on your best power suits to rub shoulders with New York's movers and shakers. The art deco-style rooms come with electronically controlled curtains and marble-clad bathrooms.

Four Seasons

SOHO

SOHO GRAND $$$$

- ✉ 310 West Broadway between Grand and Canal Streets
- ☎ 212-965 3000
  Fax 212-965 3200
- ⌂ www.sohogrand.com
- 🚇 Subway C east to Canal Street

Famous for its style, this was the first real top-notch hotel to open in the SoHo area. Cocktails and light meals are served in the Grand Bar, an intimate, wood-panelled club room, as well as the fashionable Salon, a lively lounge that is excellent for people-watching and pet-friendly, so perhaps dog-watching too.

TRIBECA

TRIBECA GRAND $$$$–$$$$$

- ✉ 2 Avenue of the Americas (6th Avenue) at Church Street
- ☎ 212-519 6600
  UK freephone 0800-028 9874
  Fax 212-519 6700
- ⌂ www.tribecagrand.com
- 🚇 Subway 1, 9 to Franklin Street

Sister property to the extremely stylish SoHo Grand, this is the first major hotel to open in the TriBeCa area. It's popular with the film crowd, thanks to its 98-seat private screening room and the annual TriBeCa Film Festival that it hosts. Amenities in the 203 rooms, including istudio 'digital lifestyle' rooms and a Grand Suite with rooftop terrace, include iPods, complimentary local phone calls and faxes, digital cable TV with movies-on-demand, Bose sound dock, and radio/CD player with library, wireless internet access, and complimentary pet goldfish on request.

UPPER WEST SIDE

MANDARIN ORIENTAL $$$$–$$$$$

- ✉ 80 Columbus Circle at 60th Street
- ☎ 212-805 8800
  Fax 212-805 8888
- ⌂ www.mandarinoriental.com
- 🚇 Subway A, B, C, D, 9 to 59th Street/ Columbus Circle

Set in the top floors of the AOL Time Warner Center on the north-west arc of the Columbus Circle, it sits steps away from Central Park and just a stroll from 5th Avenue. Inside, the luxurious rooms are simply breathtaking, with floor-to-ceiling windows offering spectacular views of the Manhattan skyline. Have fun hanging out at the trendy MObar, or flex your credit card and enjoy dinner in Asiate on the 35th floor, which offers a fusion of French and Japanese cuisine. If you're tired after your journey, behave like a celeb and book yourself a massage at the hotel spa.

TRADITIONAL LUXURY

The following hotels are all about plush furnishings, impeccable service and the right location. They are often very discreet, which is why celebrities love them, and most have the added advantage of extremely good gourmet restaurants.

GRAMERCY PARK

INN AT IRVING PLACE $$$$–$$$$$

- ✉ 56 Irving Place between East 17th and East 18th Streets
- ☎ 212-533 4600
  Fax 212-533 4611
- ⌂ www.innatirving.com
- 🚇 Subway L, N, R, 4, 5, 6 to 14th Street/ Union Square

Delightful, tiny Victorian boutique hotel. Each room has a romantic fireplace and four-poster bed.

MIDTOWN EAST

ELYSEE $$$$–$$$$$

- ✉ 60 East 54th Street between Park and Madison Avenues
- ☎ 212-753 1066,
  Fax 212-980 9278
- ⌂ www.elyseehotel.com
- 🚇 Subway 6 to 51st Street

A small hotel dating from the 1920s whose decor includes antique furnishings and Italian marble bathrooms. Home from home to movie stars, guests have use of a nearby sports club.

TOP FIVE HOTEL SPAS

Spa at Four Seasons Hotel, page 2510

Spa at Mandarin Oriental, above

The Cowshed Spa at SoHo House, page 236

The Peninsula Spa at The Peninsula New York, page 238

Plus One Spa at Trump International Hotel & Tower, page 237

NEW YORK PALACE $$$$-$$$$$

✉ 455 Madison Avenue between 50th and 51st Streets

☎ 212-888 7000

Fax 212-303 6000

🖰 www.newyorkpalace.com

🚇 Subway 6 to 51st Street

Built in 1882, the Palace rises 55 floors from its prime spot in Midtown Manhattan and is a favourite stopover for celebs visiting New York. The main hotel is in the atmospheric Villard Houses, but the adjacent Towers has the advantage of more luxurious rooms. Its new restaurant, Gilt serves modern European cuisine and the Villard Bar and Lounge is perfect for a cocktail.

If you're a smoker, make sure you ask for a smoking room as most hotels now mostly provide non-smoking rooms.

UPPER EAST SIDE

HOTEL PLAZA-ATHENEE $$$$-$$$$$

✉ 37 East 64th Street between Madison and Park Avenues

☎ 212-734 9100

Fax 212-722 0958

🖰 www.plaza-athenee.com

🚇 Subway 6 to 68th Street

What its rooms lack in size they make up for in elegant antique French furnishings. The hotel has introduced a great range of packages for tourists, including a shopping package with discounts at lots of stores including Bloomingdales and private car pick-up. The Arabelle Restaurant is also *the* place to have brunch in the city.

The posh Mark hotel does such good weekend and summer rates that you could afford to stay here and enjoy all that fabulous luxury. It's family-friendly too.

THE MARK $$$$-$$$$$

✉ 25 East 77th Street between 5th and Madison Avenues

☎ 212-744 4300

Fax 212-744 2749

🖰 www.mandarinoriental.com/themark

🚇 Subway 6 to 77th Street

In terms of luxury, it vies with the Carlyle – only this hotel is infused with Italian neo-classicism compared with the Carlyle's English gentility. The city's first really beautiful upmarket boutique hotel, its discreet service is enjoyed by a long list of celebrity clients. Unfortunately, some of them have tended to get a bit out of hand. Johnny Depp and Kate Moss had their notorious lovers' tiff here, which took its toll on the furniture before Depp was finally arrested at 5am. Fellow celebrity guests George Michael and Ali McGraw were apparently deeply disturbed by Depp's tantrum. On a happier note, such an event is a rarity, which explains why many celebs make the hotel their home-from-home when they're in New York. There's a complimentary car service to Wall Street and the Theater District for all guests, a small health club and a top-notch restaurant.

When making a booking directly with a hotel, make sure they send you confirmation of your reservation (by fax is simplest).

SHERRY-NETHERLAND $$$$-$$$$$

✉ 781 5th Avenue at East 59th Street

☎ 212-355 2800

Fax 212-319 4306

🖰 www.sherrynetherland.com

🚇 Subway 4, 5, 6 to 59th Street

A true New York secret, this is one of the grand hotels with real charm and is also the permanent home of many a celebrity. It's just undergone a multi-million dollar renovation of all its suites, with internet access in all rooms now included. It also boasts the Cipriani Restaurant, popular with ladies who like to lunch.

BOUTIQUE CHIC

These hotels are stylish and small (100 rooms or less). If you love modern design and crave the latest looks, then make sure you check them out. If you can't stay, most have great bars where you can soak up the ambience for an evening.

MEATPACKING DISTRICT

GANSEVOORT $$$–$$$$$

- ✉ 18 9th Avenue at 13th Street
- ☎ 212-206 6700
  Fax 212-660 6744
- ⌂ www.hotelgansevoort.com
- 🚗 Subway N, R to 5th Avenue

In the trendy Meatpacking District, the Gansevoort is a 187-room hang-out that's just a stroll away from Stella McCartney and some good restaurants. The feature that really makes it a place to head for is the 14m (45ft) long rooftop pool with underwater music.

MIDTOWN

BRYANT PARK $$$$–$$$$$

- ✉ 40 West 40th Street
- ☎ 212-869 0100
- ⌂ www.bryantparkhotel.com
- 🚗 Subway D, B, V, F to 42nd Street

This hide-out for the fashion pack overlooks the park that gives the hotel its name. It's just off 5th Avenue, so ideal if you are on a shopping trip and convenient for visiting all of the major sights. Inside, the rooms resemble New York lofts; think white walls, sleek Italian furniture in warm orange and ochre and cool bathrooms with giant porcelain sinks and stainless steel shelves.

Ono at the Hotel Gansevoort

CHAMBERS $$$–$$$$$

- ✉ 15 West 56th Street between 5th and 6th Avenues
- ☎ 212-974 5656
  Fax 212-974 5657
- ⌂ www.chambershotel.com
- 🚗 Subway B, Q to 57th Street

Owned by the same team behind the Mercer Hotel in SoHo, it attracts the likes of Jennifer Love Hewitt and Kid Rock to its gorgeous rooms. The ultra-modern decor is comfortable and luxurious and the hotel displays over 500 pieces of original art. The bath tubs are deep, cashmere throws adorn the beds and flat-screen TVs with DVD and CD players grace every room. Its restaurant, Town (page 169), is still a hip place to dine.

★ ★ ★ ★ **BRIT TIP** ★ ★ ★ ★
If you hire a car, bear in mind that most hotels charge a parking fee of around $30 a night.

CITY CLUB HOTEL $$$–$$$$

- ✉ 55 West 44th Street between 5th and 6th Avenues
- ☎ 212-921 5500
  Fax 212-944 5544
- ⌂ www.cityclubhotel.com
- 🚗 Subway 7 to 5th Avenue; B, D, F, V to 42nd Street

The owner-manager Jeffrey Klein is one of the most socially visible hoteliers in the city and some of his very famous friends cocoon themselves in his hotel. Based in an old gentlemen's club building, it is one of the smartest but least showy boutique hotels in New York. There's no queuing in the lobby as check-in happens in your room, which has a big TV hidden in the wall, a day bed and possibly even the latest Jackie Kennedy Onassis biography. These rooms are designed to spend time in!

Hotel Gansevoort pool

Loft at the 60 Thompson

MORGANS $$$–$$$$

✉ 237 Madison Avenue
☎ 212-686 0300
　Fax 212-779 8352
🖥 www.morganshotel.com
🚗 Subway 4, 5, 6 to 6th Avenue and
　34th Street

This Ian Schrager hotel started the boutique phenomenon and is still going strong today thanks to its unique sense of style and effortless cool. The bedrooms are apartment-style havens, all ivory, camel and taupe soft furnishings plus it has one of Manhattan's most popular restaurants, Asia de Cuba (page 169), and Morgans Bar (page 201) is certainly the hot spot to sip a cocktail.

MIDTOWN EAST

DYLAN $$$–$$$$

✉ 52 East 41st Street between Madison
　and Park Avenues
☎ 212-338 0500
　Fax 212-338 0569
🖥 www.dylanhotel.com
🚗 Subway S, 4, 5, 6, 7 to Grand Central/
　42nd Street

Located in the former Chemist's Club building, this small hotel was developed to preserve the 1903 Beaux Arts structure. A mezzanine lounge and bar overlooks the dramatic, high-ceilinged restaurant, The Chemist Club. In-room amenities include a state-of-the-art digital entertainment system with large cable TV, DVD and CD players that can access a library of thousands of video and CD titles, two-line telephones with voicemail and data port, complimentary high-speed and wireless internet, large safes and complimentary newspaper.

SOHO

6 COLUMBUS CIRCLE $$$

✉ 6 Columbus Circle between West 58th
　and 60th Streets
☎ 212-431 0400
　Fax 212-204 5005
🖥 www.60thompson.com

Overlooking Columbus Circle and Central Park, this 90 room and suite inspired urban retreat with a 60s modernist feel opened in summer 2006. This renovation was masterminded by Jason Pomerac, who opened 60 Thompson three years ago.

60 THOMPSON $$$–$$$$$

✉ 60 Thompson Street between Broome
　and Spring Streets
☎ 877-431 0400
　Fax 212-431 0200
🖥 www.60thompson.com
🚇 Subway C, E to Spring Street

A sleek, 14-storey, 100-bedroom hotel that is a great retreat from the bustling streets of SoHo. Rooms are designed for relaxing in – the best are on the top floor and have breathtaking panoramic views of landmarks such as the Empire State Building. The front patio, sheltered by stands of black bamboo, is a wonderful place to just sit and people-watch. Outstanding!

MERCER $$$–$$$$

✉ 147 Mercer Street at Prince Street
☎ 212-966 6060
　Fax 212-965 3838
🖥 www.mercerhotel.com
🚇 Subway N, R to Prince Street

A bijou 75-room boutique hotel in a Romanesque revival building slap-bang in the middle of SoHo. Offering a taste of New York loft living, it quickly gets packed with the fashionable and young corporate sets. Rooms even provide condoms in the bathroom and video games to play on the TV, and The Kitchen recreates the casual feeling of a meal at home.

SoHo House

TOP FIVE CELEBRITY HOTELS

Check out where the stars check in...
Flatotel: Coldplay, Jane's Addiction, Joan Collins, David Navarro, Stephen Gately (page 231).
Waldorf Astoria: Winona Ryder, Richard Gere, Ewan McGregor, Kid Rock, Alicia Keys, Paris and Nicki Hilton (page 229).
W New York: Cindy Crawford, Leonardo DiCaprio, Gwyneth Paltrow (see Brit Tip on page 236).
Soho Grand: Heidi Klum, Kevin Spacey, Gwyneth Paltrow, Uma Thurman (page 232).
60 Thompson: Jessica Simpson, Christina Aguilera, Matt Damon (page 235).

SOHO HOUSE
NEW YORK $$$$–$$$$$

✉ 29–35 9th Avenue between West 13th and 14th Streets
☎ 212-627 9800
 Fax 212-627 4766
🖰 www.sohohouseny.com
🚇 Subway 1, 9 to 14th Street

SoHo House is the baby sister of London's Soho House and has already proved a similar magnet for celebrities and media bigwigs with its chandeliers-meets-Corbusier decor, 24 bedrooms, Cowshed Spa and cinema. It's actually a private members' club, but if you're lucky enough to book one of the rooms you can use the members'

★ ★ ★ ★ ★ **BRIT TIP** ★ ★ ★ ★
★ For sleek New York style without the ★
★ hefty price tag, check into one of ★
★ the W New York hotels, a small ★
★ chain of five designer hotels that ★
★ have sprung up around the city. ★
★ W New York The Court (tel 212-685 ★
★ 1100), W New York The Tuscany (tel ★
★ 212-686 1600), W New York Union ★
★ Square (tel 212-253 9119), W New ★
★ York Times Square (tel 212-930 ★
★ 7400) and W New York on ★
★ Lexington Avenue (tel 212-755 ★
★ 1200) each offer exceptional ★
★ standards of minimalist-style ★
★ accommodation. You can view them ★
★ all at www.whotels.com. ★
★ ★

facilities, which includes the fabulous rooftop pool that has already gained iconic status as the set for one of the classic *Sex And The City* episodes.

THEME HOTELS

CHELSEA

MARITIME HOTEL $$–$$$$

✉ 363 West 16th Street at 9th Avenue
☎ 212-242 4300
 Fax 212-242 1188
🖰 www.themaritimehotel.com
🚇 Subway 1, 9 to 14th Street

A fun, stylish hotel where all rooms have a maritime theme; think porthole windows overlooking the Hudson River, teak panelling and blue and white nautical stripes. The 24-hour room service can be enjoyed with the latest on-demand movies or Nintendo 64. There's a sizeable roof terrace and it's in a great location for exploring Chelsea and the trendy Meatpacking District.

MIDTOWN

THE LIBRARY $$$$–$$$$$

✉ 299 Madison Avenue at 41st Street
☎ 212-983 4500
 Fax 212-499 9099
🖰 www.libraryhotel.com
🚇 Subway 4, 5, 6, 7, S to 41st Street/ Grand Central

A fabulous new hotel that, you've guessed it, has the theme of a city library. It has the feel of a cosy gentlemen's club when you first walk in, all mahogany panelling, fancy artwork and bookcases. The rooms are a revelation. Each of the 10 floors is dedicated to a category that you'd find in a real library, such as Philosophy or Art & Literature, and there are books and artworks in rooms to match the theme of each level. Original and luxurious, but pricey.

MIDTOWN WEST

DREAM $$–$$$

✉ 210 West 55th Street
☎ 212-247 2000
 Fax 212-974 0595
🖰 www.dreamny.com
🚇 Subway N, R to 5th Avenue

If you're seeking peace, tranquillity and possibly even a spiritual experience, then this new hotel promises to deliver. It's the unique vision of hotelier Vikram Chatwal

BOOKING IT YOURSELF

Of course, you can use a travel agent to make room reservations for you, but you can also do it yourself through companies that specialise in offering excellent rates at off-peak and low-peak times or can even just guarantee finding you a room during busy periods. These include:

Hotel America Ltd: Tel 08700 464010, www.hotelanywhere.co.uk/america. A British company providing hotel discounts anywhere in the world.

Hotel Conxions: Tel 212-840 8686, fax 212-221 8686, www.hotelconxions.com. You can find out about availability and price and book a room on their website.

Quikbook: Tel 212-779 7666, fax 212-779 6120, www.quikbook.com. A service providing discounts on hotels all over America. They promise there are no hidden cancellation or change penalties, and pre-payment is not required.

A great internet discount reservation service can be found at www.hotres.com and www.hoteldiscount.com or look for cheaper rates through the hotel discount service on www.usacitylink.com.

When discussing room rates with any of these organisations, always check that the prices you are quoted include the New York City hotel tax of 13.25 per cent and the $2 per night occupancy tax or 4 per cent for a one-bedroom suite.

and is all about promoting spiritual well-being, from the mind-enhancing lobby with its Subconscious Lounge to the Ayurvedic healing centre created by spiritualist Deepak Chopra. But you needn't forego the hi tech; its modern, eclectic-style rooms have 37" plasma TVs and iPod digital audio players.

THE NIGHT HOTEL $$$-$$$$$

⊠ 132 West 45th Street between 6th and 7th Avenues
☎ 212-835-9600
    Fax 212-835 9610
⌂ www.nighthotelny.com

This stylish, petite 72-room hotel is Vikram Chatwal's latest offering, inspired by the pulse and passion of the city. It offers a sense of seclusion in what feels like a private home.

THEATER DISTRICT

TIME $$-$$$

⊠ 224 West 49th Street between Broadway and 8th Avenue
☎ 212-246 5252
    Fax 212-245 2305
⌂ www.thetimeny.com
🚇 Subway C, E, 1, 9 to 50th Street

Themed around Alexander Theroux's book *The Primary Colours* (not Times Square as you might think) this brightly coloured bolthole is a the perfect place if you want to stay in a touristy area in style. Primary colours are used throughout, of course: red rooms are for lovers, blue if you're feeling

sad and yellow if you're a bit lacklustre. The colours continue through to the finishing touches, such as bowls of jellybeans in matching shades. There's a buzzing bar downstairs, where guests have included the likes of Liza Minelli.

UPMARKET

If you want your hotel to be smart and sophisticated rather than ultra-trendy or traditional, these are for you.

CENTRAL PARK

TRUMP INTERNATIONAL HOTEL
& TOWER $$$$-$$$$$

⊠ 1 Central Park West between 60th and 61st Streets
☎ 212-299 1000
    Fax 212-299 1150
⌂ www.trumpintl.com
🚇 Subway N, R to 5th Avenue

Billionaire Donald Trump's foray into hotels is a shimmering tower that houses 167 rooms and suites, as well as various shops and restaurants. The best thing about the hotel is the views of Central Park and 5th Avenue through floor-to-ceiling windows – simply spectacular. The spa is a must-visit for those in need of pampering and the staff are charming and will help you with whatever you need, from booking theatre tickets to handing you an umbrella if it's raining.

WHERE TO STAY

WHERE TO STAY

MIDTOWN

LE PARKER MERIDIEN $$$$-$$$$$
✉ 118 West 57th Street between 6th and 7th Avenues
☎ 212-245 5000
Fax 212-307 1776
🖰 www.parkermeridien.com
🚇 Subway B, D, E to 7th Avenue

A classic New York hotel in the design sense, yet with a traditional French feel, this hotel is not only in an excellent location just minutes from Central Park and Carnegie Hall, but offers great service and amenities. The rooms, which have all recently been refurbished, have a Zen-like calmness to them thanks to the minimalist and cherrywood decor. Great touches include a revolving unit, which allows you to watch the massive TV screen either in the sitting area or in the bedroom. It also has a useful desk unit, CD and DVD players.

★★★★ **BRIT TIP** ★★★★
★ ★
★ Make sure you look upwards when ★
★ you enter the lifts of Le Parker ★
★ Meridien – all three have a TV screen ★
★ offering classic film clips of Abbott ★
★ and Costello or Tom and Jerry. ★
★★★★★★★★★★★★★★★★★★★★★★★★

Even if you don't plan to use the swimming pool, you must visit its penthouse location to see the fab views of Central Park. Down in the basement is the massive Gravity gymnasium, which covers everything from Cybex training to aerobics, sauna, stretching, massage rooms, spa services and squash and racquetball courts.

Other facilities include the much-raved-about Norma's restaurant in the lobby, which serves creative breakfast dishes throughout the day (page 168). Its other restaurant is Seppi's (page 168).

Kitano

The Peninsula

THE PENINSULA $$$$$
✉ 700 5th Avenue at 55th Street
☎ 212-956 2888
Fax 212-903 3949
🖰 www.newyork.peninsula.com
🚇 Subway F to 53rd Street; 6 to 51st Street

A beautiful hotel that has undergone a massive $45-million renovation in the public areas and restaurants, as well as all of the 239 guestrooms and suites. These are of classic contemporary style with touches of art nouveau, and oversize marble bathrooms where you can watch TV from the bath. The state-of-the-art technology allows you to control your environment with the touch of a button and a water bar is on hand for hangover recovery.

MIDTOWN EAST

KITANO HOTEL $$$$-$$$$$
✉ 66 Park Avenue at East 38th Street
☎ 212-885 7000
Fax 212-447 5918
🖰 www.kitano.com
🚇 Subway S, 4, 5, 6, 7 to Grand Central/42nd Street

A first-class, Japanese-run hotel with top-notch service and a deliciously decadent, deep-soaking tub in each room. In the Murray Hill area, it has Manhattan's only authentic Japanese tatami suite.

MIDTOWN WEST

HILTON NEW YORK $$$$$
✉ 1335 6th Avenue at 53rd Street
☎ 212-586 7000
🖰 www.hilton.com
🚇 Subway B, D, F, Q to 47th–50th Streets/Rockefeller Center

After a recent $100-million renovation, the city's largest hotel now has a beautiful new façade and entrance lobby, plus two new restaurants and lounges.

The Mansfield

MEDIUM-PRICED GEMS

FINANCIAL DISTRICT

MILLENIUM HILTON $$-$$$$$
- ✉ 55 Church Street between Fulton and Dey Streets
- ☎ 212-693 2001, Fax 212-571 2316
- 🖰 www.newyorkmillenium.hilton.com

A black skyscraper geared to business, with fitness centre and a pool. For a stunning view of the harbour, ask for a room on one of the higher floors.

★★★★ BRIT TIP ★★★★
★ Hotels in the Financial District can ★
★ be especially good value at ★
★ weekends when many business ★
★ people leave the city. ★

WALL STREET INN $$$
- ✉ 9 South William Street opposite 85 Broad Street
- ☎ 212-747 1500, Fax 212-747 1900
- 🖰 www.thewallstreetinn.com
- 🚌 Subway 2, 3 to Wall Street; J, M, Z to Broad Street

An elegant boutique hotel in an old office building in the heart of the financial and historic district. Original features include mahogany panels on the walls and granite floors.

★★★★ BRIT TIP ★★★★
★ Confusingly, American hotel lifts use ★
★ the letter 'L' or the number '1' to ★
★ indicate the ground floor. The L ★
★ stands for lobby, by the way. ★

MIDTOWN

CASABLANCA $$$-$$$$
- ✉ 147 West 43rd Street off Times Square
- ☎ 212-869 1212, Fax 212-391 7585
- 🖰 www.casablancahotel.com
- 🚌 Subway 1, 2, 3, 7, 9, N, R, S to Times Square/42nd Street

Calling itself 'an oasis in the heart of Times Square', its elegant Moroccan theme includes ceiling fans, palm trees and mosaic tiles. Small, with just 48 newly renovated luxury rooms, the service is good and it also offers complimentary use of the New York Sports Club, with pool, just steps away.

MANSFIELD $$$-$$$$$
- ✉ 12 West 44th Street between 5th and 6th Avenues
- ☎ 212-944 6050, Fax 212-764 4477
- 🖰 www.mansfieldhotel.com
- 🚌 Subway B, D, F, Q to 47th–50th Street/Rockefeller Centre

A beautiful lobby with vaulted ceiling and white marble marks the Mansfield out as an elegant hotel for those also wanting the charm of a boutique establishment. The rooms have plush robes and Aveda toiletries and its M Bar, with its domed skylight and mahogany bookshelves, has been described by Zagat's as 'an off the beaten path, classy, romantic sweet spot'.

SHOREHAM $$$-$$$$$
- ✉ 33 West 55th Street at 5th Avenue
- ☎ 212-247 6700, Fax 212-765 9741
- 🖰 www.shorehamhotel.com
- 🚌 Subway F to 5th Avenue

This hotel has won awards for its ultra-modern décor following its recent renovation. It now has a new bar, restaurant, fitness centre and some more good-sized rooms.

Rick's Café at the Casablanca

ACCOMMODATION REFERENCE GUIDE

Hotel	Area	Style	Price range	page
6 Columbus Circle	SoHo	Boutique chic	$$$	235
60 Thompson	SoHo	Boutique chic	$$$–$$$$$	235
70 Park Avenue	Midtown East	Medium-priced gem	$$$–$$$$	241
Algonquin	Midtown	Excellent value	$$–$$$	245
Ameritania	Midtown West	Excellent value	$$	246
Bentley	Upper East Side	Excellent value	$$–$$$	247
Blue Moon	Lower East Side	Boutique chic	$$$	244
Bryant Park	Midtown	Boutique chic	$$$$–$$$$$	234
Carlton	Flatiron District	Excellent value	$$–$$$	245
Casablanca	Midtown	Medium-priced gem	$$–$$$$	239
Chambers	Midtown	Boutique chic	$$$–$$$$$	234
Chelsea Hotel	Chelsea	Excellent value	$$	244
Chelsea Star	Madison Square Garden	Total bargain	$	248
City Club Hotel	Midtown	Boutique chic	$$$–$$$$	234
Clarion Hotel 5th Avenue	Midtown East	Excellent value	$$–$$$	246
Courtyard by Marriott	Theater District	Excellent value	$$–$$$	246
Crowne Plaza	Times Square	Upmarket		245
Dream	Midtown West	Theme	$$–$$$	236
Dylan	Midtown East	Boutique chic	$$$–$$$$	235
Elysée	Midtown East	Traditional luxury	$$$$–$$$$$	232
Fitzpatrick	Midtown East	Medium-priced gem	$$$–$$$$	242
Fitzpatrick Grand Central	Midtown East	Medium-priced gem	$$$	242
Flatotel	Midtown	Modern luxury	$$$–$$$$	231
Four Seasons	Midtown East	Modern luxury	$$$$–$$$$$	231
Franklin	Upper East Side	Medium-priced gem	$$$	244
Gansevoort	Meatpacking District	Boutique chic	$$$–$$$$$	234
Gershwin	Flatiron District	Total bargain	$–$$	247
Giraffe	Flatiron District	Excellent value	$$–$$$	245
Gramercy Park	Gramercy Park	Modern luxury	$$–$$$$	231
Gramercy Park Hotel 17	Gramercy Park	Total bargain	$–$$	248
Herald Square Hotel	Flatiron District	Total bargain	$	248
Hilton New York	Midtown West	Upmarket	$$$$$	238
Holiday Inn Downtown	Chinatown/Lower East Side	Excellent value	$$	244
Holiday Inn Martinique	Theater District	Excellent value	$$–$$$$$	246
Holiday Inn Wall Street	Financial District	Excellent value	$$–$$$$	244
Hotel Beacon	Upper West Side	Excellent value	$$	247
Hotel Carlyle	Upper East Side	Landmark	$$$$–$$$$$	230
Hotel Plaza-Athene	Upper East Side	Traditional luxury	$$$$–$$$$$	233
Howard Johnson Express Inn	Lower East Side	Total bargain	$–$$	248
Hudson	Midtown West	Medium-priced gem	$$–$$$$	242
Inn at Irving Place	Gramercy Park	Traditional luxury	$$$$–$$$$$	232
Inn New York City	Upper West Side	Excellent value	$$$–$$$$	246
Kitano Hotel	Midtown East	Upmarket	$$$$–$$$$$	238
Larchmont	Greenwich Village	Total bargain	$–$$	248
Le Parker Meridien	Midtown	Upmarket	$$$$–$$$$$	238
Library	Midtown	Theme	$$$$–$$$$$	236
London NYC	Midtown West	Upmarket	$$$$	245
Mandarin Oriental	Upper West Side	Modern luxury	$$$$–$$$$$	232
Mansfield	Midtown	Medium-priced gem	$$$–$$$$	239
Maritime Hotel	Chelsea	Theme	$$–$$$$	236
Mark	Upper East Side	Traditional luxury	$$$$–$$$$$	233
Mercer	SoHo	Boutique chic	$$$–$$$$	235
Metro	Midtown	Excellent value	$$–$$$	246
Millennium Hilton	Financial District	Medium-priced gem	$$–$$$$$	239
Millennium UN Plaza	Midtown East	Upmarket		245
Moderne	Midtown West	Medium-priced gem	$$$–$$$$	243

Hotel	Area	Style	Price range	page
Morgans	Midtown	Boutique chic	$$$–$$$$	235
New York Hilton & Towers	Midtown West	Upmarket	$$$$$	236
New York Marriott Brooklyn	Brooklyn	Excellent value	$$–$$$	247
New York Marriott Marquis	Theater District	Medium-priced gem	$$–$$$$	243
New York Palace	Midtown East	Traditional luxury	$$$$–$$$$$	233
Night Hotel	Midtown West	Theme hotel	$$$–$$$$	237
Off SoHo Suites	Lower East Side	Total bargain	$–$$	248
On The Ave	Theater District	Medium-priced gem	$$–$$$$	243
Paramount	Theater District	Medium-priced gem	$$–$$$$$	243
Peninsula	Midtown	Upmarket	$$$$$	238
Pickwick Arms Hotel	Midtown East	Total bargain	$	248
Portland Square Hotel	Midtown West	Total bargain	$	248
Premier	Theater District	Medium-priced gem	$$$–$$$$	243
Ritz-Carlton New York	Battery Park City	Modern luxury	$$$$$	230
Roosevelt	Midtown East	Medium-priced gem	$$–$$$$	242
Royalton	Midtown	Modern luxury	$$$–$$$$	231
Sherry-Netherland	Upper East Side	Traditional luxury	$$$$–$$$$$	233
Shoreham	Midtown	Medium-priced gem	$$$–$$$$$	239
SoHo Grand	SoHo	Modern luxury	$$$$	232
SoHo House New York	SoHo	Boutique chic	$$$$–$$$$$	236
Super 8	Midtown	Excellent value	$$	246
Thirty Thirty New York City	Flatiron District	Total bargain	$–$$	248
Time	Theater District	Theme	$$–$$$	237
TriBeCa Grand	TriBeCa	Modern luxury	$$$$–$$$$$	232
Trump International Hotel & Tower	Central Park	Upmarket	$$$$–$$$$$	237
Waldorf Astoria	Midtown East	Landmark	$$–$$$$$	229
Waldorf Towers	Midtown East	Landmark	$$$$$	230
Wall Street Inn	Financial District	Medium-priced gem	$$$	239
Warwick	Midtown	Medium-priced gem	$$$–$$$$	241
Washington Square Hotel	Greenwich Village	Excellent value	$$	245
Wellington	Midtown	Excellent value	$$	246
W New York	Across the city	Medium-priced gems	$$$–$$$$$	236
Westin New York Times Square	Theater District	Medium-priced gem	$$$$	248

WARWICK $$$–$$$$

✉ 65 West 54th Street at 6th Avenue
☎ 212-247 2700
Fax 212-247 2725
🖰 warwickhotelny.com
🚇 Subway B, D, F, Q to 47th–50th Streets/ Rockefeller Center

A medium-sized hotel built in 1927 with good-quality rooms and excellent service in an excellent location. In its heyday many a Hollywood celeb stayed here, including Cary Grant. Randolph's Bar remains a favoured meeting place and a great spot for lunch or a light dinner in its recently opened restaurant, Murals on 54, which offers innovative Continental cuisine.

MIDTOWN EAST

70 PARK AVENUE $$$–$$$$

✉ 70 Park Avenue at 38th Street
☎ 212-973 2400
Fax 212-973 2497
🖰 www.70parkave.com
🚇 Subway 4, 5, 6 to 42nd Street

A beautiful, four-star boutique hotel whose motto is 'Live Life Well' and with a home-from-home atmosphere. It has a bar, restaurant and excellent room facilities as well as services such as the Mind, Body & Spa programme with in-room yoga and a nightly complimentary living room reception.

ALL WIRED UP!

Not only does America have a different style of plug, it also works on a different voltage. Ours is 230 volts, theirs is 115 volts, so you'll need a travel appliance that works on both voltages, or bring an adaptor plug with you.

FITZPATRICK $$$–$$$$

✉ 687 Lexington Avenue between East 56th and East 57th Streets
☎ 212-355 0100
Fax 212-355 1371
🖰 www.fitzpatrickhotels.com/manhattan
🚇 Subway 4, 5, 6 to 59th Street

The rooms are equipped with everything from trouser presses to towelling robes, useful after indulging in the whirlpool bath in many of them.

FITZPATRICK GRAND CENTRAL $$$

✉ 141 East 44th Street between Lexington and 3rd Avenues
☎ 212-351 6800
Fax 212-818 1747
🖰 www.fitzpatrickhotels.com/grandcentral
🚇 Subway S, 4, 5, 6, 7 to Grand Central/42nd Street

The Fitzpatrick Family Group of hotels continues its Irish theme at this hotel just across from Grand Central Station. It includes an Irish pub and you can order a traditional Irish breakfast here.

ROOSEVELT $$–$$$$

✉ East 45th Street at Madison Avenue
☎ 212-661 9600
Fax 212-885 6161
🖰 www.theroosevelthotel.com
🚇 Subway S, 4, 5, 6, 7 to Grand Central/42nd Street

Built in 1924, this classy hotel completed a $70-million renovation in 1998 in which the lobby was restored to its original grandeur with crystal chandeliers hanging from the ceiling, columns and lots of marble.

MIDTOWN WEST

HUDSON $$–$$$$$

✉ 356 West 58th Street between 8th and 9th Avenues
☎ 212-554 6000
Fax 212-554 6001
🖰 www.hudsonhotel.com
🚇 Subway A, B, C, D, 1, 9 to 59th Street/Columbus Circle

Built on the site of the former *Sesame Street* studios, this Ian Schrager and Philippe Starck collaboration is heaving with chic guests. It's loud and proud, so don't check in if you are looking for peace and quiet in the city. From the neon entrance escalator to the glowing glass floor of the Hudson Bar, you'll be in the limelight. The rooms are stylish but very small. In a great location for Central Park, the Lincoln Center and Theater District, but definitely on the west side of town so keep this in mind when considering your sightseeing plans.

THE PERFECT APPLE

A major hotel chain, Apple Core, runs five hotels in excellent Midtown locations with extremely reasonable rates of $89–199 a night. They are: Red Roof Inn Manhattan on 32nd Street, west of 5th Avenue; the smoke-free Comfort Inn Midtown on 46th Street west of 6th Avenue; Super 8 Hotel Times Square on 46th Street between 5th and 6th Avenues near the Rockefeller Center (page 64); La Quinta Manhattan on 32nd Street between Broadway and 5th Avenue; and Ramada Inn Eastside at 30th Street and Lexington Avenue.

All the hotels offer complimentary Continental breakfast, well-equipped fitness centres and business centres. In-room facilities include cable television and pay-per-view movies, free wireless internet, telephones with data port and voicemail, coffee makers, irons and ironing boards. The modern bathrooms all come with marble units and hairdryers.

Occupancy rates are above 90% – so book early through Apple Core's central reservations: tel 212-790 2710, www.applecorehotels.com

70 Park Avenue Hotel

Westin New York

MODERNE $$$-$$$$
✉ 243 West 55th Street between Broadway and 8th Avenue
☎ 212-397 6767
Fax 212-397 8787
🚇 Subway C, E, 1, 9 to 50th Street
Opened in 1998, this bijou hotel was converted from a five-storey dance studio. It's in a good location close to Carnegie Hall, though the hotel has had mixed reviews.

THEATER DISTRICT

NEW YORK MARRIOTT MARQUIS $$-$$$$
✉ 1535 Broadway at 45th Street
☎ 212-398 1900
Fax 212-704 8930
🚇 Subway N, R, S, 1, 2, 3, 7, 9 to Times Square/42nd Street
In 1998 this hotel completed a $25-million upgrade of all its rooms so each one now includes console desks, ergonomic chairs, two phone lines and voicemail. A sushi bar, Katen, is in the atrium lobby and it's also home of The View, New York's only revolving restaurant.

ON THE AVE $$-$$$$
✉ 2178 77th Street at Broadway
☎ 212-362 1100
Fax 212-787 9521
🖰 www.ontheave-nyc.com
🚇 Subway 1, 9 to 79th Avenue
This hotel is a breath of fresh air to the rather jaded Upper West Side hotel scene. It has 16 floors, 266 rooms of gorgeous

minimalism, lots of white, floating beds that appear to hover and industrial sinks with walk-in showers big enough for two. Its location, close to Central Park, is superb. It's also very pet-friendly, so the ideal place to bring your pooch. You can have food treats, water/food bowl, a list of local dog runs and parks and a list of pet stores in the area for an extra $25.

PARAMOUNT $$-$$$$$
✉ 235 West 46th Street between Broadway and 8th Avenue
☎ 212-764 5500
Fax 212-354 5237
🖰 www.paramountnewyork.solmelia.com
🚇 Subway C, E, 1, 9 to 50th Street
A hip hotel with a glorious, sweeping staircase in the lobby. The 610 rooms are small but well-equipped. The mezzanine restaurant is good for people-watching.

PREMIER $$$-$$$$
✉ 133 West 44th Street between 6th Avenue and Broadway
☎ 212-768 4400
Fax 212-768 0847
🖰 www.milleniumhotels.com
🚇 Subway N, R, S, 1, 2, 3, 7, 9 to Times Square/42nd Street
The Millennium Broadway in Times Square built this 22-storey tower in 1999 to increase its total room count to 752. The Premier has its own private entrance on 44th Street and elegant, modern guest rooms with large bathrooms, two phone lines, voicemail and a separate modem and fax machine.

WESTIN NEW YORK TIMES SQUARE $$$$
✉ 270 West 43rd Street at 8th Avenue
☎ 212-201 2700
Fax 212-201 2701
🖰 www.westinny.com
🚇 Subway A, C, E, N, R, S, 1, 2, 3, 7, 9 to 42nd Street/Times Square
A fab hotel for all types. Sophisticated sleek rooms with 'heavenly beds and baths'. It is

New York Marriott Marquis

HOTTEST NEW HOTELS...

If you're the sort of person who likes always to be in the latest place in town, then you'll want to stay in one of these happening hotels. They are scheduled to be completed by mid to late 2006 but, with planning permission in New York tougher than in former Mayor Rudy Giuliani's day, it's best to check first.

BLUE MOON $$$
✉ 100 Orchard Street, Lower East Side
☎ 212-533 9080
🖱 www.bluemoon-nyc.com

A 22-room boutique retreat that looks back to another era for its inspiration; each room is named after celebrities from the era and features that music or comedy, for example. The six suites are spacious and have balconies with fab views of the Williamsburg Bridge.

THE LONDON NYC $$$$
✉ 151 West 54th Street
☎ 212-307 5000
🖱 www.thelondon-nyc.com

The former Rihga Royal New York Hotel has been transformed into an uber hip destination; out with the tired furnishings and in with de luxe rooms with high-speed internet access. London chef Gordon Ramsey's first restaurant in the city and a concierge service by Quintessentially, Camilla Parker Bowles' son Tom's upper crust do-it-all company. This is the hot hotel for grown-ups for 07. Opening October 2006.

particularly family-friendly. Families will love the Kids Club, which gives children a sports bottle, toys, colouring books and even a bedtime story! Toddlers get a Molton Brown designer amenities box with baby wash, nappy hamper, potty seat and step stool.

UPPER EAST SIDE

FRANKLIN $$$
✉ 164 East 87th Street between 3rd and
   Lexington Avenues
☎ 212-369 1000
   Fax 212-369 8000
🖱 www.franklinhotel.com
🚇 Subway 4, 5, 6 to 86th Street

Known for its good service, this pleasant art deco boutique hotel has lovely touches in its rooms that include canopies over the beds, fresh flowers and cedar closets.

EXCELLENT VALUE

CHELSEA

CHELSEA HOTEL $$
✉ 222 West 23rd Street between 7th and
   8th Avenues
☎ 212-243 3700
🖱 www.chelseahotel.com
🚇 Subway A, C, E, 1, 2, 3, 9 to 23rd Street

A true icon of New York City, this hotel has been associated with artistic and literary types since it opened in 1912. Residents have included Dylan Thomas, Jack Kerouac, Mark Twain and Thomas Wolfe and it still pulls in the celebs – Dee Dee Ramone of the Ramones is one of a handful of live-in artistes in the heart of New York's boho community. On the darker side, Sex Pistols singer Sid Vicious is alleged to have killed his girlfriend Nancy Spungen here. Besides that, Andy Warhol filmed Chelsea Girls, the stairwell has starred in Bon Jovi and Mariah Carey videos, and room 822 was used to shoot Madonna's book Sex.

Downstairs in the basement is Serena's, a Moroccan den lounge bar, which has been attracting a new round of celebs, such as Leonardo DiCaprio and Brazilian supermodel Giselle, and is popular with the trendy Brit-pack crowd.

CHINATOWN/LOWER EAST SIDE

HOLIDAY INN DOWNTOWN $$
✉ 138 Lafayette Street at Canal Street
☎ 212-966 8898
   Fax 212-966 3933
🚇 Subway N, R to Canal Street

Well-equipped, spotless rooms available at excellent prices.

FINANCIAL DISTRICT

HOLIDAY INN
WALL STREET $$-$$$$
✉ 15 Gold Street at Platt Street

☏ 212-232 7700
Fax 212-425 0330
🖥 www.holidayinnwsd.com
🚇 Subway J, M, Z, 2, 3, 4, 5 to Fulton Street
Opened in 1999, billing itself as the most high-tech hotel in New York, complete with T-1 speed internet connectivity.

FLATIRON DISTRICT

CARLTON $$–$$$
✉ 22 East 29th Street between 5th and Madison Avenues
☏ 212-532 4100
🖥 www.carltonhotelny.com
🚇 Subway 4, 5, 6 to 28th Street
A tourist-class hotel with a view of the Empire State Building and in an excellent location for 5th Avenue and Garment District shopping. Restaurant, lounge and business services.

GIRAFFE $$–$$$
✉ 365 Park Avenue South between 26th and 27th Streets
☏ 212-685 7700
Fax 212 685 7771
🖥 www.hotelgiraffe.com
🚇 Subway 6 to 23rd Street
Small boutique hotel, in lavish colours and textures. Each floor has seven rooms, many with their own balconies adorned with fresh flowers. There's also an on-premises restaurant and access to a nearby health club for guests.

GREENWICH VILLAGE

WASHINGTON SQUARE HOTEL $$
✉ 103 Waverly Place between 5th and 6th Avenues
☏ 212-777 9515
Fax 212-979 8373
🖥 www.wshotel.com
🚇 Subway A, B, C, D, E, F, Q to West 4th Street/Washington Square
A family-run hotel with a bohemian air that overlooks Washington Square. The rooms are small but the rates very reasonable and include breakfast. Bob Dylan was known to stay here in the 1960s.

MIDTOWN

ALGONQUIN $$–$$$
✉ 59 West 44th Street between 5th and 6th Avenues
☏ 212-840 6800
Fax 212-944 1618

TOP FIVE HOTEL POOLS WITH VIEWS
If you like a swim while you're away, check into one of these establishments whose penthouse pools offer some of the best views in Manhattan.

Le Parker Meridien (page 238). The penthouse pool provides a perfect retreat for relaxation and a sun deck offers scenic views of Central Park. It's available for hotel guests free, or you can pay $50 for a day-pass to use it as well as the gym.

Mandarin Oriental (page 232). Floor-to-ceiling windows light up an inviting 23m (75ft) indoor lap pool on the 35th floor, with amazing views of the New York skyline.

Hotel Gansevoort (page 234). This trendy hotel has a suitably cool pool. Take the elevator straight to the top floor and you'll be rewarded with a 14m (45ft) heated outdoor pool that also has underwater music. There are plenty of people to watch while you have your dip.

Crowne Plaza Times Square Manhattan (1605 Broadway, between 48th and 49th Streets, tel 212-9777 4000, www.manhattan.crowne plaza.com). The 15th floor of this plush hotel houses a 15m (50ft) indoor pool, which costs $10 for hotel guests or $25 for non-residents. It has a glass roof through which you can see the skyscrapers.

Millennium UN Plaza Hotel New York (1 United Nations Plaza, 44th Street and 1st Avenue. Tel 212-758 1234, www.millenniumhotels.com). Take a trip up to the 27th floor and you'll be wowed by the wonderful panoramic views through the floor-to-ceiling windows of this 13m (44ft) city oasis.

🖥 www.algonquinhotel.com
🚇 Subway B, D, F, Q to 47th–50th Streets/Rockefeller Center
Famous for the literary meetings held here by Dorothy Parker and her cohorts, the Algonquin underwent a $45 million refurbishment in 2004 and is listed in the Michelin Guide 2006 as one of New York's top hotels.

METRO $$-$$$

✉ 45 West 35th Street between 5th and
6th Avenues
☎ 212-947 2500
Fax 212-279 1310
🖱 www.hotelmetrony.com
🚗 Subway B, D, F, N, Q, R to 34th Street
Well located near the Empire State Building,
which can be seen from its rooftop garden
terrace, this hotel is great value for money,
offering plenty of art deco style.

SUPER 8 $$

✉ 59 West 46th Street between 5th and
6th Avenues
☎ 212-719 2300
Fax 212-790 2760
🖱 www.applecorehotels.com
🚗 Subway B, D, F, Q to 47th–50th Streets/
Rockefeller Center
A well-priced hotel with excellent amenities
that include a fitness centre, coffee makers
and irons in the rooms, free local phone
calls, wireless internet and Continental
breakfast. (See The Perfect Apple on page
242.)

WELLINGTON $$

✉ 871 7th Avenue at 55th Street
☎ 212-247 3900
Fax 212-581 1350
🖱 www.wellingtonhotel.com
🚗 Subway N, R to 57th Street
The best thing about this tourist-class hotel
is its location – deep in the heart of
Midtown within striking distance of
Carnegie Hall, 5th Avenue, the Rockefeller
Center and Times Square. If you can get a
corner room with a view of 7th Avenue,
you'll understand the big deal about the
bright lights associated with the Theater
District – they're absolutely stunning viewed
from this position. Four adults can even stay
in certain rooms that cost just $210–240 for
the night and come with either two
bathrooms or one bathroom and a
kitchenette, while families can be
accommodated in rooms with pull-out
sofas. A true bargain.

MIDTOWN EAST

CLARION HOTEL
5TH AVENUE $$-$$$

✉ 3 East 40th Street just off 5th Avenue
☎ 212-532 4860
Fax 212-545 9727
🖱 www.choicehotels.com
🚗 Subway 7 to 5th Avenue; S, 4, 5, 6, 7 to

Wellington

Grand Central/42nd Street
In an excellent location near Grand Central
Station. The rooms have all the latest
business equipment.

MIDTOWN WEST

AMERITANIA $$

✉ 230 Broadway at West 54th Street
☎ 212-247 5000
Fax 212-247 3316
🖱 www.nychotels.com/ameritania.html
🚗 Subway 1, 9 to 50th Street; B, D east to
7th Avenue
Located just outside the Theater District and
near Restaurant Row. Well-appointed with
modern, comfortable rooms.

THEATER DISTRICT

COURTYARD BY MARRIOTT TIMES
SQUARE SOUTH $$-$$$

✉ 114 West 40th Street between 6th
Avenue and Broadway
☎ 212-391 0088
Fax 212-391 6023
🖱 www.courtyardtimessquare.com
🚗 Subway B, D, F, Q to 42nd Street
This hotel, which opened in 1998, is part of
the massive redevelopment of Times Square.
The spacious rooms all have a sitting area,
large work desk, two phones and in-room
coffee facilities.

HOLIDAY INN MARTINIQUE ON
BROADWAY $$-$$$$$

✉ 49 West 32nd Street at Broadway
☎ 212-736 3800
Fax 212-277 2703
🖱 www.holidayinnbroadway.com
🚗 Subway B, D, F, N, Q, R to 34th Street
Opened in 1998 on the site of the former
Hotel Martinique, this hotel is decorated in
a French Renaissance style.

WHERE TO STAY

UPPER EAST SIDE

BENTLEY $$-$$$
✉ 500 East 62nd Street at York Avenue
☎ 212-644 6000
Fax 212-207 4800
🖰 www.nychotels.com
🚗 Subway 4, 5, 6, N, R to Lexington Avenue/59th Street

A recently renovated hotel within walking distance of Bloomingdale's. Rates include breakfast.

UPPER WEST SIDE

HOTEL BEACON $$
✉ 2130 Broadway at 75th Street
☎ 212-787 1100
Fax 212-724 0839
🖰 www.beaconhotel.com
🚗 Subway 1, 2, 3, 9 to 72nd Street

Good-sized rooms with kitchenettes, plus the 25-storey hotel is well located for the American Museum of Natural History, the Lincoln Center and Central Park.

BROOKLYN

NEW YORK MARRIOTT AT THE BROOKLYN BRIDGE $$-$$$
✉ 333 Adams Street at Tillary Street
☎ 718-246 7000
Fax 718-246 0563
🖰 www.brooklynmarriott.com
🚗 Subway A, C, F to Jay Street/Borough

Thirty Thirty

Hall; N, R to Court Street; 2, 3, 4, 5 to Borough Hall just 5 minutes' walk away

This is the only full-service hotel in Brooklyn and 282 more rooms were added in late 2006. Although over the water from Manhattan, you get excellent facilities at very good prices.

TOTAL BARGAINS

FLATIRON DISTRICT

GERSHWIN $-$$
✉ 7 East 27th Street between 5th and Madison Avenues
☎ 212-545 8000
Fax 212-684 5546
🖰 www.gershwinhotel.com
🚗 Subway 6 to 28th Street

A character-crammed budget boutique with some of the best rates in the city. You can opt for plain doubles or dormitory-style rooms with 10 beds and the hotel has theatre, stand-up comedy, poetry and live music on site.

FOR SOMETHING DIFFERENT...

Abode Ltd: PO Box 20022, New York, NY 10021. Tel 212-472 2000, www.abodenyc.com. $-$$$
Unhosted, good-quality studios and apartments all over the city, but you have to book for a minimum of four days.

Bed and Breakfast (and Books): 35 West 92nd Street, Apt. 2C, New York, NY 10025. Fax 212-865 8740. $-$$
Hosted and unhosted apartments – and you may end up being the guest of a writer.

Bed and Breakfast in Manhattan: PO Box 533, New York, NY 10150. Tel 212-472 2528, fax 212-988 9818. $-$$$
From comfortable to smart and both hosted and unhosted.

Inn New York City: 266 West 71st Street between Broadway and West End Avenue. Tel 212-580 1900, Fax 212-580 4437, www.innnewyorkcity.com. $$$-$$$$
This romantic boutique retreat has just four suites, each with a kitchen, and is fantastically placed for shopping, theatres and restaurants.

Jazz on the Park Hostel: 36 West 106th Street at Central Park West. Tel 212-932 1600, www.jazzonthepark.com. $
Clean, comfortable rooms for the budget traveller. Double and 'dormitory' rooms, laundry room, rooftop terrace and garden. Price includes breakfast. Sister hostels include Jazz on the Town: 307 East 14th Street in the midst of the bars, restaurants and clubs of East Village, tel 212-228 2780 and a new hostel, Jazz on Harlem: 104 West 128th Street, tel 212-222 5773.

GRAMERCY PARK HOTEL 17 $-$$

✉ 45 225 East 17th Street at Union Square
☎ 212-475 2845
Fax 212-677 8178
🖰 www.hotel17ny.com
🚗 Subway 6, A, C, E to 14th Street

An undiscovered chic hideaway well off the tourist radar. It's where Woody Allen filmed *Manhattan Murder Mystery* and Madonna used to stay and did many photo shoots.

HERALD SQUARE HOTEL $

✉ 19 West 31st Street between 5th Avenue and Broadway
☎ 212-279 4017
Fax 212-643 9208
🖰 www.heraldsquarehotel.com
🚗 Subway N, R to 28th Street

Once the headquarters of *Life* magazine, now a small, extremely well-priced hotel near the Empire State Building and Macy's.

THIRTY THIRTY NEW YORK CITY $-$$

✉ 30 East 30th Street between Park and Madison Avenues
☎ 212-689 1900
Fax 212-689 0023
🖰 www.thirtythirty-nyc.com
🚗 Subway 6 to 29th Street

Formerly the Martha Washington Hotel, this was turned into a modern, sophisticated but affordable boutique hotel in 1999.

GREENWICH VILLAGE

LARCHMONT $-$$

✉ 27 West 11th Street between 5th and 6th Avenues
☎ 212-989 9333
Fax 212-989 9496
🖰 www.larchmonthotel.com
🚗 Subway F to 14th Street

Clean, well-sought-after Village boutique hotel. No private baths in any rooms.

LOWER EAST SIDE

HOWARD JOHNSON EXPRESS INN $-$$

✉ 135 Houston Street between Forsyth and Eldridge Streets
☎ 212-358 8844
Fax 212-473 3500
🖰 www.hojo.com

The Lower East Side can now celebrate the arrival of its first hotel – modern, without frills but incredibly well-priced. Right next door is the renovated landmark Sunshine Cinema, which was once a showplace for Yiddish vaudeville and films and is now a multiplex for art films.

OFF SOHO SUITES $-$$

✉ 11 Rivington Street between Chrystie Street and The Bowery
☎ 212-979 9808
Fax 212-979 9801
🖰 www.offsoho.com
🚗 Subway F to Delancey Street

Good-sized, clean suites with fully equipped kitchens. Well-positioned.

MADISON SQUARE GARDEN

CHELSEA STAR HOTEL $

✉ 300 West 30th Street at 8th Avenue
☎ 212-244 7827
Fax 212-279 9018
🖰 www.starhotelny.com
🚗 Subway 1, 2, 3, 9 to 28th Street

Very low budget but bright and comfy and in a great location. Corridors are bright yellow with starbursts, the carpet is red and there are dormitories or private rooms, some of which can sleep up to four.

MIDTOWN EAST

PICKWICK ARMS HOTEL $

✉ 230 East 51st Street between 2nd and 3rd Avenues
☎ 212-355 0300
Fax 212-755 5029
🖰 www.pickwickarms.com
🚗 Subway 6 to 51st Street

A cheap place to stay in a pricey neighbourhood. The rooms are tiny but the hotel does have a roof garden and cocktail lounge.

MIDTOWN WEST

PORTLAND SQUARE HOTEL $

✉ 132 West 47th Street between 6th and 7th Avenues
☎ 212-382 0600
Fax 212-382 0684
🖰 www.portlandsquarehotel.com
🚗 Subway B, D, F, Q to 47th–50th Streets/ Rockefeller Center

This hotel is under new management and they're making positive additions such as queen-sized beds and free WiFi. The rooms are small but the hotel is very near the Theater District, so convenient if that features on your itinerary.

CHAPTER 12

Parks, Gardens and Sports

New York is as famous for its parks as it is for the Statue of Liberty. Of course, Central Park is the one everyone knows about but there are many others dotted throughout the city. The parks are very busy and remarkably safe, but be prudent about going into the less populated areas and especially cautious about visiting them at night if you are unfamiliar with the neighbourhood. A great website to keep you safe and in the know is www.nycgov parks.org – it has loads of information about every park in New York.

CENTRAL PARK

This is the New Yorkers' playground and meeting place and attracts 15 million visitors every year. Its 341 hectares (843 acres) stretch from Central Park South at 59th Street to Central Park North at 110th Street, with 5th Avenue and Central Park West forming its eastern and western boundaries. It was created over a 20-year period by architect Calvert Vaux and landscaper Frederick Law Olmsted and was completed in the 1860s.

★ ★ ★ ★ **BRIT TIP** ★ ★ ★ ★
★ To find out exactly what's going to ★
★ be on in Central Park when you're ★
★ visiting, log on to www.central ★
★ parknyc.org for a complete listing of ★
★ year-round activities. ★

To enter from the south, cross the street from **Grand Army Plaza** at 5th Avenue and 59th Street. Immediately in front of you is the Pond, and then the **Wollman Memorial Rink** (62nd Street), which hosts a Victorian amusement park in the summer and ice-skating in the winter. Close by is the **Visitor Information Center**, where you can pick up free maps and schedules of events, including the series of free concerts and dramas performed at the **SummerStage** (page 257). Here also are the **Gotham**

Miniature Golf Course (a gift from Donald Trump), the dairy and the antique carousel (65th Street). To the east is the **Central Park Wildlife Center** (63rd–66th Streets) and the **Children's Zoo and Wildlife Center** (page 218).

The **Sheep Meadow** (66th–69th Streets) to the north of the carousel is much used by New Yorkers for picnics and sunbathing. To its left is the **Tavern on the Green** restaurant (page 142) and to the right is the Mall (69th–72nd Streets), a tree-lined walkway. Follow the Mall to the top and you will find the **Central Park Bandshell** (70th Street), one of the park's concert venues. Further north is the **Loeb Boathouse** (74th and 75th Streets), which is home to the **Park View at the Boathouse** restaurant (page 140) and where you can hire bikes and boats (page 253).

★ ★ ★ ★ **BRIT TIP** ★ ★ ★ ★
★ ★
★ The Philharmonic/Met Concerts are ★
★ thrilling, surprisingly tranquil ★
★ summer experiences. Join tens of ★
★ thousands of New Yorkers in laying ★
★ down a blanket on the Great Lawn ★
★ and setting up a picnic two or three ★
★ hours ahead of concert time. ★
★ The first concert of the season ends ★
★ with fireworks. ★
★ ★

Continuing north, you will come to the **Ramble** (71st Street), a heavily wooded area which leads (if you can find the way through) to the Gothic revival **Belvedere Castle** (74th Street) housing another information centre. Also here are the **Delacorte Theater**, where summer productions are presented by Shakespeare in the Park (tel 212-539 8750, www.public theater.org for tickets) and the **Great Lawn** (79th–86th Streets) where the **Philharmonic and Metropolitan Opera** concerts are held – the only time you can witness tens of thousands of New Yorkers all being quiet at the same time (page 257).

★★★★ ★ ★ ★ ★
★ A really great way to find out more ★
★ about Central Park's history and ★
★ modern-day uses is by taking the ★
★ 2-hour Big Onion walking tour (tel ★
★ 212-439 1090 www.bigonion.com), ★
★ which costs $10–15. See page 82 ★
★ for details. ★
★★★★★★★★★★★★★★★★★★★★★★★★★★

Further north again is the huge
Jacqueline Kennedy Onassis Reservoir
(86th–96th Streets). A well-kept secret is
the formal 2.4 hectare (6 acre), three-part
Conservatory Garden (104th–106th
Streets), where dozens of wedding parties
come for photographs on summer
weekends. It was bequeathed by the
Vanderbilt family, and there are free tours
and concerts in the summer.

Further details about great activities for
children and the young at heart can be
found in Chapter 9, New York for Families,
starting on page 207.

THE MAIN PARKS

Battery Park (www.batteryparkcity.org):
With a decent yet distant view of the Statue
of Liberty, this park is visited by thousands.
Situated at the southern tip of Manhattan it
is a beautiful space overlooking New York
Harbor. In the nearby Hudson River Park, the
Battery Park City Authority presents a
Sounds at Sunset summer series of poetry
readings, cabaret and classical music (tel
212-416 5394). For more information on
the park, see pages 36–37.

Brooklyn Botanic Garden

Brooklyn Botanic Garden (tel 718-623
7200, www.bbg.org): Across in the outer
borough of Brooklyn, this botanic garden is
famous for its cherry trees that bloom from
mid-March to late May – you can watch
their progress on the garden's website. More
details are given in Chapter 14, A Taste of
the Outer Boroughs, on page 261.

TOP FIVE PARKS AND GARDENS

Central Park

Battery Park

Luna Park, Union Square

Brooklyn Botanic Garden in Spring or
New York Botanical Garden for the
rest of the year

Riverside Park

Bryant Park (tel 212-768 4242,
www.bryantpark.org): This small park is a
great spot for a picnic lunch or you could
dine at the fancy restaurant here. It even

Sakura Matsui festival in Brooklyn Botanic Garden's Japanese Garden

PARKS, GARDENS AND SPORTS

Bryant Park

puts on free films and concerts on Monday nights during the summer (pages 256 and 257). The Beaux Arts-style le Carrousel – specially created to complement the park's French classical style – costs $1.75 a ride.
Carl Schurz Park (tel 212-459 4455, www.carlschurzparknyc.org): In the family-friendly Upper East Side, this park sits right next to Gracie Mansion (page 66), the official residence of the mayor of New York, and has an esplanade along the river. It is a popular destination for families and fitness fanatics, especially at weekends.
City Hall Park: Newly renovated and re-opened in 1999, this space near the fabulous Woolworth Building and civic

buildings (page 70) is charming. Parts of the park have been restored to as they were in the 18th and 19th centuries, in particular the beautiful lanterns surrounding the gorgeous Jacob Wrey Mould Fountain.
Luna Park, Union Square: This public park is the gateway to Downtown – a stone's throw from the East Village, SoHo and Greenwich Village – and as close as New York gets to a European piazza. It has an open-air restaurant (of the same name) and is right by the Union Square green market (www.unionsquarejournal.com/greenmarket. htm), one of the city's largest farmers' markets where regional purveyors sell their products at stalls in the middle of what is now one of the hippest areas of New York. The market operates year round on Monday, Wednesday, Friday and Saturday.
New York Botanical Garden (tel 718-817 8700, www.nybg.org): From antique treasures to family adventures, this extensive, wonderful garden in the Bronx is a must-see. Last year (2006) it launched the Nolen Greenhouses for Living Collections, considered the most sophisticated behind-the-scenes greenhouses in botanic gardens in America. Get there by train from Grand Central Station. More details are given in Chapter 14, A Taste of the Outer Boroughs, on page 266.

Prospect Park (tel 718-965 8951, www.prospectpark.org): A 213 hectare (526 acre) urban oasis in the heart of Brooklyn, this is an incredible park that was landscaped by the same designers as Central Park. It has a wealth of open spaces, activities, events and museums. More details are given in Chapter 9, New York for

Central Park

Families, on page 216 and Chapter 14, A Taste of the Outer Boroughs, on page 263.

Riverside Park (tel 212-870 3070, www.riversideparkfund.org): Stretching over 6.5km (4 miles) along the Hudson River from 68th to 155th Streets, this 130 hectare (323 acre) long and narrow park was designed by Central Park's Frederick Olmstead. It has a marina at 79th Street where you can have a light meal and watch the pleasure craft and houseboats.

Washington Square Park (www.washingtonsquarepark.org): In the heart of Greenwich Village, the park is best known for its bohemian and rebellious character and is very popular. It is not so much a park as an area covered in tarmac and filled with a hotchpotch of individuals who flock here to snack and people-watch. The two main attractions are the fountain and the Washington arch. More details are given in Chapter 3, The New York Neighbourhoods, on page 40.

SPECTATOR SPORTS

Ask any New Yorker and they'll tell you that they read their newspapers from back to front – that's just how important sports are to them. And they have plenty to choose between: two football teams and two baseball teams to support, plus basketball, hockey, tennis and racing. But it can be really tough to get in to watch some of the games, especially to see football's New York Giants and the Mets baseball team in action. Still, it's worth making the effort just to see another side of New York life. If you can't get tickets directly through the box offices listed below, then try TicketMaster on 212-307 7171, www.ticketmaster.com – they've got most games covered.

An incredibly expensive alternative is to try one of the companies that specialises in selling tickets at exorbitant prices – anything from $100 for a football game to $1,000 for a baseball game. They include Prestige Entertainment on 800-243 8849 or 203-622 5151, www.prestigeentertainment.com; Ticket City on 1-800-SOLD-OUT, www.ticketcity.com; or Ticket Vault on 1-877-VAULT68, www.ticketvault.com.

A third alternative is to try a ticket tout – they're known as 'scalpers' in New York – outside Madison Square Garden. However, probably your best bet is to ask the concierge at your hotel – they have an amazing ability to come up with the goods.

MADISON SQUARE GARDEN
www.thegarden.com

This venue on 7th Avenue at 32nd Street (subway A, C, E, 1, 2, 3, 9 to 34th Street/Penn Street) is home to all the following teams. Buy tickets from the Garden Box Office in person at 4 Pennsylvania Plaza or call TicketMaster on 212-307 7171.

NBA's New York Knicks basketball team: from November to June.

NHL's New York Rangers ice-hockey team: from October to April.

WNBA New York Liberty women's pro basketball team: from May to August.

Madison Square Garden is also famous for its boxing Fight Nights, and it hosts college/high school basketball matches.

FOOTBALL
The two teams are the **New York Giants** (www.giants.com) and the **New York Jets** (www.newyorkjets.com). Both teams play at the Giants Stadium at Meadowlands (201-935 3900, www.meadowlands.com) in New Jersey (get there on a bus from the Port Authority's 41st Street bus terminal at 42nd Street and 8th Avenue – 0800 772 2222). The event information hotline is 201-935 3900 and the box office is 201-507 8900 or TicketMaster at 212-307 7171, www.ticketmaster.com. You'll have just as hard a time getting tickets for the Jets as for the Giants. The season runs from September to January.

BASEBALL
Try the Yankee Stadium (page 267) in the Bronx at 161st Street (subway C, D or 4 to 161st Street/Yankee Stadium) to see the **New York Yankees** at play. The box office is 718-293 6000 or visit www.yankees.com.

The **New York Mets** play at Shea Stadium (page 271) in Flushing Meadows, Queens (subway 7 to Willetts Point/Shea Stadium). The box office is 718-507 TIXX or visit www.mets.com. The season for both teams is from April to September. In October and November, post-season games are played by the best teams for a gargantuan amount of money. It costs a fortune to get into one of these games, which is why the stands are usually filled with season ticket holders and celebs.

TENNIS
The **US Open** is held every year at the US Tennis Center in Flushing Meadows, Queens

(subway 7 to Willetts Point/Shea Stadium), from late August to early September. For tickets call TicketMaster on 1-866-OPEN-TIX or the Tennis Center Ticket office on 718-760 6200 or visit www.usopen.org. Like Wimbledon, tickets for the finals are impossible to get, but it's worth seeing some of the earlier rounds to watch how it's done American style (page 271).

HORSE RACING

One of the four local tracks is **Aqueduct Stadium** in Queens (110-00 Rockaway Blvd, Jamaica) (subway A to Aqueduct Racetrack) from November to May every Wednesday to Saturday. Free admission from January 2nd to early March. Tel 718-641 4700, www.nyra.com/aqueduct.

The $1 million **Belmont Stakes** race, on a Saturday in early June, is the major event at the Belmont Racetrack (take the Long Island Rail Road's 'Belmont Special' from Penn Station at 7th Avenue and 34th Street) from May to July. Tel 718-641 4700 ext 732, www.nyra.com/belmont.

GET STUCK IN

If you want to take part in some kind of sporting activity while in New York, your best bet is to go to Central Park. Probably the most popular sports here are boating, biking, skating and running.

BIKING

You can rent bikes from the Loeb Boathouse, Central Park, East 72nd Street and Park Drive North (tel 212-517 2233, www.thecentralparkboathouse.com) for $6 (kids)-15 per hour, including helmet, plus credit card deposit; 10am till dusk. Try tackling the 11km (6 mile) road loop that is closed to traffic at weekends. Get to the boathouse with the free trolley shuttle service every 15 minutes from 5th Avenue. For other bike rental information, see Chapter 4, What to See and Do, Bike Tours on page 72.

BOATING

Also from the Loeb Boathouse (tel 212-517 2233, www.thecentralparkboathouse.com), you can rent a rowing boat for $10 per hour with a $30 deposit – or even a chauffeured gondola for $30 per half hour.

HORSE RIDING

The 10km (6 mile) bridle path loops the Reservoir as well as the North Meadow in the Park. Riders can also take the round trip from the south-west corner of the Reservoir to the playground at the south-west bottom of the Park. Horse riding is permitted all year. For more information, contact the Claremont Riding Academy (tel 212-724 5100, www.potomachorse.com).

ICE-SKATING

The Wollman Memorial Rink, mid-Park at 62nd Street (tel 212-439-6900, www.wollmanskatingrink.com) is open from November to March and rents skates for $4.75. It's $8.50 for adults ($11 at weekends), $4.25 and $4.50 for children, $4.25 and $7.50 for seniors.

The Lasker Rink, north-Park at 106th Street, is a bit rougher but less crowded at $4.50 for adults and $2.25 seniors and students. Call 212-534 7639 or visit www.wollmanskatingrink.com/lasker.htm for information on lessons.

IN-LINE SKATING

On a hot summer's day, Central Park is filled with thousands of in-line skaters. The most popular places to skate are:

The Bandshell: for skate dancers and those who like to watch them.

West Drive at 67th Street: a slalom course has been set up here for all to try.

Wollman and Lasker Rinks: in summer these rinks are set up for the hot-shot in-line skater. Fascinating to watch, too.

RUNNING

Every day, hundreds of runners encircle the Park. If you want to run here, it helps to know the distance. The outer loop of the Park is approximately 10km (6 miles). The middle loop is about 6km (4 miles) and the Reservoir loop is about 2km (1¼ miles). The Road Runners Club (tel 212-860 4455, www.nyrrc.org) can provide information on running in New York.

SWIMMING

Cool off for free in the Lasker Pool – by far one of the favourite kids' activities in Central Park. It is open every day during the summer months. Check details on www.centralparknyc.org.

TENNIS

Anyone for tennis? There are more tennis courts in Central Park than anywhere else in Manhattan. Courts are open from April to November and a day pass to use them costs $5. Tel 212-360-8133.

CHAPTER 13

Festivals and Parades

New Yorkers love an excuse to party, from celebrating the changing of the seasons to championing their cultural roots. In fact, judging by the number of parades, open-air concerts and festivals taking place every month, it's a wonder anyone gets any work done. The good news is that you can be sure that whatever time of year you decide to visit the Big Apple, there will be some truly spectacular entertainment going on. And what's more, most of it is free!

ANNUAL AND BIENNIAL EVENTS

JANUARY AND FEBRUARY

Paint the Town
Citywide offers and discounts on everything from restaurants and theatres to accommodation from 2 January throughout February. Tel 212-484 1222, www.nycvisit.com.

Winter Antiques Show
19-28 January. 7th Regiment Armory, Park Avenue at 67th Street. Tel 718-292 7392 or 718-665 5250 or fax 212-665 5532, www.winterantiquesshow.com. Admission $20 with catalogue.
The Winter Antiques Show kicks off New York's winter season with a glitzy Opening Night Party on 18 January, but as tickets for that event start at $1,000 each your best bet is to wait until the next day to see the treasures within. From the simplicity of arts and crafts to ornate baroque clocks, you can be sure there will be fine antiques to suit everyone's taste. Private collections from all over America are also on show.

Chinese New Year Parade
From the first day of the full moon between 21 January and 19 February. Chinatown around Mott Street. Tel 212-484 1222, www.explorechinatown.com.
New York City is known for having some of the most authentic celebrations of the

Chinese New Year parade

Central Park

Chinese New Year in the US, and the festivities range from the magnificent dragon parade in Chinatown to various other performances around the city. The party continues for ten days.

Black History Month
Throughout February. A series of shows is put on to celebrate the African-American experience in New York. See the newspapers and guides for cultural events, concerts and lectures scheduled around the city, or visit www.newyorkmetro.com for detailed listings of events.

Grammy Awards
Late February. Madison Square Garden. Tel 212-465 6741, www.grammy.com.
The Grammy Awards are to music what the Oscars are to the movies. Over the years Los Angeles and New York have played tug-of-war with the Grammy Awards show and New York has won. You may not get to attend the Awards but you can go stargazing by the red carpet as celebs arrive in their limos.

★ ★ ★ ★ BRIT TIP ★ ★ ★ ★
★ A central number for New York
★ events is 212-484 1222; and a
★ website that reports many free
★ events is www.newyorkled.com. A
★ good events site for planning ahead
★ is www.new.york.eventguide.com.

MARCH AND APRIL
Whitney Biennial
March to June. Whitney Museum of American Art (page 134), 945 Madison Avenue at 75th Street. Tel 212-570 3676 or 1-800 WHITNEY, www.whitney.org. Admission $15 adults, $10 students and seniors, under 12s free. However, on Fridays

6–9pm it's pay-what-you-wish – and the queues are LONG! The next biennial year is 2008.
The exhibition's line-up of contemporary art is as controversial as Damien Hirst's cow. So for art from the apocalyptic to the ethereal and the fantastic to the political, this is a show that can't be missed.

St Patrick's Day Parade
17 March. 5th Avenue between 44th and 86th Streets. Tel 918-793 1600, www.st-patricks-day.com.
One of the bigger parades the city has to offer. If you're in town, you won't be able to miss the sea of green that goes with this

★ ★ ★ ★ BRIT TIP ★ ★ ★ ★
★ A good vantage point to watch the
★ St Patrick's Day parade is the steps
★ of St Patrick's Cathedral (page 71),
★ where the Bishop of New York
★ greets the marching bands.

annual Irish-American day. The parade starts at 11am up 5th Avenue and the festivities go on late into the night.

Greek Independence Day Parade
The Sunday closest to 25 March (when Greek Independence Day falls in the Orthodox Lent, the parade is shifted to April or even May). Along 5th Avenue to 49th Street. Tel 718-204 6500, fax 718-204 8986, www.greekparade.org.
This one's a Zorba-style parade with lots of flag waving and national dress, as well as plenty of Greek food, music and dancing.

Easter Parade
Easter Sunday. 5th Avenue between 49th and 57th Streets.
This is not an official parade, just a chance to watch strollers flaunting Easter bonnets from gorgeous to outrageous. The steps of St Patrick's Cathedral (page 71) are an

St Patrick's Day parade

FESTIVALS AND PARADES

TOP FIVE FESTIVALS & PARADES

Grammy Awards: January

St Patrick's Day Parade: March

Heritage of Pride Parade: June

Bryant Park Free Summer Season: June to August

Macy's Thankgiving Day Parade: November

advantageous viewing spot. Kick-off is at 10am, so arrive early to bag a space.

New York City Ballet Spring Season

Late April to June. New York State Theater, 20 Lincoln Center Plaza, 65th Street at Columbus Avenue. Tel 212-870 5570, www.nycballet.com. Student rush tickets (available on day of performance) $12. Tel 212-870-7766.

The New York City Ballet performs its spring season in New York before touring. Go to see the world-famous dancers, trained in the classic style of ballet masters Balanchine and Robbins.

MAY AND JUNE

See also New York City Ballet and Whitney Biennial (above).

Cirque du Soleil

May to June. Randall's Island Park. Tel 514-790 1245, www.cirquedusoleil.com. Adult tickets from $60, students/seniors $54, children $42.

Every other year, and 2008 will be one of those years, this wonderful Canadian animal-free circus hitches up its tent in Randall's Island Park on Manhattan's East River. The show's striking, dramatic mix of circus arts and street entertainment first hit New York City in 1988 and the dazzling performances have entranced audiences ever since. To help get there, NY Waterway (page 75) runs a special ferry service from Wall Street along Manhattan's East Side to Randall's Island.

American Ballet Theater

May to July. Metropolitan Opera House at the Lincoln Center. Tel 212-362 6000, www.abt.org.

Going to see the ABT at the Met is exhilarating. The majesty of the Metropolitan Opera House combines with the passion, power and movement of one of the world's most innovative dance companies to create a magical experience. The Theater also runs an ABTKids programme (see page 192).

TriBeCa Film Festival

Second week in May. TriBeCa area. Tel 866-941 FEST (3378) or 212-321 7400, www.tribecafilmfestival.org.

The 12-day TriBeCa Film Festival was founded in 2002 by Robert De Niro, Jane Rosenthal and Craig Hatkoff as a response to the attacks on the World Trade Center. The festival showcases independent movies, runs workshops and has a children's film programme. During the week, local restaurants offer cut-price meals.

9th Avenue International Food Festival

Mid-May. 9th Avenue between 37th and 57th Streets. Tel 212-581 7029, www.hellskitchennyc.com.

This festival is a gourmet's delight. Hell's Kitchen cooks up a feast of foods from around the world and hundreds of stalls line the streets selling every type of food imaginable. Go for lunch and then walk it all off by strolling on down to Chelsea's fabulous art galleries nearby.

Fleet Week

Last week in May. Intrepid Sea-Air-Space Museum (page 118), Pier 86, 46th Street at the Hudson River. Tel 212-245 0072, www.intrepidmuseum.org.

New York City Fleet Week brings thousands of sailors and marines from US naval vessels to the Big Apple. Unless you're a boat nut, it's normally not worth visiting the huge armada of US Navy and other ships that visit New York, but this week they'll be very hard to miss.

Washington Square Outdoor Art Exhibition

Late May through to early June, then again in September. Washington Square. Tel 212-982 6255.

An old and revered tradition of arty Greenwich Village, this is a huge outdoor art show with easels and food trolleys set up in the streets all around the park.

Lower East Side Festival of Arts

Last weekend in May. 155 1st Avenue at 10th Street. Tel 212-254 1109, www.theaterforthecity.nt/lesA.htm.

Deep in the heart of the neighbourhood that helped create the East Coast Beat Movement, method acting and pop art, this is a 3-day indoor and outdoor annual arts festival and carnival.

Puerto Rican Day Parade
Second Sunday in June from 11am. 5th Avenue between 44th and 85th Streets. Tel 212-484 1222, www.nycvisit.com.
This is a New York parade on a grand scale – expect more than 100,000 marchers and 3 million spectators. The largest of several Puerto Rican celebrations in the city, with 3 hours of colourful floats, music and dancing.

Broadway Under The Stars
Third Monday in June. Bryant Park, 6th Avenue at 42nd Street. Tel 212-768 4242, www.bryantpark.org or www.nycvisit.com.
Broadway kicks off New York's summer outdoor concert season with a showcase of its hottest talent performing major show songs. From then on you can experience the glamour of Broadway in the great outdoors every Thursday lunchtime. Performances are 12.30–2pm.

★ ★ ★ ★ **BRIT TIP** ★ ★ ★ ★
★ Check out the many street fairs ★
★ from spring to autumn throughout ★
★ the city with food, craft and other ★
★ stalls. Visit www.nycstreetfairs.com ★
★ and www.nyctourist.com. ★
★ ★

Mermaid Parade
Last Saturday in June. 8th Street between Steeplechase Park and Broadway, Coney Island, Brooklyn. Tel 718-372 5159, www.coneyisland.com.
The Mermaid Parade celebrates the beginning of summer. Catch the B, D or F trains to Stillwell Avenue on the Saturday following the first official day of summer to sample a wild and boisterous scene of carnival floats and costumes. The parade is followed by the Mermaid Parade Ball.

New York Jazz Festival
Mid to late June. Various clubs. Tel 212-501 1390, www.festivalproductions.net.
See some of the biggest names in jazz at various venues throughout Manhattan. Even those of you who are not true aficionados of jazz can enjoy the festival atmosphere provided by the 300 acts taking part in this event.

Heritage of Pride Parade
Last Sunday in June. From Columbus Circle along 5th Avenue and 52nd Street to Christopher Street in Greenwich Village. Tel 212-807 7433, fax 212-807 7436, www.hopinc.org.
Formerly known as the Gay Pride Parade, this parade starts off a week of events commemorating the Stonewall Riots of 1969, and the struggle of New York's gay community for public acceptance. There is a packed club schedule, fireworks and an open-air dance party on the West Side piers.

Museum Mile Festival
Second Tuesday in June. 5th Avenue between 82nd and 104th Streets. Tel 212-606 2296, www.museummilefestival.org.
Museum Mile is neither a museum nor a mile, but nine museums stretching along 5th Avenue and Central Park on the Upper East Side. All are worth a visit. During the Festival you can get into nine museums, including the fabulous Metropolitan, for free. An added perk is the fascinating street entertainment.

Central Park SummerStage
June to August. Rumsey Playfield, Central Park at 72nd Street and Central Park West. Tel 212-307 7171 for tickets to benefit concerts or 212-360 2756 for information, www.summerstage.org. Subway 1, 2, 3, 9, B, C to 72nd Street.
You can experience many kinds of entertainment for free in New York and some of the best are the free weekend afternoon concerts put on by the SummerStage, featuring top international performers. On weeknights, dance and spoken-word events are also put on in Central Park.

New York Philharmonic/Metropolitan Opera Parks Concerts.
Various sites in summer, www.nycgov parks.org Tel 212-875 5709 (Philharmonic)/212-362 6000 (Met).
These free, open-air events in parks around the city are wildly popular so arrive early to stake out a site.

Shakespeare in the Park
Late June to late August. Delacorte Theater, Central Park at 81st Street. Tel 212-539 8750, www.publictheater.org.
Plays held in the open-air theatre every summer are free. There are two each year – one Shakespeare and one American, with performances almost nightly. Although free, you still have to get tickets to see them, which are available from 1pm on the day of the performance, and the queues are long.

Bryant Park Summer Film Festival
Every Monday throughout June and August.

6th Avenue at 42nd Street. Tel 212-391 4248, www.bryantpark.org. Subway F, V, B, D to 42nd Street/Bryant Park.

Bryant Park is one of the few green spaces available in the Midtown area, and this is a summer-long series of free classical music, jazz, dance and film showings during the day and evening.

Classic films shown in the park on Mondays are a great way to unwind after a hard day's shopping or sightseeing. The lawn opens at 5pm for blankets and picnicking. The films begin at dusk.

Midsummer Night Swing

Mid June to mid July. Lincoln Center for Performing Arts. Tel 212-875 5766, www.lincolncenter.org.

Considered the city's hottest outdoor dance party, with dance-filled nights when energetic bands play everything from swing to salsa. Lots of dance instructors are on hand to give lessons in every type of dance, or you can just pop by to listen to the live music.

Celebrate Brooklyn! Performing Arts Festival

All summer. Prospect Park Bandshell, 9th Street at Prospect Park West, Park Slope, Brooklyn. Tel 718-855 7882, www.celebratebrooklyn.org.

Here's a very good reason to break out of Manhattan and visit one of the outer boroughs – a series of free music, dance, theatre and film events lasting nine weeks.

JULY AND AUGUST

See also American Ballet Theater at the Met, Thursday Night Concert Series, Central Park SummerStage, New York Philharmonic/Met Opera Concerts, New York Shakespeare Festival, Bryant Park Free Summer Season,

Fireworks above the Statue of Liberty

P.S.I. Contemporary Art Center in Queens

Midsummer Night Swing and Celebrate Brooklyn! Performing Arts Festival (above).

Summergarden Summer Restaurant Week

Mid-July. Tel 212-484 1222, www.nycvisit.com/restaurantweek.

For two weeks, more than 150 of the city's finest restaurants offer three-course fixed-price lunches and dinners at prices that reflect the year – in 2006 the cost of lunch was $24.07 (dinner $35.00).

Concerts in the Abby Aldrich Rockefeller Sculpture Garden

July and August. Museum of Modern Art, 11 West 53rd Street between 5th and 6th Avenues. Tel 212-708 9400, www.moma.org. Subway E, V to 5th Avenue/53rd Street; B, D, F to 47-50 Streets/Rockefeller Centre.

An added bonus to visiting the little gem that is MoMA (re-opened in autumn 2004 after major renovation, page 120) is the series of free classical and jazz concerts that are presented in the museum's sculpture garden every summer.

Lincoln Center Festival

Mid-late July. Lincoln Center for the Performing Arts, 140 West 65th Street. Tel 212-546 2656, www.lincolncenter.org.

A veritable feast of dance, drama, ballet, children's shows and multimedia and performance art, involving both repertory companies and special guests, at venues

Macy's Thanksgiving Day parade

inside and outside at the Lincoln Center (page 192).

Fourth of July
The Americans still insist on celebrating achieving independence from their colonial masters – and they do it in style! Throughout New York there are various celebrations going on, but by far the biggest and most spectacular is Macy's Fireworks Spectacular, which is held on the East River between 14th and 51st Streets. Tel 212-494 4495, www.macy's.com A good spot to see the $1-million, 30-minute firework extravaganza is from FDR Drive (Franklin D Roosevelt Drive).

Harlem Week
August. Along 5th Avenue from West 125th to West 135th Streets. Tel 212-262 8477, www.harlemdiscover.com.
The largest black and Hispanic festival in the world, its highlight is the street party with R&B, gospel and All That Jazz. In addition to the music, there are films, dance, fashion, sports and exhibitions. What a great way to experience Harlem!

SEPTEMBER AND OCTOBER
See also Washington Square Outdoor Art Exhibition (May and June); Thursday Night Concert Series (above).

West Indian-American Day Parade
First weekend in September. 5th Avenue to Christopher Street in Brooklyn. Tel 718-467 1797, www.wiadca.org.

Fabulous festival celebrating Caribbean culture with food (all along Eastern Parkway) and entertainment from top Caribbean artists. Brightly costumed marchers put on a special children's parade on the Saturday, with an even bigger event on Labor Day (first Monday in September).

Feast of San Gennaro
Mid September for 11 days. Mulberry Street to Worth Street in Little Italy. Tel 212-764 7241, www.sangennaro.org.
Really the best time to see what is left of the once-bustling Little Italy that is now reduced to just Mulberry Street. There are lots of fairground booths, plenty of food – look out for the cannoli-eating contest – and even more vino.

★ Parades are great fun, but they also provide perfect opportunities for pickpockets, so keep your bags and wallets close to you – and never put your wallet in your back pocket.

Columbus Day Parade
Second Monday in October. 5th Avenue between 44th and 79th Streets. Tel 212-249 9923.
The traditional celebration of the first recorded sighting of America by Europeans is now somewhat controversial in some quarters but, despite its lack of political correctness, Columbus Day still gets the big 5th Avenue parade treatment, which is well worth a view. The parade has over 35,000 participants plus celebrities – the likes of Frank Sinatra, Sophia Loren and Luciano Pavarotti have all paraded in the past.

Broadway on Broadway
Mid-September. Times Square. Tel. 212-768 1560, www.broadwayonbroadway.com.
Quintessentially New York – a free annual concert when numbers from Broadway

Greenwich Village Hallowe'en parade

shows are performed live on a giant outdoor stage by a galaxy of celebrities surrounded by TV cameras. It all ends in a big finale with loads of confetti.

Halloween Parade
31 October at 6.30pm. 6th Avenue between Union Square and Spring Street, Greenwich Village. Tel 212-475 3333, www.halloween-nyc.com.
A uniquely Village event, with the outlandishly over-the-top costumes (or lack of them!) on (or off!) many of its participants. The organisers decree a different theme each year and a lot of work goes into the amazing outfits that range from the exotic to the nearly non-existent. It attracts between 60,000 and 100,000 ghouls, ghosts and onlookers. So get creative and dress-up to join in – only those in fancy dress can march.

New York City Marathon
Last Sunday in October/first Sunday in November. Staten Island to Central Park. Tel 212-423 2249, www.ingnycmarathon.org.
Starts at the Staten Island side of the Verrazano Narrows Bridge as a mad pack of 35,000 men and women run 42km (26.2 miles) around all five boroughs, to finish at the Tavern on the Green in Central Park at West 67th Street.
If you would like to enter the marathon you need to fill out an application form, pay a small fee, and then wait to see if you get picked. You can do this through the website (above) or write to New York City Marathon, International Lottery, 9 East 89th Street, New York, NY 10128.

NOVEMBER AND DECEMBER
See also New York City Marathon (above).

Macy's Thanksgiving Day Parade
Thanksgiving Day, 9am. From Central Park West at 77th Street to Macy's (page 89) on Broadway at 34th Street. Tel 212-494 4624, www.macysparade.com.
Definitely one for the family, this is the Big Mama of all New York's parades, with enormous inflated cartoon characters, fabulous floats and the gift-giving Santa Claus himself. New Yorkers in the know like to come by and watch it being set up the night before between 77th and 81st Streets off Central Park West. The parade is even televised for the rest of America. If you miss it, you can go to see Santa in Santaland in Macy's until Christmas.

Christmas Tree Lighting Ceremony
Late November or early December. The Rockefeller Center, 5th Avenue between 49th and 50th Streets. Tel 212-632 3975, www.rockefellercenter.com.
The Rockefeller Center (page 64) in front of the towering RCA building provides the magical setting for the switching on of nearly 8km (5 miles) of dazzling lights on a huge Christmas tree. The plaza leading up to the tree is decked with lights too!

New Year's Eve Fireworks in Central Park
31 December, midnight. 5th Avenue and 90th Street or Bethsheda Fountain (Central Park at 72nd Street) are the best viewing spots. Tel 212-360 3456, www.nycgov parks.org. The hot apple cider and spirit of camaraderie begin at 11.30pm.

New Year's Eve Ball Drop
31 December, midnight, Times Square. Tel 212-768 1560, www.timessquarenyc.com
This event is a real New York classic, though you may prefer to watch safely on TV rather than be packed in with the freezing masses. Remember, Times Square is a misnomer – it's a junction, so there isn't really that much room and all the side streets get packed too. If you do manage to get a good spot, though, you'll see the giant glitterball of 180 bulbs and 12,000 rhinestones being dropped to bring in the New Year.

AMERICAN HOLIDAYS

New Year's Day: 1 January

Martin Luther King Jnr Day: Third Monday in January

President's Day: Third Monday in February

Memorial Day: Last Monday in May

Independence Day: 4 July

Labor Day: First Monday in September

Columbus Day: Second Monday in October

Election Day: First Tuesday after the first Monday in November

Veterans' Day: 11 November

Thanksgiving: Fourth Thursday in November

Christmas Day: 25 December

CHAPTER 14

A Taste of the Outer Boroughs

Those with limited time in New York may not be able to get as far as the outer boroughs of the Bronx, Queens, Brooklyn and Staten Island. But they do have a lot to offer in terms of museums, parks, restaurants, zoos, tours and atmosphere, so do go if you get a chance. This chapter will give you a few ideas.

A TASTE OF BROOKLYN

Brooklyn was once a city in its own right, until it became part of New York City in 1898. Some still refer to the event as its annexation and the borough certainly has its own unique style and language. Famous Brooklynites include Woody Allen, Barbara Streisand and Mel Brooks. There is still such a thing as Brooklynese, which is most obvious in the pronunciation of words such as absoid (absurd), doity (dirty), noive (nerve) and toin (turn).

Nowadays, many of the different parts of Brooklyn have their own unique cultures, but by far the two most important 'sightseeing' areas are Brooklyn Heights and Prospect Park (Maps 9 and 10).

BROOKLYN HEIGHTS

Whether you've had lunch or dinner, a walk across the stunning Brooklyn Bridge will certainly help the digestion. It's the most famous bridge in New York and was the world's largest suspension bridge when it was completed in 1883. The views are fantastic and strolling along the wooden walkway gives an insight into why it took 16 years to build. If you've walked to Brooklyn from Manhattan via the bridge, you'll find yourself in the heart of Brooklyn Heights. Down by the water's edge is the River Café (page 141), a refined and elegant setting to soak up fantastic views of the Manhattan skyline. Night-time is best – the twinkling lights in the skyscrapers look just like a picture postcard. Have a drink at the bar to enjoy the best views before tucking into a sumptuous supper. It is expensive and you will have to book well in advance, but it's an experience you are never likely to forget. Jackets are essential after 5pm.

The Heights themselves are home to some of the most beautiful and sought-after brownstone townhouses in New York. These were built in the early 18th century when bankers and financiers chose to escape Manhattan, yet still be close enough to keep an eye on their money. Once again, Brooklyn Heights is much in demand as an area of tranquillity close to the madness and mayhem of the city. If you walk along the Esplanade, you will see below you the former docks that were the setting for Marlon Brando's movie *On The Waterfront.*

BROOKLYN BOTANIC GARDEN

- ✉ 1000 Washington Avenue between Eastern Parkway and Empire Boulevard
- ☎ 718-623 7200
- 🖱 www.bbg.org
- 🚇 Subway 1, 2 to Eastern Parkway
- ⊙ Tues–Fri 8am–6pm, Sat and Sun 10am–6pm (Oct–Mar closes 4.30pm every day)
- $ $5 adults, $3 students and seniors, under 16s free

Right next door to Prospect Park and the Brooklyn Museum of Art, the Botanic Garden has a Rose Garden, Japanese Garden, a Shakespeare Garden and the Celebrity Path, which commemorates some of Brooklyn's more famous children. It is most famous, though, for its Japanese cherry trees and huge collection of beautiful bonsai. Relax and enjoy the vibe in its Terrace Café.

★ ★ ★ ★ BRIT TIP ★ ★ ★ ★

To enjoy some of the delicious Middle Eastern cuisine that centres around Brooklyn's Atlantic Avenue, join a tour with Savory Sojourns (page 80), whose expert guide Addie Tomei will reveal this treasure trove of sights and smells with stops at delicatessens and markets, where you can try a medley of tasty treats such as fresh pitta and grape leaves.

BROOKLYN CHILDREN'S MUSEUM

See Chapter 9, New York for Families, page 216.

BROOKLYN HISTORICAL SOCIETY

✉ 128 Pierrepont Street at Clinton Street
☎ 718-222 4111
🖰 www.brooklynhistory.org
🚇 Subway 2, 3, 4, 5 to Borough Hall
🕐 Wed–Sun 10am–5pm, Sun noon–5pm
$ $6 adults, $4 students and seniors, under 12s free

It's said that one in seven Americans can trace their family roots to Brooklyn and, as many American families originally came from the UK, it's well worth popping into this academic retreat to see if you can trace your family tree. Plus there are innovative exhibitions, educational programmes and a wonderful library.

BROOKLYN MUSEUM OF ART

✉ 200 Eastern Parkway at Washington Avenue
☎ 718-638 5000
🖰 www.brooklynmuseum.org
🚇 Subway 1, 2 to Eastern Parkway/ Brooklyn Museum
🕐 Sun 11am–6pm, Wed–Fri 10am–5pm, first Sat of month 11am–11pm, all other Sats 11am–6pm
$ Suggested donation $8 adults, $4 students, seniors and children over 12, members and under 12s free

The spring of 2004 saw the opening of a magnificent new glass entrance pavilion, complementing the beautiful 19th-century Beaux Arts building that has housed the museum since 1897. A new central lobby and public plaza have also been constructed, making the building the most visitor-friendly museum in NYC. With one of the best collections of Egyptian art in the world and well known for its African art, it was the first-ever museum to display what

Brooklyn Museum of Art

Brooklyn Heights brownstone houses

were once considered to be anthropological objects as fine art. The museum has a long tradition of collecting non-Western art and, since 1934, it has concentrated on fine art. The collections are divided into six departments that comprise Egyptian, Classical and Ancient Middle Eastern Art; Painting and Sculpture; Arts of Africa, the Pacific and the Americas; Asian Art; Decorative Arts; and Prints, Drawings and Photography.

★ ★ ★ ★ **BRIT TIP** ★ ★ ★ ★
★ A stroll along the legendary Coney ★
★ Island boardwalk to Brighton Beach ★
★ will take you to Little Odessa, a ★
★ thriving Russian community ★
★ complete with traditional ★
★ bathhouses, bookshops and ★
★ restaurants serving borscht, vodka ★
★ and caviar. ★
★ ★

The Brooklyn Museum of Art is known for its ground-breaking exhibitions and has a cinema theatre that screens movies and documentaries coinciding with the exhibitions. It also has an Education Division that organises gallery talks, films, concerts, tours and performances for children and adults. The first Saturday of each month is known as First Saturday, when a free programme of events is offered that includes a look at art, a film, activities for all the family and a live band to dance to.

It's useful to know that the museum, which has its own subway stop at Eastern Parkway, is just one stop down from Brooklyn's Grand Army Plaza. This stands in a complex of 19th-century parks and

Brighton Beach Boardwalk, Brooklyn

gardens that includes Prospect Park, the Brooklyn Botanic Garden and the Wildlife Centre. It takes about 30 minutes to get to the museum from Midtown Manhattan.

★★★★ BRIT TIP ★★★★
★   ★
★   A delicious cup of cappuccino or   ★
★ latte costs exactly the same as a cup ★
★   of filter coffee at the Brooklyn   ★
★   Museum of Art, though the sarnies   ★
★   and rolls cost around $8.   ★
★   ★
★★★★★★★★★★★★★★★★★★★★★★★★★

GRAND ARMY PLAZA AND PROSPECT PARK

✉ At the intersection of Flatbush Avenue, Eastern Parkway and Prospect Park West

☎ 718-965 8951

🖰 www.prospectpark.org

🚇 Subway 2, 3 to Grand Army Plaza; Q to 7th Avenue/Flatbush Avenue

This part of Brooklyn is one of its most beautiful areas. The enormous Prospect Park and Grand Army Plaza were laid out by Olmsted and Vaux after they'd completed Central Park, and many feel that these creations were even better. The park contains the following:

The Arch: New York's answer to the Arc de Triomphe, the elaborately carved, 24m (80ft) arch provides a grand gateway to Prospect Park, plus a majestic overview of both the park and Manhattan. It was built as a memorial to the defenders of the Union in the Civil War, and is now the base for a series of bronze sculptures that are grouped all around the Plaza, including one of John F Kennedy.

Art in the Arch: Exhibitions are held in the spring and autumn, generally featuring artwork with a distinct Brooklyn theme. The

★★★★ BRIT TIP ★★★★
★   ★
★   The Grand Army Plaza is home to   ★
★   the second largest open-air green   ★
★   market in New York. Held every   ★
★   Saturday 8am–4pm, it sells more   ★
★   than 600 varieties of farm-fresh   ★
★   fruits, vegetables, baked goods,   ★
★   dairy products and more.   ★
★   ★
★★★★★★★★★★★★★★★★★★★★★★★★★

Arch is open to the public during spring and autumn when an exhibition is on. Weekends and holidays 1–5pm. Tel 718-965 8943.

Long Meadow: At nearly a mile in length, the Long Meadow stretches from the Park's northern end at Grand Army Plaza to its western end at Prospect Park Southwest. Once the home of grazing sheep and lawn tennis and croquet players, it is now frequented by strollers, kite-flyers and the Little League Baseball. At the Picnic House you'll find WCs and picnic tables, while the Metropolitan Opera and the New York Philharmonic Orchestra put on summer events here (page 263). Call 718-965 8951.

The Long Meadow is accessible via the Grand Army Plaza and any entrance along Prospect Park West, such as 3rd Street or 9th Street. It is free to enter and is only closed 1–5am. For information on special events, call 718-965 8969.

The Bandshell: Close to the Long Meadow, this is one of the park's main attractions for live outdoor entertainment. With its three-storey-high acoustic shell, raised stage and large circular plaza, the Bandshell features food and drinks, WCs and first-come, first-served seating in the 2,000-seat plaza or

Brooklyn Museum

A TASTE OF THE OUTER BOROUGHS

★ ★ ★ ★ ★ **BRIT TIP** ★ ★ ★ ★

★ The Big Onion offers a walking tour ★
★ of the landmark district of Park ★
★ Slope, known as Brooklyn's Gold ★
★ Coast because of its fine residential ★
★ architecture and history. See page ★
★ 82 for details. ★

5,000-seat lawn. In addition to musical performances, the Bandshell hosts film events on its 6.5m (21ft) high and 15m (50ft) wide movie screen. But it is best known for the Celebrate Brooklyn! Performing Arts Festival – a series of music, dance, film and spoken word performances each June to August, which attracts nearly 250,000 people per season (page 258). For further information about Bandshell events, call the Brooklyn Information and Culture events line on 718-855 7882 or visit www.celebratebrooklyn.org. The nearest subway is the F train to 15th Street/Prospect Park Station or the 2, 3 to Grand Army Plaza.

The Ravine: One of Prospect Park's most natural features, here you will find a steep narrow gorge lined with the trees and foliage of Brooklyn's only forest. Still recovering from decades of overuse that caused soil erosion, the Ravine and surrounding woodlands have been gradually restored by the Prospect Park Alliance since 1996. You can explore on your own or take one of the weekend guided nature tours.

The Ravine is open from March to November on Saturday and Sunday 1pm–5pm, with tours at 3pm from the Audubon Centre at the Boathouse. For information on tours, call 718-287 3400. Best subways to take are the F to15th Street/ Prospect Park or 7th Avenue or the Q to 7th Avenue.

Children: Prospect Park has a wealth of activities and museums that are wonderful for children. They include the Wollman Rink, the Audubon Centre and the Boathouse, the Carousel, Prospect Park Zoo and the Lefferts Homestead Children's Museum. Full details are given in Chapter 9, New York for Families, starting on page 207.

NEW YORK CITY TRANSIT MUSEUM

✉ Schermerhorn Street at Boerum Place
☎ 718-694 1600
🕐 www.mta.info/mta/museum
🚇 Subway M, N, R to Court Street; A, C, G to Hoyt-Schermerhorn Street
🕐 Tues–Fri 10am–4pm, Wed 10am–6pm, Sat, Sun noon–5pm
$ $5 adults, $3 seniors and children under 12

This is a great museum for children and transportation buffs of all ages and is located in an old subway station in Brooklyn Heights. There is a display of old subway cars that you can get on and you can even hang on to one of the original leather straps (nowadays replaced by metal poles and bars) that created the nickname of 'straphangers' for people who use the subway. The museum has recently undergone a major renovation and now has a new art gallery, a classroom for a children's workshop, a computer lab and a reference library. The main exhibit depicts the history of buses and trolleys in the city, with interactive elements and a display of more than 200 trolley models. There is also a film about the building of the subway, old turnstiles, maps and a gift shop.

A TASTE OF THE BRONX

Diversity definitely drives the energy of this vibrant destination in the northernmost tip of the city. Nearly 50 per cent of Bronx residents are Latino, including its most famous former resident Jennifer Lopez, with the highest concentration hailing from 'the islands' – Puerto Rico and the Dominican Republic – and Mexico. However, it's also a place where traditions from Italy and Ireland continue to flourish, and a growing number of Asian immigrants are now making this area their home.

The Bronx has a scary reputation, but parts of it are very safe and have attractions that make a visit here well worthwhile. The Bronx history dates back to 1609 when Henry Hudson took refuge from a storm here. It is the northernmost borough of New York and the only one on the mainland. In 1639 Jonas Bronck, a Swedish captain from the Netherlands, settled here with his wife and servants. The story goes that when people left Manhattan to visit the family, they would say they were going to the Broncks' and the name stuck.

The horrible part is the south Bronx, but even here things are improving. In the north lies the beautiful Botanical Garden that includes a huge chunk of the original forests which once covered all of New York, and the Bronx Zoo, one of the world's leading wildlife conservation parks.

BRONX MUSEUM OF THE ARTS

✉ 1040 Grand Concourse at 165th Street
☎ 718-681 6000
✍ www.bxma.org
🚇 Subway B, D to 167th Street/Grand Concourse
🕐 Wed noon–9pm, Thurs–Sun noon–6pm
$ $5 adults, $3 students and seniors, under 12s free

Housed in an attractive glass building, the museum's collection consists of more than 700 contemporary works of art in all media by African, Asian and Latin American artists. If you want discover more about the Bronx way of life, look on the website at Sample Wednesdays, a free evening of hip-hop, film, spoken word, educational panels and performance art, which keeps the spirit of Boogie Down Bronx very much alive.

BRONX ZOO AND WILDLIFE CONSERVATION SOCIETY

✉ Bronx River Parkway at Fordham Road
☎ 718-367 1010
✍ www.bronxzoo.org
🚇 Subway 2, 5 to Bronx Park East
🕐 Apr–Oct Mon–Fri 10am–5pm, Sat, Sun 10am–5.30pm daily; 10–4.30pm for rest of year
$ $12 adults, $9 seniors and children 2–12, under 2s free. Suggested donation on Wed. Children under the age of 17 must be accompanied by an adult. Cheaper rates Nov–Mar. Congo Gorilla Forest, skyfari, zoo shuttle, butterfly garden and monorail Bengali Express $3 each; camel ride $5; bug carousel $2. Pay-One-Price ticket that includes admission and all rides, $19 adult, $14 children.

The Bronx Zoo is respected worldwide for its tradition of conservation and ecological awareness alongside the naturalistic habitats it provides, such as the African Plains where antelope roam. It is the largest urban zoo in America and houses 4,000 animals and 560 species. The Congo Gorilla Forest is a $43 million, 2.5 hectare (6 acre) rainforest, inhabited by two troops of gorillas. The latest exhibit to open is Tiger Mountain, which takes you a whisker away from the largest member of the cat family. Disney-style rides include a guided monorail tour through Wild Asia, an aerial safari, camel rides and a zoo shuttle. There is also a children's zoo. Some of the exhibits and all of the rides, apart from the bug carousel, are open only between April and October. For a tour by Friends of Wildlife Conservation, call 718-220 5141.

★ **If you want to discover more of Little Italy and the Irish neighbourhood of Woodlawn, contact Susan Birnbaum, who runs SusanSez NYC Walkabouts (tel 917-509 3111, www.dbsystems group.com/susansez). She leads tours around Arthur Avenue and beyond on her Bronx Walkabout.**

LITTLE ITALY

Technically, this area is known as Belmont or simply Arthur Avenue, but it is tagged the Little Italy of the Bronx. Take the D train to Tremont Avenue and walk east to Arthur Avenue. Treat yourself to lunch at one of the many Italian restaurants here. The old-world Belmont District is a charming area filled with shops selling every Italian delicacy you can think of, plus the Enrico Fermi Cultural Centre in the Belmont Library (610 East 186th Street at Hughes Avenue, tel 718-933 6410, www.nypl.org/branch/local/bx/ber.cfm) and the old Belmont Italian American Theater (2385 Arthur Avenue, tel 718-364 4700), which still shows films.

★ **If you're feeling peckish, pop into Mike's Deli in the Arthur Avenue Retail Market (718-295 5033, www.arthuravenue.com) for a taste of Italy.**

Afterwards, walk north on Arthur, then east on Fordham Road past Fordham University to the Bronx Park.

NEW YORK BOTANICAL GARDEN

- ✉ 200th Street and Southern Boulevard
- ☎ 718-817 8700
- 🖰 www.nybg.org
- 🚇 Subway 2, 5 to Bronx Park East. If going direct, take subway C, D, 4 to Bedford Park and then the BX36 bus or Metro-North from Grand Central Terminal.
- ◷ Tues–Sun and Mon holidays Apr–Oct 10am–6pm; Nov–Mar 10am–5pm
- $ Combo ticket $13 adults, $11 seniors/students, $5 children 2-12, under 2s free; pay as you go available at variable cost winter $1.50

★★★★ **BRIT TIP** ★★★★

★ The Botanical Garden is just a road
★ away from the Bronx Zoo – sadly
★ that is an eight-lane highway and
★ the entrances are a mile apart. In
★ the absence of a pedestrian link,
★ take a short taxi ride. Call Miles Taxi
★ Co on 718-884 8888.

Originally supported by magnates Cornelius Vanderbilt, Andrew Carnegie and JP Morgan, society folk still support these gardens today. The magnificent iron and glass conservatory, which was modelled on the one at Kew Gardens in London, has been refurbished to perfection. In the grounds, you can see the stunning Bronx River Gorge where the meandering waterway tumbles over a rocky outcrop formed by the retreat of the Wisconsin Ice Sheet. For thousands of years, New York was covered by a hemlock forest and a 16 hectare (40 acre) fragment remains in the gardens. Look out for the rock carving of a turtle drawn by the Weckquasgeek Indians many years ago.

Bronx Museum of the Arts

New York Botanical Garden

VAN CORTLANDT HOUSE MUSEUM

- ✉ Van Cortlandt Park, Broadway at West 246th Street
- ☎ 718-543 3344
- 🖰 www.vancortlandthouse.org
- 🚇 Subway 1, 9 to 242nd Street/Van Cortlandt Park
- ◷ Tues–Fri 10am–3pm, Sat, Sun 11am–4pm
- $ $5 adults, $3 seniors/students, under 12s free; free on Wed

Once an 18th century family-run plantation, Van Cortlandt House was turned into a historic house museum at the end of the 19th century by the National Society of Colonial Dames. Now you can walk through the family's public and private rooms, including a slave bed-chamber, and see the fascinating decorative art collections from the colonial and federal periods.

WAVE HILL

- ✉ 675 West 252nd Street at Independence Avenue
- ☎ 718-549 3200
- 🖰 www.wavehill.org
- 🚇 Subway 1, 9 to 242nd Street/Van Cortlandt Park
- ◷ Tues–Sun 15 Apr–14 Oct 9am–5.30pm, June and July until 9pm Wed; 15 Oct–14 Apr 9am–4.30pm
- $ $4 adults, $2 seniors/students, children under 6 free; free Sat am, Tues; daily Dec–Feb.

A scenic public garden and cultural centre, Wave Hill holds international events throughout the year, such as the Barefoot Dancing series when you're invited to move to the music from Kotchegna or folk music

Historic Richmond Town

from Bulgaria. So it's worth checking the website to see what's happening when you visit. Each Saturday Jack Chu teaches Tai Chi Chuan to beginners at 10am for $10. There's a free garden and glasshouse tour every Sunday at 2.15pm and at sunset on Wednesdays throughout June and July with entertainment and food and wine tastings from 6.30pm, free with admission.

★ ★ ★ ★ **BRIT TIP** ★ ★ ★ ★
★ ★
★ ★
★ Sports fans can take a break and ★
★ enjoy a hot dog and a drink at the ★
★ Sidewalk Café on the Plaza next to ★
★ Gates 4 and 6 at the Yankee ★
★ Stadium. ★
★ ★
★ ★

YANKEE STADIUM

✉ River Avenue at 161st Street
☎ 718-293 4300
🖑 http://newyork.yankees.mlb.com
🚇 Subway 4, C, D
🕐 Tours start at noon Mon–Sat. No reservations needed.
$ Tickets for games from $10; tours $14 adults, $7 seniors/children 14 and under

Sporting aficionados will be delighted to see the tribute to past baseball players, the field, dugout, clubhouse, locker room and press box. Babe Ruth hit the first home run in the first game played here in 1923. For details on going to a game, see page 252.

A TASTE OF QUEENS

The largest of all the New York boroughs (Map 11) at 290 sq km (112 sq miles), Queens has the highest percentage of first-generation immigrants. Given the borough's suburban look, it is hard to imagine it as the densely forested area it was four centuries ago. Then it was inhabited by the Algonquin Indian tribes, who fished in its freshwater streams and creeks, hunted game and gathered shellfish from its bays. It is also difficult to picture 17th-century Queens and the borough's early Dutch and English farmers, along with Quakers fighting for religious freedom.

Yet there remain places where such scenes can easily be reconstructed, such as at the Jamaica Bay Wildlife Refuge (tel 718-318 4340) on open marshland, once the territory of Jameco Indians and now home to many species of birds spotted along the nature walkways, and the Queens County Farm Museum (page 270). This has the largest tract of farmland left in New York and its colonial farmhouse is thought to date back to 1772.

Today, Queens is as much about the ethnic diversity of the borough and in each of the places mentioned in this section you will find many examples of the cultures of people from Asia, the West Indies, Latin America and Greece. In fact, Queens is home to the largest Greek population outside of Greece; Astoria is the Athens of the United States, with authentic restaurants and markets on the main thoroughfare of Ditmars Boulevard. Jackson Heights is a little India, with colourful sari shops, restaurants and video stores with the latest Bollywood offerings.

In fact so diverse is this sprawling borough, that the local subway line number 7 has been jokingly renamed the International Express. It's also home to JFK

Yankee Stadium

and LaGuardia Airports, so Queens is often the first entry point for millions of people to New York and the rest of the United States.

★★★★★ **BRIT TIP** ★★★★★

The Queens Council on the Arts produces an annual Cultural Guide filled with information about the borough. Order from 718-647 3377 or www.queenscouncilarts.org.

AMERICAN MUSEUM OF THE MOVING IMAGE

✉ 35th Avenue at 36th Street, Astoria
☎ 718-784 0077
🖰 www.ammi.org
🚇 Subway G, R, V to Steinway Street
🕐 Wed, Thurs 11am–5pm, Fri 11am–8pm, Sat, Sun 11am–6.30pm
$ $10 adults, $7.50 seniors and students, $5 children (5–18), under 5s free; admission into galleries free on Fridays

If you're into the making of films, then you will want to take the 15-minute train ride out to Queens to see this museum. Set in the historic Astoria Studios, which are still used today, it is home to screening rooms, rebuilt sets, costumes, props, posters and other memorabilia.

The museum is full of interactive delights, such as the perennially popular diner set from Seinfeld and a life-sized dummy of Linda Blair from *The Exorcist*, complete with rotating head. Then there's the interactive Behind the Scenes exhibit, where you can see how it's all done and even make your own short film. Catch the free film screenings on Saturday and Sunday afternoons and evenings and on Fridays at 7.30pm.

★★★★★ **BRIT TIP** ★★★★

Astoria is the heart of New York's Greek community and is filled with delis and restaurants. After you've been to the Museum of the Moving Image, head to 31st Street and Broadway for a spot of lunch.

BOWNE HOUSE

✉ 37-01 Bowne Street, Flushing
☎ 718-359 0528
🖰 www.bownehouse.org
🕐 Tues, Sat, Sun 2.30–4.30pm
$ $4 adults, $3 seniors, $2 students and children under 12

You can walk to this NYC landmark from Corona Park. Built in 1661 by John Bowne, this is the oldest house in Queens and the second oldest in New York City. It is a rare example of Dutch–English architecture, with an unusual collection of decorative arts, paintings and furniture, all of which belong to nine generations of the Bowne family. Bowne was a pivotal figure in the fight for religious freedom in the New World.

★★★★ **BRIT TIP** ★★★★

For shopping, attractions, events, tours and restaurants in Queens, click on to www.discoverqueens.info.

LITTLE ASIA

✉ Roosevelt Avenue and Main Street

The nearby jumble of Chinese, Korean, Thai and Vietnamese markets and restaurants offers everything from soft-shell turtles and bentwood bows to kimchi and wire baskets. At 45-57 Bowne Street is the beautiful Hindu Temple Society of North America (718-460 8484, www.nyganeshtemple.org), which is adorned with carvings of Hindu gods.

Dinner: Choopan Kabab House, 4327 Main Street. Tel 718-539 3180. A great place to try out Afghan fare. Alternatively, you could sample Korean food at Kum Gang San, 138-28 Northern Boulevard between Bowne and Union Streets. Tel 718-461 0909.

Nightclubs: Try Chibcha (79-05 Roosevelt Avenue, tel 718-429 9033, www.elchibcha.com, subway 7 to 82nd Street), a Colombian nightclub and restaurant. Or, if you prefer, Sunday night is Irish music night at Taylor Hall (45 Queens Boulevard, subway 7 to 46th Street). For something more exotic, there are operettas, flamenco and tango shows at the Thalia Spanish Theatre (41-17 Greenpoint Avenue, Sunnyside, tel 718-729 3880, www.thalia theatre.org, subway 7 to 40th Street).

★ ★ ★ ★ **BRIT TIP** ★ ★ ★ ★

★ For more information on the arts in ★
★ Queens, contact the Queens Council ★
★ on the Arts on 718-647 3377 or ★
★ visit www.queenscouncilarts.org. ★

LITTLE INDIA

Take the International Express – subway 7 from Times Square to the 74th Street/ Broadway station and, at 74th Street between Roosevelt and 37th Avenues at Jackson Heights, you will find this Indian haven. Stroll through the cumin-scented streets looking at the intricately embellished gold and silk on display. Two stops you should include are the Menka Beauty Salon (37 74th Street, Jackson Heights, tel 718-424 6851) where traditional henna designs are drawn on the skin, and the Butala Emporium (37-46 74th Street, Jackson Heights, tel 718-899 5590), which sells everything from Southern Asian art and children's books in Punjabi to Ayurvedic medicine and religious items.

Lunch: Travel one stop to 82nd Street in Elmhurst for an Argentinian lunch at La Fusta (8032 Baxter Avenue, tel 718-429 8222) or two stops to 90th Street station for Peruvian fare at Inti Raymi (8614 37th Avenue, Jackson Heights, tel 718-424 1938).

NEW YORK HALL OF SCIENCE

✉ 47-01 111th Street at 47th Avenue, Flushing Meadows/Corona Park at 48th Avenue
☎ 718-699 0005
⌂ www.nyscience.org
🚗 Subway 7 to 111th Street
◷ Mon–Thurs 9.30am–2pm, Fri 9.30am–5pm, Sat, Sun 10am–6pm
$ $11 adults, $8 seniors and children, $3 pre-school children. Sept–June Fri 2–5pm and Sun 10-11am, free

The bubble-shaped building features memorable daily science demonstrations and 175 interactive exhibits explaining the mysteries of digital technology, quantum theory, microbes and light and also offers slides, whirligigs, space nets and a giant teeter-totter (seesaw).

THE NOGUCHI GARDEN MUSEUM

✉ 9-01 33rd Road at Vernon Boulevard, Long Island City
☎ 718-204 7088
⌂ www.noguchi.org
🚗 Subway 7 to 33rd Street/Vernon Boulevard
◷ Apr–Oct only, Wed–Fri 10am–5pm, Sat, Sun 11am–6pm
$ Suggested donation $5 adults, $2.50 seniors/students

If you love your ballet and Balanchine in particular, you'll enjoy seeing some of the sets created by this Japanese artist, who strove to bring art and nature into the urban environment. These were Noguchi's studios and there are now more than 300 of his works on display. A fascinating spot for art and ballet buffs.

★ ★ ★ ★ **BRIT TIP** ★ ★ ★ ★

★ For an active tour of Queens ★
★ consider Oh My Gods! – Ethnic ★
★ Queens offered by Bike The Big ★
★ Apple. Stops include the House of ★
★ Jazz, Flushing Meadows in Corona ★
★ Park, the Unisphere, the Panorama ★
★ of New York City – the largest ★
★ 3-D urban model in the US – a ★
★ Hindu temple and lunch in an Asian ★
★ food court. ★

P.S. 1 CONTEMPORARY ART CENTER

✉ 22-25 Jackson Avenue at 46th Avenue, Long Island City
☎ 718-784 2084
⌂ www.ps1.org
🚗 Subway E, V to 23rd Street/Ely Avenue; G to 21st Street; 7 to 45th Road/Court House Square
◷ Thurs–Mon noon–6pm
$ Suggested donation $5 adults, $2 seniors/students

All forms of artistic expression including paintings and videos of performance art, which depict elements of American culture and life in the 20th and 21st centuries.

New York Hall of Science

QUEENS BOTANICAL GARDEN

✉ 43-50 Main Street, Flushing
☎ 718-886 3800
🖰 www.queensbotanical.org
🕓 Summer (through Oct) Tues–Fri 8am-6pm, Sat, Sun 8am-7pm; autumn and winter (Nov through Mar) Tues–Sun 8am-4.30pm
$ Free

Walk back to the north-east corner of Corona Park to see the 16 hectares (39 acres) of plants, shrubs and trees that were created for the 1939 World Fair.

QUEENS COUNTY FARM MUSEUM

✉ 73-50 Little Neck Parkway at Union Turnpike, Floral Park
☎ 718-347 3276
🖰 www.queensfarm.org
🚗 Subway E, F to Kew Gardens/Union Turnpike, then take the Q46 bus to Little Neck Parkway
🕓 Mon–Fri 9am-5pm outdoor visiting only; tours of the farmhouse are available Sat, Sun only 10am-5pm
$ Free, $2 hayrides

This 19 hectare (47 acre) site is the only working historical farm that still exists in New York and includes the 18th-century Adriance farmhouse, barns, outbuildings, a greenhouse and livestock. Free guided tours on Sat and Sun.

QUEENS MUSEUM OF ART

✉ New York City Building, Flushing Meadows/Corona Park
☎ 718-592 9700
🖰 www.queensmuseum.org
🚗 Subway 7 to Willets Point/Shea Stadium
🕓 Summer (end June-Sept) Wed–Sun noon-6pm, Fri noon-8pm; regular hours (Sept-end June) Wed–Fri 10am-5pm, Sat, Sun noon-5pm.
$ Suggested donation $5 adults; $2.50 seniors and children; children under 5 free.

The most famous exhibit here is the miniature scale model of the entire city of New York, complete with miniature lights, which turn dark every 15 minutes, and aeroplanes flying into the airports. You can rent binoculars to check out where you're staying. The museum is on the site of the 1964 World Fair and has had a recent $15 million renovation.

★ ★ ★ ★ BRIT TIP ★ ★ ★ ★

A free weekend Queens Culture Trolley (bus) takes you from the Queens Museum of Art from noon to 5pm at weekends for a journey through Flushing Meadows in Corona Park to Northern Boulevard's Restaurant Row, Corona and Louis Armstrong House and Jackson Heights.

Shea Stadium

SHEA STADIUM
✉ 123-01 Roosevelt Ave
☎ 718-507 8499
⌐ http://newyork.mets.mlb.com
Stroll through Corona Park to the home of the Mets baseball team (page 252). On the way you will see huge remnants of both the 1939 and the 1964 World Fairs, plus a series of weird buildings such as the New York Hall of Science. The park also has barbecue pits and boating on the lake. This is where Flushing Meadows plays host to the US Open tennis championship.

SOCRATES SCULPTURE PARK
✉ 21-01 Vernon Boulevard at Broadway, Long Island City
☎ 718-956 1819
⌐ www.socratessculpturepark.org
🚗 Subway N or W to Broadway/Long Island City
⊙ Daily 10am–sunset
$ Free
A great place to take children as they can climb, romp and run around these massive sculptures laid out in the park. Hard to believe it was once an abandoned riverside landfill and illegal dumpsite! It also has films outdoors in summer.

★ ★ ★ ★ **BRIT TIP** ★ ★ ★ ★
★   ★
★ **If you get thirsty on your tour then** ★
★ **pop into one of the many Irish pubs** ★
★   **that are centred in Queens. Fun,** ★
★   **friendly and lively, you're bound to** ★
★   **meet locals who'll be able to give** ★
★   **you a colourful account of life in** ★
★   **the 'burbs. Irish Circle (101–19** ★
★   **Rockaway Boulevard, tel 718-474** ★
★   **9002) or Mary McGuire's (38-04** ★
★   **Broadway, Astoria, tel 719-728** ★
★   **3434) are highly recommended.** ★
★ ★

A TASTE OF STATEN ISLAND

With its picturesque scenery, Staten Island deserves its Indian name Monacnong, which means 'enchanted woods'. It's long been a haven for Italian-American and Irish-American populations and hasn't had a vast melting pot of cultures like the other outer boroughs. But in recent years that has slowly begun to change with the population growing and diversifying. Hispanics now account for around 12 per cent of the

population, while 6 per cent is Asian.

Even if you don't have much time you should try to fit in a trip on the free Staten Island Ferry, which leaves Manhattan Island from Battery Park (page 65) and offers brilliant views of Downtown and the Statue of Liberty.

ALICE AUSTEN HOUSE
✉ 2 Hylan Boulevard, Staten Island between Edgewater and Bay Streets
☎ 718-816 4506
⌐ www.aliceausten.org
🚗 Bus S51 to Hylan Boulevard from Staten Island Ferry
⊙ Mar–Dec Thurs–Sun noon–5pm; closed major holidays
$ Suggested donation $2 per person adult, under 16s free
A unique museum in the restored Victorian house and garden of Alice Austen, one of America's first female documentary photographers. A great place to gain an insight into life in New York at the turn of the century.

HISTORIC RICHMOND TOWN
✉ 441 Clarke Ave between St Patrick's Place and Richmond Road
☎ 718-351 1611
⌐ www.historicrichmondtown.org
🚗 S74 bus from the ferry to Richmond Road and St Patrick's Place
A magnificent 40.5 hectare (100 acre) village that features buildings from 300 years of life on the island including the oldest schoolhouse still standing, which was built in 1695 (that's really old by American standards!). In the summer season, costumed interpreters and craftspeople demonstrate the chores, gardening, crafts and trade of daily life in this rural hamlet.

Staten Island Botanic Gardens

JAZZ IN QUEENS

The **Queens Jazz Trail** shows you the homes of the jazz greats, their haunts and culture. It's a great tour even if you aren't a real jazz buff, as it gives an insight into the lifestyles of another era. The tour includes a visit to the home of Louis Armstrong, the Louis Armstrong archives at Queens University (fantastic views of Manhattan's skyline) and the Addisleigh Park area, home to celebrated sports stars and top jazz and pop entertainers, including Ella Fitzgerald, Lena Horne, Count Basie, Billie Holiday, Milt Hinton and Thomas 'Fats' Waller. Other famous musicians who lived in different parts of Queens include Dizzy Gillespie, Bix Beiderbecke, Glenn Miller and Tony Bennett. The tour includes a delicious traditional soul food lunch or dinner and a jazz concert at the newly renovated concert hall at Flushing Town Hall.

If jazz really is your thing, then avoid the tourist-trap venues on Manhattan and head out to Queens for a cheap jazz night out.

Contact **Flushing Town Hall** (137 Northern Boulevard, Flushing, tel 718-463 7700, www.flushingtownhall.org) for details of the Queens Jazz Trail, $30 on the first Sat of the month 1-4pm (or $40 for a Fri Jazz night in the Town Hall plus trail the next day), forthcoming jazz concerts and the **Cultural Collaborative Jamaica** (Jamaica Avenue and 153rd Street, Jamaica, tel 718-526 3217, www.go2ccj.org). Not only is it cheaper to get into venues in Queens, but you can also usually stay for both sets rather than being forced to leave after just one.

JACQUES MARCHAIS CENTER OF TIBETAN ART

✉ 338 Lighthouse Avenue
☎ 718-987 3500
🕀 www.tibetanmuseum.org
🚌 Bus S74 to Lighthouse Avenue
🕓 Wed-Sun 1pm-5pm
$ Gallery $5, $3 seniors/students, $2 children 12 and under; grounds free

One of New York's best-kept secrets, which the Dalai Lama visited in 1991. It has terraced gardens and a fishpond. Inside, there are Tibetan, Nepalese and Mongolian arts from the 17th to the 19th century.

SNUG HARBOR CULTURAL CENTER

✉ 1000 Richmond Terrace between Tysen Street and Snug Harbour Road
☎ 718-448 2500
🕀 www.snug-harbor.org
🚌 Bus S4 to Snug Harbor
🕓 Tues-Sun 10am-5pm, closed Mon
$ $3 adults, $2 seniors/children under 12

On this plot of land once stood some rundown retirement homes for fishermen, which were going to be demolished by developers planning various money-making schemes. However, the local residents wanted it to be used for the community's benefit, and the result is a fascinating 33.5 hectare (83 acre) park containg 26 buildings modelled on historical architecture, such as Greek revival Victorian and Italian Renaissance. The various buildings are used for events throughout the year, for example

the Harmony Fair in June, a celebration of music, dance, food and cultures from around the world.

The Staten Island Botanical Park (tel 718-273 8200, www.sibg.org,) is also here with the internationally renowned Chinese Scholar's Garden, which has courtyards, pools, a Tea House and pure-flow bridge. Admission is $5 for adults, $4 students/ seniors and children.

ST MARK'S PLACE, ST GEORGE

Standing on the hill above the St George Ferry terminal, St Mark's Place is the only landmarked historical district on Staten Island. Here New York's fabulous skyline forms a dramatic backdrop to a wonderful collection of residential buildings in Queen Ann, Greek revival and Italianate styles. Visit www.preserve.org/stgeorge for a self-guided walking tour.

CHAPTER 15

Niagara Falls and Woodbury Common

M any Brits combine a visit to New York City with one or two trips to other parts of New York State. Among the most popular are Niagara Falls and the bargain shopping mecca of Woodbury Common in the Hudson Valley. This can be a simple day trip or it could be combined with a few nights' stay so that you can enjoy some of the beauties of the Hudson Valley.

NIAGARA FALLS

This spectacular falls is just a 45-minute flight from New York. There are actually two falls: the American Falls – 58m (190ft) high and 320m (1,060ft) wide – and the Horseshoe, or Canadian, Falls – 56m (185ft) high and 675m (2,200ft) wide, the average waterflow over which is an amazing 12,800 – 27,400m³ (42,000–90,000ft³) per second.

The falls were created 12,000 years ago as huge torrents of water, released by the melting ice at the end of the Ice Age, poured over the edge of the Niagara Escarpment at what is now the pretty village of Lewiston. Since then, the falls have carved their way more than 11km (7 miles) upstream, creating the Niagara Gorge.

Such is the impact of the water on the region that Niagara has its own ecosystem. The moisture that evaporates from the lakes inhibits cloud formation in summer and moderates air temperature in winter, creating a temperate climate with more days of sunshine per year than many cities in what America calls the 'sun belt'.

Little is known of early inhabitants, but the Niagara River became an important link in the French water transport systems of the 17th century and, in 1679, they built a log fort at the mouth of the river where it joins Lake Ontario. Other more solid structures followed, culminating in a heavily fortified stone chateau, now known as the French

Castle. During the 1750s, the French were so busy fighting the Native Americans that the British were able to gain control of the region in 1759 and it remained in British hands until 1796 when the US government took control.

In 1815, settlements sprang up, making the most of the fertile land and temperate climate. People soon began to see the potential of Niagara Falls as an attraction and when the Erie Canal opened in 1825, connecting the Hudson River from New York with Lake Erie, it quickly became part of a heavily travelled water route between the Atlantic and America's Midwest. In 1855, a suspension bridge was built over the gorge, further linking the east coast with the growing cities of Detroit and Chicago.

British, German and Italian settlers established Niagara village in 1848 and by 1892 it had become a city. In 1885, New York State created the Niagara Reservation parks system to preserve the beauty of the Falls and guarantee that the public would always have free access to them. Ten years later, the Edward Dean Adams hydroelectric generating station opened,

Maid of the Mist

which for the first time enabled widespread use of electricity.

Today, the Niagara Reservation gets nearly 10 million visitors a year. The Visitor Center has exhibitions and a wide-screen cinema show, which gives a thrilling introduction to the Falls. In front of the centre are the Great Lakes Gardens, which include large-scale models of the Great Lakes system created from living plants.

GETTING TO NIAGARA

There is a range of internal flights from New York to Buffalo (flying time about 45 minutes), then it's a 30-minute drive to Niagara. The flat taxi fare is $40 (plus tip and toll), but there are regular scheduled buses from the airport to the Niagara hotels and some hotels have courtesy buses.

VIEWING THE FALLS

NIAGARA RESERVATION STATE PARK

⊠ PO Box 1132, Niagara Falls, NY 14308-0132
☎ 716-278 1796
⌐ð www.niagarafallsstatepark.com
The New York State Park surrounding the American Falls is the oldest state park in America. It includes the official information centre, Cave of the Winds, Prospect Point and Observation Tower.

★ ★ ★ ★ BRIT TIP ★ ★ ★ ★
★ Get your bearings at the Park Visitor ★
★ Center, then use the Niagara Scenic ★
★ Tour Trolley to get around. ★
★ All-day tickets are $2 adults, $1 ★
★ children 6–12. In season it runs ★
★ daily 9am–10pm. ★
★ ★

NIAGARA FALLS STATE PARK VISITOR CENTER

⊠ Prospect Park
☎ 716-278 1796
⌐ð www.niagarafallsstatepark.com
☼ Summer 8am–10pm, winter 8am–6pm, closed Christmas Day and New Year
An introduction to the Falls and surrounding parks, the newly remodelled visitor centre has exhibits, tourist information, a gift shop, a café, snack bar and deli and a patio grill and WCs. The Festival Theater has a giant screen History Channel film called *Niagara, A History of the Falls*, plus there's a virtual-reality helicopter simulator ride. Entrance to the cinema show is $2 adults, $1 children (6–12). It's shown on the hour every hour 10am–8pm.

OBSERVATION TOWER AT PROSPECT POINT

Next to the Falls is the New York State Observation Tower (open late March to December 9am–8pm), which stands 60m (200ft) above the base of the Niagara Gorge and has spectacular views. From here you can also get access to the Crow's Nest ($1) by a series of stairs to the edge of the American Falls, where you can feel the spray wash over you. From the observation deck, glass-walled lifts carry you down to the base for access to the Maid of the Mist boat tour.

MAID OF THE MIST

⊠ 151 Buffalo Avenue, Niagara Falls
☎ 716-284 8897
   Fax 716-284 5446
⌐ð www.maidofthemist.com
☼ April–Oct daily 10am–8pm
$ $11.50 adults, $6.75 children (6–12), under 6s free. Includes $1 for the Observation Tower.
Without doubt, this is the top-of-the-pile

way to view the Falls – and one of the wettest, though the ticket includes a souvenir raincoat! You will be taken as close as is safely possible to the different falls and the spray – hence the name. The gorge has to be completely free of ice before boats can run, so check ahead if you're travelling in April, when the service starts; it continues until around the third week in October.

There are two boats on the American side and two on the Canadian side. Each holds 400 people and there are departures every 15–20 minutes so queues are rarely long.

★ Admission is free for under 6s to all
★ attractions in the Niagara Falls State
★ Park, including the Observation Tower,
★ Niagara Scenic Trolley, Cave of the
★ Winds and Festival Theater as well as
★ the Maid of the Mist boat ride.

CAVE OF THE WINDS TRIP
✉ Goat Island
◷ May–Oct daily 9am–11pm
$ $8 adults, $7 children (6–12), under 6s free. Children must be at least 106cm (3ft 6in) tall.

An incredible chance to soak up the Falls experience, this trip takes you closer to the waters than you thought possible. Clad in a yellow raincoat and wearing the special footwear provided, you ride in an elevator 53m (175ft) deep into Niagara Gorge, from where you follow a tour guide over wooden walkways to the Hurricane Deck, where the railing is a mere 6m (20ft) from the billowing torrents of Bridal Veil Falls. The rushing waters loom above you, dousing you with a generous spray, as you face the thundering falls head-on. Rainbows are usually visible day and night.

★ Time your visit to catch the free
★ thrilling Firework Spectacular on
★ Friday and Sunday nights at 10pm,
★ lighting up the Horseshoe Falls from
★ late May to September.

FLIGHT OF ANGELS BALLOON RIDE
✉ 310 Rainbow Boulevard South (adjacent to Niagara State Park)
☎ 716-278 0824
🖰 www.flightofangels.net
◷ Apr, May, Oct daily 10am–10pm, June–Sept 8am–12pm
$ $20 adults, $10 children, under 3s free. Special rates available on request

The newest attraction in Niagara, this is a soft adventure 15-minute ride to 120m (400ft) above Niagara in a stationary balloon giving unequalled views of the Falls. The weather is the major variable, although the balloon can withstand strong winds of up to 25 knots.

★ If you're taking a balloon ride, bear
★ in mind that the wind tends to pick
★ up late morning to mid-afternoon.

HELICOPTER RIDES
✉ Rainbow Air Inc, 454 Main Street
☎ 716-284 2800
🖰 www.rainbowairinc.com
◷ Daily 9am–dusk
$ $70 adults; 2 people per flight

A fabulous 12-minute overview of the Niagara Falls and Gorge.

NIAGARA GORGE DISCOVERY CENTER
☎ 716-278 1070
$ $5 adults and over 13s, $3 children (6–12), under 5s free

The centre showcases the natural and local history of the area, including information on the geology, interactive displays and a 180° multi-screen presentation. There are also opportunities for trail hiking, walking and biking, and a state-of-the-art outdoor climbing wall.

Niagara Falls

NIAGARA FALLS AND WOODBURY COMMON

THE SCHOELLKOPF GEOLOGICAL MUSEUM

✉ New York State Office of Parks, Recreation and Historic Preservation, off the Robert Moses Parkway two blocks north of Main Street and Niagara Blvd
☎ 716-278 1070
◷ Apr–May 9am–5pm, May–Aug 9am–7pm, Aug–Nov 9am–5pm. Closed Nov–March.
$ $5 adults; $3 children

Get an insider view of the history and geological background of the Falls at this museum, located within the park, just a few hundred metres north of the American Falls. Reach it by car, on foot or via the Scenic Tour Trolley.

WHIRLPOOL JET

✉ At the Riverside Inn, Lewiston
☎ 905 468 4800
⌂ www.whirlpooljet.com
$ $47 adults, $39 children (6–13)

This is a 45-minute white-water rapids ride from Lewiston up through the Devil's Hole Rapids to the Niagara Whirlpool. You can opt for the Wet Jet tour, which comes with a full-length splash suit, wet boots and lifejacket, or the Jet Dome tour, which gives you the white-water excitement without having to get at all wet!

★ ★ ★ ★ **BRIT TIP** ★ ★ ★ ★
★ ★
★ **If you're working to a budget you** ★
★ **can check attractions and their** ★
★ **prices in one place on** ★
★ **www.niagarafrontier.com.** ★
★ ★

OTHER ATTRACTIONS

AQUARIUM OF NIAGARA

✉ 701 Whirlpool Street
☎ 716-285 3575
⌂ www.acquariumofniagara.org
◷ 9am–5pm daily except Thanksgiving and Christmas Day
$ $7.50 adults, $5.50 children (4–12) and seniors, under 4s free

A great rainy day activity, the Aquarium is home to 1,500 aquatic animals including sharks, Californian sea lions, eels and even a colony of endangered Peruvian penguins. Sea-lion feeding times every 90 minutes, plus regular penguin and shark feeding.

For older, children, there's a trainer for-a-day programme for $150 (tel 716-285 3575 ext 214).

★ ★ ★ ★ **BRIT TIP** ★ ★ ★ ★
★ ★
★ **The Aquarium's first-floor** ★
★ **observation deck has wonderful** ★
★ **views of Niagara Gorge.** ★
★ ★

ARTPARK

✉ 450 South 4th Street, Lewiston
☎ 716-754 4375
⌂ www.artpark.net
◷ May–Aug for matinee and evening performances every day except Mon

This is an 81 hectare (200 acre) park that has its own musical theatre season, as well as presenting live theatre shows, concerts and musicals. It also has art workshops for children and adults. It is in the pretty and historic village of Lewiston, which has retained much of its character (unlike Niagara city) and is well worth a visit. Just 10 minutes from the Falls, it is also home to the Lewiston Historic Museum (469 Plain Street, tel 716-754 4214, www.historic lewiston.org). Further details from the Visitor Information Center at the Gateway to Greater Lewiston, 732 Center Street, Lewiston. Tel 716-754 9500, www.niagara-lewiston.org.

GRAND LADY CRUISES

✉ Holiday Inn, 100 Whitehaven Road, Grand Island
☎ 716-744 8594
⌂ www.grandlady.com
◷ 1 May–31 Oct
$ $34 for 2-hour lunch cruise ($17 for cruise only) and $45 for 3-hour dinner cruise May and June ($22 for cruise only).

Luxury lunch, brunch and dinner cruises on the Niagara River above the Falls.

NIAGARA AEROSPACE MUSEUM

✉ 345 Third Street
☎ 716-278 0060
⌂ www.niagaramuseum.org
◷ Summer Mon–Sat 10am–8pm, Sun 11am–5pm; winter Tues–Sat 10am–4pm
$ $7 adults, $6 seniors, $4 children, $25 family

One for buffs of anything that is metal and flies, this museum has an extensive range of artefacts and displays on the local contribution to the Apollo Lunar Landing and Agena Rocket Engines, classic aircraft engines, aircraft restoration facilities and the Aviation Hall of Fame.

NIAGARA'S WAX MUSEUM OF HISTORY

- ⊠ 303 Prospect Street opposite New York State Parking Lot
- ☎ 716-285 1271
- ☉ Summer 9am–10pm, rest of year 10am–5pm
- $ $4.95 general admission

Life-size wax figures of explorers, statesmen and others prominent in the history of the Frontier, plus a replica Native American village, old-time street and store scenes and the barrels used for going over the Falls and through the rapids.

OLD FORT NIAGARA

- ⊠ Fort Niagara State Park, Robert Moses Parkway North, Youngstown
- ☎ 716-745 7611
- ⌁ www.oldfortniagara.org
- ☉ Daily 9am–dusk (4.30–7.30pm) all year
- $ $10 adults, $5 children (6–12), under 6s free

One of the best non-Falls attractions is about 15 minutes from Niagara by car or bus. You can explore the Old Fort buildings, preserved as they were in the 1700s, see the old uniforms and watch musket demonstrations and other living-history displays. Then follow signs to the historic and picturesque village of Youngstown to browse around the shops and eateries at one of the first settlements to grow outside Fort Niagara in the late 1700s.

▐ WHERE TO STAY IN NIAGARA

ELIZABETH HOUSE BED & BREAKFAST

- ⊠ 327 Buffalo Avenue
- ☎ 716-285 1109
- ⌁ www.elizabethhousebandb.com

A Georgian-style house run by Brits within walking distance from the Falls with an outdoor swimming pool.

HAMPTON INN

- ⊠ 501 Rainbow Boulevard
- ☎ 716-285 6666
- ⌁ http://hamptoninn.hilton.com

Great location just steps from the Falls and close to a selection of good restaurants; 99 comfortable rooms.

HOLIDAY INN SELECT

- ⊠ 300 3rd Street
- ☎ 716-285 3361
  Fax 716-285 3900
- ⌁ www.holiday-inn.com

A big hotel convenient for all attractions and the convention centre. The rooms are comfortable and spacious and the hotel has a sky-lit indoor swimming pool, whirlpool, saunas and exercise equipment, plus a wedding chapel service.

RAMADA NIAGARA FALLS

- ⊠ 240 Rainbow Boulevard
- ☎ 716-285 9321
- ⌁ www.ramada.com

A full-service hotel conveniently located near all the major attractions.

RED COACH INN

- ⊠ 2 Buffalo Avenue
- ☎ 716-282 1459
- ⌁ www.redcoach.com

This has a lot of appeal because of its quaintness and the fact that it overlooks the rapids as they approach the Falls. It has only 14 suites/apartments so book well in advance.

SENECA NIAGARA CASINO AND HOTEL

- ⊠ 310 Fourth Street
- ☎ 716-299 1100
- ⌁ www.senecaniagaracasino.com

The newest and largest kid on the block; with a 24-hour casino, seductive nightclub and live music venue, this is the place for nightbirds. It also has a full-service spa.

▐ WHERE TO EAT IN NIAGARA

COMO RESTAURANT

- ⊠ 2220 Pine Avenue
- ☎ 716-285 9341

Classic American family dining, serving delicious Italian and American food at reasonable prices.

GOOSE'S ROOST

- ⊠ 343 4th Street, downtown at the corner of Niagara Street
- ☎ 716-282 6255

An unpretentious American diner serving breakfast, lunch and dinner. You can also order takeaways.

HARD ROCK CAFE

- ⊠ 333 Prospect Street
- ☎ 716-282 0007
- ☉ Daily from 11am
- ⌁ www.hardrock.com

1950s-style outdoor/indoor diner owned by local Tommy Ryan, so the boast is it's better than the chain.

LA HACIENDA
✉ 3019 Pine Avenue
☎ 716-285 2536
In the heart of Niagara's Italian district, this classic Italian restaurant has been run by the Aldo Evangelista family for decades. Delicious and well-priced food – but busy, so book in advance if you plan to give it a try.

RED COACH INN RESTAURANT
✉ 2 Buffalo Avenue
☎ 716-282 1459
🖱 www.redcoach.com
This is as posh as it gets at Niagara Falls and at lunchtime it's usually filled with local business people as well as tourists. A quaint building, good service and delicious gourmet American cuisine. However, booking is advisable.

TOP OF THE FALLS RESTAURANT
✉ Falls end of Goat Island
☎ 716-278 0340
🖱 www.topofthefallsrestaurant.com
This newly remodelled restaurant is a fabulous spot for a leisurely meal, overlooking the Horseshoe Falls. Open seasonally.

WHERE TO SHOP IN NIAGARA

PRIME OUTLETS
✉ 1900 Military Road, Niagara Falls
☎ 716-297 2022
🖱 www.primeoutlets.com
☉ Daily 9am–9pm
Little do we Brits know, but Niagara is popular for something other than the Falls: its factory outlet shopping mall, with more than 150 shops. A free, regular trolley service provides transport between the mall and Niagara hotels. Shops include Liz Claiborne, Off 5th, Reebok, Guess, Gap, Van Heusen, Brooks Brothers, Tommy Hilfiger, Levi's, Donna Karan DKNY Jeans, plus toys and shoes. Nearby is the Red Lobster restaurant, famous for its steaks and seafood.

★ ★ ★ ★ BRIT TIP ★ ★ ★ ★
★   ★
★   It's worth looking at the Prime   ★
★ Outlets website before your visit to ★
★   Niagara to check out any offers.   ★
★ ★

GETTING MARRIED AT THE FALLS

An estimated 50,000 couples start their lives together here. Locals put it down to the negative ions generated by the falling water, said to be an aphrodisiac, but it may just be its affordability!

★ ★ ★ ★ BRIT TIP ★ ★ ★ ★
★   ★
★   Check out the tourist board's   ★
★ website at www.niagara-usa.com for ★
★   information ranging from getting   ★
★   around to getting married at   ★
★   Niagara.   ★
★ ★

All you need do is get a marriage licence from Niagara Falls City Hall, 745 Main Street at Cedar Avenue, tel 716-286 4393, 9am–3.30pm Monday to Friday. There is a 24-hour waiting period after the application has been filed and divorcees will need certified copies of their most recent divorce. No blood test needed; current fee is $40.

Check out www.traveltoniagara.com and www.niagara-usa.com for information and suggestions if you're planning to get married in Niagara.

WOODBURY COMMON PREMIUM OUTLETS

For shopaholics, this American colonial-style village with more than 220 discount shops is the equivalent of paradise. For ordinary folk, it's still a wonderful place to make useful and fun purchases – and just a 1½-hour bus ride away from Manhattan. Midweek is the quietest time.

WOODBURY COMMON SHOPPING
✉ 498 Red Apple Court, Central Valley
☎ 1-845 928 4000
🖱 www.premiumoutlets.com/woodburycommon
☉ Mon–Sat 10am–9pm, Sun 10am–8pm (check the website for seasonal and holiday hours)
Upon arrival by Gray Line (tel 800-669 0051) you'll be dropped off close to the tower entrance where you'll also find the information office, pushchairs (essential with a young child on a hot day), lockers, telephones, cashpoints and WCs.

Pick up a copy of the full-colour Shopping Guide and in the centre you'll find a map with the five different sections in different colours. The colour coding is carried throughout the village, so as you walk around you can work out which area you are in by the colour of the apple above each shop sign.

The information tower is in the main red section, called Red Apple Court, which is largely dedicated to designer boutiques; to its south is Evergreen Court, home to many lifestyle stores; to the north of Red Apple Court is the Food Court and then Bluebird Court. To the left from the main entrance is the purple Grapevine Court.

Filled with the most upscale designer shops, Grapevine Court is serious droolsville territory and the first port of call for Japanese shoppers, who tend to be known as Goochers thanks to their love of Gucci. Here you'll find Betsey Johnson, Chanel, Christian Dior, Fendi, Giorgio Armani General Store, Hugo Boss, Missoni, Nieman Marcus Last Call, Off 5th - Saks Fifth Avenue, La Perla, Valentino and the Thyme To Eat Restaurant. The Cosmetics Company Store here has great deals on many brands including Clinique, Estée Lauder, Bobbi Brown, MAC, Prescriptives and Origins.

Big names in Red Apple Court include A/X Armani Exchange, Burberry, Brooks Brothers, Carolina Herrera, Donna Karan/DKNY, Escada, Giorgio Armani, Gucci, Liz Claiborne, Polo Ralph Lauren, Salvatore Ferragamo and Versace.

Good shops that you should make a beeline for in the Bluebird Court are Claire's Accessories, Bombay Outlet, OshKosh B'Gosh, Perfumania, Puma, LeSportsac, Bebe and Nike Factory Store.

In the Evergreen Court you will discover other great stores such as Lancôme - The Company Outlet, Timberland, the Zegna Outlet Store, Benetton, Banana Republic, Reebok and Claiborne Menswear.

SALES TIMES

You can save even more money on your favourite labels by heading to Woodbury at sales times. Before you go, visit www.premiumoutlets.com/woodburycom mon to check out the next sales date - there's usually one a month. However, the big sales times coincide with all the American holidays including 4 July, Memorial Day, President's Day, Labor Day Weekend, Columbus Day and the day after Thanksgiving (page 260).

Best time of all, though, is around Christmas, when some of the biggest savings are to be had - along with the biggest crowds, so arrive early!

★ ★ ★ ★ **BRIT TIP** ★ ★ ★ ★
★ Take the weight off your slingbacks ★
★ and make the most of the free ★
★ trolley that tours Woodbury - but ★
★ bear in mind they only run on ★
★ weekends. Trolley stops are shown in ★
★ the Shopping Guide. ★
★ ★

STAYING NEAR WOODBURY COMMON

The Orange County Bed & Breakfast Association offers shop-and-stay packages and can be contacted on 800-210 5565, www.new-york-inns.com.

THE THAYER HOTEL

✉ 674 Thayer Road, West Point, New York
☎ 845-446 4731 or freephone 800-247 5047
Fax 845-446 0338
⌨ www.TheThayerHotel.com

A three-star hotel at West Point - the scene of a decisive battle in the War of Independence and now home to one of the most famous officer training camps in America - with fabulous views of the Hudson River. It has comfortable en suite rooms, which have recently been refurbished, and a restaurant that's open for breakfast, lunch and dinner. The lounge overlooks the river, and drinks and light meals are served 11.30am-11.30pm Sunday to Thursday and 11.30am-1am Friday and Saturday. Shop-and-stay packages are available.

Woodbury Common

CHAPTER 16

Safety First

TRAVEL INSURANCE

The one thing you should not forget when travelling to America is insurance – medical cover is very expensive and if you are involved in an accident you could be sued, which would be very costly indeed. If you do want to make savings in this area, don't avoid getting insurance cover but don't buy it from tour operators as they are notoriously expensive. We have taken a random selection of premiums offered by tour operators specialising in North America and found that two weeks' worth of cover for one person varied in price from £42 to a staggering £90. If you're travelling for up to four weeks, the premiums go up to nearly £110 per person.

The alternative, particularly if you plan to make more than one trip in any given year, is to go for an annual worldwide policy direct from the insurers. These can start at around £60 and go up to £120, and will normally cover all trips taken throughout the year up to a maximum of 31 days per trip. These worldwide annual policies make even more sense if you're travelling as a family. For instance, cover for four people bought from your tour operator could easily cost you £160 for a two-week trip, which is little different from an annual worldwide family policy premium.

Companies offering annual worldwide insurance policies include the **AA** (0800 085 7240, www.theaa.com), **Barclays** (0800 015 4751, www.barclays.co.uk/personal), **Bradford & Bingley** (0800 11 33 33, www.bradford-bingley.co.uk/insurance), **Columbus** (0845 222 0020, www.columbus-insurance.com), **Direct Travel** (0845 605 2700, www.direct-travel.co.uk), **Norwich Union** (0800 121 007, www.norwichunion.com), **Our Way** (020 8313 3900), **Post Office** (0800 169 9999, www.postoffice.co.uk), **Premier Direct** (0845 6028002, www.alliance-leicester.co.uk) and **Travel Insurance Direct** (0870 00 55 622, www.oinc.com). Many of these companies also offer straightforward

holiday cover for a given period, such as two or three weeks, which again will be cheaper than insurance offered by tour operators.

CHECK YOUR COVER

Policies vary not only in price but in the cover they provide. In all cases, you need to ensure that the one you choose gives you the following:

➡ Medical cover of at least £2 million in America.
➡ Personal liability cover of at least £2 million in America.
➡ Cancellation and curtailment cover of around £3,000 in case you are forced to call off your holiday.
➡ Cover for lost baggage and belongings of around £1,500. Most premiums only offer cover for individual items worth up to around £250, so you will need additional cover for expensive cameras or camcorders.
➡ Cover for cash (usually around £200) and documents, including your air tickets, passport and currency.
➡ A 24-hour helpline to make it easy for you to get advice and instructions on what to do in an emergency.

THINGS TO WATCH OUT FOR

Sharp practices: In some cases your tour operator may imply that you must buy their travel insurance policy. This is never the case; you can always arrange your own. Alternatively, they may send you an invoice for your tickets that includes travel insurance unless you tick a certain box – so watch out.

Read the policy: Always ask for a copy of the policy document before you go and, if you are not happy with the cover offered, cancel and demand your premium back – in some cases you will have only seven days in which to do this.

Don't double up on cover: If you have an 'all risks' house insurance policy on your home contents, this will cover your belongings outside the home and may even cover lost money and credit cards. Check if this covers you abroad, and includes your belongings when in transit, before buying insurance for personal possessions.

MORE THINGS TO CHECK

Gold card cover: Some bank gold cards automatically provide you with travel insurance cover if you buy your air ticket with the gold card but, in fact, only the Nat West Gold MasterCard provides sufficient cover for travel in America.

Dangerous sports cover: In almost all cases, mountaineering, racing and hazardous pursuits such as bungee jumping, skydiving, horse riding, windsurfing, trekking and even cycling are not included in normal policies. There are so many opportunities to do all of these activities and more – and they are so popular as holiday extras – that you really should ensure you are covered before you go.

Make sure you qualify for full cover: If you have been treated in hospital during the six months prior to travelling or are waiting for hospital treatment, you may need medical evidence that you are fit to travel. If your doctor gives you the all-clear (the report may cost £25) and the insurance company still says your condition is not eligible for the insurance you want, shop around to find the right cover.

HEALTH HINTS

Don't allow your dream trip to New York to be spoilt by not taking the right kind of precautions, be they for personal safety or of a medical nature.

MEDICATION

If you are on regular medication, make sure you take sufficient for the duration of your trip. Always carry it in your hand baggage, in case your luggage goes astray, and make sure it is clearly labelled. If you should need more for any reason, remember that many

★ ★ ★ ★ ★ **BRIT TIP** ★ ★ ★ ★
★ Always carry plenty of water, even in
★ winter. Air conditioning and heating
★ are incredibly dehydrating and you'll
★ find yourself wanting to keel over
★ very quickly without lots of liquid. It
★ is also best to avoid drinking alcohol
★ **during the day.**
★ ★

drugs have a different name in the US, so check with your GP before you go.

IN THE SUN

Although the biggest season for New York is winter, many Brits still travel to America at the hottest time of the year, the summer, and most are unprepared for the sheer intensity of the sun. Before you even think about going out for the day, apply a high-factor sun block as it is very easy to get sunburned when you are walking around sightseeing or shopping. It is also a good idea to wear a hat or scarf to protect your head from the sun, especially at the hottest times (11am–3pm), to prevent you from getting sunstroke. If it is windy, you may be lulled into thinking that it's not so hot.

SECURITY

AT YOUR HOTEL

In America, your hotel room number is your main source of security. It is often your passport to eating and collecting messages so keep the number safe and secure. When checking in, make sure none of the hotel staff mentions your room number out loud. If they do, give them back the key and ask them to give you a new room and to write down the new room number instead of announcing it (most hotels follow this practice in any case). When you need to give someone your room number – for instance when charging a dinner or any other bill to your room – write it down or show them your room card rather than calling it out.

When in your hotel room, always put on the deadlocks and security chains and use the door peephole before opening the door to strangers. If someone knocks on the door and you don't know who it is, or they don't have any identification, phone down to the hotel reception desk. When you go out, make sure you lock the windows and door properly, even if you just leave your room to go to the ice machine.

CASH AND VALUABLES

Most hotels have safe deposit boxes so use these to store important documents such as airline tickets and passports. Keep a separate record of your travellers' cheque numbers. When you go out, do not take all your cash and credit cards with you – always leave at least one credit card in the safe as an emergency back-up and only take enough cash with you for the day.

EMERGENCIES

For the police, fire department or ambulance: Dial 911 (9-911 from a hotel room). This is a free number, even from mobiles.

If it's a medical emergency: Call the front desk of your hotel as many have arrangements with doctors for house calls. If they don't, they may tell you to go to the nearest casualty (emergency) department, but that's really not a good idea (Haven't you seen *ER*?).

Instead, you have three choices: contact **New York Hotel Urgent Medical Services** on 212-737 1212, www.travelmd.com, **Dial-a-Doctor** on 212-971 9692, or walk in or make an appointment at a **DOCS Medical Center**. There are three in Manhattan: 55 East 34th Street (tel 212-252 6000), 1555 3rd Avenue (tel 212-828 2300) and 202 West 23rd Street (tel 212-352 2600).

If you need a pharmacy: There are several 24-hour pharmacies, mostly run by the Duane Reade chain. The most centrally located 24-hour pharmacy is at 224 West 57th Street at Broadway (tel 212-541 9708, www.duanereade.com), near Columbus Circle.

If you need a dentist: You can call 212-679 3966 or 212-371 0500. If you need help after hours, try the 24-hour Emergency Dental Associates on 212-972 9299.

British information services: 845 3rd Avenue, NY, NY 10022. Fax 212-745 0359. This is the information service of the British embassy in Washington and acts as the political, press and public affairs office of the New York Consulate-General, which covers the states of New York, New Jersey, Connecticut and Pennsylvania.

Cabs in New York

Using a money belt is a good idea and, if your room does not come with its own safe, leave your valuables in the main hotel safe.

SAFETY IN CARS

Unless you have a driver, a car in New York is not a good idea. If you do hire a car, however, be sensible. Never leave your car unlocked or leave any valuable items on the car seats or anywhere else where they can be seen. Always put maps and brochures in the glove compartment as these will be obvious signs that your car belongs to a tourist.

NEW YORK STREET SAVVY

It may surprise you to know that New York City remains the safest big city in the USA, according to the FBI. Although the city is nowhere near as dangerous as it used to be, it is still a large city and there are always people on the lookout for an easy opportunity. To reduce your chances of becoming a victim of street crime, follow these simple guidelines:

➡ Always be aware of what is going on around you and keep one arm free – criminals tend to target people who are preoccupied or have both arms laden down with packages or briefcases.

➡ Stick to well-populated, well-lit areas and, if possible, don't go out alone.

➡ Don't engage any suspicious people, such as street beggars, in conversation, though you can tip buskers if you wish.

➡ Visible jewellery can attract the wrong kind of attention. If you are a woman wearing rings, turn them round so that the stone or setting side is palm-in.

➡ If you're wearing a coat, put it on over the strap of your shoulder bag.

SAFETY FIRST

Central Park in winter

→ Men should keep wallets in their front trouser or inside coat pockets or in a shoulder strap.

→ Pickpockets work in teams, often involving children, who create a diversion.

→ Watch out for pickpockets and scam artists especially in busy areas, as you would in any big city.

→ Do not carry your wallet or valuables in a bumbag. Thieves can easily cut the belt and disappear into the crowds before you've worked out what has happened.

★ ★ ★ ★ ★ ★ ★ ★ ★
★   ★
★ **It cannot be stressed enough that** ★
★ **you should only ever walk about** ★
★ **with as little cash as possible –** ★
★ **and never, ever count your money** ★
★ **in public.** ★
★   ★
★ ★

→ A useful trick is to have two wallets – one a cheap one carried in your hip pocket or bag containing about $20 in cash and some out-of-date credit cards, and another hidden somewhere on your body or in a money belt containing the bulk of your cash and credit cards. If you are approached by someone who demands money from you, your best bet

is to get away as quickly as possible. Do this by throwing your fake wallet or purse in one direction, while you run, shouting for help, in the other. The chances are that the mugger will just pick up the wallet and run off rather than chase after you. If you hand over your wallet and just stand still, the mugger is more likely to demand your watch and jewellery, too. This advice is even more important for women, who could be vulnerable to personal attack or rape if they hang around.

Having given you some essential safety advice, however, it is important to remember that this is very much common sense and applies if you are travelling almost anywhere in the world, especially in a major city. New York is a busy, feisty city but it is a great holiday destination and no doubt you'll have a brilliant time and want to come back for more!

Mounted police

Index

Page numbers in *italics* refer to illustrations or maps. Those in **bold** refer to major references.

PHOTOGRAPH ACKNOWLEDGEMENTS

60 Thompson/Full Picture 202 top, 235 top; 70 Park Avenue Hotel 242; Peter Aaron/Esto for the Jewish Museum 126 bottom; Bart Barlow/NYC & Company Inc. 6; Steve Brickles 47, 70 bottom, 91, 94, 95, 99, 103, 107, 110, 115, 139, 143, 162, 163, 166, 167 top, 170, 174, 175 bottom, 178 bottom, 183 bottom, 186 top, 195, 203 bottom, 222, 223, 226, 283 bottom; Chelsea Savoy 219; Le Cirque 138; G Davies/NYC & Company Inc. 255 bottom; Jake Dobkin (www.bluejake.com) 70, 182 bottom, 254; D Finnin/American Museum of Natural History 118 top; Four Seasons 86 top, 135, 199 bottom, 231 bottom, 247; Frick Collection 123 top; Darren McGee/NYC & Company Inc. 119 bottom; Jeff Greenberg/NYC & Company Inc. 2, 7, 10 top, 11, 18, 19, 27, 35, 38, 39 bottom, 43 bottom, 50 bottom, 51 top, 54 bottom, 55, 62 top, 63 top, 66 top, 67, 71 bottom, 74, 75, 78 top, 79 top, 82, 83, 87, 90, 102, 114, 119 top, 131, 175 top, 179 top, 187 bottom, 190 top, 191 top, 214, 215, 250 top, 251 top, 263 top; Mick Hales/Metropolitan Museum of Art 122 top; HK Hotels 234 bottom, 239 bottom; Adam Husted/Brooklyn Museum 263; Andy Innyc 51 bottom; Ithaka 178 middle; Knitting Factory 194 top; Gayle Lackman 183 top; Eric Lagnel 234 top; Mark Leet/NYC & Company Inc. 42; Leonardo.com 230 top, 231 top, 235 bottom, 238, 239 top, 243 bottom, 246, 255 top; Lower East Side Tenement Museum 210; Kevin McCormick/NYC & Company Inc 63 bottom; Macy's East Inc./NYC & Company Inc. 259 top; Larsen Maher 218 bottom; Manhattan Oriental Hotel Group 10 bottom, 198, 202 bottom; Marquee 203 top; Meet 167; Mesa Grill/NYC & Company Inc. 178 top; New York Aquarium 218; New York Convention and Visitors Bureau 274; New York Hall of Science 270 top; Niagara Falls Convention and Visitors Bureau 275; NYC & Company Inc. 34, 39 top, 43 top, 46 top, 50 top, 54 top, 59, 62 bottom, 66 bottom, 71 top, 79 bottom, 86 bottom, 118 bottom, 122 bottom, 123 bottom, 126 top, 127, 134, 179 bottom, 186 top, 187 top, 190 bottom, 191 bottom, 199 top, 211, 250 bottom, 258 bottom, 259 bottom, 266, 267, 271, 282, 283 top; Michael N Paras/NYC & Company Inc. 270 bottom; Joseph Poberiskin/NYC & Company Inc. 31, 251 bottom; Tom Powell Imaging 130; PS1 Contemporary Art Center 258 bottom; Ray Jackson/Bernstein Associates/NYC & Company Inc. 78 bottom; Ritz-Carlton 230 bottom; Ritz-Carlton Hotel 14 ; Ruby Foo's 182 top; Mark Thomas 58; Tavern on the Green 142; Linda Turley/NYC & Company Inc. 194; Universoul Circus 207; Uwe Ditz Photography/NYC & Company Inc. 46 bottom; W Hotels 206; Waldorf Astoria/NYC & Company Inc. 15; Westin New York Hotel 243 top; Woodbury Common 279; Zoe 171.